Divorce For Dummies

M000024579

Divorce decisions in a nutshell

You face many tough decisions when negotiating a divorce agreement. In most cases, the basic questions you need to ask yourself boil down to the following:

- Where will you both, and your children, all live afterwards?
- Who will the children live with or will you share their day-to-day care?
- If you agree on the children living primarily with one of you, how will they keep in contact with their other parent?
- Which one of you will pay child support and how much will the child support be?

- How long will the child support last?
- Will maintenance (spousal support) be paid? If so, to whom and how much?
- How long will the maintenance payments last?
- What are your assets?
- What are your debts?
- How will you divide your assets (for instance, your home, cars, pensions) and how will you share out the paying off of your debts?

Important organisations and helpful resources

The following list of resources may be of some help as you're going through your divorce. Keep this information in a handy place (maybe under a refrigerator magnet or inside a phone book):

Legal and mediation resources

- Solicitors Family Law Association, www.sfla.org.uk, 01689 850227
- Law Society, www.lawsociety.org.uk, 020 7242 1222
- Law Society of Scotland, www.lawscot.org.uk, 0131 226 7411
- Law Society of Northern Ireland, www.lawsoc-ni.org, 028 9023 1614
- UK College of Family Mediators, www.ukcfm.co.uk, 0117 904 7223

- National Family Mediation, www.nfm.u-net.com, 08456 013 034
- Family Mediators Association, www.fmassoc.co.uk, 0117 946 7062
- Family Mediation Scotland, www.familymediationscotland.org.uk, 0131 558 9898
- Comprehensive Accredited Solicitor Mediators, www.calmscotland.org.uk
- Mediators Institute Ireland, www.mediatorsinstituteireland.ie, 00353 01 6618488

Financial resources

- Legal Services Commission, www.justask.org.uk, 020 7813 1000
- Scottish Legal Aid Board, www.slab.org.uk, 0131 226 7061
- National Debt Helpline, www.nationaldebtline.co.uk, 0808 808 4000
- Consumer Credit Counselling Service, www.cccs.co.uk, 0800 138 1111
- Payplan, www.payplan.com, 0800 389 3431

- Money Advice Scotland, www.moneyadvicescotland.org.uk, 0141 572 0237
- National Association of Citizen's Advice Bureaux, www.adviceguide.org.uk, 0207 833 2181
- Citizens Advice Bureaux Scotland, www.cas.org.uk, 0131 550 1000
- Citizens Advice Bureaux Belfast, www.citizensadvice.co.uk, 028 9050 3000

For Dummies: Bestselling Book Series for Beginners

Divorce For Dummies®

Cheat Sheet

Contact Centres and resources for non-resident parents

- National Association of Child Contact Centres, www.naccc.org.uk, 0115 948 4557
- Family Mediation Scotland, www.family mediationscotland.org.uk, 0131 558 9898
- Families Need Fathers, www.fnf.org.uk, 020 7613 5060
- Match (Mothers Apart from Their Children), www.matchmothers.org

Counselling and support resources

- Relate, www.relate.org.uk, 01788 573 241
- Relate Northern Ireland, www.relateni.org, 028 9032 3454
- Couple Counselling Scotland, www.couple counselling.org, 0131 558 9669
- Catholic Marriage Care, www.marriagecare. org.uk, 020 7371 134
- ACCORD (Northern Ireland Catholic Marriage Care), www.accordni.co.uk, 028 9023 3002
- Jewish Marriage Council, www.jmc-uk.org, 020 82303 6311
- Muslim Marriage Council, www.sajid@ imamsajid.com, 01273 722 438
- British Association of Counselling and Psychotherapy, www.counselling.co.uk, www.bacp.co.uk, 01788 550 899
- National Council for the Divorced and Separated, www.ncds.org.uk, 07041 478 120
- Department of Constitutional Affairs, Marriage and Relationship Support Directory, www.lcd. gov.uk/family/marsup/famtxtfr.htm

Resources if you have children

- The Child Support Agency Information Service, www.csa.gov.uk, 0845 600 6610
- CAFCASS (Children and Family Court Advisory and Support Service), www.cafcass.gov.uk, 020 7210 4400
- NCH Action for Children, www.nch.org.uk, 020 7226 2033
- National Council for One Parent Families, www. oneparentfamilies.org.uk, 0800 018502
- One Parent Family Scotland www.opfs.org.uk, 0131 556 3899
- Gingerbread, www.gingerbread.org.uk, 0800 018 4318
- Grandparents Association, www.grandparents-federation.org.uk, 01279 444964
- Parentline Plus, www.parentlineplus. org.uk, 0808 800 2222
- Parentline Scotland, www.children1st.org.uk, 0808 800 2222
- Parent Network Scotland, www.face.stir. ac.uk, 0131 555 6780
- Reunite, www.reunite.org, 0116 2555 345
- Childline, childline.org.uk, 0800 1111
- Children First (Scotland), www.children1st. org.uk, 0131 337 853

Resources if abuse is a risk

- Womens' Aid Helpline, www.womensaid. org.uk, 08457 023 468
- Muslim Women's Helpline, www.mwhl.org, 0208 908 3205
- Scottish Women's Aid, www.scottishwomen said.co.uk, 0131 475 2372
- Women's Aid Northern Ireland, www.niwaf.org, 028 9024 9041
- Men's Advisory Project, 028 9024 1929

Copyright © 2004 John Wiley & Sons, Ltd. All rights reserved.
Item 7030-7.
For more information about John Wiley & Sons, call (+44) 1243 779777.

For Dummies: Bestselling Book Series for Beginners

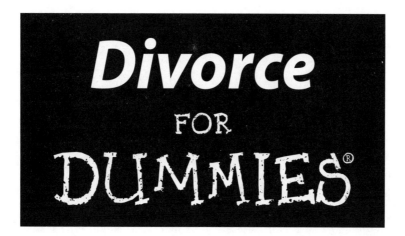

by Thelma Fisher, Hilary Woodward, John Ventura, and Mary Reed

JOHN WILEY & SONS, LTD

Divorce For Dummies®

Published by
John Wiley & Sons, Ltd
The Atrium
Chichester
West Sussex
PO19 8SQ
England

Email (for orders and customer service enquires): cs-books@wiley.co.uk

Visit our Home Page on www.wiley.co.uk or www.wiley.com

Wiley also publishes its books in a variety of electronic formats. Some content that appears in print may not be available in electronic books.

British Library Cataloguing in Publication Data: A catalogue record for this book is available from the British Library

ISBN: 0-7645-7030-7

Printed and bound in Great Britain by Biddles Ltd, Kings Lynn

10 9 8 7 6 5 4 3 2 1.

WILEY

About the Authors

Thelma Fisher was one of the first practitioners in the UK to apply the process of family mediation to divorcing couples. She had previously qualified and worked as a social worker and couple counsellor after graduating in English Literature and Language at King's College London. From 1981 to her most recent role as chair of the UK College of Family Mediators, she pioneered both the professional practice of mediation and its place in the Family Justice System, setting up one of the first family mediation services in Swindon before moving on to help create family mediation's early literature and training while a social work lecturer at the University of Bath where her special interests included the effects of separation and divorce on children. In 1989 she was appointed the first director of the national network of services that later became known as National Family Mediation. She played a key role in advising parliament on mediation in the discussions leading up to the Family Law Act 1996.

Thelma has lectured on mediation in many countries, including Canada, Norway, France, Bosnia, Croatia, Serbia and The Republic of Macedonia. In the UK she has regularly addressed national and international conferences and frequently appeared in the national media. She has published articles on family mediation in the *British Journal of Social Work*, *Family Mediation* and *Family Law*. She edited two editions of a standard textbook on family mediation, *Family Conciliation within the UK,* (Jordan Publishing, 1990 and 1992) and a UK edition of the influential American textbook by John Haynes, *The Fundamentals of Family Mediation,* (Old Bailey Press 1993). She is also the author of *National Family Mediation Guide to Separation and Divorce: The complete handbook for managing a fair and amicable divorce*, (Vermilion 1997). She was awarded the OBE in 1997 and made a Fellow of Kings' College London in 2000. She and her husband had three children and she has two grandchildren. She enjoys poetry and singing!

Hilary Woodward was brought up in Hertfordshire, and did her first degree in Sociology and Anthropology at The London School of Economics and Political Science in the Sixties. She worked on a variety of research projects with the Institute of Education, Medical Research Council and Institute of Psychiatry. Following the birth of her son, Joe, in 1973 she started working on a casual basis for a London firm of solicitors, before making the decision to train as a full-time lawyer. She was admitted to the Solicitors Roll in January 1982, and specialised in family law for over twenty years. She was a partner and then consultant in private practice in Bristol with Henriques Griffiths until her retirement from private practice in June 2003, having headed a growing and well-respected family department for most of that time. She has been an active member of the Solicitors Family Law Association and on the local committee for many years. She trained and practices as a family mediator with Bristol Family Mediation, one of the first family mediation services in the country. She is now a governor and honorary treasurer for the UK College of Family Mediators. She has contributed to a number of family law research projects, most particularly with Professor Gwynn Davis on the Ancillary Relief Outcomes study for the Lord Chancellor's Department in 1999 and on the FAINs study for the Legal Services Commission in 2002. She enjoys spending time when she can at her small village house in the Cevennes in France, and is a regular member of her local tennis and health clubs.

John Ventura is an authority on consumer advocate law and financial issues. He earned degrees in both law and journalism from the University of Houston. He currently operates three law offices specialising in bankruptcy, consumer law, and personal injury in the Rio Grande Valley. He has written eight books on consumer and small-business legal and financial matters, and is the author of *Law For Dummies* (Wiley). In addition, he writes a regular column for a Texas business journal and hosts a weekly radio program on legal issues.

John has been a frequent network TV show guest on CNN, CNN-fn, and CNBC, and has done numerous national and local radio programs. He has provided expert opinion for publications including *Money*, *Kiplinger's Personal Finance Magazine*, *Black Enterprise*, *Inc.*, *Martha Stewart's Living*, *The Wall Street Journal*, and *Newsweek*.

Mary J. Reed has ghost-written numerous books on money and legal matters and has been a regular contributor to *Home Office Computing* and *Small Business Computing* magazines. She is the owner of MR_PR, a public relations and special events firm based in Austin, Texas. Prior to starting her own business, Mary was vice-president of marketing for a national market research firm, public affairs and marketing director for a women's health-care organization, and public relations manager for an award-winning regional magazine. She holds a bachelor's degree in political science from Trinity College in Washington, D.C., and a master's degree in Business from Boston University.

Sandy Cartwright, a family lawyer in Austin, Texas, acted as a Special Contributor to the US edition of this title.

Dedication

This book is dedicated to The Rt Hon the Baroness Hale of Richmond, DBE, otherwise known as Brenda Hale, the first female Law Lord, who has made a remarkable contribution to the development of family law and family mediation over the last twenty years.

Authors' Acknowledgments

We are grateful for the help of the following people in contributing their specialised knowledge and experience to this book:

Fiona Garwood, who contributed much of the material on divorce law in Scotland, has been a family mediator for 20 years with Family Mediation Lothian (lothian@familymediation.freeserve.co.uk). Fiona also works as an Assistant Director for Family Mediation Scotland (www.familymediationscotland.org.uk), where she is responsible for mediation training and standards. Her work includes research into the involvement of children in mediation and referrals from court to family mediation services. She also provides training for mediators and other professionals and writes articles for mediation journals.

Leonard Mair is an experienced family law solicitor. He heads the family law team in Morton Fraser one of Scotland's leading firms of solicitors based in Edinburgh (www.morton-fraser.com). Leonard trained and practised as a mediator with Family Mediation Lothian. He specialises in high net worth negotiations.

Sheena Bell was a member of the Northern Ireland Family Mediation Service since its inception in 1987 by the N.I. Marriage Guidance Council (later Relate, NI). She held all the professional posts within the service during the ensuing years – mediator, intake worker, co-ordinator, supervisor and trainer – until June 2000. She runs, with 3 mediator colleagues, an expanding private practice in Family Mediation, does consultancy work, supervision and training in Family Mediation. She also mediates workplace disputes and has a private counselling practice.

Gregg Taffs has been a financial adviser for 17 years. Gregg started with the insurance division of Barclays Bank before leaving to become an independent financial adviser for Solace Associates (www.solace.uk.com), providing specialist advice to high net worth clients focusing mainly on investments and pensions.

Our thanks go to Alison Whiles of the family department and Pauline Horne in the estates department, both of Henriques Griffiths solicitors, Bristol, for their help and encouragement.

We are grateful to Marian Roberts, from the UK College of Family Mediators, One Plus One, Relate and the National Council for One Parent Families for special advice and to the many dedicated organisations whose work we have read and whose Web sites we have consulted. We have tried to acknowledge them all in one place or another in the text

A special thanks goes to Abbey books for chasing up all the titles, publishers and dates for Thelma, and Pete Jeffries from CAFCASS for explaining all the roles of these chaps.

We also thank our long suffering spouses for enduring the time we have spent on our computers late into the night!

Publisher's Acknowledgments

We're proud of this book; please send us your comments through our Dummies online registration form located at www.dummies.com/register/.

Some of the people who helped bring this book to market include the following:

Acquisitions, Editorial, and Media Development

Executive Editor: Jason Dunne

Executive Project Editor: Caroline Walmsley

Project Editors: Amie Jackowski Tibble, Daniel Mersey

Copy Editor: Kate O'Leary

Editorial Assistant: Samantha Clapp

Technical Editors: Alan Markham, Karen Bruce Lockhart

General Reviewer:

Cover Photos: © Owaki - Kulla/CORBIS

Cartoons: Ed McLachlan

Production

Project Coordinator: Bill Ramsey

Layout and Graphics: Andrea Dahl, Stephanie D. Jumper, Michael Kruzil, Heather Ryan

Proofreaders: Carl William Pierce, Dwight Ramsey, Brian H. Walls

Indexer: TECHBOOKS Production Services

Publishing and Editorial for Consumer Dummies

    Diane Graves Steele, Vice President and Publisher, Consumer Dummies

    Joyce Pepple, Acquisitions Director, Consumer Dummies

    Kristin A. Cocks, Product Development Director, Consumer Dummies

    Michael Spring, Vice President and Publisher, Travel

    Brice Gosnell, Associate Publisher, Travel

    Kelly Regan, Editorial Director, Travel

Publishing for Technology Dummies

    Andy Cummings, Vice President and Publisher, Dummies Technology/General User

Composition Services

    Gerry Fahey, Vice President of Production Services

    Debbie Stailey, Director of Composition Services

Contents at a Glance

Table of Contents

Introduction

. . . .

Divorce is on the rise around the world, and the UK is no exception. Despite divorce having become so commonplace, most people are almost completely at a loss over what to do if *their* marriages are breaking up. Overwhelmed by confusion, anger, fear, and resentment, many divorcing spouses panic over the changes occurring in their lives (and the lives of their children) and end up making emotionally and financially costly mistakes that could have been avoided if they had had more information. Others turn what could have been an amicable break-up into a cut-throat battle. They end their marriages bitter, angry, and a whole lot poorer at a time when this isn't necessary at all.

But divorce isn't about winners and losers, and it doesn't have to include huge legal bills either. With the right information, tools, and advice (and the proper attitude), you and your spouse can work out the terms of your divorce with a minimum of expense, stress, and emotional upheaval. In this book, we tell you how it can be done.

Why You Need This Book

Dip into this book and you can discover the following:

- ✔ What to do first before you file a divorce petition
- ✔ Family law and divorce law basics, including how divorce laws may vary throughout the UK (though you should always defer to your solicitor)
- ✔ Facts to consider when you're deciding on how you'll care for your children, maintenance, child support, and the division of your assets
- ✔ Mistakes to avoid and insights into effective negotiating
- ✔ Tips for finding a solicitor who is competent *and* affordable
- ✔ Advice for keeping your emotions as well as your legal expenses under control, including tips for using mediation and other non-confrontational methods for getting through your divorce as amicably as possible
- ✔ For the small percentage of you who are involved in hostile divorces and have to sort out your differences through a court, this book can prepare you for the courtroom experience
- ✔ Advice for minimising the potential negative effect divorce may have on your children, and suggest ways to rebuild a new life for yourself after divorce.

Foolish Assumptions

Because you've picked up this book, we're assuming that you've come to the realisation that your marriage has what may be insurmountable problems and you're seriously considering a divorce. Or perhaps you're already separated and are ready to take legal steps to end your marriage. We're not going to give you reasons for why you should or shouldn't get divorced – those are decisions you need to make yourself. However, we do give you advice on how to start and get through the whole divorce process while handling its ups and downs as gracefully as possible.

The law is known for having very specific, impenetrable language – often it's impossible to understand unless you're a lawyer (and sometimes, even if you are). Divorce law is littered with obscure words, so we always give you a definition and you can find most of them in the glossary at the end of the book. We don't save you from them altogether, however, as you'll meet up with them at times. Someone recently wrote how when you travel by ship you may be initially embarrassed to use words like 'stern' and 'starboard' but may end up casually saying them because no-one seems to be astonished or impressed when you do. You may acquire some of that ease yourself, and thankfully, many lawyers belong to the 'plain speaking' brigade and we definitely approve of that. Keeping in line with plain speaking, we alternate between 'he' and 'she' instead of using 'he or she', which can get confusing.

How This Book Is Organised

You can use this book in either of two ways. You can read it cover to cover, and never skip a beat on the subject of divorce, or you can pick it up when you need an answer to a particular question or want to know more about a certain subject. For even easier reading, it's organised into six parts.

Part 1: Trouble in Paradise

This part of the book helps prepare you for dealing with a seriously troubled marriage and reviews your options if you're in a failing relationship. It provides information on gathering facts about your family's finances and honing your money management skills before you get divorced. This part also offers you an overview of family and divorce law and the responsibilities that parents have towards their non-adult children. We close this part with a chapter on separation – to save your marriage, or as a prelude to divorce.

Part II: Divorce Preliminaries

The second part of *Divorce For Dummies* tells you how to prepare yourself for the divorce process and has specific advice for the spouse who initiates a divorce and for the spouse who gets the bad news. It devotes a full chapter to telling your kids that mum and dad won't be living together any more and helping them get through your divorce as painlessly as possible. Lastly, this part provides advice on coping with the emotions you will inevitably feel and dealing with the reaction of your friends and family.

Part III: Decisions, Decisions

Once your divorce has begun, you have to make some important and sometimes tough decisions: Will you pay or receive spousal support? Where will your children live, and if it's not with you both in your separate households, how will you make sure that they stay in touch with both parents? What about child support? How will your marital property be divided up? These questions aren't to be taken lightly, but their answers should be easier to reach after you read the chapters in this part of the book.

Part IV: Working Out the Terms of Your Divorce Agreement

This part of the book is a must-read whether you and your spouse negotiate most of your divorce yourselves or you each hire lawyers to do most of the negotiating for you. You'll find out about the benefits and drawbacks of negotiating yourselves, and discover the many benefits of using mediation to help settle your divorce. We tell you how to find an affordable solicitor and what you should expect from her, and what she expects from you. For those of you heading for divorce court, the final chapter in this part tells you what to expect before, during, and after your divorce terms are decided by a judge.

Part V: After Your Divorce Is Finalised

After your divorce is wrapped up, you still have paperwork to deal with and money matters to handle. Plus, you now face the prospect of getting by on your own. You may also face problems with your divorce agreement or with your spouse failing to adhere to court orders or the plans you made for your children or spousal maintenance. This part provides advice for these and other common post-divorce problems. Finally, we include a chapter that explains the value of pre- and post-marital agreements if you marry again.

Part VI: The Part of Tens

The first chapter in this part points you to great Web sites where you can find out more about divorce and the many organisations out there to help you. The second chapter offers advice for helping your kids cope in the aftermath of your divorce. You'll also find practical tips for how to put your divorce behind you and move forward with your life. The final chapter offers help on building and sustaining a mutually fulfilling relationship in the future.

Icons Used in This Book

This icon lets you know about something especially useful that can save you time, money, or energy as you're going through your divorce.

Make a note when you see this icon – it indicates if there's something you should keep in mind as you make your way through the divorce process.

Stop and read this information to steer clear of mistakes and pitfalls that are common in divorce.

For those of you who like as much in-depth information on a subject as possible, you may want to make a point of reading this material.

This icon highlights scenarios we've seen (or heard about in the news) that may help you realise you're not alone as you go through your divorce.

If you live in Scotland or Northern Ireland, pay close attention when you see this icon. The laws in these two countries are slightly different from those in England and Wales and we've highlighted the major differences with this icon. Many of the laws are the same throughout the UK however, so don't depend on these icons for the whole picture.

Where to Go from Here

The divorce process is never an easy one, but we do our best to give you the information you need to make it as smooth as possible. However, as with any legal issue, make sure you talk things over with your solicitor before making any major decisions, as the laws evolve over time and you need the most up-to-date information possible.

Part I
Trouble in Paradise

'It's my wife calling — she wants a divorce.'

In this part . . .

1f your marriage is rocky and you think you're heading for a breakup, this part of the book provides information to prepare you for the divorce process. (Because divorce may not be an option for some of you, we also talk about marriage as well as divorce issues.) We also offer information on what to do if you're a victim of domestic violence.

We provide you with some solid advice for getting your finances together (whether or not you're divorcing), an overview of your legal rights and obligations during the divorce process, plus some basic information on family law in general and divorce law and procedure in particular. This part ends with a chapter on separation, which you may opt for as a last-ditch effort to save your marriage or use as a prelude to – or in lieu of – divorce.

Chapter 1

Your Divorce Roadmap

In This Chapter

▶ Understanding the basic requirements of the law

▶ Caring for your children

▶ Making decisions about home, money, pensions, and possessions

▶ Locating who is out there to help you

▶ Getting ready for life after divorce

The word 'divorce' literally means 'turned aside'. You may be contemplating 'turning aside' from your spouse or facing the effects of your spouse 'turning aside' from you. You could be forgiven for thinking of divorce as a negative mirror image of your marriage. Getting a divorce means taking apart, bit by bit, all the things you and your spouse put together over the years. It's like watching your married actions in reverse – unmaking the promises, telling your families an unwelcome story, enacting the end not the start of your relationship, perhaps selling the home you once struggled to buy, and sharing out the care of any children you were thrilled to have together.

You could look at your situation in a more positive light. Think of it as holding up a mirror to yourself during a major life crisis. With this mirror in front of you and this book in your hand, we hope you can watch the expression on your face change from uncertainty to determination to self-confidence. To get through your divorce with as little difficulty as possible, you need good information and an optimistic outlook. This, we hope, sums up what we have written. Because divorce takes its toll on you, in Chapter 9 we give you some ways to look after yourself as you work your way through the process.

Divorcing Is a Process

Like most crises, your divorce is a process not an event. It has a beginning, a middle, and – yes, eventually – an end. In this book we give you a map of the whole process of divorce – from the moment you decide that your relationship is in serious trouble to the moment your divorce is finalised – and we even offer some tips for dealing with the changes in your life afterwards. Because everyone is different, we give you a variety of routes. This chapter is a bird's-eye view of the whole landscape to help you choose where to start.

As we do not always spare you hard words (check the Glossary at the back of this book if you come across a word you're unsure of), neither do we always spare you hard problems to overcome and hard decisions to take. We provide ways to avoid creating problems where there needn't be any, and warn you when difficult decisions are ahead. No matter how hard you try to dodge them, when you come across decisions that must be made, you need to be prepared.

If it's at all possible, we recommend you go for a co-operative divorce, but we know it can be difficult and you may end up in court with a fully-contested divorce (see Chapter 5). One of our favourite solicitors is a wonderful mediator, but if she is representing someone in a full hearing, then she is very, very tough. So when it comes to your divorce, we are not bland – nor are we cynical. However, we are realistic about what divorce means for you.

Getting to the Bottom Line: The Law

The legal effects of both marriage and divorce are to change your legal status. In the eyes of the State, you changed once from a single person to a married person and divorce changes you back again. However, only a judge in a county court or high court can change your status back to being single. That is the bottom line of divorce law.

Because you collect responsibilities by being married, the law is accompanied by a stack of documents and a series of routine court procedures to make sure that you give the judge the information required for your divorce to be granted with the minimum of unfairness to either you or your spouse. If you have kids, the law is there to protect them – so divorce law has links to family law.

The basis for divorce law in England and Wales

The law that governs divorce if you live in England and Wales is the Matrimonial Causes Act 1973, and in Scotland it's the Divorce (Scotland) Act 1976. In both cases, the only ground for divorce is the irretrievable breakdown of your marriage, but you must establish that by one of five facts:

- Your spouse has committed adultery and you find it intolerable to live with him or her.

- Your spouse has behaved in such a way that you cannot reasonably be expected to live with him or her.

✔ Your spouse has deserted you – for a minimum of two years.

✔ You have been separated for at least two years and your spouse consents to a divorce.

✔ You have been separated for at least five years.

Chapters 4 and 5 spell out the legal aspects of marriage and divorce in more detail.

The divorce rate in the UK hit a seven-year high in 2002. The total number of divorces was 147,735 (13.3 per cent per 1,000 of the married population) which was 2.7 per cent up on 2001. And a fifth had been divorced before compared with 11 per cent in 1981.

Changing the focus on children

The law about children changed radically when the Children Act 1989 was passed. This law shifted the focus away from deciding 'parental rights' to the notion of 'parental responsibilities'. You do not have rights over your children, which you then can fight about at divorce; rather you have responsibilities for your children which you do not shed when you divorce. Accordingly, the law stopped talking about *custody*, which the court would grant to one parent, and *access* which was granted to the parent who does not 'get' the children. Instead, the law now encourages parents to decide for themselves what is in the best interests of their children, where they live (their *residence*) and how they'll have *contact* with the parent they aren't living with.

Divorced or separated parents now have more flexibility in working out their arrangements and many children now live with both parents at different times according to whatever works best for them. Of course, if you and your spouse cannot agree, then the court decides and the law spells out what factors the judge must consider in making her decisions.

Chapter 5 goes into more detail about the Children Act 1989 and what it means for your family, and Chapter 10 covers the ways you can plan for your children's care.

Understanding the differences in UK law

You may be surprised to learn that divorce law, procedures, and courts differ in some respects in England and Wales from those in Northern Ireland and even more so in Scotland. The divorce laws themselves are similar but the Scottish laws about children and property are significantly different. At the time of writing, Northern Ireland is waiting to change its divorce law while the Northern Ireland Assembly is suspended. We have given you the main legal differences where they occur but we don't have sufficient space to spell out the minor – but important – differences in the law and procedure in detail. Therefore, if you live in Scotland or Northern Ireland, we recommend that you consult a solicitor for those further details.

Starting the Divorce Process

The chances are that if you could have prevented your marriage from breaking down you would have done so. If you're still not 100 per cent sure that divorce or separation is what you want (or have to accept) then you might start at Chapter 2. Here, we give you suggestions for trying to improve your relationship if there is a chance of saving it or at least for thoroughly testing the inevitability of its end. We suggest some alternatives to divorce, such as separation, but emphasise that you should not leave your home without first thinking through the consequences that we spell out in Chapter 6.

If you've decided that your relationship is over, there's no turning back, and you're ready to take legal steps to end your marriage – have a look at Chapter 7. Where Chapters 4 and 5 give you the legal background, Chapter 7 starts you on the path, with tips on everything from telling your spouse it's over to working out your family's financial situation and how that will be affected by your separation.

We urge you to make sure everyone stays safe. A relationship breaking down can be the result of abuse or can be the trigger for abuse. In either case, your safety, your spouse's safety, and your children's safety are paramount. Chapter 2 tells you how and where to find help if abuse is a risk in your household. Gone are the days when what went on in other people's homes was treated as their business alone. Nowadays the police treat all domestic violence as a crime and take it very seriously.

Separating when you never married

Cohabitation is on the increase every year. If you're in a long-term relationship where you and your partner are living together but never married and you're thinking of ending the relationship, you'll still find much of this book useful. But there are warnings for you throughout. If you part, the law doesn't protect your individual interests as strongly as if you were married. For example, you won't be able to claim ongoing financial support from your ex-partner, and, unless you have your name on the deeds to your home, you may not be able to claim a share of it. Chapter 4 might be the place for you to start. A solicitor specialising in this area of law can give you more advice.

The end of your relationship can trigger overwhelming feelings – including grievances and fear that your security is ebbing away – and your emotions can get out of control. Your children are likely to sense what's going on around them even if your outbursts of anger don't land directly on them. You'll find crucial information about the steps to take to protect yourselves in Chapter 2.

Finding Your Way Through Your Divorce

After you have started the divorce ball rolling by informing your spouse, getting a full picture of your financial situation, and ascertaining what both your expectations are for your lives after the divorce, you and your spouse need to work out how you want to handle extricating your lives from each other. The serious stuff that you have to sort out falls broadly into these categories:

- **Money,** including your salaries and pensions – and your debts
- **Your house,** if you have one
- **Your possessions,** including everything from your car to your CD collection
- **Your children,** if you have them

We have gone into detail on how to handle all these issues, though we don't spend so much time on possessions (such as pictures and CDs). Dividing these can feel like a sword in your soul but in the long run these things are replaceable. You may also have other things of value, like cars or a business or other properties. For the most part, anything owned by either or both of you before, during, or after your marriage (even an inheritance) can be viewed by the court as belonging to both of you and open to claim, so it all needs to be entered into the calculations. Chapter 3 helps you get to grips with working out what you have and what you owe, and you can find advice on dividing up your possessions in Chapter 11.

Looking at your financial picture

When you come to sorting out your finances, it is very important that you do not look at each item in isolation from the others. We discuss your salaries, pensions, houses, mortgages, assets, and debts under separate headings because there are differences in the options you have for sorting them out. But they are not actually separate issues if you look at them within your total financial situation. As you collect information about what you earn, own, and owe, you will build up a big picture of what comes in and what goes out and how that looks when you try to divide it. The information you find in Chapter 11 can help you understand your whole financial picture. Chapter 12 covers the issue of spousal maintenance, including if it's an option in your situation and if so, who's likely to pay it, and who's likely to receive it (and how much).

When we started practising in the divorce field, divorcing spouses couldn't divide up their pension benefits. Your pension was your own, you had earned it, and it didn't belong to your spouse. What turned the tables were most probably the efforts of wives who had no pension in their own right (often because they gave up work to look after their children) and lost any future share of their husband's pension on divorce. In a passionate debate in the House of Lords in 1996, the law was changed. Now your pensions can be calculated and shared at the time of your divorce. We describe your options in Chapter 11.

Keep the following list in mind when you're thinking about dividing up your finances:

- ✔ It's not wise to decide what to do about your house, without thinking about your future ability to pay for it.

- ✔ It isn't wise to exchange information about pensions and do a deal without thinking about your future earning capacities.

- ✔ It's not wise to disregard your debts and commitments when you think about your current income.

- ✔ It's not wise to hurry over decisions without weighing up their impact on each other and on how much money you have coming in and how much you will have going out once you are apart.

Chapters 7, 11, 14, 16, and 17 all have things to say about gathering up the different parts of your financial information and fitting it together to give you the clearest picture of your financial situation – before your divorce, and after.

If you end up with very little money to live on after your divorce, you may be able to get some financial support from the government in the form of welfare benefits and tax credits. We give you information on these support benefits in Chapters 7 and 15. You may also be eligible for legal aid during your divorce and Chapter 15 tells you what it covers and how you qualify for it.

Caring for your children

If you have non-adult children, the end of your marriage is not the end of your family. Your young children may think of your 'family' as it was before you parted and may dream that you are all still together even if they know that you aren't. In the 1970s, most commentators thought that every divorce harmed a child. Since then there have been more than 215 reputable pieces of research into the effects of divorce and separation on children that have revealed that 'it all depends'.

In essence, research suggests that your children are most at risk of lasting damage to their well-being, self-esteem, happiness, and future prospects if you subject them to a lot of conflict – especially if you don't resolve the conflict and your kids think it is about them. If you and your spouse can co-operate, both keep in loving touch with your children, keep them informed appropriately about what is happening, listen to them, and continue to support them as well as you can financially and practically – despite your own distress – your kids should do well. They won't be happy while things are changing – none of us likes change that is out of our control – but they will grow through your divorce.

If you're worried that your children are very confused and unhappy and torn between you and your spouse, you might suggest that they talk through your divorce with someone outside the home. Have a look at Chapter 8 for ways to help your children through your divorce. You can also find out about counselling and support groups for children by contacting your local Relate (www. relate.org.uk) or a local Family Mediation Service (www.nfm.org.uk).

Chapters 8, 10, and 13 give you lots of important information to help you make decisions where your children are concerned. They also cover what you can do if you and your spouse are not able to manage things as you would wish for your children. In such circumstances, a judge and CAFCASS (the Children and Family Court Advisory and Support Service) will help you and the judge to reach decisions about your children. (See Chapter 18 for how to handle taking your divorce through the court process.)

Raising your kids is expensive. Chapter 13 talks specifically about child support – but all the factors concerned with money and property will have an impact on your children. You can work to maximise what you have for their benefit rather than spend your resources on fighting each other. Keeping their interests in mind throughout your divorce will protect your children, as far as you can, from poverty.

Children talking about divorce

As we say, how your children fare depends a lot on how you manage your divorce. Here are two contrasting examples of what children have said about their new lives when asked about them in a study lead by Carol Smart at the University of Leeds (www.leeds.ac.uk/family):

✔ A 15-year-old girl living with her mother after her divorce said, 'I have this image of really nice parents...but our family definitely isn't like that. It's stressful because nobody really gets on ....' When describing that she lives with her mother and her mother's new partner and their new baby, she says, 'She doesn't listen...he gets at me,' and concludes, 'it's just like I'm a person who lives here...sort of like a tenant.'

✔ In contrast, a boy of eight said of his separated family: 'Good fun...we laugh at quite a lot of things. We've got a new cat and a garden...Mum laughs more...it's quite an ordinary family...it was good when they split[ted] up because they used to argue a lot...it's better now, lots better...it's nice to be with Mum and Mel and I get to see Daddy Pete in London and he phones us.'

Getting the help you need

Though you can choose to go it alone (see the section 'Taking the road less travelled: going it alone' later in this chapter), you don't have to get through your divorce on your own. There are heaps of people out there who can help you negotiate your way through it. Among them are the following:

- ✔ **Relationship and other counsellors:** Relationship counsellors don't set out to 'put you back together' unless that is what you both want. Accredited counsellors are very well trained and can guide and support you while you work out what you want to do individually about your relationship, work with you together to improve your marriage, or support you after it has ended. If you're interested in trying counselling, or just finding out how a counsellor can help you, Chapter 2 tells you how to find the help you want.

- ✔ **Solicitors and barristers:** Most family solicitors work to the Solicitors Family Law Association Code of Practice and are now also guided by a Law Society protocol that strongly encourages a conciliatory approach. Furthermore, specialist family judges don't appreciate combative solicitors and barristers in their courts. Chapters 15 and 17 give you information about how to choose and work with your solicitor to achieve a fair and – as far as possible – even-tempered divorce and, if you have children, focusing on their needs. Chapter 15 also sets out the role of the Community Legal Service in helping you gain access to legal services and pay your legal bills, if you are eligible.

Your solicitor's job is to be your personal legal adviser, so you and your spouse need to have different solicitors representing you. He should also guide you through the steps you need to take, keeping in mind how you want to play things during your divorce. He should give you the advice and information you need to make decisions about your future – but you make the decisions. He also acts as a signpost to other forms of help if you need it and, if necessary, prepares and supports you if your case comes to a full hearing. Chapter 18 talks you through what happens if you take your case to court.

- ✔ **Family mediators:** A mediator's job is to work with you together as a couple. The unique characteristic of mediation is that it can keep the lines of communication open between you. If you can still communicate with each other then it's likely you can problem-solve together. You're able to part on better terms if you work together than if you pull up the drawbridge and prepare the boiling oil.

Joint problem-solving not only cuts down your legal costs but, if you have children, it helps you continue to talk to each other as their parents. Bitter disputes about children can often be resolved in a single mediation session because you may suddenly hear your worst fears, such as 'I'm afraid I'll lose the children', replicated in the words of your spouse. Chapter 16 tells you how mediators work, how they can help you – and when it isn't such a good idea to use them. We are both family mediators and, in our experience, mediation is very effective in helping divorcing couples reach an agreement quickly and with a minimum of conflict.

✔ **Children and Family Court Advisory and Support Service (CAFCASS) officers:** If you have children and your divorce goes to court, you'll probably come across a CAFCASS officer. These officers of the court are trained to focus on the needs of your children and to report to the judge to help her decide what order to make. You might be referred to a CAF-CASS officer by the judge if she wants to know more about you and your children before making a decision. Chapter 18 tells you more about this stage of your divorce.

✔ **Judges and magistrates:** Family judges who work in the county or high courts and magistrates who work in family proceedings courts all now have specialist family training. Your imagination may run riot when you think of judges and magistrates, but you will usually find that they are sympathetic as well as experienced and knowledgeable. At the same time they can be clear and stern if they are faced with abuse or violence. Chapter 18 describes what role a judge plays in your divorce.

Taking the road less travelled: Going it alone

Though it's possible for you to get a divorce without getting any legal help, we don't recommend it unless everything is straightforward and you are in absolute agreement and fully trust each other's grasp of the issues, or you haven't been married long enough to acquire many assets and you have no children. Before you go down the route of a do-it-yourself divorce, look at Chapters 3 and 7, which set out what factors you need to consider. Chapter 14 also gives you guidance on how you can sensibly negotiate with each other to cut down on the cost of professional help. Remember that with your solicitor's help you can still get a 'quickie' divorce so that you don't need to attend court in person and we think (we would, wouldn't we!) that family solicitors and family mediators are too good these days to disregard.

Moving on to Pastures New

After you have your final decree, you can begin a new phase of your life. Chapter 19 gets you thinking about ways to get back in the swing of things – perhaps with a new job, or a rediscovered hobby, or spending more time with your kids. However, even after your divorce is final, you may need to take action to implement your decisions. Chapter 20 spells this out, including help with solving persistent post-divorce problems.

Because your life doesn't end when your marriage does, at some point you may think about getting into a new relationship. You might be scared that because this relationship didn't work out you won't be able to make any relationship work. However, this just isn't true. Part V is the place to start when you're ready to think about moving on. Chapter 23 can help you ensure that things are as easy as possible for your kids. For tips about moving on after your divorce and ways to avoid divorce the next time around, have a look at Chapters 23 and 24. If you're ready to think about marriage again, we offer some guidelines for putting your expectations on paper (in the form of pre- and post-marital agreements) in Chapter 25.

Fitting together your family life after divorce can be an awe-inspiring challenge, especially if your new household collects children from two (or more) previous families. Even finding words for your new life can be difficult – 'single again', 'stepfamily', 'one-parent family', or even 'blended family'. None of these labels reflects all the possibilities. However, your new lives will gradually fall into shape and you will look back and say 'How did I ever get through all that?' – because you have!

Gearing Up for Your Divorce

Now – what's your most immediate concern? Do you need to ask your spouse to leave the family home? Are you desperate for someone to talk to? Is money, or the lack of it, your biggest worry? Are you still unsure whether divorce is the only road ahead? Take some time away from your daily routine and have a good think about your situation. Whatever issue you come up with – that's your starting point. The Cheat Sheet at the front of this book provides you with details of a whole range of organisations that can help you, from finding a solicitor to providing a counsellor to talk to you or your children. Alternatively, you can use this book to help you decide what to do first. You will survive your divorce, and we're here to help you through it.

Chapter 2

What to Do First When Things Start to Go Wrong

Marriages rarely die overnight. Almost always, the destruction of a marriage happens little by little, over time. If your marriage is in really serious trouble, any discussion, cooperation, or compromise may be impossible, and you may have no option but to end it yourself, possibly against your spouse's wishes.

To help bring some objectivity and common sense to your situation so that you can gain a true appreciation of how bad (or not so bad) things really are, this chapter reviews some of the common signs of a marriage in crisis and highlights your options for dealing with relationship problems. We also address the steps you can take if the pressures in your troubled relationship cause your spouse to turn abusive or violent.

Recognising the Signs of Trouble

When your marriage is going through a tough time, you may find yourself wondering whether it's an instance of the 'for better or for worse' your marriage vows alluded to, or whether your relationship is truly on the rocks. Although no test exists that can tell you whether your problems are typical reactions to the stress and strain most marriages experience at one time or another, or whether they point to more serious issues, troubled marriages do tend to exhibit many of the same characteristics. Do any of the following statements apply to your marriage?

- ✔ In your mind, your spouse just can't do anything right anymore.
- ✔ You argue or fight constantly.
- ✔ You've lost the ability or the willingness to resolve your marital problems.
- ✔ Resentment and contempt have replaced patience and love.
- ✔ You've turned from lovers into flatmates.
- ✔ One or both of you is having an affair.
- ✔ You go out of your way to avoid being together and, when you are together, you have nothing to talk about.

Don't panic if you find that your marriage exhibits some of these characteristics – you're not necessarily heading for a divorce. However, you do have cause for concern and you and your spouse, first separately and then together, have to assess your options and decide what to do next.

Marital problems can trigger depression, feelings of vulnerability and power-lessness, anger, and sleep problems, any of which can impede clear thinking and sound decision-making. A counsellor or therapist can help you deal with these disturbances so that you can move forward. The British Association for Counselling and Psychotherapy (www.counselling.co.uk) can help you locate one in your area.

Should I Stay or Should I Go?

Many couples opt to stay married after their relationships have failed – perhaps you fall into this category. Maybe you feel it's important for your young children to be raised in a two-parent household, or you can't afford a divorce straight away. Or you're feeling pressure from family and friends to stay together. Maybe your faith forbids divorce, or possibly you've come to an understanding that allows you and your spouse to lead separate lives but remain under the same roof. Perhaps you're still together because you're afraid of what life will be like if you're single again. Fear of the unknown may motivate you to tolerate a situation that would be unbearable to others.

If your home is full of tension and anger because of your marital problems, you may be doing yourselves and your children more harm than good by staying together.

Never stay in a marriage if your spouse has or is threatening to harm you or your kids physically. At the very least, separate and give your spouse an opportunity to get professional help. If you are afraid that leaving may trigger violent behaviour in your spouse, contact the Women's Aid Helpline (08457 023 468, www.womensaid.org.uk), the Scottish Women's Aid (0131 475 2372/ 2389, www.scottishwomensaid.co.uk), Women's Aid in Northern Ireland (028 90 24 9041, www.niwaf.org), or the Muslim Women's Helpline (0208 908 3205, www.mwhl.org). All these groups provide information in several languages as well as English. See 'What to Do if Things Become Abusive or Violent' later in this chapter for more information.

Trying to Work Things Out

If you decide to stay in your marriage, you have two basic options: You can try to improve your relationship; or you can grit your teeth, shut down your feelings, and put up with things the way they are. The first alternative is almost always the better choice. To give your relationship a chance, try taking a short break from one another or going for marriage counselling. Neither of these options is mutually exclusive, so you may want to try both.

Taking a relationship mini-break

Sometimes what you really need when you just can't get on and your emotions are running high is a short time apart – a day or two, a long weekend, maybe even a holiday on your own. At the end of your time apart, you may have a whole new attitude toward your relationship and a renewed commitment to it.

Use the time apart to calm your emotions, assess your situation, and put your marital problems in perspective. Think about whether you are giving your spouse adequate attention and affection. Try to assess why you aren't getting on and your own role in those difficulties. Analyse the kind of arguments you are having – what you tend to argue about, how often you argue, and when – to determine if any patterns emerge.

If you spend your time apart with a close friend or family member, choose that person carefully. Avoid anyone who does not like your spouse or resents your marriage. If you are looking for advice from the person you will be spending time with, the friend or family member should be impartial and someone whose judgement you trust.

Going for relationship counselling

Saving your marriage may require more than just taking a break from your spouse. If only it could always be that easy! You may need to re-establish or improve communication between the two of you, so that you can begin a productive dialogue about what has gone wrong in your relationship and why and what you can both do to improve things.

Timing is everything when your marriage is falling apart. Don't wait until your marriage is damaged beyond repair to get professional help.

Finding a qualified relationship counsellor

Working with the right counsellor can help save your marriage; doing so can save you and your spouse months or even years of anguish while you try to decide what to do about the problems in your relationship.

Choose your counsellor carefully. Several national relationship counselling agencies exist and can tell you how to find a counsellor in your area. These agencies are not-for-profit organisations that offer counselling on a sliding-fee scale for couples, families, and individuals. Just knowing there may be a way out of your situation without having to resort to divorce can take some of the pressure off and make it easier for you to address your marital problems. Here are some places to start when you begin looking for a qualified relationship counsellor:

- **The British Association of Counselling and Psychotherapy:** (www. counselling.co.uk) can give you a list of accredited counsellors in your area, along with details about their qualifications, background, and specialisms.

- **The national Relate office:** (01788 573241, www.relate.org.uk) or the Relate office in your area offer all sorts of help for relationship problems.

- **Your faith community:** You can find details for counselling within many different faiths at www.lcd.gov.uk/family/marsup/famtxtfr.htm).

- **Local counselling resources:** Try contacting any of the following – Relationship Counselling for London (020 7580 1087, www.counselling 4london.com), Couple Counselling Scotland (0131 558 9669, www. couplecounselling.org), Scottish Marriage Care (0141 222 2166, www.scottishmarriagecare.org), or Relate Northern Ireland (01232 323454).

- **Referral from a friend or relative:** Lots of people have been through relationship counselling and can recommend a professional who has helped them through their difficulties.

Be sure that the person you decide to work with is someone both you and your spouse feel comfortable with. You may have to share intimate and painful information about yourselves with the counsellor that you choose.

If your spouse won't go with you to talk to a relationship counsellor, go by yourself. You may learn things about yourself as well as new relationship skills that can help improve your current marriage or prepare you for a happier relationship or marriage in the future.

Getting comfortable on the counsellor's couch

Remember that everything you say in counselling is confidential, and it's a place you should feel comfortable to talk about your problems. You can also try less intimate kinds of relationship counselling such as group sessions. The Association of Marriage Enrichment (www.ame-uk.org.uk) runs courses for small groups on improving relationships, resolving conflicts, and changing behaviour and attitudes. The courses are usually weekend or week-long retreats with experienced leaders and other couples focused on exploring ways of improving their relationships.

When your marriage has derailed, it's difficult to step back and objectively assess what's going on and determine what changes to make. A trusted and experienced counsellor can provide invaluable assistance. The right counsellor can help promote discussion and mutual understanding. He or she can also offer insights into your problems, help you both come to an agreement about what to do about those problems, and even teach you new marriage skills.

Your spouse's unwillingness to attend counselling sessions with you may signal that he or she isn't willing to change or is no longer committed to your marriage.

When Staying Isn't an Option

Living together while you try to resolve your marital differences and save your marriage may be an unrealistic option for you. Instead, you may decide to separate or live apart for a while.

Separating before making a final decision

Separating can provide you with an opportunity to find out what it's really like to live in separate residences. Meanwhile, the door is still open for getting back together. However, separation can also be a prelude to divorce.

Before you separate, it is a good idea to protect yourself by talking with a family solicitor beforehand, especially if you want spousal or child support during your separation. The solicitor can warn you about anything that might jeopardize your standing in a divorce if you both decide to end your marriage.

You can opt for either of two types of temporary separation – with or without a separation agreement:

- ✓ **Separating without an agreement means you simply begin living apart.** When you and your spouse clearly anticipate that your separation is temporary and that you will eventually reconcile, separating without an agreement may be your best option.

- ✓ **Separating with an agreement is recommended if you view your separation as the first step towards a divorce and have no plans for reconciliation.** Your solicitors work with you both to formalise your separation and put the agreed terms in writing. Remember that in the UK the same solicitor cannot advise both of you.

A separation agreement is often preferable for many financial and legal reasons:

- ✓ You formalise the terms of your separation including whether or not one of you will help support the other financially while you are living apart; how you will deal with the arrangements for where your kids will live, how they will see the parent not living in the home, and how you will work out child support. If you plan to change your financial or housing situation then the agreement can cover these changes as well.

- ✓ By spelling everything out you minimise the potential for conflict while you're separated. It can also protect you against either of you acting independently to the long-term disadvantage of the other – by selling valuables you own together or taking an unfair disadvantage of a joint bank account, for example.

- ✓ If one of you breaks the terms of your separation agreement, the court can help enforce the agreement under contract law – your separation agreement is a contract between you and your spouse.

- ✓ Fewer issues will have to be decided on if you end up eventually getting a divorce. A judge always has the final discretion but is more likely to enforce your agreement if you can each show that you've had independent legal advice and you've fully and frankly disclosed your financial positions to each other.

Dating others while you are separated is usually not a good idea because your spouse may then be able to divorce you on the grounds of adultery or behaviour.

Chapter 6 can give you more information about separation agreements. If you and your spouse agree to divorce on the basis of your separation you will have to live apart from one another for at least two years. Check out Chapter 5 for more about the grounds for divorce.

Separating permanently with no intention to divorce

If divorce is not an option for you, you can opt for a permanent separation called a *judicial separation*. People very rarely use judicial separations these days and even more rarely for financial reasons. The process for getting a decree of judicial separation is similar to the process for getting a divorce. You and your spouse can still work together to negotiate the terms of your separation and work out, as appropriate, the division of your marital property, the arrangements for the children, child support, and maintenance for one of you by the other. You can use solicitors to help you negotiate such an agreement within the judicial separation proceedings and take this agreement to court. The key difference between a judicial separation and a divorce is that, when all is said and done, if you only separate you're still married. You cannot therefore remarry. Judicial separation simply releases you from the duty to cohabit.

Getting your marriage annulled

A *nullity decree* is a court action that either voids your marriage or proclaims that it was never legally valid in the first place, as if the marriage had never taken place, or that the marriage is treated as void from the date of the nullity decree. If you have young children from that relationship, it won't modify or cancel your parental responsibilities to your children. To get a *nullity decree* you have to prove to the court that your marriage is either void or voidable.

Legal annulments do not equal religious annulments

Legal annulments and religious annulments are two different animals. In some religions, if you divorce and want to remarry, your religion will not recognise your new marriage unless your old marriage is religiously annulled. Religious annulments are most commonly associated with the Roman Catholic faith. For religious purposes, you may need a religious annulment as well as a civil divorce.

The most common criteria for nullity include:

- ✔ At the time of your marriage one of you was already married
- ✔ Your spouse was under 16 when you got married
- ✔ You weren't respectively male and female
- ✔ You didn't comply with certain formal requirements, such as filling out marriage forms properly, or getting married in a licensed venue (see Chapter 4 for the requirements you need to meet)
- ✔ Either of you is incapable of consummating the marriage (by having sex) or refuses to do so
- ✔ You did not give your valid consent to the marriage
- ✔ Your spouse was suffering from a sexually transmitted disease in a communicable form at the time of your marriage
- ✔ Your spouse was pregnant with another man's child at the time of your marriage ceremony. You won't be granted a nullity decree if, for example, you knew about the pregnancy beforehand and you still went ahead with the marriage.

If you want a religious annulment, then you must apply to your church's authorities. Remember that this does not, in itself, count as a legal divorce or judicial separation. Chapter 6 can tell you more about religious annulments and Jewish Gets.

Getting a divorce

Your final option when your marriage is failing is to get divorced, ending your marriage and many of your rights and responsibilities regarding your spouse that are associated with it. Each chapter of this book provides information that can help you get through the divorce process as painlessly as possible.

What to Do if Things Become Abusive or Violent

Sometimes when a marriage is falling apart one spouse begins to be abusive, threatening the other with violence or becoming physically violent. If this happens in your marriage, take the threats or the violence very seriously. Ignoring them can literally be a matter of life or death!

What is meant by domestic abuse?

Domestic abuse or domestic violence is often thought of only as involving physical harm. Nowadays abuse is understood to include more than physical harm. If you have experienced emotional or verbal abuse and have felt seriously undermined or threatened as a result, then you will know the personal costs of this.

Call the police

Domestic abuse is a crime. If you are harmed by your spouse or threatened with harm, call your local police station. One or more police officers will be sent to talk with you and prepare a police report. If it is obvious that you have been abused, the police may arrest your spouse on the spot, persuade your spouse to leave, or at least help to defuse the situation.

Although they are in a very small minority, some police officers believe that domestic violence is not a matter for the police – it's a private matter between a husband and wife. However, the police themselves can now be dismissed if they're found guilty of domestic violence. Therefore, if you call the police for help and the responding officers seem reluctant to prepare a police report, calmly request that one be prepared and get the officers' names and numbers. If the officers continue to refuse, it will be helpful to have this information when you contact their superiors. Official police policy is to treat domestic violence just as seriously as, if not more seriously than, any other crime.

Get an injunction against your spouse

Injunctions are a form of court order. An *occupation order* (also known as an injunction or ouster order or *interdict* in Scotland) is a court order that can force your spouse to leave your home, or forbid your spouse to enter or come within a certain distance of your home, or restrict his or her rights within the home. The court may attach a power of arrest which will allow a police officer to arrest your spouse if he or she breaches the terms of the order.

The court very rarely makes an occupation order without giving your spouse an opportunity to tell his or her side of the story. This may mean going back for a second hearing. During the hearing, the judge decides whether to grant you an occupation order by reading your statements and hearing your evidence on oath and by reviewing any police or medical reports relating to your situation. The judge has to weigh up the harm to each of you, or your children, in deciding to make an order.

If you get an injunction prohibiting your spouse from entering your home, don't be tempted to let him or her back in again. A judge won't take kindly to your allowing your spouse to breach the order, and may even think twice about giving you further protection if you do allow him or her back in and trouble ensues.

You can also ask the court for a *non-molestation order*, which means that your spouse must not harm you, or trouble you, or use violence towards you or your children. Sometimes the court recommends a violent or abusive spouse to enter an alcohol or drug addiction rehabilitation programme or to attend an anger management course. A CAFCASS Officer (Children and Family Court Adviser) may be asked to arrange this if the abusive spouse agrees.

It can be easier to get a protective order against your spouse if police reports are on file. The reports can also help if you file criminal charges against your spouse. If the court attaches a power of arrest to any part of the order, you or your solicitor have to make sure that a copy of the order and power of arrest are lodged with your local police station. The order is not effective until your spouse has had proper notice of it.

If you need immediate protection and the courts are closed because it's a weekend, evening, or holiday, your solicitor can get an order from a local magistrate or judge that the police can act upon. It stays in effect for just a few days until you can go back to court again.

If you get an occupation or non-molestation order, or both, but your spouse refuses to obey them, call the police and your solicitor immediately. Your spouse may then be arrested and criminally prosecuted, or your solicitor may apply to the court for your spouse to be sent to prison. To make certain that the police will arrest your spouse if the situation requires it, keep a certified copy of the court order with you at all times.

It is possible to ask a judge or magistrate for an anti-stalking order that can help protect you if your spouse is following you, waiting for you outside your home, making threatening or harassing phone calls, or displaying other sorts of behaviour in order to intimidate and frighten you.

There are certain circumstances when it may be appropriate for you to accept an *undertaking*, or solemn promise to the court, from your spouse to do something, such as to leave the home or to not use violence, instead of having a court order against him or her. An undertaking has the same force as an order, except that you cannot have a power of arrest attached to it. But if your spouse breaches his or her undertaking to the court, or fails to comply with an order, he or she will be in contempt of court. The remedies for contempt of court include a fine, or, more seriously, committal to prison. Always consult your solicitor about the pros and cons for you of an order or an undertaking, especially if your spouse is in breach.

File criminal charges

If your spouse has already been physically violent to you, in addition to getting a non-molestation order from the court you may file criminal assault charges against him or her. Taking both actions will provide you with different and overlapping protections. The police also have the power to charge your spouse if he or she is persistently harassing you.

Go to a refuge

If you are afraid to remain in your home despite an occupation or non-molestation order against your spouse, consider going to your local refuge. You can take your young children with you. Refuges don't publish their addresses for safety reasons, but you can find your local refuge's phone number from the police, the telephone directory, your local Housing Department, or your local Social Services Department.

If you are in a crisis situation (your spouse has just beaten you or is threatening to) and you can get to a phone or use your mobile, call the Women's' Aid Helpline (08457 023 468, www.womensaid.org.uk), the Scottish Women's Aid (0131 475 2372/2389, www.scottishwomensaid.co.uk), the Muslim Women's Helpline (0208 908 3205, www.mwhl.org), or the Men's Advisory Project Helpline (028 9024 1929). The person answering the phone will calm you down, advise you on how to handle the situation, and call the police for you. It is wise to find and keep their number handy in case you need it.

The Women's Aid Web site is a very good source of information and includes guidance on how to remove any evidence that you'd contacted the Web site. The Women's Aid Helpline tells you how to find out about resources in your area for victims of domestic abuse and for individuals who are afraid that their spouses may become abusive.

Other safety measures you can take

In addition to keeping the phone number of your local refuge, here are some other things you can do to protect yourself if your spouse has been abusive in the past and you are afraid you will be harmed again, or if your spouse is threatening you with violence for the first time:

- ✔ Hide an extra set of keys, some money, and some clothes in a safe place in case you need to get out of your home quickly.
- ✔ Always have in mind a safe place to go that your spouse does not know about.

- ✔ If you have children who are old enough to understand, tell them that if you say a certain 'code word' that's a signal for them to run to a neighbour's house or call the police.

- ✔ Tell friends and family about the abuse. Sharing this information with others diminishes the power of some abusers.

- ✔ Join a support group. The people on the other end of the Women's Aid Helpline can help you find a group in your area or you can call your local refuge for information. Joining a group may give you the resolve you need to deal with your situation in a decisive manner.

- ✔ Testify in court against your spouse.

If you are seeking help to stop your own violence, contact Change – an organisation for men learning to end their violence – on 01324 485 595.

Chapter 3

Wise Up to Your Family's Money Matters

*W*e'd all like to believe that till-death-do-us-part wedding vows guarantee that every marriage will last forever. But these days the reality is that about one in three marriages ends in divorce. So it makes sense for every married and about-to-be-married person to be prepared not only for the possibility that his or her marriage may end in divorce but also for the financial consequences that can follow. At a minimum, your preparation should include the following:

✔ Becoming familiar with your family's finances

✔ Learning how to manage your money

✔ Working to maintain a positive credit record in your own name

✔ Building and maintaining marketable job skills

Understandably, you may view marrying with the possibility of divorce looming over your happy union as pretty cynical. But, when you understand how *not* being prepared for the end of your marriage can affect you and your children, you'll be convinced that the advice we give you on what you can do to minimise the impact of divorce on your life is wise (albeit unromantic).

Consider this: your lack of preparation may force you to stay in a bad marriage because you can't support yourself or because you don't have the financial resources to live on your own. And, without the right preparation, you may be at a disadvantage when the time comes to work out the financial details of your split. Plus, when you are single again, you may have a hard time building a financially secure life for yourself.

This chapter also offers advice about protecting yourself from the financial fall-out of divorce and preparing to earn your own living or make more money after a divorce. If you are a stay-at-home spouse or if you put your career on the back burner during your marriage, pay special attention to this information.

If you think a divorce may be in your future, the sooner you can put the advice in this chapter into action, the better prepared you'll be, financially and legally, for life on your own.

Here are some facts that should motivate you to take action. A wife's lack of financial know-how can cost her dearly when she gets divorced. The National Council for One Parent Families report in *One Parent Families Today, the Facts* that women are more likely than men to have a lower standard of living after divorce – even when you compare women who live with their children after divorce with the proportionally fewer men who do. For example, only 34 per cent of single mothers with children under five are employed compared with 60 per cent of single fathers, and of these women, 28 per cent will be part-time workers compared with only 10 per cent of men.

Although the differences become less pronounced as children grow, they still persist. In part, this is because women, in addition to working part-time more frequently, tend to have lower-paying jobs, and they find it harder to work because of the high cost of childcare. They may also lack the financial know-how, confidence, or credit record they need to build a good life for themselves after they are divorced.

It Takes Two to Manage (Or Mismanage) Money

Don't rely entirely on your spouse to pay your household bills, reconcile your chequebook, make investment decisions, and so forth. You need to share these responsibilities. At the very least, you should know what bills need to be paid, how much is in your bank accounts, and where your money is invested. Here's why:

- **Your spouse may resent having to shoulder all the responsibility for managing your family's finances.** This resentment can cause trouble in your marriage.

✔ **Your spouse may not be a good money manager.** You and your children may be harmed by your spouse's bad decisions. In addition, your spouse's financial mismanagement may damage _your_ credit record – not just his or her own.

✔ **If you or your spouse become incapacitated by a serious illness or accident, the other may be unprepared to manage your family's finances.** As a result, you may make costly financial mistakes.

✔ **You'll have fewer arguments over money.** If you're both fully aware of your financial situation, there's not as much to argue over.

✔ **You're more apt to notice a drain on your resources.** In a worst-case scenario, if your spouse is having an extramarital affair or has a problem with gambling, drinking, drugs, or the use of Internet chat rooms – all of which cost money – the money has to come from somewhere. If you're aware of your financial situation, you're more likely to see exactly where it's coming from.

✔ **You'll be prepared to make good decisions if you and your spouse negotiate your own divorce agreement.**

✔ **Your divorce will be more expensive if you don't know what your financial situation is.** If your divorce is not co-operative and your solicitor lacks the information he or she needs to handle it, that information will have to be acquired through the time-consuming and potentially expensive _disclosure process_. The formal disclosure process helps the parties of a divorce get the facts of a legal action so that neither side takes the other by surprise. To find out more about the disclosure process, see Chapter 5.

✔ **Your spouse has free reign over the family finances, which could harm you.** For example, your spouse could waste your cash and assets or hide them from you so that they aren't included in your divorce negotiations. For more on hiding assets, read Chapter 11.

✔ **After your divorce, you may be without the financial resources and information you need to build a new life for yourself.** Keeping track of your family's finances will help you to keep track of your own.

Financial Fundamentals: What You Must Do First

To play an active, informed role in the management of your family's finances, you must have certain information about your household finances, as well as basic money management skills and other resources important to your financial life and well-being. Check out Chapters 7 and 11 for more tips on understanding and managing your financial situation after your divorce.

Find out what you have and what you owe

You don't have to be a chartered accountant to work out your family's financial worth. You just need to find out what your family's debts and assets are. A debt is something that you owe, like your mortgage, or your credit card bill, or your car payments, not to mention the 20 quid you borrowed from your best friend. An *asset* is a thing of value. Depending on the type of asset, you can use it to purchase something else, you can sell it, or you can use the asset as collateral for a loan. An asset can be tangible – such as cash, property, vehicles, antiques, fine jewellery, or art – or intangible – such as stocks, bonds, or pension benefits. Any assets should be registered in both of your names. Get a notebook and make a list of the following:

- ✔ Your total household income and the source(s) of that income

- ✔ The cheque and savings account numbers that you and your spouse use and the bank(s) in which those accounts are held

- ✔ Your family's significant assets and the approximate value of each. Your home and your pensions are often the biggest. See Chapter 7 for a worksheet to help you work out your assets

- ✔ How your *joint assets* are titled or deeded – joint tenancy with right of survivorship or tenancy in common (described in the sidebar 'Joint property and your rights to it')

- ✔ Your family's debts – whom you owe and how much

- ✔ Where financial and legal documents important to your family are stored, including bank records, tax returns, wills, titles and deeds, mortgages, loan agreements, insurance policies, and documentation pertaining to any investments, stocks, shares, bonds, and mutual funds you or your spouse may own, as well as paperwork relating to the pension plans either of you participate in. (See Chapter 11 for more details.)

- ✔ What your credit record says about you and your spouse

- ✔ The names, addresses, and phone numbers of your solicitor, bank, accountant, financial adviser, and stockbroker, if you have them

- ✔ Basic information about your spouse's business, if your spouse is self-employed, including its legal form, assets, and liabilities.

Have an understanding with your spouse that you share fully all of your household's financial information with each other and that all financial records are kept in a place that is readily accessible to both of you.

Pensions: A Thumbnail Sketch

In the UK there are many different sorts of pension schemes, and the sort that you or your spouse are members of affects the benefits available to each of you when you divorce. Pensions and the laws associated with them are complicated, and the following is only a simplified guide.

You are entitled to a basic *State Retirement Pension* if you've paid, or been credited with, National Insurance contributions. The amount that you're entitled to depends on your contributions. You may have an additional state pension called the State Earnings Related Pension, or SERP, depending on how much you earn and what you've contributed to National Insurance contributions as an employee. In addition, there are a variety of other non-Government pension schemes are available:

✔ *Occupational pension schemes:* Most of these are contracted out of SERPs, but then the employers have to pay a guaranteed minimum pension or provide protected rights equivalent to SERPs. Occupational pensions fall into one of two main categories:

- The *final salary scheme,* or *defined benefit scheme* is the traditional type of retirement plan that you imagine receiving along with a gold watch after 50 years of loyal service to an employer. Because they're expensive for employers, final salary schemes are not as widely available in the private sector as they used to be.

- A *money purchase* or *defined contribution scheme* is the type of retirement scheme that many employees are offered these days. Participation in a money purchase scheme isn't automatic; if your employer offers one and you want to participate, you have to enrol in it. If you do enrol, you, your employer, or both of you, contribute money to your scheme.

✔ *Retirement Annuity Contracts:* A form of pension available up to July 1988 mainly if you were self-employed or your employment didn't offer an occupational pension scheme. It's possible to convert the contract to a *personal pension scheme.*

✔ *Personal Pension Scheme:* This has been available since July 1988 to both the employed and self-employed, subject to certain Inland Revenue limits to your contributions as a proportion of your income.

✔ *Stakeholder plans:* Introduced in April 2001, these plans are low cost portable personal pensions plans available to people who weren't previously eligible to participate in a pension scheme, such as part-time and lower paid employees or people who aren't earning but who can afford to contribute.

✔ *Small self-administered schemes:* Known as SSASs, these plans are a form of pensions available only to company directors, who have a more than a 20% shareholding in their company and who can't be a member of the company's occupational pension.

✔ *Unapproved Schemes:* Available as a top-up pension to certain highly paid senior executives who have reached the earnings limit set by the Inland Revenue.

✔ *Additional Voluntary Contributions:* May be paid by an employee into a separate scheme administered by the employer or into a free-standing scheme, when the employee's contributions aren't up to the maximum percentage of his or her income permitted by the Inland Revenue in the occupational scheme.

✔ *Section 32 buy-out policy:* A pensioner can ask the pension scheme administrators to buy out their pension benefits by purchasing an annuity with an insurance company.

Draw up a spending plan and stick to it

Knowing how to manage your debts and assets is essential so that you have enough money to pay your bills each month, don't take on too much debt, and accomplish the most with any money you may have left over. Being a good money manager means knowing how to do the following:

- ✔ Develop and manage a household spending plan. (See the sidebar 'Budgeting basics' to understand more about spending plans, and see the table coming up for a sample form designed to help you keep track of your finances.)

- ✔ Manage your chequebook and your balance statements. If you don't keep track of how much money is in your account by recording each cheque you write, all account deposits and withdrawals and then reconciling your account balance with your monthly bank statements, you can lose money in bounced cheques.

- ✔ Use credit wisely. Although credit can help you purchase necessities you couldn't afford otherwise, using credit too often or not understanding the terms of credit before you apply for a credit card or get a loan from a bank, credit union, or finance company can land you in trouble.

- ✔ Make sound investment decisions with stocks, bonds, mutual funds, property, and so on. Even if you use professional stockbrokers, financial advisers, and estate agents to help you manage important investments, you should know enough about your investments so that you can intelligently evaluate their advice.

Using the following forms, total how much you spend in a month. For help developing and using a budget, you can also check any household budget programs such as 'Quicken'.

Sample Form for a Household Spending and Savings Plan

Fixed Monthly Expenses	*Amount (£)*
Rent or mortgage	_____
House and contents insurance	_____
Ground rent	_____
Car purchase payments	_____
Other finance agreements	_____
Other insurance	_____
Children's allowances/activities	_____
Childcare	_____
TV licence and channel subscriptions	_____
Other monthly commitments	_____
Total	£ _____

Variable Monthly Expenses*	Amount (£)
Groceries	_____
Utilities	_____
Telephone (including mobiles)	_____
Petrol/diesel	_____
Clothing	_____
Credit card payments	_____
Dental, optician, or medical costs	_____
Magazines and books	_____
Church or charitable donations	_____
Personal expenses (haircuts etc.)	_____
Internet use	_____
Recreation (including sports and meals out)	_____
Miscellaneous	_____
Total	£ _____

Periodic Expenses*	Amount (£)
Education	_____
Car tax and insurance	_____
Other insurance	_____
Taxes	_____
Household repairs	_____
Birthday and holiday gifts	_____
Entertaining	_____
Subscriptions	_____
Total	£ _____

Estimate the entire year's periodic expenses and divide by 12 for the monthly amount

Total monthly household expenses	£ _____
(The three previous totals from this table combined)	
Net monthly household income	£ _____
Surplus or deficit (net household income minus total monthly expenses)	£ _____
Surplus allotted for savings	£ _____
Surplus allotted for investments	£ _____

Draw up a Household Income Sheet

It is wise to count up your income from all sources for both of you so that you can check that your spending plan isn't over-spending your income. Any money you have left over in the month will also help to decrease your debts as you approach the possibility of divorce. You will need to list everything on the form. You can download financial worksheets similar to these from www.divorce.uk.com. See Chapter 7 for help with checking the values of your assets and liabilities.

Sample Household Income Sheet

Your gross salary/wages for the year:

Full-time employment	£ _____
Part-time employment	£ _____
Subtotal (A)	**£ _____**

Your deductions for the year

National insurance	£ _____
Income tax	£ _____
Pension contributions	£ _____
Other deductions (union subscriptions, charitable donations, health insurance)	£ _____
Any share save options that you are paying for	£ _____
(Remember that these will usually be optional and you may not be able to afford to continue with them after your divorce)	
Subtotal (B)	**£ _____**

Calculate your net available income

Subtotal (A)	£ _____
Less Subtotal (B)	£ _____
Net available income	**£ _____**

Additional employment-related income

Bonus/commission (not included above)	£ _____
Other fringe benefits from your employment such as car allowances, or contributions towards a computer or office at home	£ _____

State benefits

Child benefit	£ _____
Working tax credit	£ _____
Child tax credit	£ _____
Disability benefits	£ _____
Rent or council tax rebates	£ _____

Other sources of income

Rental income from property	£ _____
Trusts	£ _____
Dividends	£ _____
Fees	£ _____
Casual payments	£ _____
Maintenance or child support from a previous spouse	£ _____
Total	**£ _____**

*Divide the total by 12 to work out your monthly income

Owning a house

When you get divorced, the law in England and Wales (unlike in Scotland – see Chapter 11 for why this is) views all that you owned before you entered the marriage plus all that you acquired during the marriage as potentially open to claim by both of you. This means that the judge has to take all assets into account, regardless of whose name they are in or when they were acquired. If you have children, the judge also views your house as your home – it's still a home for you and your children rather than simply a financial asset. Have a look at Chapter 11 for help in working out what to do with your house when you divorce.

Registering the deeds to your home

Check whether the deeds to your home, and to any other property that you own, are in both of your names. You need to formally register your interest in the property if your name is not on the deeds. You can get most of the information and forms that you need from the Information Centre at the Land Registry headquarters (0207 917 8888, or 0191 301 3500, or try their Web site: www.landregistryonline.gov.uk). Here's a step-by-step guide to what you need to do to register your interest:

- ✔ **Find out whether the property is registered at the Land Registry and which district it's registered in.** You can find this out from the deeds or paperwork relating to the property. If you don't have access to the deeds, contact the Land Registry for a SIM form (an application for an official search of the index map), then complete and return it with your fee to the Land Registry. The reply will tell you whether the property is registered or not, and if it is, the title number.

- ✔ **To add your name to a registered property, ask the Land Registry for an MH1 form (notice to register your interest in a matrimonial home).** Then complete and return the form to your district Land Registry with the fee of £2.

- ✔ **To register your interest in a property if you find it's not already registered, you need a K2 form (application for registration) from the Land Charges Department of the Land Registry.** Complete and return the form to the Land Charges Department with your fee of £1 payable to HM Land Registry.

Keep a copy of all of your applications and any replies with the deeds. In both these cases you're registering your rights of occupation in the matrimonial home, but you're also preventing your spouse from dealing with the property without any reference to you.

✔ **The process to register your interest in a property other than the matrimonial home is similar to step 2, but slightly more expensive.** You just need different forms: a CT2 form if the property is already registered (and the £40 fee to register), and a K3 form if it isn't (still at £1). You also need to have a legitimate claim to the property. Contact your solicitor for help in proving that you do.

Finding out about your mortgage

You probably have one or more mortgages on your home. The type of mortgage you have doesn't really matter when it comes to working out what to do with your house. However, you do need to know how much you owe, what the payments are, and how much longer they need to be paid. If the information isn't to hand, check with your lender.

Budgeting basics

Developing a spending plan isn't difficult. It's simply a matter of recording your monthly household expenses, tallying them up, and then comparing them to your monthly household income. To get a comprehensive picture of your monthly expenses, review your chequebook stubs, your bank statements, including direct debits and standing orders, your current account withdrawals, and your cash receipts. To get a true picture of your expenses, look at several months' worth of information.

Some expenses are fixed, whereas others change every month and other expenses occur periodically throughout the year. To budget for periodic expenses, divide the total annual cost of each periodic item by 12. That gives you a monthly cost to include in your budget. To budget for variable expenses, tally up a few months' worth of what you're spending – on groceries, for example – or preferably a year's worth for the utilities, and divide by the number of months you kept track to get an average.

Your total *net* monthly household income is the actual amount of money available to spend (*gross* income less taxes and other deductions). That income can include wages and salaries, investment income, or child support.

Try using a form like the one in this chapter to record your income and expenses. If the total amount of your monthly expenses exceeds your total household income each month, you need to reduce your expenses or increase your income to avoid serious financial trouble.

If your budget shows that you have a surplus of cash at the end of the month, then you can pay off your debts more quickly, put more money into savings and investments, or spend some of the money on things you or your family really want or need.

One final comment about spending plans: Developing one may not be difficult, but living with one can be really tough if you don't exercise self-control. In the end, a spending plan is only as good and as useful as the discipline you put behind it!

If one of you is keeping the house, the other should try to remove his or her name from the mortgage so that he or she is not liable and eligible for another. Your lender is likely to agree to remove your name from the existing mortgage if you have a good track record and the person remaining has enough income or if there is enough equity in the property to cover the mortgage. Chapter 11 tells you more about dealing with your mortgage when you divorce.

Deciding what is fair

During your divorce, you can either decide for yourselves what is a fair distribution of your assets and income (Chapter 14 offers help on how to do this); use the assistance of a mediator in working out the financial terms of your divorce (see Chapter 16 for info on mediation); or your solicitors can negotiate this issue on your behalf (Chapter 17 has the scoop on dealing with your solicitor). As a last resort, you can leave it to a judge to decide (read Chapter 18 for a taste of what happens when you go to court).

When making a decision a judge must give priority to the needs of any children of the family and in addition may weigh up a whole range of factors:

Fairness is relative and varies from divorce to divorce. The most common criteria for working out who gets what include:

- How much each of you earns or could earn in the future, and your other financial resources
- Your financial needs, obligations, and responsibilities now or in the future
- Your current standard of living
- The value of your property
- The contribution each of you has made to your marriage – and, as it should, being a full-time homemaker or stay-at-home parent counts
- The pension benefits to which each of you may be entitled
- The length of your marriage
- Your age and your health
- In very rare instances, the judge may weigh up how either of you have behaved in the marriage

The law may treat inheritances and gifts to a spouse during marriage as joint property, including any future inheritances that are certain and foreseeable. Your personal injury settlement may also not be beyond claim by your spouse.

Joint property and your rights to it

You can own joint real estate or property in two ways. How you own that joint property affects your rights when the time comes to split it up.

- **✔ Joint tenancy with the right of survivorship.** Under a joint tenancy, each owner owns all the property. If your spouse dies, his or her share automatically goes to you, no matter what your spouse's will says, and vice versa. A property held under a joint tenancy bypasses a will. Most married people own property in this way.

- **✔ Tenancy in common.** In this sort of joint ownership, often used by cohabiting couples, each of you has a distinct share. If the size of your share is not defined, then it will probably be assumed that it is 50 per cent unless you can prove otherwise. The important point to remember is that either of you can leave your share by will or intestacy (when there is no will). Your spouse can do what he or she wants with his or her share of the property – give it away, sell it, trade it, use it to collateralise or secure a loan, or encumber it with some sort of claim.

So if you don't want your spouse to have your share of your house on your death, you need to make sure that you own your house under a tenancy in common and that you leave a will saying who is to receive your share. To change your ownership from a joint tenancy to a tenancy in common, send a notice to your spouse telling him or her that that is what you are doing. If your property is registered, you must then register the change at your district Land Registry by means of Form 75, known as *a restriction*. If your property is not registered, you need to put a copy of the notice with the title deeds. This process is known as 'severing the joint tenancy'.

Finding Out What You Need to Know

If you review the list of 'financial-ought-to-knows' earlier in this chapter and realise you're the one who doesn't know the answers, don't panic. You can get up to speed in several ways. Start with your spouse. Ask him or her to sit down and describe your family's finances in as much detail as possible, show you where key documents and other important records are kept, and answer your questions.

If your spouse seems threatened by your sudden interest in the family finances, try alleviating that concern with an explanation of why you want to know. Explain that if you know more about your family's finances, your spouse will not have to shoulder all the burden for managing your money. Also, you will be better able to make wise decisions for the family if your spouse becomes incapacitated or dies.

Review your family's financial records and documents, including information stored on your home computer (many households use personal finance software to help them manage their money). If you don't know where your tax returns are filed and your spouse won't tell you, you can obtain copies by writing to the Inland Revenue.

Money management and personal finance courses are a good resource for increasing your financial skills and knowledge. Your local community college or university may offer classes for little cost. Also, many investment companies and financial advisers offer investment seminars as a way to attract new clients or develop additional business from their current client base. These seminars are usually free, and no purchase is required. However, these advisers often assume that their audience has a better-than-average knowledge of investing, not to mention better-than-average money to invest!

Another possible source of financial education is the Citizens Advice Bureau (CAB) office in your area. Some of these offices offer low-cost to no-cost money management classes, including classes on how to develop and use a budget.

If you, or you and your spouse, owe a lot of money and are having trouble paying your bills, your local CAB advisers may be able to help you work out more affordable payment plans with your creditors so that you can get out of debt. The less debt you have going into a divorce, the less potential for problems after your divorce. Look for your local CAB in the telephone directory. Alternatively, there are several helplines you can use:

- ✔ **Citizens Advice Bureau:** www.adviceguide.org.uk
- ✔ **National Debtline:** 0808 808 4000, www.nationaldebtline.co.uk
- ✔ **Consumer Credit Counselling Service:** 0800 138 1111, www.cccs.co.uk
- ✔ **Payplan:** 0800 389 3431, www.payplan.com
- ✔ **Money Advice Scotland:** 0141572 0237, www.moneyadvicescotland. org.uk

Bookstore shelves are overflowing with titles about personal finance and investing. Even if you're a financial novice, you can find many books written for people just like you. An A-level course on personal finance has recently been proposed. Or you could just read Alvin Hall's *Your Money or Your Life* for tips on managing your finances.

Although a financial seminar or adviser can certainly inform you of the pros and cons of different money management ideas, you and your spouse may not agree about things like how much to spend and how much to save and what is an acceptable amount of credit card debt. A marriage counsellor may be able to help you resolve those disagreements. Or this may become an item to negotiate about in mediation. Chapter 16 can tell you more about mediation. Differences about money can affect the quality and financial stability of your marriage and can impact your life long after your divorce.

Maintaining Your Employability

Even though two-income families are becoming the norm in today's society, many women, and a growing number of men, choose to be full-time homemakers and stay-at-home parents for at least some point during their marriage. If you are one of them, be aware that in today's fast-changing work world your job skills can quickly become rusty or even obsolete and you may lose many of your work or professional contacts as well.

To protect yourself while you are out of the job market, try to do what you can to keep your job skills up-to-date, and also develop new ones, if possible, even if you have no immediate plans to work outside the home. You may also want to begin preparing for a new career. Your local school, community further education college, or university continuing education department are all potential sources of training and education.

At the very least, learn how to use a computer, if you are not already computer literate. Most jobs these days assume or require that you have at least some computer skills.

Don't lose yourself in your marriage by always making your needs secondary to your family's. Taking care of and developing yourself is not necessarily selfish. By doing so, you gain the confidence and the resources – both inner and financial – to rescue a failing marriage, end a bad marriage, or take care of yourself if you are widowed. In other words, hope for the best but be prepared for the worst.

Working part-time is another option for building and retaining your job skills and professional contacts. A part-time job helps you build a CV. Plus the money you earn can fund a savings account in your own name, provide extra income to help pay your family's bills, or help finance your children's education.

Being prepared to enter the work world as quickly as possible, perhaps once your children have started school, is important now that life-long spousal support is rare. The more quickly you can land a good job and earn a good living, the better off you will be.

Building a Positive Credit Record

Your *credit record* is a record of how you manage the credit accounts that you maintain in your name or that you share with your spouse. Those accounts may include bank credit cards, bank loans, store cards, and so on.

One or both of the 'big two' credit bureaus, Equifax or Experian, or a third, CallCredit, has your credit history stored in a computerised database. (See the sidebar 'Contacting the credit bureaus'.)When you apply for a bank loan, credit card, or some other form of credit, the creditor reviews your credit record to make sure that you aren't likely to be a risk. If problems do exist, obtaining credit at reasonable terms – or any credit at all – may be difficult.

Creditors look not only at how much credit you are servicing but also at your credit limits. In other words, if you have a credit card with a limit of £1,000, even if you are not carrying a balance on that card, the fact that you *could* run one up is something that creditors consider when evaluating whether or not to extend credit.

Having good credit in your own name (not just *joint credit* that you share with your spouse) plus your own trouble-free credit record are essential in preparing for the possibility of divorce. Here are some of the most important reasons why:

- Without your own credit record it can be difficult – maybe even impossible – for you to obtain a bank loan or a credit card, purchase a home, or rent a car, if you get divorced. Also, because some employers and insurance companies review credit records as part of their decision-making process, you may even find it tough to get the insurance or job you need! Although you can build your own credit record after your divorce, the process takes several years.

- When you and your spouse share joint credit, both of you are legally responsible for those accounts. That means that if your spouse mismanages that credit, your credit record, as well as your spouse's, is damaged.

- If your divorce agreement requires that your spouse pay off certain debts you were both liable for and if your ex-spouse fails to meet that obligation, the creditor can still try to collect the money from you.

  If, prior to your divorce, you or your spouse close all of your joint accounts and you later tell those creditors that you would like credit with them in your own name, they can require that you re-apply for credit if the joint accounts were based on your spouse's income. If you don't already have a credit record that reflects credit in your own name, you will likely be denied the credit you want.

Some single men and women with their own credit and bank accounts close them when they marry, open joint bank accounts with their spouses, and apply for joint credit. If your spouse fails to pay one of his or her individual debts, therefore, the creditor can try to get paid by coming after *your* share of the marital property, not just your spouse's share.

There is no law saying that when you get married you and your spouse must merge your finances!

TECHNICAL STUFF

Selecting the best credit card

If you plan on paying your credit card balance in full each month, go for a card that offers you a grace period of at least 25 days. (A grace period is the time you have to pay the card balance before you're charged interest.)

If you expect to – at times – carry a balance on your credit card, shop for one with a low annual percentage rate (APR). Pay attention to how that APR is calculated. Most companies base their APR on an *average daily balance,* including new purchases. That method works out better for the credit card company than it does for you. The most consumer-friendly APR calculation method is the *adjusted daily balance* method. The average daily balance *not* including purchases method is second best. Steer clear of cards that use the *two-cycle average daily balance* method to calculate APRs – they cost you a bundle in finance charges. Information about the APR calculation method should be included in a credit card offer's small print.

It isn't always the best idea to go for the card with the highest credit limit and using a credit card to finance a major purchase is an expensive financing alternative. You're better off saving up for something or getting a bank loan. Also, having a high credit limit can jeopardize your opportunity to obtain an important loan for other credit in the future. As an incentive some companies offer 0 per cent interest for the initial period (often up to six months) either on purchases or transfers. Whilst this can be very useful as you build your credit record they need to be monitored carefully as the grace period may be shorter than standard and penalties for late payment may be higher.

Don't be tempted by credit card offers touting special benefits such as product rebates, frequent flier miles, and so on. To take advantage of these offers, you'll probably have to charge a lot on the credit card first, and some cards with added benefits tack on high APRs, a short grace period, or other unfavourable terms of credit. Other things to look out for include:

- Avoid cards with a high annual fee or one that escalates after a certain period of time.

- Avoid cards that charge you high penalties if you don't make your payments on time, or if you don't use your card often enough.

- Steer clear of cards that increase the annual rate you pay if you're late with your payment or if you exceed your credit limit.

- If you have access to the Web log on to www.moneyfacts.co.uk to obtain an up-to-date list of the credit cards with the lowest interest rates. Best buy lists are also shown in the money pages of the national press, such as Wednesday's *Daily Mail*.

Establishing a Credit Record of Your Own

Before you begin the credit-record process, request a copy of your credit report from any of the credit bureaus listed above. It would also be good to know what's in your spouse's credit report, but your spouse has to agree to order it. However, your credit reports alone provide you with information on most of your joint debts as well as your individual ones. They just won't tell you about your spouse's individual or separate debts.

Review your credit reports carefully for errors and omissions. If you find any problems, write to the agency informing them of the correct situation. If you used to have credit in your maiden name, make sure that this credit is a part of your credit history. If it's not, ask that the credit bureau add that information.

If some of the joint accounts in your credit history reflect late payments or even defaults due to your spouse's mismanagement of those accounts, you may be able to distance yourself from that negative information by preparing a 'Notice of Correction.' This can be an explanation of up to 200 words on what has occurred and why. Any future lender will see the notice when they search your report. Send the notice to each of the two main credit bureaus (see the sidebar 'Contacting the credit bureaus'). The notice you provide becomes a permanent part of your credit record.

Avoid using any of the agencies that offer to rebuild your credit, especially those that state that, for a fee, they are able to remove detrimental information from your record. If they sound too good to be true, they most likely are.

Once you have resolved any difficulties in your credit record continue to build a solid credit history. You can do this by applying for a small unsecured loan (£500) from your bank/building society and repaying it over a reasonable period (12 months). Let the degree of crisis in your marriage dictate how quickly you pay back what you borrow.

If the bank won't loan you money without a co-signer, don't ask your spouse – you will end up linking your credit to your spouse's. Ask a relative or close friend to co-sign instead.

After you pay off a loan, you should take a few more steps to secure a good credit history:

- ✔ Take out another small loan – this time not co-signed – in your own name.

- ✔ Order a copy of your credit report from each of the credit bureaus to make sure that they reflect your loan payments. If they don't, ask the bank to report your payment history to the credit bureau it works with.

- ✔ Apply for one or more store cards, as they tend to have a more relaxed application process. Beware, though – interest rates are high. Do not overspend and repay the debt quickly.

- ✔ Apply for a credit card, preferably with a 0 per cent interest rate, and ensure that you make regular payments within the grace period.

- ✔ Always proceed with caution, as too many applications for credit in a short period can temporarily damage your credit file.

Being an *authorised user* on your spouse's accounts will *not* help you build your own credit history. That's because being an authorised user means that you get to use the credit but you have no legal responsibility for the account.

Contacting the credit bureaus

You can obtain a copy of your credit record from any of the credit bureaus by writing to them at the following addresses and providing your name, address, and date of birth and enclosing a £2 cheque or postal order.

- Consumer Help Service, Experian, PO Box 8000, Nottingham NG1 5GX, www.experian.com

- Consumer Enquiries, Equifax Europe plc, PO Box 3001, Glasgow G81 2DT, www.equifax.com

- Callcredit plc, 1 Park Lane, Leeds, West Yorkshire LS3 1EP, www.callcredit.co.uk

To ensure that you obtain *all* the required information, use the following statement:

'I am writing under section 158(1) of the Consumer Credit Act 1974. Please send me a copy of my file, including any information held about me under any linked addresses.'

If there are any errors on the report you can apply to have them removed. If for instance a county court judgement is registered but has been satisfied, apply to the county court for a 'Certificate of Satisfaction' (in Scotland it's called a Scottish Decree), send proof of payment from the individual or organisation that took the case to court (called 'the pursuer' in Scotland) to the Registry Trust with a £4.50 search fee. All rating agencies will receive notification of the change within four weeks and adjust their records. If a credit account has been settled but this has not been recorded, you need to contact the company in question and ask them to notify the rating agencies.

Check to make sure that any jointly-held credit is recorded in your individual names rather than Mr & Mrs R. Smith. Ask the creditors to begin reporting information on these accounts in your name as well as your spouse's. Assuming that these accounts have positive payment histories, having them in your credit file may help you build your own credit history.

Chapter 4

Family Law Basics

. . . .

In This Chapter

▶ Following the evolution of family law

▶ Understanding the legal side of marriage obligations

▶ Finding out about the role of family law courts and lawyers

▶ Examining your parental responsibilities

. . . .

*T*he rules of the game for marriage, separation, and divorce, as well as those that apply to parent–child relationships, fall under the heading of *family law.* Among other things, family law establishes the ground rules for what makes a marriage or divorce legal, sets out the obligations of one spouse to another, and defines the basic responsibilities that you as parents have toward your children, such as supporting them financially even after your marriage has ended.

This chapter provides an overview of the laws that apply to beginning and ending your marriage. It also offers a brief historical perspective on how those laws have evolved to accommodate and reflect society's changing values.

Check out www.divorce.co.uk for easy-to-understand advice and information on a variety of divorce-related legal and emotional issues.

Changing Laws for Changing Times

In the past few decades we've witnessed dramatic changes in our society's lifestyles, values, and attitudes. Among those changes was the movement of women out of the house and into the work world. In turn, fathers began playing a more active role in the care and bringing up of their children. As a result, lawmakers and family law courts began to re-evaluate their attitudes towards arrangements for children and financial support between spouses.

Ending the blame game

Since the 1970s, it has been possible to obtain a divorce without blaming your spouse if you're willing and able to wait until you've been separated for two years – if your spouse consents to the divorce. (You need to wait five years if your spouse doesn't.)

In the 1990s the Lord Chancellor, Lord Mackay, proposed a new divorce law which would remove 'fault' allegations from divorce altogether to minimise the opportunities for blame and bitterness. Although the resulting Family Law Act 1996 was passed by Parliament, it was never fully implemented – chiefly because the new Act was very controversial. So many additional steps and stages were introduced into what used to be a simple divorce process that the next Lord Chancellor, Lord Irvine, dropped most of the Act – except for the parts concerning domestic violence and public funding for mediation. As a result, it's still possible – necessary, even – to base a divorce on fault unless you're willing and able to wait for a minimum of two years.

Recognising children's rights

In 1989 the government passed The Children Act, which radically shifted the emphasis from parents' *rights* in respect of their children to parents' *responsibilities* towards them. The Act came about partly in response to an increasing awareness of the damage that was being done to children who were caught in the bitter disputes of their parents, or who lost touch with one parent. The Children Act emphasised the rights of the children rather than the rights of the parents, radically changing the way caring for children is handled in divorce cases.

Managing child support

As the number of single parent families grew in the latter half of the last century, so did the demands on the state for financial support. As a result, the government introduced the Child Support Act 1991, devising a formula for the calculation of child support payable by each parent and shifting most of the power for deciding child support issues from the family courts to an administrative agency known as the Child Support Agency (CSA). The main aim was to make parents more responsible for the financial support of their children following divorce or separation, and also to reduce the costs of litigation. The Child Support Act has been only partially successful in achieving its aims, and the formula had to be greatly simplified in 2003 – partly to minimise the scope for the administrative errors and delay which have dogged the Agency since its inception. Have a look at Chapter 13 for more on child support and the CSA.

Supporting your spouse

Attitudes towards spousal support have also changed over the past few decades, with a growing number of women earning their own money. Orders for spousal maintenance have become less common, and judges are now expressly required by statute to consider whether or not to dismiss such claims on divorce. Nominal maintenance orders – such as 5p per year – may still feature, mainly to leave open the possibility for claim by a spouse whilst there are dependent children. Spousal support and maintenance are fully explained in Chapter 12.

Tying the Knot

People typically think of marriage as a romantic relationship and most marriages do start out that way. However, marriage is also a financial and a legal relationship. In fact, the financial and legal aspects of marriage last long after the romance fades and those aspects of marriage become paramount if you decide to legally separate or get divorced.

Carrying a licence to marry

If you're reading this book, you're likely already married and considering divorce, and you may not care what your responsibilities should have been when married – you want us to cut to the chase! But knowing what you're responsible for *during* marriage helps you better understand your responsibilities after divorce.

You're required by the state to give notice of your intention to marry in order to ensure that there are no legal objections, such as a previous marriage that hasn't been dissolved. (So if you want to remarry, make sure your divorce is finalised first!) Your notice can take any of the following forms, depending on where you want to get married.

- ✔ **A registry office wedding:** If you're planning a marriage in a registry office, then you must give prior notice of your intention to the Registrar.

- ✔ **A religious wedding ceremony:** The person conducting your wedding ceremony can tell you whether or not he or she is also licensed to act as Registrar, in which case you don't need to contact the registry office. (If you get married in the Church of England, your Banns, announcing your marriage and giving the opportunity for objection, will then be called in the parish churches where you each live.) If the person conducting your religious ceremony isn't licensed for civil marriages, then you must also inform the registrar and additionally arrange a registry office marriage.

✔ **Another approved marriage venue:** If you plan to marry in a secular venue other than the registry office (for instance, an approved hotel) then the organiser will tell you how to inform the Registrar.

In all these situations, you need to show proof of your age, identity, and address. If either of you have been married before, you need to give evidence that the marriage has ended – by showing proof either of your divorce or your former spouse's death.

You can't legally marry under the following circumstances:

✔ You're under 16 years old. You also need to have your parents' consent if you're under 18 – unless you live in Scotland.

✔ You're planning to marry a close relative such as your parent, sibling, grandparent, child, or grandchild.

✔ You're already married to someone else – that's called *bigamy*.

✔ You aren't respectively male and female (see the sidebar 'Same-sex relationships').

After you're married, you receive a certified copy of your marriage certificate to show that you're legally married. If you don't have a copy and need one for your divorce, the original marriage certificate is kept at the church or registry office and they should be able to give you a copy.

Many couples these days choose to live together without marrying. The law relating to co-habiting couples is very different to that relating to married couples. You can read more about living together in the sidebar 'Living together without being married' later in this chapter.

Same-sex relationships

Same-sex marriages are not currently allowed in the UK but the government has made proposals to allow same-sex couples to register their partnerships. If these proposals become law, same-sex couples who register will gain rights and obligations very similar to those of married couples.

Understanding your marital rights and responsibilities

After your marriage ceremony, you and your spouse have a legally binding marital contract with one another. With that contract you have agreed to assume a number of important financial and legal obligations to one another. The contract also entitles you to certain legal rights as spouses. Some of those obligations and rights include the following:

- ✔ **You have an obligation to support each other financially.**

  The law does not say how you must provide the financial support or how much support you have to provide. Furthermore, if you are a spouse based at home, the courts are likely to view the work you perform in taking care of your home, bringing up your children, or supporting your spouse's career as contributing financially to your marriage.

- ✔ **You have an obligation to provide financial and other support for your children.**

- ✔ **You have the right to choose where, when, and how you fulfil your legal obligations to your children, within limits.**

  For example, the authorities don't mind if you raise your children as vegetarians, but they will intervene if they have reason to believe you're starving them – in fact you may lose care of your children as a result. And although you're free to choose your own doctor, if the authorities decide that you're withholding lifesaving medical treatment from your child, the authorities may intervene.

- ✔ **You have an obligation to provide for your spouse on your death.** If you don't make provision, your spouse can make a claim against your estate.

- ✔ **You are exempt from testifying against each other in court.**

- ✔ **You have a right to certain retirement and state benefits.**

- ✔ **You have a right to register your spouse's death and to claim bereavement benefits and fatal accident damages.**

- ✔ **You have a right to succeed to a tenancy.**

Agreeing to the terms before you marry

You may attempt to limit or extend your marital obligations towards one another by signing a *pre-marital* or *pre-nuptial* agreement before you marry. For example, before you marry you may agree that you don't have any financial rights to a business which your future spouse has owned for some years before you knew each other. However, the courts in England and Wales aren't bound by such agreements if there is a later disagreement between you. The judge may only take the agreement into account as part of the wider picture if he or she feels it is fair to you both to do so. Chapter 21 covers pre-marital agreements in more detail.

Living together without being married

You may often hear about living together – also known as co-habitation, or 'common law marriage' – in the same context as marriage. However, under UK law, there is no such thing as a common law marriage no matter how long you've been together. Many couples living together think that they have similar rights, obligations, and protections to married couples if they separate but that is not the case – except with regard to your children. As parents, your responsibilities in the eyes of the court are the exact same towards your children regardless of marriage. If you're not married and you separate, you don't have to go through a legal divorce process. Some other big differences for co-habitants are the following:

✔ You have no obligation to share any part of your estate (that is, everything that you own) with your co-habitant when you die, unless you have been living together for at least two years up to the date of your death, or your co-habitant can prove that he or she was financially dependent upon you. (In Scotland, there is no two-year provision – you can go to court to establish 'widow' or 'widower's rights to your unmarried partner's assets after living together for any length of time.)

✔ You won't automatically be entitled to your co-habitant's pension. Some pension schemes, however, do allow claims from co-habitants.

✔ Your property ownership rights, if you share a property together, are governed by trust and property law, not by family law. That means that if you do not have your name on the deeds, you may not be entitled to anything, even if you have children together. (Your dependent children, however, may have a claim.)

✔ You have no legal right to claim maintenance or ongoing financial support for yourself.

✔ As a father, you don't have legal parental responsibility for your children unless you have a court order, or a written agreement registered at the Principal Registry of the Family Division, or – since 1 December 2003 – you have registered the birth of your child with the mother. Only the natural mother automatically has parental responsibility.

Though rare, it's possible in Scotland to establish a common law marriage if you were both free to marry, lived together for a reasonable time, and you can show that almost no-one realised you weren't married. However, it isn't easy to prove, and depends on showing consent to marriage – if your partner for instance didn't believe in marriage, you wouldn't have a common law marriage. This can be important for inheritance as well as for the financial consequences of divorce.

Marrying in a religious ceremony

Though not necessary to be legally married, a religious ceremony is customary in all faith communities. However a religious marriage ceremony is only also a legal marriage if the minister who performs the ceremony and the place where it is being held is registered for marriage. If it isn't, you must also have a civil marriage in a registry office. Therefore, if you only had a religious ceremony in an unlicensed venue, you may not be considered legally married!

If you got married abroad, your marriage will generally be legally recognised here so long as your marriage complies with the laws of the country where you got married.

Mick Jagger contested Jerry Hall's divorce application in July 1999 on the grounds that their Hindu wedding was a ceremony and not a marriage. Rumour has it that this was so he wouldn't have to pay as much support in the settlement as he would've if they were legally married. In the end, Jerry Hall didn't proceed with the divorce action in order to avoid, so they say, having to give evidence about the history of their tumultuous relationship. The two settled out of court.

Knowing What the Law Says about Children

The Children Act 1989 concentrated on *children's* rights, requiring a change in the language we use to refer to their care. The phrases 'custody', 'care and control', and 'access' were abandoned, as they imply that children are possessions to be shared (or fought over) by their parents. Instead the legal system, and gradually the media and general public, use the terms 'parental responsibility', 'residence', and 'contact', which encourages divorcing parents to think of their children as people, rather than possessions to be fought over. Read on for full explanations of these terms.

Understanding parental responsibility

If you are married, the law says that both of you have parental responsibility – meaning that you both have a responsibility to provide for the moral, physical, and emotional health of your children. This responsibility includes

- Providing your children with food, clothing, medical care, and a place to live

- Disciplining your children

- Ensuring that your children receive at least minimal education (college is not required) in a state or private school or at home

- Choosing your children's names and religions

The law in Scotland presumes that, after your divorce, you and your ex-spouse will consult each other on what's best for your children, as you were presumed to do when you were married. Your responsibilities as parents in Scotland are to

- Safeguard and promote your child's health and well-being

- Provide direction and guidance for your child

- Maintain direct contact and personal relations with your child if you're not living together

- Act as your child's legal representative

- Consult your child about his living arrangements to the extent he can understand, particularly if he's over the age of 12

Throughout the UK, these obligations remain yours regardless of whether you and your spouse separate or divorce. Usually your parental obligations remain until your child becomes a legal adult at the age of 18. See Chapter 10 for more about parental responsibility.

There's no place like home – determining residency

As parents, during the divorce process you need to settle your children's *residence* – the arrangements about where and with whom the children will live. You have three options to choose from:

- **Sole residence:** The children live with one parent. For example, they are based with their mum.

- **Joint residence:** The children live with two people together. In this example, they live with their mum and stepdad.

- **Shared residence:** The children split their time between both parents' households. In this case, they might spend one week living with their dad and the next week with their mum.

Research has shown that children are usually better off living with both of their parents in one way or another.

Keeping in contact with your kids

If your children live with you and you are separated from their other parent, you're expected to allow your kids to have some degree of contact with him or her. Most parents will have *direct contact*, spending time with their children. However in some cases, such as where there have been allegations of abuse, the children won't have physical contact but may have *indirect contact*, exchanging letters or phone calls instead. Studies show that it's very important for their emotional development that your children do not lose touch with either of you, so direct contact with both parents is optimal.

Putting the children first

The law says – whether you're married or not – you have to give priority to your children's needs when you make any major decisions concerning them. Their welfare must always be your paramount consideration.

When a judge looks at the residence and contact arrangements you and your spouse are recommending to see if they're satisfactory, her highest priority is the child's best interests. The judge has to consider a checklist of factors, when asked to make such decisions, including:

- The wishes and feelings of the child concerned, in light of her age and understanding
- Her physical, emotional and educational needs
- The likely effect on her of any change in her circumstances
- Her age, sex, background, and any characteristic which the court considers relevant
- Any harm which she has suffered or is at risk of suffering
- How capable each of her parents is in meeting her needs
- The range of powers available to the court

During your divorce proceedings, a court won't make an order about your child (for example, about residence or contact) unless the judge thinks it is in your child's interest for the court to do so. This *no order principle* is based on the view that you know your children better than anyone else and are therefore better placed than the court to make a decision on your child's best interest.

Child abduction

Taking a child from the person who has care of him without that person's consent is a criminal offence. Consult a solicitor immediately if your child is abducted, especially if you believe your ex or soon-to-be-ex is the culprit and may take your child to a country outside England and Wales.

Both the Hague Convention and European Convention agree that decisions about custody should be made in the country where the child resided before the abduction. This means that if you and your kids live in England but your ex-spouse abducted your son to Morocco, the residence and child care decisions made in England take priority.

Several cases dealing with this subject have received media coverage in recent years, and Sally Field brought the issue to light further in the film *Not Without My Daughter.*

Distinguishing One Lawyer from Another

If you are involved in a family law dispute, it is likely that at some point you will have dealings with lawyers, whether they are representing your spouse or yourself. The two main sorts of lawyer that you will come across in England and Wales are *solicitors* and *barristers.* Chapters 15 and 17 have advice on finding and working with your solicitors and barristers, but following are brief descriptions of the differences between the two.

✔ **Solicitors:** Your first point of contact with a lawyer will almost certainly be with a solicitor. Solicitors are legally qualified and trained professionals who advise and represent you in all non-court matters. They can write letters on your behalf to your spouse or their solicitor; they can negotiate and help prepare your case for court if necessary. A solicitor has many capable and educated people working with her as she assists you, including legal executives, trainee solicitors, and paralegals. You may encounter some of these key players when working with your solicitor.

We strongly recommend that if you're considering divorce, you choose a lawyer who specialises in family law and preferably is a member of the Solicitors Family Law Association (check out their Web site for a list of solicitors in your area: www.sfla.org.uk).

✔ **Barristers:** With your permission, your solicitor may instruct a barrister, often referred to as counsel, to give an opinion on your case or to represent you in court. Barristers aren't usually involved with the day-to-day running of your case – that will be left to you or your solicitor – but it is their job to keep particularly up to date with developments in the law and to act as skilled advocates. Experienced solicitors will sometimes perform both roles.

Barristers are called *advocates* in Scotland.

Courting Justice

When you're getting legally separated or divorced, or if you're in a family law dispute of another kind, your legal issue falls under the jurisdiction of one or more different courts. If some aspect of your separation or divorce ends up in court, the judge decides on the issue after a hearing or trial. A jury trial is not an option and most family proceedings take place in private. Your solicitor can advise on which court is the most appropriate for you, or on whether the proceedings need to be transferred from one court to another.

- ✔ **The Family Proceedings Court:** Proceedings about children may start in the Family Proceedings Court, the family wing of the Magistrates Court, unless divorce or separation proceedings have already begun in another court, such as the County Court. (Usually all the proceedings are heard by the same court.) The Family Proceedings Court is often used for issues regarding children, especially if the local authority is involved. The Family Proceedings Court also has power to grant limited financial relief if you are separating from your spouse but not yet planning to divorce.

- ✔ **Criminal Courts (Magistrates and Crown Courts):** If you pursue criminal charges against your spouse for harassment or physical abuse, those charges will be heard in the criminal courts. In most cases that will be the Magistrates Court but in very serious cases it may be the Crown Court. Your spouse may be sent to prison if the court finds them guilty of serious violence or abuse.

- ✔ **The County Court:** This court deals with almost all divorce or separation proceedings, but it must be designated as a divorce County Court. You don't have to issue the divorce proceedings at the County Court in the area where you live, although it's usually more convenient. However, issues regarding children must be dealt with in the jurisdiction where the children currently live. A district or circuit judge of the County Court hears your case.

- ✔ **The High Court:** Your divorce or separation proceedings only go to the High Court if there's a lot of money involved or your case involves a particularly complex issue, such as a foreign marriage. A district judge or circuit judge who's authorised to sit in the High Court hears your case.

AROUND THE UK

The Scottish court system

The court system in Scotland is very different from the one in England and Wales. In Scotland there are no County or Magistrates Courts. Most divorce and family actions are handled by the *sheriff courts:* the local courts found in major towns and all cities throughout Scotland. The sheriff courts handle both civil law actions, which include family, divorce, and public law cases, and criminal law cases. If your case goes to court, you need to instruct a local solicitor to act for you and an advocate to represent you in court.

Some divorces are heard in the highest civil court: the *Court of Session* in Edinburgh. Cases usually go to the Court of Session when there's a lot of money involved or an unusual point of law to be decided. You need a specialist solicitor advocate to represent you in the Court of Session and cases take longer and cost more than actions in the sheriff courts.

Chapter 5

Divorce Law Basics

· ·

In This Chapter

▶ Meeting the minimum requirements for a divorce

▶ Waiting two years or blaming your spouse

▶ Examining the three basic kinds of divorce

▶ Finding out what happens if your divorce ends up in court

▶ Finalising a divorce

· ·

*Y*our divorce may be your first encounter with the legal system (except for that appearance in court for the odd traffic offence). Understandably, the prospect of dealing with lawyers, courts, and legal jargon can be fairly intimidating.

One of the best ways to steel yourself for what's to come and boost your self-confidence is to find out about the laws that apply to divorce and the legal processes involved in getting a divorce. With that in mind, this chapter provides an overview of the basics of divorce law and some of the key decisions you need to make to comply with the requirements of the legal system.

So, the first thing you should know is that the main act that deals with divorce in England and Wales is the Matrimonial Causes Act 1973. This Act is the basic framework for divorce, and deals with whether or not you can get divorced and provides guidelines for you, your solicitor, your mediator, and the courts to follow. In Scotland, the key piece of legislation is the Divorce (Scotland) Act 1976, and in Northern Ireland, the divorce law is spread over several different Orders.

Not Just Anyone Can Get Divorced

To get a divorce in England and Wales, you have to meet some minimum requirements. These are

✔ One or both of you must be habitually resident in England or Wales for a minimum of one year. However, if you can show that England or Wales is your country of *domicile* (your usual home, even though, for example, you are working abroad), you need only be resident for six months.

✔ You or your spouse have not initiated similar proceedings in any other country anywhere in the world.

✔ You have been married for a minimum of one year.

In Northern Ireland, the minimum period is two years. There is no minimum in Scotland.

✔ Your marriage has irretrievably broken down.

Understanding irretrievable breakdown

The court will accept that your marriage has irretrievably broken down if you can establish that any one of the following five facts applies to you:

✔ **Your spouse has committed adultery and you find it intolerable to live with him or her.**

Adultery means sexual intercourse between a man and a woman, one or both of whom are married and not to each other. You cannot petition on the basis of your own adultery. Adultery is easier to prove if your spouse is prepared to admit to it. Sometimes a spouse is prepared to admit to adultery if you promise not to pursue any claim for costs. You don't have to name the third party, but if you do, that third party has to be given notice and allowed to respond. You cannot rely on adultery as a basis for divorce if you and your spouse have lived together for more than six months after you first learnt of the adultery, unless the adultery is continuing.

✔ **Your spouse has behaved in such a way that you cannot reasonably be expected to live with him or her.**

To cite behaviour as your basis for divorce, you need to provide the court with at least three examples of behaviour by your spouse which you have found unacceptable, and preferably give dates. If the behaviour is extreme, such as serious violence, one incident may be enough. Other examples of behaviour include drinking or gambling to excess; constant verbal abuse; refusal to have, or excessive demands for, sexual intercourse; or complete lack of financial or other support.

The test is whether the court thinks it is unreasonable to expect you to continue living together. It is not an absolute bar to divorce if you have lived together for more than six months since the last incident of behaviour, but the court takes account of this fact, and it may undermine your claim that the marriage has irretrievably broken down.

✔ **Your spouse has deserted you – for a minimum of two years.**

Divorces based on desertion are relatively rare. You have to prove that your spouse has refused to live with you for at least two years without good cause. Any attempt at reconciliation for up to six months does not count against you, but you have to add any periods of reconciliation onto the two-year period leading up to your petition.

✔ **You have been separated for at least two years and your spouse consents to a divorce.**

You have to establish not only that you have not lived together for the two years leading up to your petition, but also that you believed that the marriage was over at the time you separated. You can live under the same roof as your spouse for part or all of this time, but you need to satisfy the judge that you have lived as separate households. It is not enough just to stop sleeping together; you need to prove that you no longer eat meals together, do chores for each other, or generally function as a couple. You also need written confirmation of your spouse's consent to divorce.

A reconciliation for up to six months won't prevent you from getting a divorce on this basis, but you have to add the period of reconciliation onto the two-year period leading up to the divorce petition. For example, if you and your spouse separate in January 2004 and hope to divorce two years later, but then you have an unsuccessful reconciliation for three months, you can't petition for divorce until April 2006 – two years and three months after your original separation.

✔ **You have been separated for at least five years.**

The same conditions apply to a divorce on this basis as they do to a divorce based on two years' separation except that you do not need your spouse's consent.

You don't have to blame your spouse for the breakdown of your marriage if you can wait for two years before filing your petition. You still need to try and agree all the key issues between you, preferably before you separate.

The Office for National Statistics records that in 1991, nearly a third of divorces were granted on the grounds of adultery, whereas in 2002 that proportion had dropped to 22 per cent. The Office attributes this to the rise in the use of mediation, whereby couples are more likely to choose the no-fault basis for divorce of two years' separation.

The vast proportion of petitions for divorce go through on an undefended basis, even when they are based on adultery or behaviour – allegations made in a petition rarely affect the outcome of the other key issues in your divorce, namely the arrangements for your children and finance. Keep in mind that allegations of fault increase the potential for bad feeling between you, however.

Resolving Basic Divorce Issues

You and your spouse need to decide on several fundamental issues during your divorce. Although it is technically possible to finalise your divorce before resolving all children and financial issues, it is usually wiser to wait until all such issues have been resolved. Some of the reasons for this are

- ✓ **Your children need to know what the arrangements are going to be for them.**

- ✓ **Until your divorce is finalised, you and your spouse are next of kin.** If your divorce is finalised before you have sorted out the benefits you have as next of kin, such as retirement or insurance rights, you may lose these important benefits.

- ✓ **If you don't have your name on the title deeds to your home, you may lose any matrimonial rights you have registered.** See Chapter 3 for how to register your interest in a property that isn't in your name.

- ✓ **Unless and until a final financial order is made in the divorce proceedings, either one of you may pursue financial claims against the other many years after the divorce itself has been finalised.** Your ex-spouse may also claim against your estate on your death, if he or she has not remarried and believes that you haven't made reasonable provision for him or her. If you want to avoid those possibilities, you must have a final order settling all financial and property matters between you and dismissing all future claims, including those on death.

- ✓ **If you remarry following your divorce, you can't make any financial claims against your ex-spouse unless you have reserved those claims in your petition for divorce.** This is known as the *remarriage trap,* and it is a particular risk if your spouse started the divorce proceedings and you agreed to them going through on an undefended basis. If you subsequently remarry without having secured from the court a final order with regard to all financial and property matters, you are prohibited from pursuing your claims at a later date. You are also at a severe disadvantage should your ex-spouse decide to pursue his or her financial claims against you.

Your decisions should include answers to the following questions:

- ✓ **How will your property, pensions, and debts be divided up?** If you are unable to agree on a division, complex laws, plus a wide discretion on the part of the judge in applying those laws to your case, can make deciding who gets what a complicated undertaking, especially if you and your spouse have managed to amass a considerable amount of assets. (See Chapter 11, to help you work out how to divide up your assets.)

- ✓ **Will one of you pay spousal support or maintenance to the other?** If so, how much will the payments be and for how long will they continue?

If you are an older woman who has never worked outside the home during your marriage or has not done so in many years, you may have difficulty finding a well-paying job after you are divorced. Therefore, getting an adequate amount of maintenance for a long enough period of time – possibly the rest of your life – is essential to your maintaining an acceptable post-divorce lifestyle. However, if your divorce is rancorous, your spouse may fight against paying you the maintenance you think you need. (See Chapter 12 for more on maintenance.)

✔ **If you and your spouse have dependent children, how will residence and contact be handled?** These issues can be some of the most emotional in a divorce. Some spouses, if they are unable to agree on arrangements, fear that if they do not become the resident parent, they will no longer play a meaningful role in the lives of their children; others may view fighting for the children as a way to get back at their spouses. See Chapter 10 for more about making decisions on the arrangements for your children.

✔ **What arrangements will you make for child support?** Since 1993, the Child Support Agency (CSA) has taken over most of the powers with regard to child support from the courts. The CSA calculates child support according to a formula, which is described in Chapter 13. You don't have to wait for divorce proceedings to apply to the CSA; you just have to be separated. Even if you and your spouse agree the question of child support without going to the CSA, it is a good idea to be aware of the formula.

If you and your spouse can work together to resolve these issues, your divorce can be relatively quick and inexpensive. If you can't work together, or if your divorce has complicating factors (your property or debt is substantial, for example), bringing your marriage to an end can take time and money. In a worst-case scenario, you must look to the courts for help.

The Ground Rules of the Divorce Court

The divorce laws and statutory guidelines provide a framework and set boundaries for resolving the basic issues that you need to decide when you separate. In other words, those laws and guidelines are actually quite flexible, within certain limits:

✔ As you work your way through the divorce process, you and your spouse have a considerable amount of leeway when you decide on most of these issues, as long as you are both *in agreement*.

✔ As you address the division of your family property, spousal support, and child residence and contact, assume that a *family law judge* is looking over your shoulder. This means that whatever you decide about these matters should give priority to the needs of your children and be fair to you both. Your decisions should reflect an appreciation of what the judge would probably decide if your divorce issues were to end in a full hearing. You can find more on the guidelines used by judges when they decide about money and property division in Chapter 11 and on children in Chapter 4.

Second-guessing family law judges can be tricky because judges have considerable discretion in how they interpret the law and the weight that they give to the various statutory guidelines in each case. As a result, approaches may vary somewhat from one court to another or even from one judge to another in the same court.

You can appeal a judge's decision, but an appeal can be hard to justify legally and may be risky. Plus, appealing means more delay and legal fees.

Divorce law helps resolve legal and financial issues. The law won't resolve the anger, guilt, fear, or sadness you may feel. Don't look to the legal system to do that for you or you'll be left feeling disappointed and frustrated when your divorce is over.

One Objective (But Many Ways to Get There)

The goal of any divorce is to end a marriage. That goal can be achieved in many ways, however. You can work together to make your divorce process as easy and inexpensive as possible, or you can turn it into an expensive battle full of anger, unreasonable demands, and uncompromising behaviour.

Divorce is a process, not an event. Just what path your divorce process takes is up to you and your spouse. Here are your basic options, all of which are described in more detail in the sections that follow:

- ✔ **Option 1 – the co-operative divorce.** You and your spouse work out the terms of all the key issues of your divorce together. One of you files an agreed divorce petition and you ask the court for a consent order regarding your property. You can also use a mediator or engage solicitors, or even hire both a mediator and solicitors, to help you work out the details and formalities, but you still keep things friendly.

- ✔ **Option 2 – the difficult divorce.** You and your spouse can't agree on all the key issues in your divorce. You may be able to avoid a full hearing by resolving your differences with the help of solicitors or through mediation (see Chapter 16).

- ✔ **Option 3 – the fully contested divorce.** At this point, you lose control of one or more of the key issues in your divorce. They are now in the hands of a divorce court judge. Luckily, the minority of cases end up this way.

Your divorce can be a combination of two or even all three divorce options we just listed. For example, you and your spouse may work some things out together, engage solicitors to negotiate other aspects of your divorce, and then have a judge resolve the issues on which you're deadlocked.

Many couples committed to working things out themselves with minimal help from lawyers also use *mediation* as a way to help them structure their divorce negotiations and reduce the opportunity for emotions to get in the way of reason. (See Chapter 16 if you feel that you and your spouse can benefit from mediation.)

The co-operative divorce

A *co-operative divorce* is the divorce option that is easiest on your cheque-book (and on your emotions). With co-operation, filing a *divorce petition* (the legal paperwork that initiates a divorce) will be little more than a formality, since your spouse won't object to the petition. A straightforward uncontested divorce should be completed within three to six months.

Using collaborative law

A relatively new option for working out the terms of your divorce outside of court in a friendly manner is available through a process called *collaborative law*. You, your spouse, and your respective lawyers (who must be trained in the collaborative law process) sit down together to reach a settlement on all the issues of your divorce. Unlike mediation, no neutral third party is involved. After you hammer out an agreement, your divorce petition and agreed order is filed with the court. The benefits of this approach include:

✔ Lower costs

✔ Less stress for you, your spouse, and your lawyers

✔ Creative solutions to divorce issues

✔ Increased cooperation between spouses

✔ A positive foundation from which to build a post-divorce relationship if you and your spouse share young children

The drawback to using collaborative law to negotiate your divorce is that if you and your spouse are unable to come to an agreement and need the court's involvement, the lawyers you have been working with must withdraw from your case and you have to find new lawyers. That does not mean that you begin the divorce process all over again however, as you can take the information you collect with you for use by your next solicitor. To find out more visit www.collab.law.uk.

You and your spouse work together to structure agreements relating to your children and to your finances that you both think are fair. If you reach an agreement about your children that is clearly in their interests, the court is unlikely to interfere, and no further formalities will be involved. After you agree on the terms of your final financial settlement, you or your solicitors file the agreement with the court as a draft consent order for the approval of the judge. Providing the judge approves the draft order neither you nor your spouse should need to attend court. It can all be done by post. Judges approve most draft orders if you've both had some independent legal advice, and the agreement does not on the face of it appear to be unfair.

The difficult divorce

If any of the key issues in your divorce are contested, lawyers are almost always involved. For example, you may have a hard time accepting that your spouse is blaming you for the breakdown of your marriage when you know that you are both equally responsible. You may ask your solicitors to negotiate on the contents of the petition or on the question of costs. Most lawyers will tell you that it's rarely worth arguing over the divorce itself (that is, over the *reason* for the end of your marriage) – if you both agree that the marriage has broken down; the reason for the divorce rarely affects the way the judge deals with any of the other issues such as the children or money. These days, only a tiny number of divorce petitions are fully defended.

If you and your spouse can't agree over the arrangements for your children or for your finances, you can go to mediation to resolve the issues or ask your solicitors to try to negotiate a solution for you. More correspondence and paperwork mean that the difficult divorce takes longer to complete than the co-operative divorce and is more stressful for you – and it costs more.

The fully contested divorce

The fully contested divorce is more emotional, time-consuming, and expensive, and involves more paperwork and legal red tape than your other options. It can exhaust both your emotional and your financial resources. Also, the animosity between you and your spouse probably won't go away after your divorce is final, and you may have difficulty even carrying on a polite conversation when it's all over.

The main issues that you might contest are the following:

> ✔ The basis of the petition itself (see the section on 'Understanding irretrievable breakdown' earlier in this chapter). It's now rare for the basis of the petition itself to become fully contested

✔ The arrangements for your children

✔ The arrangements for your money and property

✔ Your personal protection or the short-term occupation of your home, if your safety, or that of your children, is under threat

If any aspect of your divorce ends with a full hearing, you're more likely to end up revisiting the terms later on. Doing so not only takes money and time but may also mean that you can never really put your divorce and your failed marriage behind you.

Initiating the Divorce Proceedings

Every divorce starts the same way – one spouse sends or *files* a *petition* with the court. If you do the filing, you are called the *petitioner* and your spouse is the *respondent*. In Scotland, the divorcing parties are known as the *pursuer* and the *defender*. If your petition is based on your spouse's adultery, you do not have to name a third party, but if you do, he or she will become known as the *co-respondent*. (The Law Society has recommended changing the words simply to 'husband' or 'wife' for clarity.)

When is a divorce not a divorce?

A civil divorce which is valid according to UK law may still not be enough for the purposes of your church or faith community if you want to remarry according to your faith. For example, a divorced Catholic who wishes to remarry in the Catholic Church must obtain a religious annulment first. If you're Jewish, you remain married according to Jewish religious law unless you also have a religious divorce, known as a Get. A Muslim needs a religious divorce under the Islamic law of Shariah in order to remarry. Check the requirements for divorce with your own religious authorities if you wish to end your marriage according to your faith.

Not surprisingly, a divorce that takes place in the UK must comply with UK law to be valid. A divorce that takes place outside the UK will generally be regarded as valid here if it has complied with the divorce laws of the country in which it has taken place, and there were some proceedings giving both spouses adequate notice and an opportunity to respond. A Muslim divorce, for example, by a *bare talaq* (a single unilateral declaration of divorce by a husband) isn't regarded as valid in the UK; but an application by a wife to a judge of the Shariah Court, or a divorce which otherwise complies with Islamic law, is regarded as valid if both parties have consented or have had proper notice and an opportunity to respond. Check with your solicitor if you're not sure if your divorce is legally valid here.

In your petition, you establish the facts and the issues of the divorce as you see them, and indicate what you want financially from your spouse. This *ancillary relief* may include maintenance (or *periodical payments*), lump sums, property and pensions for you, and maintenance or lump sums for your children. You can also claim costs. If you want to activate these claims, you must make a separate formal application to the court.

Even if you think it's unlikely that you will want to make a formal application, preserving all your possible claims in the petition is still a good idea. Otherwise, if you change your mind later, you have to get the permission of the court first to make the application. That will cost you extra time and money, especially if your spouse objects.

When you file a divorce petition, you are actually initiating matrimonial proceedings against your spouse. As the *petitioner,* you pay at least the initial court costs of your divorce. If you also make a formal application and your case ends up in court, you present your side first.

Unless your divorce is based on fault, you will both probably pay your own legal and court costs. However, you can try to agree between you a provision that your spouse reimburse you for all or part of your costs. You need to include the claim for costs in your petition. If you are publicly funded, you do not have to pay any costs up front, but you may be liable for them in the long run because public funding usually takes the form of a loan rather than a gift. For more about costs and public funding, see Chapter 7.

Remembering your marriage certificate

When you file a petition for divorce, you are required to file a certified copy of your marriage certificate at the same time. If your divorce goes through, the marriage certificate remains on your divorce file with the court. If you cannot find your marriage certificate, you can apply for another certified copy from the church or registry office where you married. You need to provide your full names, the date of your marriage ceremony, and a fee (currently £6.50).

Including a Statement of Arrangements for the Children

If you have any children in your family, you must file a statement detailing the current and proposed arrangements for them, including

- ✔ Where they will live
- ✔ Where they will go to school
- ✔ Child support

✔ Contact

✔ Whether they have special health or educational needs

'Children of the family' includes not only the children of you and your spouse, but also any children of either of you, or of anyone else, if the children have lived with you and been treated as children of the family. The statement has to be filed with the court at the same time as the petition.

Serving and receiving the papers

After a petition is filed, your spouse must be formally notified. The notification can be accomplished in a number of ways:

✔ **The most common way is to ask the court to post a copy of the papers to your spouse.** The court sends a copy of the petition and any statement of arrangements to your spouse with an explanation of the proceedings and a form of acknowledgment for your spouse to return.

✔ **A rarer alternative is to ask the court bailiff to serve the papers personally.** You need a special form for this request (Divorce 96), a description or recent photograph of your spouse, and a court fee. This option is best if you anticipate difficulties in proving that your spouse has received the papers.

✔ **You can hire your own private process server to serve the papers personally on your spouse.** This is more expensive and only necessary if there is a lot of hostility between you, or you have to make an urgent application.

✔ If you are having real difficulty in proving 'service'(formally presenting the documents) upon your spouse, the court will sometimes allow *substituted service* – the papers are delivered to a particular address that the judge thinks the respondent is likely to receive mail from. The judge may even *dispense* with service if he or she is satisfied that you have made every possible effort to trace your spouse and failed.

Once your spouse has received the papers, they have eight days within which to return the *acknowledgement of service* to the court detailing whether they

✔ Consent to the divorce

✔ Intend to defend it

✔ Object to any claim for costs in the petition

✔ Agree with the arrangements for your children

The form also gives the details of any solicitor engaged by your spouse.

If your spouse intends to defend the divorce, they have 21 days to file an *answer.* They also need to file a cross-petition if they agree that the marriage has broken down but not for the reasons you've stated. In addition, when adultery is the basis for your petition, either your spouse needs to admit to the adultery on the acknowledgement of service, or you will need some other strong evidence.

You will need your spouse's signed consent on the acknowledgement of service if you are basing your petition on having been separated for two years. Your spouse can defend a petition based on two or five years' separation on the grounds that financial matters need to be resolved first, or that he or she will suffer hardship if the divorce is granted. The court will then have to deal with those issues before the divorce can be finalised.

Signing the affidavit in support of petition

The court will forward a copy of the acknowledgement or statement of service to you or your solicitor. You then need to sign a statement on oath confirming the contents of your petition and statement of arrangements, and saying whether you are pursuing any claim for costs. This is known as the *affidavit in support of petition.* Attach a copy of your spouse's acknowledgement of service or the bailiffs' certificate of service to your affidavit.

An affidavit is a statement that is signed on oath in front of a solicitor or an officer of the court. You cannot sign the affidavit in front of your own solicitor – you must pay a fee to a solicitor for witnessing your signature (about £5 per document and £2 per attachment) but the officer of the court will not charge you for this service. Send your sworn affidavit to the court for the judge to check. The judge then certifies whether you are entitled to a divorce, and whether the arrangements for your children are satisfactory.

The initial writ or summons in Scotland is simply a formal statement of the reasons for your divorce, your financial claims, and requests for orders in relation to your children. A writ is served by recorded delivery post or personally by Sheriff Officers in the Sheriff Court or Messengers at Arms in the Court of Session. No acknowledgement of service required. In Northern Ireland, the petitioner is not permitted to give evidence by written statement alone: He or she has to attend court personally to give evidence to the judge.

If you and your spouse are not already legally separated but will begin living apart now that your divorce has begun, it's best to have a written agreement that details your living and financial arrangements and how you will handle child-related issues during the divorce process. (See Chapter 6 for more about separation.)

Divorcing in Scotland

Scotland has two kinds of divorce actions: The simplified procedure and the ordinary procedure.

✔ **The simplified procedure is sometimes known as the 'do-it-yourself divorce'.** To qualify to use the simplified procedure, you must have no children of the marriage under 16 years old or any financial claims between you and your spouse. Also, no other ongoing actions may exist between you.

You can ask for the forms for the simplified procedure from the local sheriff clerk's office or from the Citizens' Advice Bureau (CAB) or from your own solicitor. The forms and guidance on filling them can be downloaded from the Scottish Courts Web site: www.scotcourts.gov.uk. There is a fee for using the simplified procedure, which is explained on the forms. Doing your divorce yourself is a lot cheaper than using the ordinary procedure, but you should still seek legal advice at the outset. as you may lose rights you are entitled to only on or before the divorce is granted.

✔ **The ordinary procedure is for divorces where you have children under 16 years old, financial claims between you and your spouse, or both.** The person who raises a divorce action is called the *pursuer*. You can be a *party litigant* (someone who brings or defends a court action without a solicitor). However, it is wise to use a solicitor to act on your behalf to raise a divorce action under the ordinary procedure. You can find a solicitor to act for you from the Law Society of Scotland: www.lawscot.org.uk. It is worth considering a solicitor who specialises in family law matters. Some of these solicitors are members of the Scottish Family Law Association: www.fla-scotland.co.uk.

Under the ordinary procedure, actions can be defended or undefended. In a defended action, the *defender* (the person against whom the action is raised) opposes the pursuer's claims and/or raises his or her own counter claim against the case or parts of the case raised by the pursuer. It is unusual for the grounds for divorce to be defended, but there are defended actions relating to arrangements for children and financial matters.

In an undefended action, the defender does not oppose the pursuer's claims or raise counter claims, and the action can be dealt with by affidavit evidence – by a statement, sworn on oath in front of a notary public (an official who is authorised to certify documents). For this type of action, you need a witness. If you and your spouse have an undefended divorce, you may have matters on which you disagree. These matters can often be negotiated by your solicitors through correspondence.

Getting Through the First Stage: The Decree Nisi

After the judge has granted the certificate confirming that you are entitled to a divorce and that the arrangements for your children (if any) are satisfactory, the court fixes a date for the *decree nisi*. On that date, a judge reads out in open court the names of the couples who are to be divorced and the basis of their divorces. That completes the first stage of your divorce. You do not have to attend court, and the court will send a copy of the decree and any agreed order for costs to you and your spouse or your solicitors.

If an argument occurs between you and your spouse over who should pay the costs of the divorce, either of you can make written representations to the court or request a short appointment with the judge. The judge will usually order the respondent to pay the costs of the petitioner if he is satisfied that the petitioner has proved the adultery, behaviour, or desertion alleged.

On the rare occasions the judge identifies a major problem over the arrangements for the children or over the basis for the divorce, he may direct that further evidence be filed, or that the parties attend before the court.

Finalising Your Divorce with the Decree Absolute

You can apply to the court for your final decree of divorce, known as the *decree absolute,* not less than six weeks and one day from the date of your decree nisi. The court won't grant the decree absolute before then unless there are exceptional circumstances. If you wait more than 12 months to apply for the decree absolute, you have to file a statement giving the reasons for the delay. You should keep your decree absolute in a safe place as you may need it in the future (to remarry or apply for a passport, for example).

The effect of your decree absolute is that you and your spouse are no longer next of kin and you will be free to remarry. If you have made a will naming each other as an executor or beneficiary, the will becomes invalid in those respects. You should make or review your will at that stage, if you have not already done so. See Chapter 19 for more about wills and estate planning.

You may want to delay the application for your decree absolute until you have resolved all financial issues. See the section 'Resolving Basic Divorce Issues' earlier in this chapter for the reasons why this may be a sensible decision for you.

If you are the respondent and your spouse has not applied for the decree absolute within three months, you may apply to the court instead, giving your reasons for making the application. The judge will grant the application if he is satisfied that there is no good reason for the delay.

Remember that, if you are the petitioner, you can stop the divorce at any time, even up to the date of the decree absolute. If you and your spouse reconcile, or you start having doubts about whether a divorce is really what you want, you can either simply do nothing further, so that the divorce does not progress, or you can apply to the court to dismiss the petition. If you reconcile after the decree nisi has been pronounced, you can ask the court to rescind the decree. However, by then, if it is only you who is having second thoughts, and your spouse does still want a divorce, he or she can apply to the court for the decree absolute as described in the section above.

In Scotland, there is no decree nisi there is only one decree of divorce. If you are granted a divorce by a judge, you're divorced from that date.

Agreeing to Disagree: What Happens After You Decide to Litigate

When your divorce is not co-operative and you are in dispute with one another, you, your spouse, and your lawyers will work your way through a very specific legal process. At its most extreme, the process culminates with a court-ordered judgement after a fully contested hearing. However, at any point during the process, you and your spouse can reach an agreement regarding all of the issues in your divorce and avoid a full hearing.

Emergency applications

If you are in urgent need of an order from the court because you have reason to believe that your spouse is disposing of assets in order to defeat or reduce your claims, you can apply to the court for emergency relief. You must provide evidence to support your claims in the form of a written statement. Depending on the urgency and merits of your application, the judge may either grant an immediate order to protect your assets, or insist on notice first being given to your spouse or to a third party who will be directly affected. You and your spouse then have to argue the application in front of the judge.

If you or your children need protection from the court because you are suffering abuse or violence from your spouse, and are at a real and immediate risk of harm, you can ask the court to grant you a non molestation or occupation order. This order may forbid your spouse to threaten, harass, or use violence towards you or your children and may require your spouse to leave the home or allow you to return. Such an order usually lasts for about six months. A judge rarely orders anyone to leave their home without hearing both sides of the story first. (See Chapter 2.)

So that you understand some of what's to come, the following information offers a brief overview of each stage in the divorce process if any issue goes all the way to court. Chapter 18 goes into more detail about the conduct of the final hearing if you get to that point.

Formal Applications to the Court: Financial Issues

Family law protocol requires solicitors to make every effort to resolve the issues between you. But if you and your spouse are unable to agree on the financial arrangements either during or after your divorce, either of you may issue a formal application to the court, known as an application for *ancillary relief*. Your application should state briefly what you are applying for, such as maintenance – or *periodical payments* – for yourself, lump sums for yourself or your children, a property adjustment or pension order. This application is known as the *Form A*. Applications for child support are not now usually included on the Form A. (For more on child support, see Chapter 13.)

If you live in Scotland or Northern Ireland, check with your solicitors how financial applications are made there, as the laws have subtle – but very important – differences from those in England and Wales.

On receiving your application and court fee, the court fixes a timetable and a date for your first appointment with a judge, usually three to four months ahead. With regard to the timing of applications for ancillary relief, you need to bear in mind a few points:

- ✔ You cannot apply for ancillary relief until after the divorce petition has been issued.

- ✔ The court cannot make any final orders for capital, property, or pensions until after the decree nisi has been granted.

- ✔ The order can't take effect until after the decree absolute has been granted (although your solicitor may be able to find a way round this restriction for you).

- ✔ In Scotland, capital and property orders have to be made before the divorce decree is issued.

Once the court has issued the application, you and your spouse, or your solicitors, are sent a copy of the application and the timetable. You or your solicitors are responsible for promptly sending a copy of the application to the landlord or mortgage lenders of any property, and to the administrators of any pension fund that you are claiming.

The powers of the court

Following is a list of the main financial orders that a court can make:

- **Maintenance pending suit:** Regular financial spousal support until the final decree of divorce.
- **Periodical payments:** Regular spousal support after your divorce.
- **Lump sum:** A fixed sum, in one or more instalments, for you, your spouse, or your children.
- **Periodical payments for a child:** Regular payments of child support (through the CSA).
- **Property adjustment:** The sale, transfer, or an adjustment of an interest in property.
- **Pension provision:** Dividing between you or attaching an interest to a pension fund.

Filing statements

You and your spouse must complete a statement of means on a standard form known as the *Form E,* including the following details:

- Background including your full name and address, date of birth and occupation, your children's names and dates of birth, and details of any other court proceedings between you and your spouse or about the children
- Assets – listing everything you own, including your property, savings, income, valuables, and pensions
- Liabilities – listing everything you owe, including mortgages, credit card debts, and outgoings
- Needs, for income, capital, property, or pensions
- Contributions to the family, whether financial or otherwise
- The orders that you are seeking
- Special factors if any

You also have to attach proof of your means including copies of valuations; mortgage, pension, and bank statements; payslips and P60; business accounts; and so on. You must send one copy of everything to the court and one to your spouse or solicitor by the date specified by the court, usually about six weeks before your first court appointment.

If you are in urgent need of maintenance, you can apply to the court for an earlier *interim* appointment. You do not have to file a full Form E for this, but you do need to give the court enough information to make a decision. That decision usually lasts until your divorce has been finalised or until the final financial order has been made.

Two weeks before the first court appointment, your solicitors must file with the court and exchange with each other

- ✔ A chronology, or timeline of events

- ✔ A concise statement summarising what you see as the main issues in the case

- ✔ A questionnaire saying what further information or documents you believe your spouse should disclose

- ✔ A *Form G* to say whether you want the judge to give some informal guidance on the case at the first appointment, or on a later appointment

The first directions appointment – or FDA

About two weeks after filing with the court, you and your spouse attend your first court appointment with your legal representatives, also known as the first directions appointment (FDA). This appointment is a good opportunity for you to discuss all the issues and the steps needed to resolve them. In court, each lawyer has a chance to address the district judge; if you made the application, your lawyer goes first. The judge may ask questions to clarify the issues. You don't have to say anything; usually your lawyers do the talking for you.

The judge then makes *directions* about the future conduct of your case, and will set dates for compliance, either as agreed or as he thinks best. These directions are geared towards identifying and resolving the main issues as quickly and cost-effectively as possible, and may relate to any or all of the following:

- ✔ Valuations of property

- ✔ Which questions and requests for documents you must reply to

- ✔ Further evidence or reports (such as a pension actuary report) that are required

- ✔ The next court appointment

The court allows about 15 minutes for each appointment unless your case is complex and your lawyers have asked for longer. At the end of the appointment, your lawyers have to give the judge a written estimate of your costs.

The financial dispute resolution appointment – or FDR

You and your spouse must comply with all the judge's directions before you return to court a second time. In addition, you must each send to the court copies of any offers of settlement that you have made. The main aim of the second appointment, known as the *financial dispute resolution appointment* or *FDR,* is to help the two of you settle and avoid a full hearing. The judge gives some guidance on the likely outcome based on the court papers and offers, but without hearing any oral evidence from either of you. Again, your solicitors must give the judge a written estimate of your costs.

The judge who deals with this appointment cannot deal with the final hearing, if there is to be one, because he has been privy to offers that have been made between you on a *without prejudice* basis – that is, offers made without prejudicing any claims in your Form Es.

In more straightforward cases, such as one where you and your spouse have agreed on all or most of the relevant factual information before the first appointment, you can ask the judge on a Form G to combine the first appointment with the financial dispute resolution appointment. This should save you both time and money. The court doesn't allow you to postpone any of these appointments without a good reason.

Disclosure

Lawyers use the *disclosure* process to help you determine the facts of a case. Depending on what you want to learn through disclosure, the lawyers may use a variety of formal legal tools, some of which are described in this section.

The disclosure process can take a short time, especially if the facts of your divorce are clear and undisputed and all the important documents are attached to your Forms E; or it can last many months. Some form of disclosure will take place no matter whether your divorce is co-operative, difficult, or fully contested.

Protocol requires that you and your solicitors co-operate over all reasonable requests for disclosure in order to minimise costs and the risk of a contested hearing. If you disregard such protocol, and your case goes to court, you may be penalised on the question of costs.

Disclosure can be dealt with directly between you, through your mediator, or through your lawyer. What follows is a description of the process as it is usually dealt with through lawyers.

Voluntarily providing your spouse's lawyer with the information he or she requests is less painful than going through the formal disclosure process. Plus, this way you save time and money. Disclosure can be formal or voluntary depending on whether

- ✔ Your lawyer has to force your spouse's lawyer to provide certain information relating to your divorce issue through a court order (or if your spouse's lawyer has to do the same).

- ✔ The two lawyers agree in writing to willingly exchange all the information you need to work out the terms of your settlement.

- ✔ Your lawyers need to formally acquire additional information relating to your case from other sources.

- ✔ Your divorce is amicable (in which case less need exists for formal disclosure) or contentious.

Voluntary disclosure

Voluntary disclosure occurs when your lawyer asks your spouse's lawyer (or vice versa) for financial, legal, medical, or other information and the information is provided voluntarily without the need for a court order. The particular types of information your lawyer asks for depend on the issues involved in your divorce.

Ideally, most of the disclosure in your divorce will be voluntary because formal disclosure can be time-consuming and expensive, depending on just how much formal disclosure either lawyer wants. Your solicitor may have to complete extra paperwork, formulate questions to ask your spouse or others, and then review and analyse all of this information.

Formal disclosure

Witness summonses, statements, questionnaires, and notices for the production of documents are all formal disclosure tools. The following list tells you what each of these terms means:

- ✔ **Witness summons:** A legal document requiring someone to attend a court hearing or trial. Anyone who ignores a summons faces legal penalties.

- ✔ **Statement:** A statement by a witness, made out of court and filed with the court. The witness is either under oath or has to confirm in the statement that he believes that everything that he is saying is true, and that he is aware that the statement will be used in the proceedings.

- ✔ **Questionnaires and notices to produce documents and other information:** Written questions for the respondent prepared by the applicant's lawyer or vice versa, seeking information or documentation on a relevant issue. Questionnaires deal specifically with issues that are being disputed in the case, and the costs involved in producing the information must be proportionate to the benefits being sought.

Depending on the issues that have to be resolved before your application can be determined, any number of individuals may be involved in the disclosure process. The information provided by accountants, valuers, actuaries, employers, business associates, bankers, and so on may be used to help resolve questions regarding the value of your marital property, spousal support, business, or pension, for example.

After orders are made for the various forms of disclosure, you may not ask your spouse for any further disclosure, and vice versa, without the prior permission of the judge. The Form E and ancillary relief procedure described in the previous sections are designed to make the disclosure process as efficient and cost-effective as possible.

Such formal disclosure is most common in divorces involving spouses who are unwilling to co-operate with one another. However, even if your divorce is amicable, you may be required to do a limited amount of formal disclosure in order to

✔ Narrow the scope of your negotiations by identifying exactly where you and your spouse disagree, and the particulars of your disagreements. The more that you know you agree on, the less you have to negotiate or litigate later, and the less your divorce will cost.

✔ Assess the strengths and weaknesses of your position versus your spouse's.

✔ Assess how well your spouse is likely to perform on the stand if your case goes to a full hearing and your spouse is called to give evidence.

✔ Get your spouse to admit to certain activities or to establish certain facts. If your case goes to a full hearing and your spouse gives evidence that differs from what he or she said during the disclosure process, your lawyer can use the discrepancy to undermine your spouse's credibility.

The court won't allow you to go on a fishing exercise just for the sake of it. You and your spouse will have to justify the information that you are seeking and demonstrate that it's essential for the judge to determine the issues in your case.

Full hearings

If you and your spouse can't agree a final settlement, you have to go to court with your lawyers and any witnesses to enable a judge to make a final decision on the issues between you. (Only about 10 per cent of all financial divorce cases get to this stage.) Your lawyers outline the facts and the arguments, and you must give evidence on oath. The lawyer representing the applicant has the first and the last say. All the relevant applications, orders, statements, reports, and documents are usually agreed upon and filed with the court in advance, for the use of all concerned at the hearing.

Giving evidence

Although you may wish you didn't have to give evidence, you will almost certainly have to do so if you want to have any chance of persuading the judge to make the order that you want. Here are some tips on how to manage the situation:

✔ Tell the truth, even if it hurts.

✔ If you do not understand a question, say so. Ask that it be repeated or restated.

✔ Give your answer and nothing more – no extra facts and no elaboration. Providing more information than you are asked for may hurt your case.

✔ Be polite and don't argue with your spouse's lawyer.

✔ Direct your responses towards the judge. The judge records your evidence, and it is the judge who decides the issues.

Your lawyer listens when you give your evidence. If your lawyer objects to a question, and the judge accepts the objection, don't answer it. A tactical and legitimate reason for your remaining silent probably exists.

The judge's decision – the order or judgement

After listening to your lawyers' opening and closing statements; hearing evidence from you and your spouse and from any witnesses involved in your case; and reviewing any reports, documents, and other written information entered as evidence, the judge makes an order or *gives judgement* on the issues in your case.

The judge may announce his decision immediately at the end of the hearing, or, more rarely, he may take time to consider all the evidence and announce his decision at a later date.

The judge also has to decide who is to be responsible for the costs of the case. After the judge has given judgement but before he decides on the question of costs, your lawyers may produce copies of any *without prejudice* offers that you have made and argue that the other party pay the costs from the date of the offer, if the offer was as good as the judgement made. Offer letters produced in this way must specify that they may be produced in support of an application for costs after the judgement has been given. These offers are sometimes known as *Calderbank* offers, or offers made *without prejudice save as to costs*. The judge should take any such offers into consideration, but he has the ultimate discretion to decide the question of costs, taking all the circumstances into account.

The rules relating to orders for costs in family matters are complex and are being reviewed by the government. You should be guided by any advice your lawyers give you. Orders for costs against one party in favour of the other are more common now than they used to be, but it is rare that you recover 100 per cent of the costs that you expend.

If you and your lawyers strongly disagree with the order or judgement made, you can appeal the decision. You have a limited amount of time to file your appeal, usually 14 days for financial decisions and seven days for decisions about your children. Remember, that appeals are risky, and involve yet more time, money, and stress for both of you. They also almost certainly reduce the financial resources that you are seeking to share between you.

Formal Applications to the Court: Issues Regarding Your Children

Private disputes about children follow a different procedure from those about money and property. If you and your spouse can't agree on the arrangements for your children, such as where they will live, how much they will see of the other parent, or where they will go to school (Chapter 10 gives you advice on how to make these decisions), one of you files a formal application with the court known as a C1. The C1 gives basic details for yourself, your spouse, and your children, and the reasons why you are making the application.

The court sends a copy of the application to your spouse, or to his or her solicitor, and your spouse has 14 days to acknowledge it, saying whether he or she wishes to oppose the application or make any other application.

The court arranges an initial appointment at which the judge tries to clarify the issues between you, see if any agreement can be reached, and, if not, make any necessary directions for the conduct of the case.

A CAFCASS officer or Family Court Adviser

CAFCASS stands for *Children and Family Court Advisory Support Service*. A professional social worker who works as a CAFCASS officer and specialises in children matters, is available at the first court appointment to see you and your spouse in private, to try to help you sort out any disagreements. It's up to you whether you speak to a CAFCASS officer, or reach any agreement, but the judge will probably encourage you to do so.

If you and your spouse can't agree on a suitable arrangement, the judge usually directs each of you to file with the court and exchange with each other a written statement by a certain date, usually 14 to 28 days hence. This statement sets out in more detail what you are asking the judge to decide and why. The judge may order a CAFCASS officer to investigate and file a report on the issues in dispute, usually within three months (depending partly on the workload of the local CAFCASS office).

The next court appointment following the filing of the report – sometimes called a *pre-trial review* – gives you, your legal representatives, and the judge an opportunity to review your case and make any agreed orders. If you still cannot agree on any of the issues, the judge fixes a final hearing.

Social workers, psychiatrists, your friends or your spouse's friends, the police, grandparents, and others may be included in the disclosure process in children cases. (Refer to the section 'Disclosure' earlier in this chapter.)

The final hearing in children matters

The final hearing in children matters follows a similar pattern to that for financial matters, with your lawyers presenting the facts and arguments to the judge, and evidence being given on oath by you, your spouse, and any witnesses. If a CAFCASS officer has filed a report, they may be called to answer questions that your or your spouse's lawyer may have of them. At the end of all that, the judge makes a decision.

An order for costs is rarely made against either party in children matters. In most cases, each party takes responsibility for their own costs.

Cases involving children are always heard in private and all statements and reports will be confidential to you and your legal representatives. If either of you disclose the contents of such statements or reports to anyone else, you may be in contempt of court and liable to be committed to prison. The courts take very seriously the need to protect children from any outside interference with their well-being, and they expect you to do so, too. However, note that this privacy doesn't apply in Scotland, where the procedures are in any event very different, although the Court may grant orders preventing publication in the media.

Chapter 6

Separation: A Healthy Breather or a Prelude to Divorce?

In This Chapter

▶ Understanding what being separated means

▶ Exploring the pros and cons of separation

▶ Reviewing your separation options

▶ Making reconciliation work

Separation is more than just a matter of living apart from your spouse. It is an important step with legal, financial, and emotional ramifications that requires plenty of advance planning. Separation can be the beginning of the end to your marriage, or the start of a better-than-ever union. Either way, don't take the decision to separate casually.

Before separating, you need to understand fully the pros and cons of such a change in your living arrangements. You and your spouse should also be clear about the direction you anticipate your separation will take you – toward reconciliation or to a divorce court. Otherwise, you may be setting yourself up for disappointment and more heartache.

You're Married, But Only Sort Of

Separation is the equivalent of marital limbo. You don't live with your spouse and you may even feel single again – but you're *still married.* All the formal 'benefits' of being married, like spousal inheritance, pension rights, and death benefits remain intact during a separation. However, your relationship has changed. When you live apart, you see one another less frequently, are less accountable to one another for your comings and goings, and what you do and don't do at home. After separating, you and your spouse may try 'dating' each other in an effort to put the spark back in your marriage, or you may avoid any contact unless it's absolutely necessary.

Dating your spouse – and especially having sex with your spouse – while you're separated can jeopardise your grounds for divorce. The courts understandably question the credibility of a divorce based on allegations of adultery or behaviour if you're still dating your spouse. Consult your solicitor before you go on that hot date. However, if you are informally separated with the intention of reconciling there is no real danger in dating your spouse.

Why should you separate?

Couples separate for many reasons. Sometimes those reasons are well reasoned and logical; other times they are based on fear or misguided hope. Sometimes, you and your spouse have no other option. Among the most common reasons for separating are the following:

- ✔ You want to find out what living on your own feels like.

- ✔ You need time to assess your commitment to your marriage away from the day-to-day stress and responsibilities of the relationship.

- ✔ You want to send your spouse a strong message that things have to change if you are going to stay married. (For example, your spouse has a substance abuse problem and has been unwilling to deal with it.)

- ✔ Your spouse wants a divorce but you don't. By agreeing to separate you hope to delay or even prevent the end of your marriage.

- ✔ You've agreed to divorce but must separate for two years (see Chapter 5).

- ✔ You anticipate an amicable divorce but living with your spouse until your divorce is official is emotionally impossible.

- ✔ You and your spouse are estranged and can no longer continue living under the same roof.

- ✔ Your spouse has become physically violent and you are afraid for your or your children's safety.

- ✔ You can't afford to get divorced yet.

- ✔ You have religious objections to divorce.

The drawbacks of separating

Although separating certainly has its pluses, living apart from your spouse can have its drawbacks, too. So before you agree to separate, consult a family law solicitor experienced at handling divorces and separations (see Chapter 7 for advice on how to find a solicitor). In addition, try to determine if any of the following situations apply to you.

- Your individual living expenses will increase after you and your spouse separate.

- Your new place – if you're moving out – may not be nearly as plush as your former home.

- Your children may have a hard time understanding that 'daddy and mummy are spending some time apart'.

- You may not have enough money to live on if you do not have your own source of income.

- You may end up paying for certain expenses twice if you separate legally and then later get divorced.

- You may give your spouse grounds for a divorce based on your behaviour or desertion if you separate against your spouse's wishes.

- You may still be treated as a married couple with regard to pensions, life insurance, and contractual obligations. However, a carefully worded separation agreement written by a family law solicitor can help address these issues.

If your spouse agrees to pay certain debts while you are separated and fails to do so your creditors may have a legal right to come after both of you for payment. Furthermore, if your spouse gets into debt while you are separated you can be held responsible for the debt even if you have a written agreement to the contrary. If you end up paying that debt, you may be able to claim reimbursement from your spouse later.

Any assets that you acquire following your separation may still be taken into account as assets on your divorce – that is to say, your spouse can still make a claim on them even though he or she may not have contributed in any way. Consult a family law solicitor first in order to gain a clear understanding of the pros and cons of separating given the particulars of your situation.

Talk it over before you separate

Both of you together should discuss the reasons for your separation (assuming that you can have a calm and productive conversation) and make it clear why you're separating – as a prelude to a divorce or as a last-ditch effort to save your marriage.

Try not to harbour any illusions about the final outcome of your separation. That way, you can focus on achieving your goals for the separation. If you and your spouse are uncertain whether separating is your best move, a relationship counsellor (see Chapter 2) may be able to help you decide what is best for you both, and a family law solicitor can help with the legal issues.

Initiating a Separation

Whether you are drawing up a formal separation deed (see the section 'Protecting Yourself When You Separate Informally' later in this chapter), or just separating informally, always try to agree on the terms of your separation before you move out. Make a note of the date that you or your spouse move out of the home. Even if you decide to live separately under the same roof, you need to note the date that you start the new arrangements. This date may be important later, particularly if your separation is going to form the basis of your divorce.

Often, the spouse who wants the separation is the one to move out of the couple's home. However, if your spouse is the primary carer of your young children, you should consider being the one to move so that the lives of your children are disrupted as little as possible.

Protecting Yourself When You Separate Informally

You can separate on an informal basis, or you may be able to agree the terms of separation in writing between you through a formal *separation deed*. Although a separation deed is usually best in that it will be contractually binding, if the following statements apply to you an informal separation may be all that you need:

- ✔ You and your spouse both earn a good living and can comfortably support yourselves.
- ✔ You have no dependent children from your marriage.
- ✔ You do not share joint bank accounts nor jointly owe a great deal of money.
- ✔ You are confident that your separation will be relatively brief and amicable.

If you opt for an informal separation, you should nevertheless set ground rules for your time apart and make them part of a written agreement that you both sign and date. (Make sure that you both keep a copy of your final signed agreement.) An informal separation agreement can help protect you from the potential repercussions of a civilised separation turned sour.

Identify any issues that may disrupt the peacefulness of your time apart and determine ahead of time the best way to deal with those potentially disruptive conflicts. Working out solutions to possible problems in advance minimises the potential for disagreements and misunderstandings during your separation.

There are a few practical steps that you might want to take when one of you leaves the home, in order to save you both some time, cost, and inconvenience later:

✔ **Get your gas, electricity, and phone meters read so that you can apportion the bills at a later date if you need to.** If you think that the separation might go on for a while, have the bills put into the name of the spouse who is remaining in the home.

✔ **Let your council tax authority know the date on which you or your spouse leave.** The remaining spouse may then be able to claim a 25 per cent reduction in the council tax bill as a sole adult occupier, and the one that is leaving will not retain liability.

✔ **Take your personal valuable documents with you.** Don't forget your medical card and passport.

✔ **Take details or copies of financial documents that might become important if there are any claims between you.** For example, you'll need your mortgage account number and copies of joint policies (see Chapter 7 for a list of important documents you may need during your divorce process).

✔ **Decide how you are going to manage any joint bank accounts between you.** Consider asking the bank to freeze the account if there is any risk of misuse so that you can only draw on it with joint signatures (see Chapter 11). Make sure that any important direct debits and standing orders are covered first.

✔ **Make an agreed inventory of the main contents of your home.** You will never remember everything that's there and you may have to agree how to divide up your possessions at some point. Also, you'll have a record if anything goes missing.

✔ **Notify the Inland Revenue if you aren't planning on getting back together.** They'll probably treat you as a single person for income tax purposes.

✔ **Talk to your solicitor to find out if there are any other important steps that you should take to protect yourself.** Everyone's circumstances are different.

If your spouse mismanages your finances while you are separated your credit rating (and not just your spouse's) may be damaged. You must be sure your separation agreement states that your spouse will *not* include your name on any new financial or bank accounts and will *not* sign your name on any documents – especially financial documents – during your separation.

Formalising Your Separation Agreement

You absolutely must have a written statement, such as a formal separation agreement, that spells out the terms of your separation if you are separating permanently as an alternative to divorce. Make sure all of the terms of your separation are in black and white and enforceable by law – you need to protect yourself from miscommunication or future disagreement on what the terms of the agreement are. Your solicitors can draw up the agreement for you, and you don't need to go to court.

Having a legal separation deed or agreement is always a good idea, even if your separation is amicable and you both hope to reconcile: If either of you fails to live up to the terms of the agreement you can ask the court to help enforce it. Any of the following situations can be made easier if the terms of your separation are stated in a formal separation agreement:

- ✔ You and your spouse are so estranged from one another that communication and co-operation are impossible.
- ✔ You don't trust your spouse to live up to his or her verbal promises.
- ✔ You want financial help from your spouse while you are living apart.
- ✔ You have dependent children.

The longer you live apart, the greater the chance that your relationship with your spouse will deteriorate. Your spouse may become involved in a new romantic relationship and abandon your reconciliation plans. Or you may find it harder to co-operate with one another as time goes on. At times like these, having a written separation agreement can help prevent the total breakdown of your relationship.

You may have to ask a judge to decide the terms of your separation if you and your spouse can't come to an agreement. If there are major financial matters you can't agree on, such as what happens with the house, you may have to resort to divorce or judicial separation proceedings (see 'Not Quite Divorce: Judicial Separation' later in this chapter). A legal separation agreement can serve some very practical purposes especially in regard to your finances:

- ✔ A well-written separation agreement can help limit your liability for any debts that your spouse may rack up during your separation.
- ✔ A separation agreement can provide for the continuance of certain spousal benefits including health insurance and continued access to credit on a shared account.

A judge is more likely to enforce your agreement if you can each show that you have had independent legal advice on the terms of your agreement, and that you have fully and frankly disclosed your financial positions to each other.

Try the art of compromise

You will probably find that give and take works better than strong-arm tactics when you are working out the terms of your separation. In other words, don't expect to get everything you ask for. Refusing to compromise is likely to backfire – you may end up in court where the judge will have the final word – and you have no control. That said, you should be aware of provisions it's helpful to include in your separation agreement and provisions that you should avoid if possible.

What to put in a separation agreement

A legal separation agreement can address most, if not all, of the same issues that a divorce agreement covers, including

- ✔ child support
- ✔ child residence and contact
- ✔ spousal support
- ✔ the division of marital property and debts

If you separate and then decide to divorce, all or some of what you include in your separation agreement can be converted into your divorce agreement, subject to the final discretion of the judge.

As long as you are still married, you should be able to claim any rights as a spouse that you may have to your spouse's pension, and your spouse can also nominate you for the death in service benefits.

Safeguard your liquid assets

A *liquid asset* is cash or something that can be quickly converted to cash. That includes the cash advance on your credit card, a bank account overdraft, as well as investments that allow you to write cheques against them. Be sure that your agreement gives you ready access to the liquid assets you and your spouse own. You may need them during your separation to help pay bills, put food on the table, or cover unexpected expenses – especially if your income is low and you will be receiving little or no spousal support.

Liquid assets can work both for you and against you. If you can draw on these assets, then your spouse probably can too, and you could end up being liable for your spouse's overdraft.

Men – and women – behaving badly

If there were rules of proper behaviour for separated spouses they'd include the following dos and don'ts. Ignoring these ground rules can turn an amicable split into a hostile one, derail any plans for reconciliation, and even weaken your position when the time comes to negotiate your divorce. To avoid such problems, take heed of these separation don'ts:

✔ **Don't get involved in a serious relationship** – especially if it means that you spend less time with your young children. And don't bring a romantic interest home for the night when the children are staying with you. If your spouse finds out about your love affair, it's likely to increase any hostility he or she may already be feeling toward you.

✔ **Don't bad-mouth your spouse, ever!** You're likely to upset your kids if they hear you. Plus, nothing short of spousal abuse will annoy a judge more quickly than learning that you've been saying disparaging things to your children about your spouse.

✔ **Don't do things that you know will be hurtful to your spouse.** Ultimately, the person you hurt most may be yourself!

✔ **Avoid sexual relations with your spouse without first understanding the potential ramifications of doing so.** Once you've filed the petition for divorce, you may weaken your grounds for divorce if you're sleeping together. Furthermore, you may mislead your spouse into thinking you want to reconcile.

And, while you're at it, keep in mind these separation etiquette dos:

✔ **Keep the lines of communication open between you and your spouse.** Even if you can't agree about anything it's more likely you'll sort things out quickly if you know where you both stand on the big issues.

✔ **Allow your spouse to spend plenty of time with your kids if they live with you (unless your spouse has been abusive).** If you have a separation deed, the chances are that it will state when and where your spouse can see the children.

✔ **Meet all of your obligations to your spouse and children without fail.** They're depending on you, and may not trust you in the future if you don't.

Be careful about what you sign

Question anything in a separation agreement that you do not understand. Don't agree to any provision in your agreement because 'it's good enough for now' or because you 'can live with the arrangement for a while'. Separation agreements often become the basis for divorce agreements. Once something is in a separation agreement, it can be difficult – if not impossible, to have that provision voided or modified. Unless the problems your separation agreement caused were obvious and significant you and your spouse must agree to the change.

Think whether you need to give yourself some room to manoeuvre by clearly indicating in writing whether the separation agreement binds you to the same terms in your final divorce agreement.

Not Quite Divorce: Judicial Separation

If you live in England or Wales, you can ask the court for a decree of judicial separation instead of a formal separation deed or a divorce. A decree of judicial separation releases you and your spouse from living together, but does not allow you to remarry.

You may want to apply for a decree of judicial separation if you have religious objections to divorce or want the financial remedies without freeing your spouse to remarry. However, decrees of judicial separation are increasingly rare these days. Chapter 5 tells you about the financial remedies that are available to you on divorce and judicial separation.

The procedure for judicial separation is exactly the same as with a divorce, with three exceptions:

- ✔ **You do not have to prove that the marriage has irretrievably broken down.** So if you don't want to say that it has, judicial separation is for you.

- ✔ **There is only one decree, not two.** That is the decree of judicial separation rather than the decree nisi and decree absolute of divorce.

- ✔ **The court has slightly different powers to make financial orders than it does for divorce.** The powers include orders for maintenance, capital and property. In most cases you preserve your claims against your spouse's pension, unlike divorce, but you will be treated as if you were divorced for inheritance purposes.

If you decide to go for a divorce at a later date, you can use the basis of your judicial separation petition as the basis of your divorce petition – but, be warned, you will end up *paying twice* for almost the same work.

If You Kiss and Make Up

You may possibly breathe a huge sigh of relief after you have separated but, conversely, you may begin to miss certain aspects of married life. When you are now living in a smaller place surrounded by rented furniture and just a few items from your home, you may long for the old familiar comforts. You may miss your children if they're not living with you, or wish you had your spouse's help when you're overwhelmed with all of the responsibility of caring for them if they are. Or you may realise that you truly love your spouse and are willing to do what's necessary to repair your marriage.

For any or all of these reasons, you and your spouse may decide that living together is better than living apart. And, like many couples who reach that conclusion, you can reconcile and end your separation.

Stuart and Sarah separated when Stuart had an affair and Sarah then began an affair in retaliation. However they found they were meeting every day to sort out things about their children. They eventually realised, in discussion with a mediator, that they were contriving to be together because that was exactly what they both wanted once they had got over their hurt pride.

Reconcile for the right reasons

Be sure that you are reconciling because you both really want to – not because you feel guilty, are scared to be alone, or are tired of doing your own laundry. Initially after you've reconciled you may feel a sense of exhilaration and renewed hope for your future as a couple. But sooner or later the old problems in your relationship are likely to resurface and you may respond to them in the very ways that contributed to your marital troubles in the first place. So take a positive step to address the problems before they get out of hand. Have a look at Chapter 24 for tips on making your relationship work.

Fortify your relationship with counselling

Despite your happiness at being together again, both of you may be harbouring anger, hurt, doubt, and distrust toward one another as a result of your separation. Although these feelings are quite natural under the circumstances, they can get in the way of rebuilding your marriage. Therefore, if you are really serious about staying together and repairing your marriage, see a therapist or relationship counsellor if you aren't already doing so. (See Chapter 2 for help with finding a relationship counsellor.)

You are more apt to make your marriage work the second time around if you begin therapy or counselling while you are still in the honeymoon phase of your reconciliation. Working things out is a lot easier when you're more motivated to make your marriage a success.

Part II
Divorce Preliminaries

'I haven't seen my husband since the divorce,
but there's always something around that
reminds me of him.'

In this part . . .

Your marriage is definitely over and now it's time to take action. Chapter 6 gives you advice for breaking the news to your spouse, help in determining what you want out of your divorce, and practical ways of estimating and preparing for what divorce will cost you (both personally and financially). Chapter 7 tells you how to help your kids cope with the changes your divorce will bring to their lives. And, finally, to ease some of the stress and pain, Chapter 9 provides suggestions on how to deal with your emotions.

Chapter 7

Setting Your Divorce in Motion

. . . .

In This Chapter

▶ Telling your spouse that you want to call it quits

▶ Working out your financial situation

▶ Determining what you want from your divorce

▶ Estimating the cost of your divorce

▶ Protecting your assets in case your divorce gets hostile

. . . .

*W*hen you definitely know that you're heading for a split, you can't begin preparing for the divorce process too soon. You need at least a general idea of what's to come in order to negotiate a fair divorce agreement intelligently. If you head into your divorce unprepared, you're likely to feel overwhelmed and panicky. Taking a proactive stance helps alleviate some of the natural anxiety you feel about your divorce.

Conducting your divorce amicably benefits everyone. Therefore, we offer practical advice for talking about divorce with your spouse to give yourselves the best chance of a fair divorce process. We also provide tips for getting your money matters in order and ensure that you have the info you need to get a fair and adequate divorce settlement. (Chapter 3 has more information on general financial preparedness.) If you can co-operate in collecting financial information and making joint financial decisions, including covering the cost of your divorce, you can maximise your resources to meet your needs in the future. It's hard not to panic about money, but staying calm and working it out with cool heads pays off.

Breaking the News to Your Spouse

You and your spouse may have tried just about everything to resolve your problems. Maybe you've decided to call it quits because things are simply not going to get better. Or perhaps only one of you is ready to end the marriage. If you are the one who wants to end your marriage, the way you break the news to your spouse can have a big influence on whether your divorce will be amicable or contentious. It can also help set the tone for your post-divorce relationship, an important consideration if you have dependent children.

Maintaining your composure

Telling your spouse that you want a divorce isn't easy, particularly if the news comes as a shock or if your spouse has been hoping that somehow, some way, you can work out your marital problems and stay together. The following suggestions may help you ease into that conversation and help your spouse accept the news as calmly as possible:

- ✔ **Quietly and slowly tell your spouse your reasons for wanting to end your marriage.** Review what you consider to be the problems in your marriage, what you may have done to try to fix them, and why you feel that your efforts have not worked. Even if you've covered this same ground many, many times before, go over it again.

- ✔ **Avoid blaming your spouse for the end of your marriage (as difficult as that may be).** Avoid accusatory or derogatory language and try to steer clear of starting an argument.

- ✔ **As much as possible, speak in terms of how _you_ feel.** It's hard to argue with someone about his or her feelings. If your spouse does try to argue with you, reiterate your feelings and intentions, over and over again if necessary.

If a calm conversation is impossible because your spouse is simply too upset about the idea of divorce, tell them that you would like to talk again later. Your next conversation will probably be a little easier to take. You may need to have a few conversations concerning your intention to divorce before your spouse finally accepts the news.

Making sure your spouse hears the news from you first

Your spouse should find out about your divorce plans from you first and not through the rumour mill (from mutual friends, relatives, or even your kids). Second-hand news is a cruel way for your spouse to find out that their marriage is ending and a sure way to make for a bitter divorce.

If you have already filed a petition for divorce, tell your spouse that you've done so before he or she receives the divorce papers. If you can't tell your spouse in person or with a phone call, write them a letter. It's preferable that you compose the letter, not your solicitor. A solicitor's letter is too impersonal and your spouse may be angry that you didn't bother to write it yourself. If your spouse holds a grudge, it can make your divorce negotiations even more difficult.

Waiting until your spouse is ready to begin negotiations

Don't expect to begin negotiating your divorce agreement as soon as you tell your spouse the news. It may take weeks or even months before negotiations can begin. Be patient and move slowly. Remember, you've probably been thinking seriously for some time about divorce and may have even begun preparing for that change. Therefore, you're probably much more prepared to end your marriage than your spouse is.

Your spouse's initial reaction is more likely to be anger, shock, and disbelief rather than the desire to get cracking on the divorce proceedings. Give your spouse a chance to let the news sink in and time to do some preparation before you actually set your divorce in motion.

If you move too fast, feelings of guilt or remorse, or anger or abandonment, may result in bad decisions that you both will regret later. You may concede too much to your spouse or be too willing to compromise. Your spouse may make unreasonable demands out of anger and spite. Feeling pressure from you, your spouse may panic, engage a solicitor straight away, and turn your divorce into a hostile battle when it wasn't necessary.

However, waiting for the right time may not be possible or practical. You may not be able to hold off until your spouse is ready to co-operate. Your spouse may never be ready, or you as a couple may be so estranged that being civil and working co-operatively is impossible.

When you're both ready, have a general discussion about the issues in your divorce – particularly whether you want to negotiate yourselves, use mediation, or use solicitors to negotiate for you – and try to develop a timetable for beginning the process. Unless both of you feel in control of your emotions and ready to talk, don't push him or her to iron out the details of your divorce straight away. For example, if you can wait for your divorce until after two years of separation (see Chapter 4), your divorce can more easily be co-operative because neither of you will have to blame the other.

Jane was so shocked and hurt by her husband's attempts to end their marriage that they clung to each other for several days, allowing the reality to dawn. Their reaction gave them time to get onto a more even keel. It led to their co-operating over telling their children and working out the practical and financial consequences for the family.

Keeping cool if your spouse initiates the divorce

Even if the writing has been on the wall for months or even years, finding out that your spouse wants a divorce can send you into an emotional tailspin of shock and disbelief. As time goes on, you may vacillate between feelings of anger and sadness, or anger and depression.

The sooner you can face facts and move forward, the better off you both will be. Although feeling sorry for yourself is an understandable response to finding out that your marriage is ending, especially if you didn't want it to end, thinking of yourself as a victim will not help you face up to your situation. Allowing yourself to become obsessed about 'the unfairness of it all', how you've 'been wronged', and 'what could have been' will prevent you from working out a reasonable divorce agreement. Feeling sorry for yourself for too long may even drive away your friends and family members at the time when you may need them the most. If keeping cool seems impossible, find a good counsellor (see Chapters 2 and 9 for tips on locating one).

As you work through your emotions and begin dealing with the practical realities of your divorce, avoid angry recriminations and do not insult your spouse. And don't force yourself either to spend time together or to remain apart; do what makes you feel most comfortable.

Pulling Together Your Financial Information

From the law's perspective, your divorce, in practical terms, is about arrangements for your children and an equitable sorting out of your finances. Ideally, these issues should be resolved before your divorce is finalised.

To finalise a divorce in Scotland, all the arrangements must be made ahead of time! If all matters of capital and spousal maintenance have not been dealt with when the divorce is granted it will be too late.

Complete and accurate financial information is essential to your obtaining an equitable divorce settlement. You need this information whether your divorce is amicable or rancorous, and whether you negotiate a settlement agreement with your spouse or place your family's future in the hands of a judge.

Without adequate financial information you may not get either your fair share of assets or a reasonable amount of spousal or child support. If your spouse holds all the financial cards, deciding when to raise the stakes, when to hold steady, and when to close is a guessing game. If you guess wrongly, you may end up with less than you deserve.

Listing what you own

One of the first things to do in preparation for your divorce is develop a comprehensive picture of your financial situation. Determine exactly what you and your spouse own, and what your assets are worth. To create a full portrait of your finances, make a list of all your household assets and note a current market value for each. *Current market value* is the amount you can get if you sell an asset at the present time.

You may have already prepared a list of your assets, but that list may need updating once your divorce becomes a reality. You or your spouse may have sold assets or purchased new ones, the value of your assets may have changed, and you may have paid off debts or acquired new ones.

 If you have a family accountant, financial adviser, or stock broker, he or she can help you pull together the information and documentation you need for a full list of your assets. Have a look at the Asset Worksheet in this chapter to help make sure you are not forgetting anything.

Asset Worksheet

Family home

Joint or sole ownership?
Current value
Type of mortgage(s) (e.g. repayment or interest only)
Less mortgage(s)
Gross equity

Other properties

Joint or sole ownership
Current value
Type of mortgage?
Less mortgage
Gross equity

Any savings scheme linked to your mortgage

Type of scheme (e.g. endowment policy, pension or PEP)
Joint or sole
Estimated maturity value and date
Current surrender value

Household furniture and furnishings worth over £500 each

Type
Value if sold

(continued)

Asset Worksheet *(continued)*

Life or other insurance policies

Company where policy is held
Type of policy
Estimated maturity or death value
Surrender value (if any)

Stocks and shares

Name of holding
Joint or sole
Number of shares
Total value

Bank, building society, savings accounts, PEPs, TESSAs, ISAs

a) Bank or company
Joint or sole
Current balance or value

b) Bank or company
Joint or sole
Current balance or value

c) Bank or company
Joint or sole
Current balance or value

d) Bank or company
Joint or sole
Current balance or value

National savings certificates and bonds including premium bonds

Type of bond
Joint or sole
Current value

Vehicles (cars, caravans, boats etc worth more than £500)

Joint or sole
Value if sold

Trusts and foreseeable inheritances

Joint or sole
Current value

Valuables

Joint or sole
Value if sold

Business interests

Nature of interest/business
Estimated value
Money owed to you
Debtor
Amount owed

If your divorce is amicable and you and your spouse are committed to a fair settlement, you can create your list of assets together by assembling documents to prove that you own certain items and what they are worth. You'll need these documents throughout your divorce as solicitors, mediators, and the judge will all need to see them:

✔ **Documents for your home**

- Two or three valuations for your house

- Title deeds or copy of land registry entry. (See Chapter 3 for how to find out if you have these or how to apply for them if you don't.)

- Mortgage deeds and recent mortgage statements

✔ **Documents for endowment policies or other insurance policies**

- Schedules

- Current estimated maturity valuations

- Up-to-date surrender or sale valuations

✔ **Documents for pensions policies**

- Policy booklet and schedule

- Statements, including cash equivalent transfer values (CETV, see Chapter 11)

✔ **Other documents you may need**

- Share certificates and recent share price listings

- Bank and building society statements and passbooks with current balances

- All vehicle log books and valuations

- Documents relating to any other investments, valuables, or assets and their valuations

- Bank deposit box details

Working together will save time and help ensure that you don't overlook anything. In this case, two heads definitely *are* better than one. To make certain that your list is comprehensive, look through your home safe and bank safe deposit box (if you have them) for titles to property, deeds, securities, or other documentation relating to your ownership of valuables and property.

You can download asset and income worksheets from www.divorce.co.uk to help you integrate what you both earn, possess, and owe with what you will each need in the future, including the future costs of your children (see the section 'Creating income and expenditure sheets' later in this chapter).

Listing what you owe

Your family's financial portrait is only half-finished until you list and value your household debts, which may include

- ✔ Credit card debt
- ✔ Bank overdrafts and loans
- ✔ Hire purchase and other finance agreement commitments
- ✔ Mortgage or secured loan commitments
- ✔ Tax arrears/Inland Revenue debt
- ✔ Timeshare charge arrears
- ✔ Store card debts
- ✔ Catalogue debts
- ✔ Other personal loans, including student loans and business loans for which you or your spouse are personally liable

Without a list of your debts, you may forget about smaller debts, such as your store card, or anything that's being paid off slowly by direct debit from your bank account. When you've put together your complete financial picture, you're able to divide up your debts as well as your assets – making sure neither of you is left with the lion's share of either.

Gathering miscellaneous financial documents together

To collect together your assets and debts, you will need to refer to a variety of other financial and legal documents in addition to bank and savings account statements. Those documents include

✔ Copies of your tax returns for the past three years

✔ Copies of all life insurance policies in which either of you is listed as a primary or contingency beneficiary or owner

✔ Documentation about investments such as stocks, shares, PEPs, TESSAs, ISAs, bonds, and mutual funds

✔ Pension booklets, rules, and statements

✔ Copies of any financial statements you prepared separately or together when applying for a loan

✔ A copy of your will and your spouse's will

✔ Profit-and-loss statements and balance sheets for any business in which you, your spouse, or both of you have an interest and copies of related partnership agreements or articles of incorporation

✔ Copies of any pre-nuptial or post-nuptial agreements you have signed

After you locate all the documents you need, keep them together in a safe place. If you use a mediator or a solicitor to help negotiate your divorce, they need to see all this information and documentation. The more information you and your spouse willingly share with each other, your mediator, and your solicitors, the less information your solicitor will need to secure through formal disclosure, and the more money you'll save. (We talk about disclosure in Chapter 5.) Make sure you both have copies of all the documents.

In Scotland you should also identify when and with what funds (inherited, gifted, or earned during the marriage) any assets were acquired. The solicitor is mainly interested in the assets and debts which existed on the day you and your spouse separated (the *relevant* date), not what you have when you go to see him. See Chapter 11 for more about the relevant date.

Creating income and expenditure worksheets

Assuming that you and your spouse negotiate child support, spousal support, or both, either on your own or with a mediator or solicitor, you need to know the actual take-home payfor both of you, and your investments, pensions, inheritance, child support from any previous marriages, bonuses, state benefits, tax credits, and other sources of income. And you must know how you both spend that income.

To determine how much money is coming into and going out of your household, have a look at Chapter 3, which gives you instructions, and samples to follow.

If your spouse won't cooperate with you in the budget development process, you may have to take your best guess for certain types of income and expenses by using bank statements, cheque stubs, and credit card receipts.

Planning for Your Life After Divorce

If it is likely that you will be separating before you begin divorce proceedings, you need to sort out some sort of plan for your future. See Chapter 6 for actions you should both take before one of you actually leaves.

An important aspect of planning for divorce is thinking about what life will be like after your marriage has ended and what you want out of your divorce settlement. You may want to consider the following:

- ✔ How much will you need to spend on your children's everyday expenses, out of school and recreational activities, including holidays and school trips. Remember that costs are paid by both parents in most of the arrangements you make for your children (see Chapters 10 and 13).

- ✔ How much will you need for living expenses after you are divorced? (Think about developing a post-divorce budget that projects the income and expenses you anticipate.)

- ✔ What adjustments do you need to make in order to make ends meet and live a happy life on your own?

- ✔ Do you have adequate job skills if you plan to re-enter the job market after not working for several years?

- ✔ Where can you get those job skills? How long will it take to get them and how much will that education cost? (Remember to count educational expenses into your post-divorce budget, as well as any transport and child care costs you may incur while you are developing your job skills.)

Although thinking about these things when you are preoccupied by more immediate issues is tough, having at least a general plan for your post-divorce life helps you better define your divorce priorities and determine what you really want financially from your divorce and what you are willing to give up.

Deciding on your goals and priorities

Write down your divorce goals and priorities in their order of importance. Then put the list away in a safe place. After a month or so, when you've had some time to think, take another look at your list. You'll probably find that you want to add, subtract, or re-order a few items.

When you're thinking about what you really want out of your divorce, try to be realistic. Don't ask for the moon, but then again, don't be a martyr. The expenditure list in Chapter 3 can help you keep your feet on the ground when you're thinking about what you want versus what you need.

Spend some time thinking about the kind of divorce you want and what you are willing to do to get that divorce, and articulate your desires to your solicitor. For example, ask yourself the following questions (and have a look at the chapters we've referenced for help in coming up with the answers):

- ✔ Are you willing to go all the way to a court hearing to get the top items on your list of divorce priorities, or is a negotiated settlement more important to you? (Chapters 14 and 16)

- ✔ What decisions are in your children's best interests, and how are you going to work with your spouse to achieve that? (Chapter 10)

- ✔ How important is it to you to have a good relationship with your spouse after the divorce? How important is that to your children? (Chapter 10)

- ✔ Do you absolutely have to have the children living with you all the time, or are you willing to share their care with your spouse? (Chapter 10)

- ✔ Do you have to stay in the family home, or might you and the children be better off somewhere else? And how near do you and the children need to be to your work, schools, friends, family, and ex-spouse? (Chapter 10)

- ✔ Realistically, how big a house do you need for you and the children for the next few years, and what can you afford? (Chapter 11)

- ✔ What are your minimum and maximum income needs, and what do you see as the optimum division of your time between your work, your children, and your other commitments? (Chapter 11)

- ✔ How much of a priority is it for you to provide now for your longer-term security, such as when your children leave home or you reach retirement age? (Chapter 11)

- ✔ What difference will it make if you or your spouse remarry or co-habit? (Chapter 20)

- ✔ How much time and money are you prepared to spend on your divorce? (Read on for how much it's likely to cost.)

If you're clear about the kind of outcome that you want for your divorce, you'll be better able to choose a solicitor who can help you achieve it. (See Chapter 15 for tips on choosing the solicitor that's right for you.) You'll also be able to provide your solicitor with direction and feedback during the divorce process. If you use the first solicitor you hear about with little or no thought to your goals and priorities, terminating your marriage may end up being more stressful, lengthy, and expensive than you ever imagined.

How Much Do You Have to Spend to End Your Marriage?

If you aren't careful, the thousands of pounds you spent on your wedding and honeymoon may be a mere pittance compared with the cost of your divorce. How much it will cost to end your marriage depends on a number of factors:

- **Whether your divorce is amicable and co-operative, or bitter and contentious:** The more you and your spouse can agree on, the less you will have to spend on solicitors, barristers, legal fees, and court costs. If your divorce is contentious, your solicitor may have to make a number of applications and court appearances. It will take your solicitor time to prepare each application and yet more time to argue each one out before a judge, and you will have to pay for all of that time.

- **The area you live in:** Legal fees will cost you more if you live in a city, as the overhead costs of most city firms of solicitors, especially in London, are higher and they cover the cost by charging you more.

- **The reputation and experience of the solicitor who represents you:** More experienced solicitors and barristers with 'winning' reputations can command bigger fees than those lawyers who have not been practising as long or who do not have established reputations as family law specialists. On the other hand, they may help you settle things much more quickly and efficiently. At the very least, make sure that your solicitor is a specialist family lawyer and preferably one who belongs to the Solicitors Family Law Association and works to their code of practice and protocol.

- **How many of your divorce terms you and your spouse can work out together:** It's almost always more economical if you and your spouse can negotiate your finances together rather than pay your solicitors to do all the work on your behalf.

- **Whether you and your spouse get into a battle about the children, which can be very expensive:** Co-operating over the plans for your children will save you the expense of your solicitors working out the fine details or the full costs of going to court.

- **The amount of assets and debts you need to divide up and their complexity:** Depending on the debts and assets involved, you may need to hire a valuer, financial adviser, forensic accountant, actuary, or other professional to help with your divorce.

- **Whether you or your spouse are hiding any assets:** If you are, then you may get involved in the potentially spiralling expense of formal disclosure proceedings.

✔ **Whether you and your spouse are willing to settle your divorce out-side court or whether one or both of you is determined to have a court hearing:** If one of you is bent on a fight, it will cost both of you.

✔ **The legal strategies of your solicitor and your spouse's solicitor:** You may choose a consensus-seeking family lawyer only to find that your spouse has chosen one who is adversarial or inexperienced in family law. Your solicitor may then have to change tack.

✔ **Whether you are eligible for any sort of public funding or legal aid:** The charging rates of solicitors and barristers doing publicly-funded work are fixed annually by the government and are normally much lower than private charging rates.

The least it will cost

If your divorce is extremely simple – you and your spouse have little or noth-ing to negotiate, you have no children or no children still at home, no marital property, few debts, neither of you is asking for spousal support, and you are willing to complete most if not all of the paperwork yourself – you can get divorced for just a few hundred pounds, maybe even less.

Even if you own property or owe debts, your divorce may cost you no more than one to two thousand pounds, if you and your spouse work out the terms of your divorce together after you have each had an initial consultation with your solicitors or the help of a professional mediator. Your solicitors will review your final agreement and formalise the agreement. Public funding reduces the cost even further. (Chapters 14 and 16 provide helpful informa-tion if you want to negotiate on your own or in mediation.)

Pinpointing the cost with multiple estimates

To get a better idea of the likely cost of your divorce, you may get estimates from several family solicitors. When you are inquiring about or meeting potential solicitors (see Chapter 15), ask for fee estimates based on several divorce scenarios. That will help you to decide whether to hold out for a particular property settlement, child arrangement, or specific amount of maintenance.

By using the solicitors' estimates, you can do a very basic cost-benefit analysis comparing the value of what you may gain should you pursue a particular goal compared with how much it would cost you to get it. However, no solicitor can guarantee that you'll get the outcome you want, regardless of how much money you spend.

The most it will cost

Be prepared to spend a whole lot more money on your divorce if you and your spouse fight every step of the way, or if your divorce is complicated and active involvement of your solicitors from start to finish is essential. In this case, you may be looking at legal bills in five figures. At the end of a prolonged child residence battle, legal bills have been known to rise to £10,000. If you and your spouse go into battle over complex financial matters, those bills could *triple*.

The private hourly rate of an experienced family law solicitor can range from £100 to £500 or more, depending on where they practice and their level of experience. Some solicitors handle very straightforward and amicable divorces for a flat rate as low as £500 per case and a mediation case can average a few hundred pounds. Rates for publicly-funded work range from about £45 to £100 per hour, depending on the work involved, the complexity, and whether your solicitor is based in London or elsewhere. (As with everything, London rates are more expensive than anywhere else in the UK.)

Do what you can to avoid a battle about your children. Not only will it be extremely expensive, but the battle may cause your children to suffer long-lasting emotional damage. If you are considering such a battle, analyse your motives, perhaps with the help of a counsellor (see Chapter 2 for help in finding a counsellor). After some serious reflection, you may decide that you're confusing your own needs with your children's – or that you are using the kids as a way of getting back at your spouse. Refer to Chapter 8 for a thorough look at what your children's needs can include and to Chapter 10 to see what your alternatives are for child care.

Help from public funding or legal aid

If you are on a low income or have no income apart from your spouse's, you may be able to apply for financial help. We give you full details in Chapter 15 about what you need to qualify and how you can use public funding. The Legal Services Commission, www.justask.org.uk (or the Scottish Legal Aid Board if you live in Scotland, www.slab.org.uk), may be able to help with funding your legal and mediation costs.

Most forms of legal aid for family disputes are more like a loan than a gift. So, for example, if you're granted public funding to take your case to court, or for your solicitors to negotiate on your behalf, you have to pay back all your court and solicitor's costs out of any money or property that you receive as part of your settlement. This *legal aid charge* or *statutory charge* (also known as a *claw-back*) almost always applies regardless of whether your final settlement is by consent or fully contested. However, the one exception to this rule is that if you're eligible for public funding for mediation, you don't have to pay back any of the costs incurred by your mediator or solicitor so long as you reach an agreement in mediation and you and your solicitors go along with that agreement. This exception is an incentive for you to reach an agreement in mediation and to stick with it.

Receiving state benefits and tax credits

The fact of the matter is that, after a divorce, the pot of money you were living on when you were married has to be split between two households. You can try to cut back on your expenditure and you can try to increase your income, but you may not be able to avoid being hard up. If you have children, the drop in income and increase in expenditure will affect them too.

The good news is that the government provides some safety nets to protect you financially. Public financial support includes *income support* and tax credits and benefits to help you provide for yourselves and your children, and to encourage you back into work where possible. Be aware of these benefits when you make arrangements for your family after divorce. All the professionals who have a contract with the Legal Services Commission have training in welfare benefits and tax credits because these benefits are such an important part of many divorced families' lives at one time or another.

Here we briefly summarise the main benefits and tax credits that you may be entitled to depending on your means and circumstances. For more information, pick up leaflet GL23 from your post office, try the Web site: www. inlandrevenue.gov.uk/taxcredits, or make an appointment with your local Citizens Advice Bureau. See Chapter 13 for a detailed explanation of the benefits you may be eligible for if you have children.

- ✔ **Child Benefit:** A non-means tested benefit, payable on a weekly or four-weekly basis to anyone responsible for a child living with them under the age of 16, or under 19 and in full-time education.

- ✔ **Child Tax Credit:** Paid to the main carer of a child under 16, or under 19 and in full-time education, the Child Tax Credit depends on your means. An amount is paid for each child in your household, plus extra for a disabled child or child under one year old.

- ✔ **Working Tax Credit:** You may be able to claim Working Tax Credit, depending on the number of hours that you work (you need to work at least 16 hours if you have a dependent child or 30 if you do not). Your income. Working Tax Credit is more generous if you have children and you are their main carer, and you may be able to get help with childcare costs when you are at work. Maintenance or child support paid to you by your spouse or ex-spouse won't be taken into account as income.

✔ **Income Support:** You can claim Income Support if you have less than £8,000 capital, work less than 16 hours per week, aren't in full-time education, and have income below a prescribed amount. Income support is a passport to several other benefits such as free prescriptions, housing benefit, council tax benefit, and legal aid. You may also be able to borrow money from a social fund for certain essential household items.

Rules and levels of Income Support are liable to change, so check with the Inland Revenue to make sure your information is up-to-date.

✔ **Job Seekers Allowance:** To claim Job Seekers Allowance you must be over 18, unemployed, and available for work. You won't be treated as available for work if you have a dependent child living with you under the age of 16. Rates of payment depend on your National Insurance Contributions or are calculated in a similar way to Income Support.

✔ **Housing Benefit:** If you live in rented accommodation, are responsible for the rent, have less than £16,000 capital, and your income is below a prescribed level, you may be entitled to help towards your rent up to a maximum of 100 per cent of the eligible rent for your area (that may be less than the rent that you are contracted to pay).

✔ **Council Tax Benefit:** If you are responsible for the council tax on your home, have less than £16,000 capital, and your income is below a prescribed level, you may be eligible for help towards your council tax, up to a maximum of 100 per cent. You should in any event claim a 25 per cent reduction if you are a single adult occupier.

✔ **Disability Benefits:** There is a range of benefits available if you are temporarily or permanently disabled. It is always best to get specialist advice if you think you may be able to claim.

✔ **The New Deal:** Special deals are available to help single parents back into work, particularly if you have been on Income Support for more than six months. According to users, one of the most helpful features of the scheme is the personal adviser you are given to help you find work.

Anticipating a Hostile Divorce

If you suspect that your divorce will be a knock-down, dragged-out fight, or if you're certain your divorce won't go smoothly, you may need to take some defensive measures.

Opening a bank account in your own name

If you share a savings account with your spouse and you are concerned that she may abuse the account, you might want to withdraw some of the money in the account – maybe half, depending on your needs and the amount in the account – and deposit it in a new account in your own name. Make sure that you have a clear record of any such transactions.

After your spouse learns that you have taken money out of your joint account and placed it in your separate account, expect some fireworks that may make your divorce negotiations more difficult. If you withdraw an unreasonable amount of money (and just what 'unreasonable' constitutes is something your solicitors might have to advise you on), you may end up increasing the costs of your property settlement.

Make sure you have enough money in your current bank account to cover your monthly expenses. Bounced cheque charges and angry creditors are among the last things you need right now.

Closing or freezing your joint accounts

Cancel credit card accounts if your spouse is also a card holder. If you can't close an account because of an outstanding debt that you can't pay, return your card to the credit card company and explain that you won't be responsible for debts on the account beyond the current balance.

If you both have a joint account, ask your bank manager to freeze it so that you can only draw on it with joint signatures. Banks shouldn't be able to close a joint account without both of your consent. Make sure that you make arrangements for essential direct debits and standing orders first. Also, if you and your spouse have an overdraft limit with a bank or credit card, cancel or reduce these limits. Inform your spouse of what you've done and ask her to tear up her card or return it to you or the credit card company.

Finding a safe place for your important personal property

If you think that your spouse may try to damage, destroy, or steal your personal property out of anger or revenge, find a safe place to hide your valuables. That can be a safe deposit box in your name, the home of a trusted friend or family member, or any other place your spouse can't access.

If your spouse steals or damages your personal property, you may be able to claim the value of that property from your spouse in any financial proceedings between you. Your solicitor can also use evidence of your spouse's destructive behaviour as leverage on the question of costs during your divorce negotiations or at the end of the final hearing.

Building your individual credit

Individual credit – credit in your own name – is essential to your having a life on your own. Building a decent credit record takes time. If you don't have individual credit when you close your joint accounts, you may have to wait several years before you have access to credit on the best terms. (See Chapter 3 for more information on building your own credit record.) Check to make sure that any jointly-held credit is recorded in your individual names rather than Mr & Mrs R. Smith. And ask your creditors to begin reporting information on these accounts in your name as well as your spouse's. Assuming that these accounts have positive payment histories, having them in your credit file may help you build your own credit history. This is distinct from being an authorised user, which does not build your own credit record.

Protecting your mutual assets from being wasted by your spouse

If your spouse is angry about your divorce or wants to get revenge, he or she may try to use up your joint assets rather than allow you to get a portion of those assets in your divorce. If you are concerned that this may happen, consult a family law solicitor straight away about what steps you can take to safeguard your joint assets. Avoid maintaining large unprotected cash balances in your joint accounts or your solicitor may be able to apply for an injunction and request an emergency hearing if the property in question is at real risk from your spouse.

Identifying sources of ready funds

Protecting your legal rights when you're involved in a hostile divorce takes lots of money. If you seriously fear that your divorce will be hostile, start identifying the financial resources you have at your disposal at once, including your separate savings account, stocks, shares, or bonds; borrowing against your insurance policy funds; getting a second mortgage on property you own in your own right; borrowing money from family members; and anything else along those lines. Keep a record of all your transactions as you will be expected to account for them in any financial proceedings. Talk with an accountant or your financial adviser about the tax consequences and other implications of selling stocks or shares, borrowing against any insurance funds, or taking a second loan on any property you own.

Chapter 8

Helping Your Children Get Through Your Divorce

· ·

In This Chapter

▶ Putting your children's feelings first

▶ Deciding when the time is right to break the news

▶ Talking to all your children at once or each child individually

▶ Preparing for your children's responses and questions

· ·

Remembering to put your children first can seem like a tall order, especially if the break up of your marriage is full of conflict. After all, you have your own emotions to deal with, financial and legal matters to resolve, and worries about what the future may bring. Nevertheless, your children depend on you for the care and support they need to be happy and secure and to grow into well-adjusted adults.

In this chapter, we help you address your children's personal needs during your divorce and offer advice for minimising any emotional trauma they may experience. We also offer guidance on when and how to tell your children about the end of your marriage and alert you to some of the ways your kids may respond to the news.

Remaining Sensitive to Your Children's Feelings

When you get divorced, you and your spouse aren't the only people affected by the change in your marital status. Your divorce means the end of family life as your children have known it up to now, something that has been their mainstay. They may feel anxious and be thrown of balance for a time – toddlers may revert to more childish behaviour, school children may lack concentration, older children may be more than usually moody or angry. These early reactions should pass unless the insecurity continues and is compounded by conflict.

There are four ways you can best protect your children from the long-term damage of divorce by ensuring the survival of their self-esteem:

- ✔ **Don't get your children caught up in your adult arguments.**
- ✔ **Don't subject your kids to the insecurity of a succession of changes in their living arrangements.**
- ✔ **Make sure that your children don't lose either of you without very good reason.**
- ✔ **Keep your kids in the picture about what's happening with your family.**

Be reassured, however that this does not mean that every child who experiences adversity is damaged by it. Your children can be resilient if they are given your help and support. Your children may well experience a drop in household income. They may have to move out of their home and neighbourhood, attend a new school, and make new friends. You may not have been able to keep them totally clear of a fraught – even hostile – home environment. You may have to come to terms with the fact that your divorce is their first experience of your doing something for your own sake and apparently not theirs. However, your job is to do all that you can, co-operatively whenever possible, to prevent your children, resilient or vulnerable, from feeling anxious, unloved, and insecure.

What your kids may fear (but not be telling you)

During and after their parents' divorce, young children in particular may become fearful that terrible things may happen to them or believe that they are in some way responsible for the break up of their parents' marriage. Some of the more common fears and misconceptions children have about divorce include the following:

- ✔ The parent I no longer live with will disappear from my life.

- ✔ My parents' divorce is my fault.

- ✔ If I am really good, my parents will get back together.

- ✔ I have to choose between my parents. I can't have a relationship with both of them after they are divorced.

- ✔ My parent's new partner will replace my other real parent.

- ✔ A new stepbrother or stepsister is going to replace me.

Understanding the thoughts that may be going through your children's minds can keep you alert to any signs that they are having trouble coping with your divorce.

When, What, and How to Tell Your Children What Is Happening

Both you and your spouse need to convey in words and deeds that you will always be there for your children. They may fear that they will lose one of you in a divorce or that one or both of you will somehow abandon them and they will have to fend for themselves. Make sure that your reassurances are realistic and your promises are more than hot air. You want your children to trust you.

There are several ways for you to tell your kids, and some are better than others. At the very least, consider the following options for making the conversation go smoothly:

- **Agree on what you're going to say.** It's best if you and your spouse can take the time together to decide what you are going to say about your divorce before you talk with your kids. Getting your story straight first means that you don't contradict one another or argue while you break the news to your kids.

- **Tell your children as a couple.** If at all possible, you and your spouse should tell your children about your divorce together, even if it requires putting your animosity aside for a while. Telling them together conveys to them that although your marriage may be ending, you can co-operate as parents and that they still have a family – just a different kind of family – and you will both remain actively involved in their lives.

- **Be fair to one another.** You should both agree that when you talk with your children – whether together or separately – neither of you will blame the other for your break up or encourage your kids to side with one of you against the other. Both these scenarios are unfair to your children and can cause them a great deal of hurt. When you criticise their other parent, you are criticising someone they love. Your comments can also backfire on you – your children may side with the parent you have criticised and not with you.

- **Be honest with your children about why you are getting divorced.** But remember to keep their ages in mind and don't tell them things about your adult relationship that they neither understand nor need to know. Tell them as much as they need to know and no more. If you haven't been able to hide the discord in your marriage, you may want to acknowledge what your children already know by saying something like, 'We know that you've heard us fighting a lot and here's what is going to happen...'

Don't hide the fact that life is going to be different for everyone in the family because of your divorce. Prepare your children for some of the changes to come. Then reassure them that your divorce hasn't changed, and won't change, your love for them, and that you will continue to be involved in their lives. But don't promise them things you can't deliver.

✔ **Be very clear with your children that your divorce has absolutely nothing to do with them.** Young children may feel somehow responsible for the divorce and assume that if only they had behaved better you wouldn't be ending your marriage. A Web site available especially for children, www.itsnotyourfault.co.uk, may help them (or you) understand better what is happening in your family.

✔ **Don't let emotion get the better of you.** Try not to get emotional when you tell your children about your divorce. Watching a parent cry, shout, or get very upset can be frightening for your children. Don't add to their anxiety with a highly charged account of what has been going on. You're likely to make them more concerned about your emotions than their own. As a consequence, your kids may not let you know exactly what they are feeling.

Finding help with telling your kids

If you need help deciding what to say to your children, talk things over with their health visitor (if you have a child under school age), their teacher (if they are at primary school and the relationship is a good one), or a school or children's counsellor if they are of secondary school age. You can also ask your local Relate office (www.relate.org.uk) or local Family Mediation Service (www.fmassoc.co.uk) what service is available in your area or use a mediator to help you work out together what you are going to say.

Helping your children cope with the news

If your children are having trouble coping with the news of your divorce, they may need a great deal more cuddling if they are young and extra time and attention if they are a bit older. Adolescents may seem to take the news in their stride or protest vigorously, which can make it hard to give them the support and understanding they need – but you mustn't stop trying to reach out to them. Levelling with your teenage children as much as you can conveys respect for their growing maturity and helps them to grow – but not if you're tempted to confide in them to get them on your side!

Getting help from someone else

Sometimes helping your kids isn't that simple. When your children need more than you, at the time, can give them, consider first involving a loved grandparent (UK research studies have shown many grandparents to be the people closest to children at such a time) or another trusted adult who's especially close to your kids. Support groups for children whose parents have separated can be helpful to older children.

Tell your children's teachers, baby-sitters, other carers, the parents of their close friends, and any other adults they see regularly about your divorce plans. Informing these people will help them understand that any significant changes in your children's behaviour may be due to your divorce. Ask these adults, for their part, to keep you informed of any changes they notice in your children.

In some areas there are groups or short courses for divorcing parents where you can learn about children's reactions to divorce, effective parent–child communication, and resources that can help parents and their children. Find out from your local Relate or Family Mediation Service if there are support services in your area.

TIP

Resources to help you and your children

Many resources – books, leaflets, and Web sites – are available to help you and your children cope with your divorce.

For books, you may find *Good to Talk* by Bren Neale and Carole Smart (Young Voice, 2001), based on research done at the University of Leeds, helpful. You may also find *What's at Issue? Families* by Bridget Lawless (Heinemann Library, 1999) and *Caught in the Middle: Helping Children to Cope with Separation and Divorce* by Anne Charlish (Cassell Illustrated, 1997) useful. You can find further lists of books for children on several Web sites mentioned in this chapter or from a general divorce Web site: www.divorce-online.uk.

These Web sites may help your older children:

✔ www.itsnotyourfault.org

✔ www.coping-with-life.org.uk (a Rotary Web site)

✔ www.young-voice.org

✔ www.nyas.net

✔ www.thesite.org.uk

You may also find these Web sites useful:

✔ www.e-parents.org

✔ www.parentlineplus.org.uk

You can download excellent free leaflets for children from the government Web site: www.lcd.gov.uk/family/divleaf.htm. You'll find a leaflet for 5–8 year olds called 'Me and My Family'; for 8–13 year olds, 'My Family's Changing'; for older children 'My Family's Splitting Up – a Guide for Young People', as well as a leaflet for parents called 'Parents and Children'; these can all be downloaded free. This collection of leaflets should also be available from local county courts and magistrates' courts and from divorce and family agencies such as Family Mediation Services and CAF-CASS offices.

For help over the phone, try the ParentlinePlus helpline (0808 800 2233).

Keeping your kids out of the argument

Watch your own behaviour in the presence of your children. What you choose to do (or don't do, as the following list tells you) can either help reassure them that things will be okay or can add to their anxiety about the future.

- ✔ Don't fight with your spouse when your children are around.
- ✔ Don't say negative things about your spouse to your children or to someone else within hearing distance of your children.
- ✔ Don't get highly emotional around your children about your divorce or your life after the divorce. You risk increasing their insecurity and fear about the future.
- ✔ Don't use your children as go-betweens between you and your spouse.
- ✔ Don't interfere in your children's relationship with your spouse by trying to manipulate them into thinking of you as the 'good parent' and your spouse as the 'bad parent'.
- ✔ Don't put pressure on your children to take sides.
- ✔ Avoid making big changes in your children's daily routines. As much as possible, keep everything in their lives just as it was. Children generally don't like change, and divorce is change enough.
- ✔ Don't spoil them because you are feeling guilty or because you want to get them on your side. And although you may feel tired, don't let discipline slip.
- ✔ Avoid making your children your confidantes. Keep your adult worries and concerns to yourself or share them only with other adults.
- ✔ Don't look to your children for comfort. It should work the other way around.
- ✔ Don't expect your child to become 'your little man' or 'your little woman' about the house. Your children are children not surrogate spouses. But don't let them off normal chores, either. If there are fewer hands to do things, share out the tasks. Involving them appropriately can help them to cope with change. We all cope with change better when we have something useful to do.

Deciding when to tell your children

You may tend to put off doing things that are unpleasant or that you don't feel confident about (most people do). So, you may come up with countless reasons to put off telling your children about your divorce. However, make sure that you tell them before anyone else does. They need to hear the news from you, in your own words. And, in the same breath, you need to reassure them that you will always love them and take care of them.

TECHNICAL STUFF

Staying positive

A child's self-esteem is a precious thing and so is yours. Being too negative can destroy your self-esteem as well as your children's.

An American professor, John Gottman, invites couples into his studio for a weekend and measures the ratio between negative and positive statements in their conversation. Guess what? He has arrived at a startling glimpse of the obvious. If the ratio of positive to negative statements is five to one or more, then he can predict that the relationship will survive. He claims 94 per cent success in his predictions over a period of about 20 years' study.

Imagine being the child who hears his parents saying mostly negative things about each other or about him. Hearing negative things about his parents or himself may well be the key factor in losing his self-esteem. And the ratio of negative to positive is likely to get worse when there's a divorce.

So here are some things you can do to protect your own and your child's self esteem:

✔ At a contact handover, listen to yourselves talking together for about ten minutes and count the ratio of positive to negative statements you all make.

✔ If you notice more negative than positive statements, reverse your own ratio next time. You may well find your ex-spouse becomes more positive too!

✔ Practise turning a criticism into a positive statement. For example, 'You're always late and I never know when you are coming! How do you think that makes Mary feel?' can become 'I appreciate your commitment to keeping in contact with Mary, and I find it really helpful when you arrive within 15 minutes of when we expect you'.

✔ Say what you think and feel rather than guess negatively what your spouse may be thinking and feeling – even if you feel you know them (and their thoughts) so very well! However, stay as positive as you can. Rather than, 'You always look so bad tempered when I arrive. Do you really hate me now?' try saying instead 'I find it hard coming to collect Mary but I appreciate the fact that you let me come'.

✔ Be specific rather than generalise. Don't say, 'There you go! You always look on the black side'. Say instead, 'I feel that you're looking too much on the black side'.

The right time to talk with your children about the changes to come depends on their ages and on the circumstances of your divorce. For example, if your spouse announces that he or she has already filed for a divorce and is moving out the next week, you need to tell your children about the split sooner and not later.

Informing your older children

Bear in mind that if you have older children (secondary school age and older) they usually need to be told sooner than very young children – assuming that you have some control over the timing of your conversations with your them. Older children are more likely to learn about your divorce by overhearing a conversation or by coming across divorce-related papers, and partly because they're better at sensing that 'something is up'. They are also better at managing information over a period of time, digesting it, and coming up with explanations that they can live with – although they may sound more worldly-wise than they feel. When you're certain that you are divorcing and have worked out at least some of the details, especially those that affect your children, talk with them as soon as possible.

Don't, however, discuss your divorce plans with your older children until you have talked the plans over with your spouse. It's unfair and inappropriate to make them confidantes and try to seek their advice and opinions. If you need advice and counselling, go to an adult source. (See Chapter 9 for suggestions on finding a counsellor.)

Don't overlook the responses of your adult children. They will still be shaken by a divorce, even if you have tried to wait until they have left home or gone to university. Like any children, they need to be told in a sensitive way. Your adult children may feel that the home they left is no longer there for them at a time when they haven't yet established themselves anywhere else. They may also seem to lose confidence in marriage (possibly explaining why many younger people choose to cohabit instead).

Talking to your younger children

If you have toddlers and primary school children, avoid telling them about your divorce plans too far ahead of the date when you and your spouse plan to begin living apart. Young children have a different sense of time from adults and older children; for them, a week can seem like a month and a month can seem like a year. If you tell your younger children too early, you risk intensifying the anxiety they have over knowing that their lives are going to change in ways they don't yet understand. As well, avoid using words like 'court' and 'law' because young children will associate them with wrongdoing, perhaps without your realising it.

Regardless of their ages, whenever possible don't wait until just before you and your spouse begin living apart to break the news to your children. *Worse than that is if one of you leaves without any explanation at all.* Instead, tell them far enough ahead of the day you plan to separate so that they have time to process your news, ask you questions, spend time with both of you in a relaxed manner, and enjoy your affection. All of these things are essential preparation for the changes ahead.

Telling your kids individually or all together

Should you tell your children about your divorce all at the same time, or have separate conversations with each of them? Only you can make that decision, but in this section we give you arguments in support of each approach.

Discussing your divorce as a group

If your children are close in age and maturity, telling them all together has important benefits:

- ✔ **It can help foster a 'we're all in this together' attitude among your children.** That feeling can be both a comfort and a source of strength to them.

- ✔ **If all of your children learn about your divorce at the same time, each of them knows exactly what his or her siblings know.** This may not seem important to you, but if you tell each of them separately, they may worry that they don't know what their siblings know or that you are going to treat them differently from everyone else in the family.

Talking to each child alone

If your children have significant disparities in their ages or levels of maturity, it's advisable to have individual talks with them so that you can tailor an appropriate message.

Be sure to tell each child that you are having a similar conversation with his or her siblings. Unless your children are very young, they are probably going to talk with one another about what you have told them. Therefore, your message about why you are getting a divorce and what is going to change or stay the same in their lives should be consistent. If you tell each child something different, you'll only add to their anxiety and confusion.

Anticipating Your Children's Responses

You can't predict how your children will react to the news of your divorce. Their reaction depends on their ages and maturity levels, their personalities, and their relationship with you, among other things. Interestingly enough, however, you may find that their emotions mirror yours and may include any or all of the following:

- ✔ Disbelief
- ✔ Anger
- ✔ Fear
- ✔ Sadness
- ✔ Depression
- ✔ Rejection

To help keep an eye on how well your children are dealing with the news of your divorce, try to spend some extra time with them (but not in an interfering way). The time you spend together gives your children the opportunity to express their feelings and concerns about their daily lives in their own time. Your children will possibly will drop things out at odd moments of intimacy – young ones in the bath or at bedtime; older kids in the car or even while washing up.

Listening to your children

Your children need to feel that they are being listened to while you are in the midst of your marriage break up. You must find time to be in touch with their thoughts and feelings especially when they are finding it difficult to put these into words. Don't anxiously put words into your children's mouths but listen to how they are making sense of what is happening to them.

You may find it hard to hear what your children may say at times. For example, they may say 'Didn't daddy love me, then?' or 'If you had not been so cross all the time, mummy wouldn't have left'. You might be tempted to defend yourself by launching into explanations, but the important thing is that you hear and respond warmly to the anxiety behind their comments and that you are not judgemental. Then your kids are more likely to open up to you so that you can comfort and reassure them.

After your children find out about your divorce plans, they may begin to feel isolated and cut off from their friends. They may feel as though they're the only children whose parents ever got divorced and may be embarrassed about what's happening to them.

Although your children may appear to be coping, don't assume that they're not having trouble at school or at play, or won't have trouble later on. Stay tuned in to their mood swings or any changes in their behaviour that may be a sign of emotional distress. See the section below on 'Recognising signs that your children are finding it hard to cope'.

The art of 'active' listening

If you have never before concentrated on listening attentively to your children, now is the time to start. Good, 'active' listening requires your being attuned to the feelings behind your children's comments and questions, and then letting them know in a non-judgemental way that you heard what they were saying.

Active listening doesn't mean preaching or lecturing, and doesn't necessarily involve analysis or problem solving. Its purpose is to encourage your children to open up to you and to tell you what they think about your divorce.

Active listening promotes a feeling of love and trust between you and your children, something they need in order to deal with their parents' divorce.

If you separate before your divorce is final, your children should visit the parent who moves out as soon as possible so that they can reassure themselves that their parent is all right and is still their parent. Young children have been known to worry that the parent no longer at home gets enough to eat, for example.

However, if your children refuse to visit their other parent or seem reluctant to do so, don't force them. Contact should always be beneficial – not done for the sake of it. Under normal circumstances, your children should have the other parent's new address and phone number but in some rarer instances there could be strong reasons for keeping this from them, for example if there has been violence or abuse or you have reason to fear that there will be. (Refer to Chapter 2.)

If you or your spouse fought openly and often during your marriage, your separation may of course be a relief to your children as well as to you and represent a positive, though strange, change in their lives.

Recognising signs that your children are finding it hard to cope

If you're divorcing, you need to be familiar with the more common signs of emotional distress in children and be on the lookout for them in your own children so that you are ready to step in as soon as possible. When children behave in the following ways, they're asking for help.

Toddlers and pre-school children may

- ✔ Revert to more childish behaviour, such as bedwetting, thumb-sucking, and crying.
- ✔ Have trouble sleeping in their own room or have nightmares.
- ✔ Develop behaviour problems at home or with other children.
- ✔ Become fearful of leaving you.

Primary school children may

- ✔ Say they feel ill more than usual so that they can stay at home from school (headaches and stomach aches are particularly common).
- ✔ Choose one parent to be angry with and choose another to cling to for comfort.
- ✔ Begin spending more time alone in their rooms and less time playing with friends.
- ✔ Participate in fewer classroom activities.

Secondary school age children may

- ✔ Withdraw from friends and family.
- ✔ Develop non-specific illnesses or nervous habits such as nail-biting.
- ✔ Spend more time alone in their rooms.
- ✔ Express anger towards the parent they think is responsible for the divorce.
- ✔ Try to behave like a surrogate spouse to the parent they feel has been wronged.
- ✔ Develop behaviour problems (such as getting into fights) at school, outside school, or at home.
- ✔ Become more rebellious (for example, truanting, smoking, drinking, experimenting with drugs, or staying out late).

Although you may have no cause for alarm if your children are under stress for a short period of time, if your child's obvious discomfort is prolonged or grows worse, you do have cause for concern. Alcohol and drug abuse, delinquency, or criminal actions require immediate attention because these can put your child and others in danger. Read Chapter 2 for help on finding a counsellor or someone else who can help you and your child.

Handling your children's questions

After you tell your children about your divorce plans, give them an opportunity to ask questions. If they ask you something that you can't answer, say so by admitting that you don't know or it's too soon to tell. When appropriate, tell them that you will give them an answer by a certain date or as soon as you can. Be careful in explaining that you are divorcing because you and your spouse don't love each other any more – you don't want your children to think that you could therefore stop loving them. You must reassure your children that you love them, and will continue to do so.

During one of our mediation sessions, Sam, a ten-year-old boy, protested when his mother said she would tell him why she and his father were divorcing when he was older and would understand. He shouted 'You tell me now even if I don't understand!' So she had to try.

Your children's initial questions will probably relate to how your divorce will change their lives and what will stay the same. For example, depending on their ages, they may want to know

- ✔ Where will they live?
- ✔ Will they still go to the same school?

- ✔ Will you and your spouse still live in the same town?

- ✔ Will they spend time with each of you?

- ✔ Will you continue to be involved with their favourite sporting activity?

- ✔ Can they continue their music or dance lessons?

- ✔ How will you share parenting responsibilities?

- ✔ Can they still go on school trips?

- ✔ Will there be enough money?

- ✔ Where will their dog or cat live?

Don't be surprised if your children don't ask you many questions at first. Learning that you are getting a divorce will probably come as quite a shock, even if they already know that you and your spouse are having marital problems and even if they have plenty of friends with divorced parents. Your children may need time to let the news sink in before they're ready to ask you questions.

Understanding how children vary with age

Your older children may come to you with questions after they have shared your news with friends, especially if their friends' parents are divorced and their friends tell them what the divorce experience was like for them.

There are many resources available for older children, and it may be better to leave them around rather than thrust them eagerly on your reluctant adolescents. Here's a list of some of the books they may find helpful:

- ✔ *Divorce is Not the End of the World* by Zoe Evan, and Sue Ellen Stern (Tricycle Press, 1997) for 9–13 year olds

- ✔ *What Do You Know About Divorce and Separation* by Pete Sanders and Steve Myers (Franklin Watts, 2000) for 7–14 year olds

- ✔ *Parent Problems!* by Bren Neale and Amanda Wade (Young Voice, 2000), which gives children and young people's views on divorce

Your younger children may have a hard time grasping the concept of divorce and find it hard to understand that you and your spouse will always continue to love them and care for them. If you have, for example, said that you no longer love each other, they may begin to think that love for them can also just stop. They may ask you the same questions over and over, which can really tax your patience. You will need to understand that at that moment your children need constant reassurance.

You can help your younger children deal with your divorce by reading them age-appropriate books that deal with the subject. A very wise child psychiatrist once said that one of the things that helps children cope with trauma is if they construct a story about it or an explanation for it that they can then live with comfortably. You can gradually help your children to do this.

One parent we know made up a story to help explain to her five-year-old that she and her husband were separating. The story was about a water nymph falling in love with a fire sprite. They couldn't live together because one needed water and the other air. However their child, a water sprite, could live with each of them, separately.

We recommend the following titles to help your younger children acknowledge and express their fears and worries about your divorce and the changes divorce brings:

- *Separation: Divorce* by Janine Amos (Cherrytree Books, 2002) for 5–10 year olds

- *How Do I Feel About My Parent's Divorce* by J. Cole (Franklin Watts, 2001) for 5–11 year olds

- *Dinosaurs Divorce: A Guide for Changing Families* by Marc Brown and Laurence Krasny Brown (Little, Brown & Co., 1988) for 3–7 year olds

'No one tells us anything'

Let your children know that you are willing and available to talk with them about your divorce and answer their questions whenever they want.

Four hundred and sixty-seven children from the west of England, aged between five and 16, were interviewed for a study published in 2001. A quarter of them whose parents had separated said no-one talked about the separation when it happened. Only 5 per cent said they were given full explanations and the chance to ask questions!

If your kids seem reluctant to ask questions, take the initiative by talking with each of them individually about your divorce and asking them if they have questions about it. Obviously, if you have always enjoyed an honest, open relationship with your children they will be more willing to discuss their fears and concerns than if you never before expressed an interest in finding out what they were thinking or having a meaningful conversation with them.

If you need help finding ways to communicate with your children, try any of the following titles:

✔ *But I Want to Stay With You* by Jill Burrett (Simon & Schuster, 2000), which is about communicating with your children

✔ *Good to Talk* by Bren Neale and Carole Smart (Young Voice, 2001)

✔ *Where's Daddy?* by Jill Curtis (Bloomsbury, 1996), which offers advice about how to tell children of all ages about a divorce

✔ The government leaflet for parents and for young children at the Web site: www.lcd.gov.uk/family/divleaf.htm

If your children have gone through a divorce before, don't assume that it's easier for them if you are divorcing the second time round. The second divorce may trigger the very same emotions they experienced during your first divorce. Their lives are again disrupted by changes in their lifestyle and the discomfort of living with two adults who are preoccupied with the end of their marriage. You have to do the same things to help them through it.

Chapter 9

Taking Care of Your Emotional Self

In This Chapter

▶ Preparing yourself for the emotional ups and downs

▶ Staying in control of your feelings

▶ Keeping in contact with family and friends

*F*or better or worse, your marriage is an important part of your life and ending it isn't easy – whether you initiate the divorce, it's a mutual decision, or your spouse is the one who chooses to finish it.

As the reality of your divorce sinks in, clear and rational thinking may become difficult, if not impossible. Focusing on your day-to-day activities and getting a good night's sleep may become increasingly hard to do. You may find yourself distracted by questions such as: Will I have enough money to survive? Where will I live? How will the children be affected? Will I ever marry again? This chapter helps you understand the emotions you are likely to feel and provides you with suggestions for how to keep them under control.

Preparing for the Emotional Ups and Downs

Getting divorced can be an emotional roller coaster ride: One day you feel angry, sad, depressed, and guilty, and the next you feel hopeful and confident. Your feelings may even change from morning to afternoon, or from hour to hour. They will probably be most intense at first, and gradually ease up over time. You may also experience the same sorts of emotions when you separate.

Because divorce is a highly personal experience, there is no way to predict exactly how you will respond to it. Nevertheless, you'll probably experience at least a couple of the following emotions:

✔ Sadness or grief over the loss of your relationship

✔ Anger toward your spouse for past slights and oversights

- Embarrassment that your marriage is ending, especially if you've always tried to portray yours as the perfect marriage

- A sense of failure and disappointment that you couldn't make your marriage work

- Fear of the effect your divorce may have on your children and yourself (especially if it's been many years since you were single or if you've never lived on your own)

- Guilt if you initiated the divorce

- A sense of rejection or abandonment if your spouse initiated the divorce, especially if he or she left you for someone else

- Depression

Even if you no longer want to be married to your spouse, you may still experience some sense of loss. The more you understand your feelings, the better you'll be able to put your emotional response in perspective, handle it in a positive way, and prevent your emotions from derailing your divorce.

Understanding the Stages of Grief

Maybe now you feel as though you will never get over the loss of your marriage, but in time you will. When you lose a loved one – whether it's your spouse or the marriage itself – you must progress through a series of stages in order to get over the loss and heal emotionally. The stages listed below apply to the loss of anything or anyone that is especially important in life, including the loss of a marriage:

- **Shock and denial:** Even if you knew that your marriage had problems and that your spouse was unhappy, the news that he or she wants a divorce can feel catastrophic. *Divorce?* That's something that happens to other people, not to you! If the decision to divorce is a mutual one, you may still find it difficult to comprehend that your marriage is actually ending. You may vacillate between thinking that it's all just a silly misunderstanding and that you and your spouse can work things out. You may also find yourself questioning your judgement (were you too naïve?) and the assumptions you made about your marriage and your spouse (were you too trusting?). You may also feel anxious about all the changes about to take place in your life and unprepared to deal with them.

- **Anger:** Anger commonly follows shock (although not with everyone). Anger is a normal response, especially if your spouse initiates the divorce. In addition to being angry with your spouse, you may be angry with yourself. Expressing your anger is a healthy way of relieving some of the pressure you feel. Keeping your anger bottled up can lead to depression.

Punching a cushion or just shouting loudly can help you let off steam. Exercise is also a great way to burn off some of that anger; swimming laps, running, or kickboxing can help to release some of the tension you're feeling.

When you can't seem to shake your anger, and especially if you become confrontational or violent, seek the help of a counsellor immediately. It is imperative that you confide in someone who can help you put your feelings in perspective.

✔ **Depression:** You're bound to feel low during various points in your divorce – this is another perfectly normal response to a difficult life situation. However, if your depression won't go away or grows worse, if you begin drinking too much to numb your feelings, or if you're having thoughts of suicide, seek immediate help from your doctor or a counsellor. You may need help to get through the tough times and out of your depression. Refer to Chapter 2 for ways to find a good counsellor to help you.

✔ **Bargaining (avoiding reality):** At times during the healing process, you may respond to your divorce by trying to strike bargains with your spouse or yourself. In desperation, you might promise to do just about anything to keep your marriage together and to make the pain go away. *Avoid making such deals.* If your spouse accepts your offer and you stop your divorce proceedings, you're only postponing the inevitable. The promises you make may be impossible for you to keep, and you may find that you are more miserable than ever in your marriage.

✔ **Sorrow:** If you're feeling sad about what divorce is taking away from your life, it's important to realise that no situation lasts forever. The future holds possibilities for your own new way of life and for your children, who are always moving forward anyway. You may find another partner, or a new career or job, or you may be able to pursue an interest that you were not able to develop during your marriage – and you should be the wiser for what you have gone through.

✔ **Understanding and acceptance:** Eventually, you will begin to accept your divorce. If you choose to divorce after two years' separation, providing you have made sensible arrangements during the period, you are more likely to be in a state of mind to negotiate with your spouse than if the divorce happens quickly while emotions are high. If you can't resolve your emotional conflict until after your divorce is over and have to wait until then before you experience peace of mind, don't worry: This is normal.

Understanding each of the stages you pass through when you're recovering from divorce won't make your pain go away, but it might help you to know that other people have felt the same way you do. At times, you may feel you are going crazy or that life will never be normal again. However, knowing what to expect and finding out that countless other people in your situation have gone on to find happiness in life can be very reassuring.

Because your judgement may be somewhat impaired during the early stages of the healing process, try to avoid making important decisions when you are still feeling unstable. If important decisions must be made, seek some objective input from a trusted friend or family member.

Keeping Your Emotions in Check

How you handle your emotions can mean the difference between creating a fulfilling life for yourself as a single person and remaining stuck in the past. It can also mean the difference between helping your children cope with the situation and jeopardising their happiness. You can end up bitter, angry, and defeated, or you can emerge from your divorce a stronger and more self-confident person – the choice is up to you.

How your emotions can affect you

You need to recognise the possible negative effects of not dealing with the emotions you're feeling. Letting your emotions go unchecked can

- Impede your ability to make sound decisions
- Sap your energy at the time you need it most
- Prevent you from recognising and acknowledging how you may have contributed to the demise of your marriage
- Make you more apt to acquiesce when it comes to your divorce negotiations, especially if you feel wracked with guilt and remorse
- Drive away your friends and family

Ways of getting through the tough times

Here are some steps you can take to help yourself move through the emotional healing process as quickly as possible.

- **Reach out to close friends and family members, or join a support group.** Your friends and family are there to help, and talking to other people who are going through the same things you are can be a great source of comfort.
- **Keep a diary or journal.** The process of recording your thoughts and feelings can have a calming effect and help you gain a new perspective about your life.

✔ **Spend more time with your kids.** Making your children an even more important part of your life than they already are helps reassure them that your divorce in no way diminishes your love for them and that you will continue to be a part of their lives, no matter what.

✔ **Exercise.** Physical activity helps release endorphins, which help lift your spirits naturally. You will also be physically healthier.

✔ **Get re-acquainted with friends you may have lost touch with after your marriage began failing.** Catching up with friends you haven't seen for a while can help give you some perspective and remind you that things – other than your divorce – are happening elsewhere in the world.

✔ **Set up some counselling sessions for yourself.** Counselling can help you to put your marriage in perspective and assess what went wrong. Then you can think more clearly about what the future many hold. (See Chapter 2 for information on locating a counsellor.)

Women tend to be better than men at building emotional support systems and admitting when they need help. Men have a tendency to try to 'tough it out' by repressing their emotions instead of confronting what is bothering them. Whatever your sex, you need to acknowledge what you're feeling, however you choose to do so.

Dealing with the Response of Your Family and Friends

No doubt most of you will share the news that you are getting divorced soon after you've made your decision. You may even discuss the pros and cons of divorce with them beforehand. Your family may offer you the greatest support after a marriage break-up, both practically and emotionally. If they are also grandparents they may be good at looking at the experience through the eyes of your children and offer them a safe port in the storm.

Although you should expect your family to support you through tough times, don't take their support or patience for granted. If they help you out, let them know that you appreciate their generosity and stay alert for ways that you can return their favours. Also, try to be sensitive to just how much you can lean on them – everyone has his or her limits – and avoid crossing that line.

Your decision to divorce shouldn't affect your close friendships either; your true friends will remain friendly no matter what your marital status may be. But be ready for those friends and family members who may view the divorced you a little differently to the married you.

Meeting with disapproval

Some people may suggest, in general terms, that you haven't tried hard enough at your marriage. However, they need to understand that had you been able to avoid divorce, you probably would have done so.

If you have kids, you'll probably maintain a relationship with your ex-spouse and his family. Whether you have children or not, you may want to keep in touch with your ex-spouse's family. You and your spouse need to talk about this in order to adopt an agreed approach so that communication is still possible on all sides, especially when needed.

Keeping grandparents

Children and grandparents usually want to keep in touch with each other. Most parents want to share their children with their own parents from time to time. Why should children lose their grandparents just because your marriage is over? Their grandparents will be deeply affected if this should happen and it deprives your children of a part of their history and sense of security. You could also lose a valuable source of support.

However, the relationship between you, your ex-spouse, your children, and their grandparents may need careful managing. If it's possible for all the adults to conduct themselves with sensitivity and forbearance, then your children stand to gain much. If there's a lot of tension around, there's also the risk that your ex-spouse's parents may give you a hard time or cast you as the villain of the piece and you might need to ignore this for the sake of their 'grandparenting' relationship with your kids.

If your friends become more distant

Almost inevitably, some of the friends and acquaintances you and your spouse shared as a couple will feel uneasy about how to continue their relationships with both of you after your divorce becomes common knowledge. Others may seem more distant when you cross paths. That sort of behaviour can be very hurtful, especially if you are already feeling rejected.

If certain friends are important to you, consider making the first move – invite them over for coffee, ask them if they want to play tennis or go shopping, or invite their children to come and play with yours.

Sorting out tensions

There is no better way of sorting these future relationships out than to talk about them with your spouse and agree to be generous if you can. You may be able to establish some ground rules about not inviting your mutual friends to take sides (this may be harder with family). If it is hard to talk over the issue and you choose to use mediation, then it may be a topic to put on the agenda (see Chapter 16 for more on mediation).

If you can't agree at all, it is better that you initiate the topic with friends, family, and neighbours; make plain that you wish to continue your relationship as normally as possible while the break-up is taking place. You could say that you appreciate that it may be awkward at times but that you value their friendship and hope very much that it will continue until everyone is in calmer waters.

Part III
Decisions, Decisions

'His form's certainly suffered since his divorce.'

In this part . . .

The decisions you need to make during your divorce will be some of the most difficult of your entire life. You'll have to make arrangements for where your kids will live and how you and your ex will take care of them, divide up your marital property (and debt), give consideration to whether either of you should pay maintenance to the other, and plan for your children's financial support. Because you may end up with less money to share between you, we also give you information about welfare benefits and tax credits you may be eligible for. This part of the book provides guidance for making all of those decisions, with one important caveat – you still need the guidance and advice of your own family solicitor about how to sort out many of these matters fairly and within the law.

Chapter 10

Deciding Who Cares for Your Children

*G*rappling with decisions about the future care of your children can consume every ounce of your patience and resolve. If negotiating your arrangements seems about as likely as winning the lottery, we offer some encouraging statistics. Estimates show that over 80 per cent of all divorcing parents negotiate their own arrangements – either by themselves, with the help of a mediator, or with legal help – and the chances are you can too.

The law is clear in all decisions about children at the time of divorce: *Your children's best interests must be paramount.* These decisions aren't questions of who wins or loses, but what's best for your children. Put aside any longings and fears for yourself as a parent while you think about your children's needs. Try to take a cool look together at what will suit your children best.

Deciding for Yourselves

If you have children, you don't stop being parents just because your marriage has ended. If you and your spouse can decide one thing and one thing only in your divorce, decide how you will care for your children. Here we offer you just a few of the reasons why *you* – and not a judge – should make these decisions. (More information on negotiating your own divorce terms outside a courtroom is provided in Chapters 14, 16, and 17.)

- ✔ **If you do go to court, you have no guarantee that you will get the arrangement you want.** The judge may make no order or a different order from the one you were hoping for.

- ✔ **The courts are reluctant to make decisions about children unless it is absolutely necessary.** A judge or sheriff asked to make a decision about a child can try a number of alternatives to a court decision to settle the dispute between you. Have a look at the section 'Finding a Way Forward When You Can't Agree' later in this chapter for some of the options.

- ✔ **No matter how well-intentioned they may be, because of their case-loads, most family court judges can devote only a very small amount of time to making these important decisions.** The judge usually thinks you know your children best and therefore will encourage you to make the decisions.

- ✔ **In England and Wales, judges rely on the advice of a family court adviser (*a CAFCASS officer*).** If there is a serious dispute with irreconcilable claims by each parent, the family court adviser may interview other people in your children's lives, such as teachers or grandparents, before reporting back to the judge.

- ✔ **A serious court battle can become extremely costly, stressful, and time-consuming, and have long-lasting effects.** One reason for the great amount of money and time involved is the testimony of any experts that are asked to give their opinions. You are normally expected to pay for their time even if you are granted public funding (legal aid). Chapter 15 has more on legal aid.

- ✔ **Members of your extended family, friends, associates, people in your children's lives, and others may be brought into court.** Your children may have to be seen by the CAFCASS officer or even by the judge. (In the Principal Registry of the Family Division, the biggest family court in London, judges routinely see children who are over nine years old.)

Of the estimated 80 per cent of divorcing couples who come to a negotiated agreement about their children, many start off thinking they will wage a battle. But either they lack the financial resources to do so or deliberately avoid such a battle for fear of the emotional harm a court hearing would have on their children.

Understanding Parental Responsibility – Much More Than Just 'Custody'

The law regarding children radically changed in 1989 when it shifted from talking about parental *rights* over children to talking about parental *responsibility* for children. (Refer to Chapter 4 for more about the legal aspects of parenting.) As a result, making decisions about your kids requires you to think and act on two levels:

- ✔ How you and your ex will both continue to be responsible for the big decisions for your children
- ✔ How you will arrange for their day–to-day care

Day-to-day arrangements are now referred to as *residence* and *contact* instead of 'custody' (or 'care and control') and 'access'. Not only have the words changed, but so have the concepts behind them. The law encourages people not to treat children as possessions to be fought over, but as human beings and citizens in their own right. Overlooking your children's needs and wishes is all too easy if you end up locked into a fight over possession of them.

Despite the change in legal terms, the media continues to refer to 'custody' and 'access' and most people still use those terms. They're no longer used in court and you're unlikely to hear them used during your divorce proceedings. Because you want to sound as if you know what you're talking about when you walk into your solicitor's office, we won't use them either.

The law expects you and your ex-spouse to continue to be responsible for your kids after your divorce. Parental responsibility means that you share obligations for the big decisions concerning your children's home, education, discipline, financial support, medical care, choice of name and religion, and other important matters. Sharing this responsibility means that you have to be able to talk to each other after your divorce is over.

If in practice you decide to share decision-making authority about some things but not others, avoid conflict and misunderstanding after your divorce by clearly spelling out the areas of shared decision-making. For example, you may agree that you will both decide on your children's non-emergency medical or dental treatment only when the treatment involves invasive procedures, or about any psychiatric and psychological treatment, or that you will share decision-making if it comes to consenting to your children getting married or enlisting in the armed forces before they're 18.

Only rarely is parental responsibility ever removed by a court from a parent. At present other adults such as a stepparent or grandparent can only acquire parental responsibility if they have an adoption or residence order – that is, an order that the child live with them.

Deciding Where Your Children Will Live

As well as being responsible for the big decisions about your children's lives, you also need to arrange for their day-to-day care. You're required by law to decide *residence*, or where your kids will live, and *contact* – how they'll keep in touch with their non-resident parent. As with other decisions about their lives, your children's needs come first. Deciding arrangements is like a jigsaw – you must fit together a number of very different pieces in some sort of order. Some of the pieces you should take into account are

- Your children's needs and way of life
- Your and your ex-spouse's working lives and the amount of time you have to spend with your kids
- Your soon-to-be-divided pot of money
- Your future separate housing

Consider who did what in your family before you and your spouse decided to separate and then see what has to change.

Staying primarily with one parent

Almost gone are the days when judges assumed that mothers were the only ones to look after small children. Many men take a much greater part now in the day-to-day care of their children, before and after divorce. In most cases after divorce or separation, however, children still spend more of their time with one parent than the other – usually their mother. About 12 per cent of fathers live with their children after divorce.

If you decide that living primarily in one place with one parent suits your kids, you'll probably agree, as most parents do, that they should see their other parent as often as they need. No child wants to lose a loving parent. However, every family is different and you need to think through how things will work best in your situation.

Having your children live with you all or most of the time and being responsible for making the day-to-day decisions about their lives makes sense if your spouse can't be actively involved with them after your divorce. But be aware that having your kids living with you all the time can be fraught with problems, especially if your spouse ends up with very limited contact but would have preferred to be a more involved parent after your divorce. Bear in mind some of the potential consequences of being a non-resident parent:

- ✔ In living with one parent, non-resident parents often feel excluded from their children's lives.

- ✔ About 40 per cent of non-resident parents slowly drift away from their children, especially if they remarry and start new families. When that happens, the divorced couple's children no longer have the benefit of a relationship with two birth parents and their extended families; and the non-resident parents often come to feel that they are no longer necessary to their children.

- ✔ Some non-resident parents begrudge paying child support if contact is more limited than they wanted.

Then again, the resident parent's situation isn't always a bed of roses. Consider the following:

- ✔ As most parents on their own can tell you, shouldering all or most of the day-to-day responsibilities of raising children can be a tremendous burden – particularly if you are working full time or going to college. Juggling child care, work, and college, not to mention housekeeping and keeping your garden tidy, all on your own, can leave you feeling completely drained at the end of each day.

- ✔ You may have little quality time to give your children, much less any time for yourself.

- ✔ Your kids may spend more time in day care, after-school care, or at home by themselves than when you were married and your spouse could help out. In such situations, some children end up doing more of the cooking and housework and playing parent to their younger siblings.

Whether you're a resident or non-resident parent, it's not an easy road. You can find advice and information on how to manage alone with your children from the National Council for One Parent Families Helpline on 0800 018 5026 and they also have a good Web site: www.oneparentfamilies.org.uk.

You can also check out your local Citizens' Advice Bureau to find out if there is a branch of Gingerbread in your area. This self-help organisation gives support to parents on their own with children.

If you're a resident of Scotland and are looking for some more local help, try the One Parent Family Scotland Web site at `www.opfs.org.uk`.

Non-resident parents often feel a sense of loss – of control, intimacy, routine, and role. However, if you communicate with your ex-spouse, you are much more likely to maintain close relationships with your children.

Coping with being a non-resident mother

Although they're in the minority, some mothers don't seek to have the primary care of their children. Whatever the reason for not being the resident parent, many non-resident mothers say that they find the community around them less understanding in this situation than towards non-resident fathers. MATCH (Mothers living Apart from Their Children) has a good Web site (`www.matchmothers.org`) and you can write to their e-mail address: `enquiries@matchmothers.org`.

Staying in contact as a non-resident father

A researcher wrote in 1993 that divorce 'splinters fatherhood into many fragments' when fathers become non-resident parents. As a non-resident father, you have three options for handling your relationships with your kids and your ex-spouse:

- ✔ Lose contact with both your children and your ex
- ✔ See your kids but have no contact with their mother
- ✔ Keep in contact with your kids and with your ex

Contact the Parentline Plus Helpline on 0808 800 2222 or visit their Web site on `www.parentlineplus.org.uk` for more information. You can also contact Families Need Fathers on their Web site: `www.fnf.org.uk`.

Mum's the word: A bias against fathers?

In a recently published book of essays *Children and their Families: Contact, Rights and Welfare* (Hart, 2003), Bob Geldof claims that the courts act in secret and against fathers. He recounts that he was told, to his disbelief, after his marital break-up with Paula Yates how lucky he was to see his children for two hours a week!

He went on to fight a long court battle with his ex-wife after she left him for the Australian rock singer Michael Hutchence but they eventually agreed to share the care of their daughters Fifi Trixibelle, Peaches, and Pixie as they had done before. In 1998, the courts granted him a residence order.

He says that parents should care for their children after divorce on a 50:50 basis. UK law does not prescribe how care should be divided but leaves it to parents or to the courts to use their judgement in the best interests of the children. The debate about whether courts in their discretion favour mothers more than fathers is currently very much a live one.

Living in two households

Increasingly parents choose to share the day-to-day care of their children on a more equal basis. You may hear this called 'shared care' or 'shared residence'. Both terms are correct and we use them interchangeably. (See Chapter 4 for more on these terms.)

If you don't want your kids to live with one parent and just visit the other, think creatively. Can you share out their care between you in a different way?

The benefits and pitfalls of sharing day-to-day care

The benefits of sharing care with your former spouse are obvious: Your children get to maintain their relationships with both of you, and you both remain actively involved in your children's lives. Nevertheless, sharing care has some potentially serious drawbacks, including the following:

- ✔ **Shared residence is relatively expensive.** You and your former spouse both need to provide your children with a place to sleep and a place to store their clothes and other belongings when they are at each of your homes (unless you want them living out of suitcases and boxes). Plus, you each have to provide your children with separate sets of clothing, toys, and other items that they use regularly.

  Your kids may prefer to live with one of you most of the time. By the time your children reach adolescence, they may get frustrated with switching back and forth between homes. Living in one place gives your children ready access to all of their belongings – and their friends will always know where to find them.

- ✔ **You and your spouse must communicate and co-operate with one another much more than you would if they were living with one of you most of the time.** You'll still have to put aside your differences and work together to agree certain rules and regulations for your kids so that when they're with either parent, the same basic rules apply.

- ✔ **Shuffling back and forth between your home and your ex-spouse's home can be hard on some children.** This is especially true for very young children, because they may feel constantly unsettled. They often think of 'my mum's house' or 'my dad's house' but have trouble with the idea of 'my house'.

One for you, one for me – splitting up siblings

Rarely do siblings live in different homes. However, sometimes older children want so much to stay in their own homes and schools with their friends that they will stay with whichever parent is living there or nearer, even if the parent moving out is going to be looking after the rest of the children. If you decide to separate your kids from their siblings, this is likely to be for such special reasons. Halving the number of children between you in order to be fair to you both is not a good reason!

For most children, not living with both parents in the same house after a divorce is hard enough, but separating siblings from each other can feel cruel to them. Nevertheless, separating your kids may just make sense in certain situations – for example, if a child needs special attention from one of you during a difficult time.

Although you can change the residence arrangement at any time if you agree to do so and the change is in your children's interests, it will be up to a judge to decide if the change is merited if you and your ex don't see eye-to-eye. Most judges are reluctant to alter a residence arrangement unless the children's best interests are at risk.

Making shared care work

To make shared residence arrangements work, you and your spouse must do something you may have had a hard time doing recently while you were married – get on with each other! To determine if you and your spouse have what it takes to manage sharing your children's day-to-day lives while living separately, read the following rules:

✔ **Avoid post-divorce warfare.** Arguing over your children can be emotionally devastating for both you and them. When you do have disagreements about your kids, talk things out. Don't shout them out, especially when your children are within earshot.

✔ **Don't use your children to try to get back at your former spouse.** Your marriage is over – it's time to move on. If you can't forgive and forget, you have no business sharing their care.

✔ **Respect one another's parenting abilities and styles.** You may not like the way that your ex-spouse parents your kids but unless he or she endangers the children or unless you have good reason to believe that he or she is harming their emotional, scholastic, or sexual development, how your ex-spouse acts as a parent is up to them. Plus, if you criticise your ex's parenting abilities, you can expect to hear some criticism of your own parenting.

✔ **Support one another's efforts to learn new parenting skills.** Even if you were both active, involved parents, each of you probably had primary responsibility for certain things – one of you may have got the children dressed in the morning and prepared their lunches while the other helped with their school projects and got them ready for bed. Now, you may have to learn new skills so that you can do all of those things you used to share.

✔ **Agree on a schedule for when the children will live with each of you and stick to it.** Children depend on predictability. At the same time, don't be inflexible.

✔ **Mind your own business when your children are with their other parent.** Don't check up to find out what time your ex-spouse got the children to bed, what they ate for dinner, or to tell your ex what the children should wear to school the next day. Your ex-spouse is in charge of your children when they are at his or her home.

✔ **Support one another as parents.** Don't let your kids play one of you off against the other in order to get what they want, and don't criticise your ex-spouse in front of your children.

Residence decisions and their financial implications

There are several generous state benefits and tax credits available to supplement the income of families with children. See Chapter 7 for a summary of these. However, the agencies that administer the benefits and credits will not share them equally between you even if you and your spouse are sharing the care of your children equally. The Inland Revenue, for example, pays the tax credits to the person who receives the Child Benefit, and that will usually be the mother unless you agree otherwise.

The Child Support Agency treats the person who receives the Child Benefit as the parent with care, and requires the other parent to pay child support at the rate of 50 per cent of the full liability even though you might be sharing their care equally. If you have only one child, then only one of you will be able to claim the Child Benefit, but if you have more than one, you and your spouse may agree that you claim the Child Benefit for at least one child each. In that way you may each be able to claim the full range of benefits and credits and eliminate the need to pay each other child support. Most benefits and credits vary in amount according to the number of children you have living with you and your income, so you may need help working out what arrangement is best for you and how to maximise your income in this way. Your local Citizens Advice Bureau should be able to advise you. You'll find their details in your local phone book.

Consulting your children

If your children are mature enough to know their own minds and especially if you and your ex-spouse are planning to share their care, you may need to consider their preferences. Your kids may have already let you know what they think, directly or indirectly, but if they haven't and you want to know their feelings on the matter, talk it over with them. Decide beforehand whether to talk with them together with your ex-spouse or separately.

In Scotland the Children (Scotland) Act 1995 expressly requires you – and the courts, if they have to make decisions about a child – to consult your kids about your plans and take into account their views regarding decisions being made about them. If your child is old enough that the court thinks she is capable of understanding and you have raised an action in court that directly affects her, she will most likely receive a notice from the court about the action. This notice includes an invitation for your child to express any views to the sheriff on an 'F9' form. Her views are usually kept confidential by the sheriff, however they may be disclosed in court. A child over twelve is considered capable of conducting proceedings alone unless it is shown otherwise. Your child may therefore become a third party in court in a dispute between you and your spouse. In addition, any child – usually (but not necessarily) over the age of 12 – may instruct a solicitor to act on her behalf, and she may apply to the Scottish Legal Aid Board for financial help to do this.

Despite good intentions, research has shown many parents don't manage to talk to their kids about their plans and many children regret this later on. You might put some options to them and pay close attention to their reactions. Listen carefully to their views. Keep in mind that some children – even older ones – avoid such situations and you may find it easier to talk while doing something together, such as cooking dinner or walking the dog. Make the occasion as easy as you can. When you do talk to them about residence arrangements, keep the following things in mind:

- ✔ **If you ask your kids directly who they want to live with, they might automatically say 'you' because they don't want to upset you.** They may also feel that they are rejecting one parent by choosing the other. Make clear that it is your responsibility to weigh up all the factors and make a decision, but you do want to hear what they have to say about their future.

- ✔ **Your children may base their ideas on unfounded assumptions.** For example, they may think they'll be able to get away with more if they live with the parent they perceive as a lax disciplinarian or as more indulgent. They may believe that one of you has an emotional need to live with them and will put 'your' needs before their own.

   Also be sure that your children's preferences are not the product of revenge. For example, if you're leaving the marriage for someone else and your children know about it, they may want to stay with your ex-spouse out of loyalty to him or her and frustration with you.

- ✔ **Your kids may tell your spouse the exact opposite of what they tell you, if you choose to talk to them separately.** Whether it's because they are saying what they think you each want to hear or that they're playing you off against each other, you and your ex-spouse may hear different things from the children. The best remedy for this problem is to keep the lines of communication open between you and your ex.

- ✔ **Your children trust you.** Avoid bribing your children into spending more time with you by making glorious promises about what their lives will be like if they do, and avoid making your children feel guilty by telling them how sad and lonely you'll be if they don't choose to be with you more often. *When*, not if, they realise you manipulated them, they won't be able to trust you in the same way.

- ✔ **Your children love both you and your ex-spouse.** Do not slag off your ex in front of your kids no matter what you feel. Your kids don't need to hear what you think of their other parent. If you need to vent any anger or bitterness towards your ex, talk to anyone other than your children.

- ✔ **Your children very much want to please you, which means that you have to recognise if they are telling you what they think you want to hear, or if they're saying what they really feel.** It is wise not to ask them outright who they want to live with until they are old enough and mature enough to honestly assess what they really want and feel comfortable communicating that information to you.

Have a look at Chapter 16 for how mediators can help you consult your children if you are having problems doing it on your own.

Keeping in Contact with Your Children

You and your ex-spouse may decide that sharing day-to-day care isn't the best option for your children and having them live with one of you most of the time is the way to go. If your children live mostly with one of you, you and your ex will have to work out the arrangements for contact between the kids and their non-resident parent. The legal term for a child's right to keep in touch with their non-resident parent is *contact*.

Contact usually means that children see their non-resident parent on a regular pre-arranged basis, perhaps weekly or fortnightly, either by visiting or staying overnight, as well as on bank holidays, birthdays, and maybe during part of their school holidays. You may develop more flexible arrangements as the children become more independent, depending on how near to each other you are. If you and your spouse work out your own arrangements for your children, you can agree to anything you want so long as it is in the children's best interests. However, because a certain amount of planning is usually necessary, contact generally takes one of the following forms:

- ✔ **Staying contact:** Children stay overnight with their non-resident parent – usually in that parent's home on pre-arranged days and times and often at an agreed frequency, for example on alternate weekends.

- ✔ **Visiting contact:** The kids meet their non-resident parent, often at that parent's or a relative's home, usually for an agreed period of time on a regular day and at a pre-arranged frequency, for example every Sunday.

- ✔ **Supervised contact:** The children meet their non-resident parent somewhere that is supervised by another parent-agreed or court-approved adult, for example by a grandparent or by a member of staff in a Contact Centre. (For more about Contact Centres, see the following sidebar 'Using contact centres'.) Supervised contact, when it takes place, is usually ordered by the court.

- ✔ **Indirect contact:** Children keep in touch with their non-resident parent by means of letters, presents, telephone calls, e-mails and so on, without actually physically meeting.

These options for contact carry with them decreasing degrees of closeness. You may opt for a mixture of them all or change between them at different times – cooling contact a bit if there is a new partner, intensifying contact if your child misses his non-resident parent a lot or needs some special time. You should agree any arrangements beforehand with your ex-spouse if they are to work well for the children.

Arranging for your children to stay close to both of you is vital to their short- and long-term well-being. The only proviso under the law is that the contact must be *beneficial* to the child. (See the section 'Allowing indirect contact only' later in this chapter.) Indirect contact may be preferable if direct contact isn't beneficial, unless there are unusually strong reasons for a court to stop the relationship altogether – which is rare.

Contact can be hard to arrange if you end up living a long way away from your ex-spouse. Seeing your children at your ex-spouse's home may seem the only option but this will only work if you have a good relationship with each other. It may be better to spend the time with your children in some other way. (For the financial costs of contact, see Chapter 13.)

The conventional picture of a dad meeting his kids at McDonald's for a quick Happy Meal need not be the one you fall into. However, maybe you don't have anywhere else convenient to meet or you haven't used enough imagination. Or maybe your children love it! It doesn't really matter where you see your kids, as long as you're spending your time together well.

Making your arrangements work for your children

Study after study shows that children do well when they have the affection and attention of both parents. In addition, they may suffer long-lasting emotional, developmental, and personal damage if their parents continue to act out their negative feelings toward one another after they are divorced.

Positive male and female role models help your kids develop into well-adjusted adults. Therefore, for their benefit, do what you can to help ensure that your children have an opportunity to maintain a strong relationship with both of you – even if you dislike or distrust each other.

The following list offers some suggestions for how to help maintain a positive relationship between your kids and your ex:

- Agree on a visiting schedule that's as generous as possible. Also, let your older children have some control over when they spend time with their non-resident parent. Keep a record of the plan in both homes where they're easy to spot, perhaps on the fridge doors.

- If you're the resident parent, encourage your kids to phone their other parent, but let them have some say in when and how often they do so. They should be able to share their good news and their concerns, to get that parent's advice, or to get help with homework. Phoning shouldn't become a chore, duty, or only for bad news.

✔ If you are the non-resident parent, try to agree a schedule for when to phone your kids so that the calls are looked forward to and your ex-spouse doesn't feel that they are disruptive.

✔ Make sure that you both see school reports and share out homework assignments or projects whenever you can.

✔ Make sure both of you attend parent-teacher events.

✔ When you take photos of your children, get extra copies made for your ex-spouse.

✔ If you are the resident parent, let your ex-spouse know the dates and times of your children's school plays, and athletic events.

✔ Invite your ex-spouse to your children's birthday parties, and to share other important dates with you and your children.

Encouraging your kids and your ex to maintain a good relationship can be tricky, especially when you don't have a good relationship with your ex. Here are some tips for avoiding points of tension:

✔ Don't try to shut your ex-spouse out of your children's lives by placing needless restrictions on their time together.

✔ Let your ex-spouse know of any big changes in your life – like a new partner moving in. Don't let your kids tell them first if you can avoid it.

✔ Let your ex-spouse know well ahead of time when you will be taking children away for the weekend or on holiday.

✔ Keep your ex-spouse informed of your children's medical problems.

✔ Consult your former spouse about the important decisions in your children's lives.

✔ Do not have arguments on the doorstep.

✔ Don't pass angry messages in written notes for your children to deliver. Your kids might get curious and have a read, and if they don't, they'll still find it hard when their other parent opens the note!

✔ Take care when you phone your ex. If you wish to sort something out with your ex-spouse and you think there might be a row, make the call after bedtime. Imagine what it's like for your kids to listen to one half of the row.

✔ Don't argue at the school gate. Your children will be mortified if you do so in front of their friends or teachers.

✔ Don't forbid your children to spend time with your ex's new partner. If you do, you will force your ex-spouse to do things without your children, which could add to the stress they may already be feeling.

Remember that the worst experiences for children after divorce are losing contact with a loved parent, and experiencing conflict between you – especially conflict that is not resolved and conflict that involves them.

Tackling potential contact problems

Regrettably direct contact can sometimes become a sensitive issue for you, even with a court order. For example, as a non-resident parent, you may be tempted to deliberately return your kids later than arranged, pick them up late, cancel plans to spend time with them, or withhold child support – just to get back at your ex. If you aren't the resident parent your ex-spouse may refuse to allow you to see the children or place unreasonable restrictions on contact. Often the only way this emotionally charged duel can end is if one of you takes the other to court.

The judge sees contact as your child's right, not a right of either parent to have it or bar it. In most cases, the judge is very keen to make contact work if it's likely to be beneficial and safe for the children and she may ask a CAF-CASS officer (family court adviser) to help determine if this is so. The judge may order supervised contact if she feels that the well-being of your child warrants this. Supervised contact may take place at a *contact centre*. It is worth noting that there is rarely any purpose in going to court to try and make your non-resident ex-spouse see his or her children.

Using a contact centre

Contact centres have been set up in many places to provide a safe place for children to meet their non-resident parent, when contact could otherwise be harmful or upsetting for the child. For example, it may be a good idea for you not to meet your ex-spouse at the time of contact, so you can arrive and leave the contact centre at different times. Being together with your children in a contact centre, which is friendly and has a whole range of toys and facilities for making drinks and even meals, can be a more positive experience for both you and your children than walking round the playground.

Most of these centres are run voluntarily. The contact centre staff, sometimes with the help of a CAFCASS officer, will work out with you how to make contact enjoyable for your children. They may also be able to provide for supervision if a court order requires it. Contact centres have a protocol for how they can best be used. In England and Wales the National Association for Child Contact Centres (NACCC) makes clear that they offer safe contact and are available when there is no other solution (Web site: www.naccc.org.uk; Tel: 0845 450 280). In Scotland, contact centres are connected with Family Mediation Scotland. www.family mediationscotland.og.uk.

Deciding if contact puts your children (or you) at risk

If your ex-spouse has threatened you or your children with violence or abuse, or you've experienced it, you must tell the judge who will investigate the risk before deciding whether or not to stop or continue contact. A judge can order that a contact centre is used if she thinks contact should still take place. Evidence suggests that contact can sometimes trigger episodes of violence that can be dangerous to you and frightening to your children. You should take threats seriously and report them to the CAFCASS officer if he or she is involved or otherwise to your solicitor or to the Social Services Department Child Protection Unit who have a duty to investigate. See Chapter 20 for more on dealing with threats and abuse.

Some non-resident parents feel that their ex-spouses have denied contact unreasonably and even alienated their children from them. This is the time to be honest with yourself if you are the parent with care, in case it's your anger and hurt that govern your temptation to refuse to allow contact, rather than fear for your own or your children's safety.

Allowing indirect contact only

When you have good reason to believe that your ex-spouse, the non-resident parent, will harm or endanger the children, contact *should* be restricted or even prohibited. Indirect contact can consist of letters and cards or phone conversations and e-mail and text messages as long as they haven't been forbidden by the court. Indirect contact may be ordered in situations in which the non-resident parent has a history of

- ✔ Mental, physical, or sexual child abuse
- ✔ Child neglect
- ✔ Criminal activities
- ✔ Mental or emotional instability
- ✔ Alcohol or drug abuse
- ✔ Exhibiting explicit sexual behaviour in front of children

If allegations of abuse surface in a divorce, the court usually appoints a CAFCASS officer to represent the children. This independent person conducts an investigation into the allegations and prepares a report to help the judge make the decision whether to allow contact. When contact is restricted by the court, you may be ordered to have contact with your children at a contact centre. Sometimes indirect contact by letters and cards provides the link for the child and parent when other means are ruled out.

Some parents cruelly and maliciously use unwarranted accusations of child abuse or molestation by their spouses as a way to try to deny that parent contact to their children. If you are unfairly accused, get legal help from your solicitor or contact Families Need Fathers at 134 Curtain Road, London EC2A 3AR, www.fnf.org.uk.

Stopping contact altogether

A big decision for a judge to make is whether contact should be stopped altogether. It is important to understand that your children's right to contact with their non-resident parent is not for contact at all costs, but for *beneficial* contact. Research findings indicate that some mothers so much want their children not to lose contact with their fathers that they may agree to contact arrangements even though these are dangerous to themselves and the children. If there are signs that your kids are frightened of contact or refusing to go, then these signs must be taken seriously and dealt with. If you're concerned for your or your children's safety, contact your local refuge (see Chapter 2 for further information on dealing with abuse).

Burying the hatchet for your children's sake

When you and your spouse use contact as a vehicle for expressing your negative feelings for each other, you're inflicting emotional damage on your children. Children hate to see their parents fighting and, more important, tend to blame themselves for the discord. Those feelings can create many problems for your children, including a loss of self-esteem, emotional distress, and even marital troubles of their own in the future.

Avoid this scenario at all costs! Your children deserve the opportunity to have both of you in their lives. Remember, a bad spouse does not necessarily equal a bad parent. Using your children to get back at your ex-spouse is a form of punishment for your children. You and your spouse must act like mature adults and put your children, not your hurt and angry feelings, first.

If you suspect your ex-spouse of child abuse

If you think that your ex-spouse is abusing your children, talk to a solicitor immediately. The solicitor can advise you of the appropriate steps to take, which may include any of the following:

- Contacting the police

- Starting criminal proceedings against your former spouse, and stopping all communication with him or her

- Asking the court to prohibit your ex-spouse from having any future contact with your child until your allegations are investigated

- Having your child examined by a doctor

- Taking photos of any unusual marks, bruises, or cuts on your children that you believe are evidence of the abuse or molestation

- Asking the court to put pressure on your spouse to undergo evaluation and treatment for chemical dependency, alcohol abuse, psychiatric problems, or anger management

- Reporting your allegations to your local Social Services Department Child Protection Team immediately

Going the Extra Mile with a 'Parenting Plan'

Like a growing number of divorcing parents, you may wish to use a *parenting plan* in addition to agreements. A parenting plan is a detailed, written description of how both of you will be involved in the lives of your children after your divorce. In this way, your parenting plan can help you to avoid conflict and legal fights. (See Chapter 16 for how to use a parenting plan as part of mediation.)

Try using the excellent tools for developing a parenting plan provided by the Department for Constitutional Affairs. Write to Freepost, PO Box 2001, Burgess Hill, West Sussex RH15 8BR for a copy, or download it from the DCA Web site at www.dca.gov.uk/family/divleaf.htm. The plan is free, and you may want more than one copy.

The DCA parenting plan booklet contains both information on how to develop a plan and spaces to fill in to help you develop a plan of your own. You can use it as a guide and not complete it all or you can use it, as intended, as a way of spelling out how residence and contact are going to work in your situation. It is a tool you can use with your children.

Putting it all into the plan

Parenting plans spell out, in as much detail as you want, how each of you will be involved in your children's lives after your divorce. A good plan, such as the one recommended by the DCA, includes the following:

- **How you are going to communicate clearly with each other and your children:** How to talk about changes, how to make plans, remembering not to row or blame each other in front of your children, who explains what to your kids, and listening to them.

- **What your living arrangements will be:** Who lives where, travel arrangements to and from your homes and who will pay for what, who pays for and has the number of your children's mobile phones, setting rules for them (for instance, the rules on smoking, cycling helmets, times for bed, going out alone, and staying out late) and who baby-sits.

- **How your children will stay in contact with you both:** What happens when you need to postpone a visit, how to handle telephone calls, and how to keep in contact with other family members and anyone else.

✔ **What your children's religious or cultural upbringing will include:** What their religious education will consist of, what arrangements to make for religious festivals, or speaking family languages other than English.

✔ **How to deal with plans for special days:** Including birthdays, weddings, funerals, anniversaries, and so on.

✔ **Where your children will go to school and what to do about out of school activities:** How will the school be informed, how will both of you keep in touch with the school, how to make choices about schooling – examinations, course choices, school trips, and so on.

✔ **How to handle holidays:** How to agree them, travel arrangements for them, and plans for who will have the children for school in-service training days, and so on.

✔ **What to do about keeping your kids healthy:** Who will arrange dental and other check-ups, special health needs, and regular treatments; who will care for them when they are ill; what to do in an emergency.

✔ **What to do about pets.**

✔ **How to review your plans from time to time.**

The DCA plan ends with a checklist for who is paying for what and how. It also lists a number of places to go for help and further information if you need it.

Improving your living arrangements with a parenting plan

A parenting plan can be useful to you for a number of reasons. A good plan does all of the following:

✔ Provides a visible arrangement that all of you – parents and children – can see.

✔ Helps you and your ex-spouse to be more realistic about the amount of time and energy you need to care for your children on a day-to-day basis as single parents.

✔ Encourages you to get all your post-divorce parenting issues out on the table (acknowledging those issues and resolving them together, before your divorce is final, is best).

✔ Minimises the potential for post-divorce strife by helping you antici-pate and resolve potential areas of conflict before they develop, and by spelling out on paper, before you are divorced, every detail that may make or break your agreement.

✔ Lets you establish mutually agreed procedures for resolving any post-divorce conflicts that develop relating to your kids.

✔ Allows you and your ex-spouse to express your long-term goals for your children. For example, your parenting plan could state the following goals: 'It is our goal to support our children to the fullest extent possible in their school and extracurricular activities' or, if you are committed strongly to some issue, 'It is our goal to limit the amount of time our children spend watching TV and playing computer games, and to encourage outdoor activities, reading, and conversation to the fullest extent possible'.

Making the plan flexible

If you and your spouse negotiate a parenting plan, avoid making your plan so rigid and inflexible that it cannot bend and change to meet the developmental needs of your children. Remember that what your children need from each of you changes over time, depending on their personalities and their ages.

Your plan should also be flexible enough to respond to the changing circumstances in your own lives. That flexibility may include changing when or how often your children spend the night at your home and appropriately passing more of your decision-making responsibilities to them as they grow. These and other plan adjustments could be necessitated by changes in your professional lives, a serious illness or accident, changes in your living situation or finances, or changes in your children's needs.

Satisfying the Judge About Your Arrangements

Your divorce cannot be granted until a family judge has considered the arrangements for your children and decided that they are satisfactory. You or your solicitor specify the arrangements in a separate statement when you file your petition for divorce. You may base the arrangements on your Memorandum of Understanding (the concluding document; see Chapter 16 for more information on what this covers), developed in mediation, or on your parenting plan. If the judge is satisfied, she will grant what is called a *Section 41 certificate* or *certificate of satisfaction*. You do not normally need to go to court for this, but if you cannot agree or if the judge is not satisfied with your suggested arrangements, a date will be set for a court hearing.

If your children are under 16 when you decide to separate or divorce in Scotland, you as parents can decide between you what arrangements are best for them, though you are required to take into account their views depending on their age and maturity. A child over twelve is presumed to be sufficiently mature, but younger children views must also be considered. (Refer to the section 'Consulting your children' earlier in the chapter for more on this.) If you cannot agree on the arrangements and use a court, any arrangements the court makes for your children are governed by the principles of the Children (Scotland) Act 1995. This Act is based on similar principles to the Children Act 1989 which applies in England and Wales. Chapter 4 gives you more information about the Children Act 1989.

Finding a Way Forward When You Can't Agree

It's understandable if you and your spouse are at loggerheads over the arrangements for your children. After all, your decision-making may be complicated by any number of things going on in your head:

- Fear that you may be squeezed out of your children's lives if you do not participate equally in all ways on decisions regarding them

- Guilt over how your divorce will affect your children

- Anger at your spouse

- Concern that if you don't see your children every day, your influence in their lives may diminish or they won't be well cared for

- Worry that over the coming years you'll miss out on the special moments in your children's lives

- Fear that if a new man or woman comes into your spouse's life, that person will try to take your place when you're not around

If you and your spouse can't agree on the best way to care for your children, putting the issue in the hands of a judge is not your only alternative. You can try mediation to help you plan as parents together, even if you are not on good terms. (In fact, if you apply in England and Wales for financial assistance from the Community Legal Service (legal aid) you are required to attend a meeting with a mediator to see if mediation is suitable before you are granted financial aid for a lawyer to represent you in court.) Even if you take your case to court you may still be referred to an information meeting about mediation. (Chapter 16 explains how mediation works.) If you take up the option of mediation, research shows that you are very likely to agree arrangements for your children.

If your case goes to court, the judge is likely to ask a CAFCASS officer to talk to you about your arrangements for your children and to report back to the court on the meeting. The CAFCASS officer may try to help you resolve your dispute if you're close to resolution. Sometimes attendance at court can trigger a settlement. Your solicitors might also work together to find a solution while you are at court.

If you take your case to court in Scotland, the courts aren't allowed to make decisions about your children unless it's absolutely necessary. Any sheriff who is asked to make a decision about a child can try a number of alternatives to a court decision to settle the dispute between you, such as

- ✔ **Refer you to a family mediation service for information about that service.** You are still free to decide whether or not you want to try mediation to help you to reach agreement with your spouse about your children. The sheriff can refer you to mediation at any stage in the proceedings.

- ✔ **Ask for a report on your family circumstances and those of any children from a person known as a reporter.** This report provides extra information to help the sheriff make a decision based on the welfare of your children. It's feasible that when the reporter interviews you, your ex-spouse and your children, a solution may become possible. The reporter can explain this in the report or can make recommendations to the sheriff about how the situation can be resolved.

- ✔ **Hold a child welfare hearing, which both you and your ex-spouse, as parents, must attend.** The sheriff will take an active role and may use this hearing to see what possible basis there may be for agreement between you and your ex. If your children have indicated a wish to express their views, they will usually attend the hearing.

- ✔ **The sheriff must hold an options hearing before a case goes to proof – when evidence is lead by both solicitors at a formal court hearing.** Like the child welfare hearing, the sheriff will take an active role and seek any possible routes to agreement on the disputes between you and your your ex-spouse as parents.

Preparing for a court hearing

Before you go to court, think twice (and maybe three or four times) about whether a court battle is *really* worth the expense and the stress it will create for you and your children. Maybe it's time to settle out of court. However, for many reasons – both good and bad – some parents want to limit the time their former spouses can spend with their children after a divorce. Others want the sole right to make decisions about their children, or seek a residence order that's not consistent with the roles they've played in the lives of their children so far, perhaps to avoid paying child support.

If you're concerned that your spouse may try to limit your right to continue playing a meaningful role in your children's lives after you're divorced, or if you want to limit your spouse's involvement in your children's lives after your marriage has ended, you may be heading for a court battle. If that seems likely, you can take action now to improve your position:

- ✔ **Become aware of the general guidelines that judges use to make decisions about children.** The Children Act 1989 – or the Children (Scotland) Act 1995 – is the basis for decisions about children. You can find more about these Acts in Chapter 4.

- ✔ **Stay involved in all aspects of your children's lives.** This includes participating in parent-teacher events, taking your children to the doctor, dropping them off or picking them up from the childminder, nursery, or school, being home at night to feed and bathe them and get them to bed, and helping them with their homework.

- ✔ **Be there for your children so that they view you as a 'go-to' parent.** They need someone they can count on for emotional, physical, and psychological support and for general care giving.

Questions you can expect a judge to ask

If you take your dispute to court and it has not been resolved by other means, the judge, informed by the CAFCASS officer, will probably consider most, if not all, of the answers to the following questions before deciding on the arrangement that's in your children's best interests:

- ✔ Where are your children living now?

- ✔ What kind of relationship do your children have with each of you? To whom do they turn for help or support when they have problems?

- ✔ During your marriage, how did you and your spouse share parenting responsibilities? Were you both actively involved in your children's lives – bathing, dressing, and feeding them, helping them with their homework, playing with them, talking with them and helping them resolve their personal problems, attending parent-teacher meetings, taking them to their doctor appointments, handling their emergencies, and so on?

- ✔ What arrangements do you and your ex-spouse want and can you co-operate with one another on behalf of your children after your divorce?

- ✔ Where will you each be living after your divorce and what kind of home life can you offer your children?

- ✔ Do any of your children have special educational or health care needs? How do you and your spouse deal with them now?

✔ What hours do you work and does your work require you to travel? Do you think your work and travel schedule will change after your divorce?

✔ How stable are your finances?

✔ Do you suffer from any mental or physical problems?

Orders a judge can make

The judge is bound by the Children Act to avoid delay, and will intervene if she thinks that your children are likely to suffer from you or your solicitors dragging out the decision-making process. If you have not been able to agree about where your children should live or how they are to see their non-resident parent, the judge can make the following orders (but remember that a judge won't make an order unless it's in your children's best interests):

✔ **Residence Order:** This order states which of you your children should live with.

✔ **Contact Order:** This states how your children should keep in touch with the parent that they don't live with.

The judge can attach conditions to residence and contact orders if she thinks it's in your children's best interests. For example, if the judge thinks there is a risk of abuse or threat of violence, she may order supervised contact. You, your solicitor, or a CAFCASS officer will then arrange contact at a contact centre or in the presence of some other trusted person, such as a grandparent.

If you have special concerns that you disagree upon or want to have the weight of a court order behind, a judge can make orders in addition to those setting out residence and contact, that are in the children's best interests:

✔ **Specific Issue Order:** The judge can make an order to cover one specific issue. For example, the judge can order that your children should go to a specific school.

✔ **Prohibited Steps Order:** This order prohibits a specific thing, for instance that your children cannot be taken out of the country.

✔ **Other orders:** It is possible for a judge to make an order prohibiting any further applications for residence or contact if, for example, she considers that such applications might be thoroughly unmerited or harmful to your children. These orders are rare however.

The court does not like changing a child's surname unless you can show that a change is clearly going to benefit your child. It is not enough to say that you are going to remarry and want your child to take your new surname.

Neither of you may get the children

Although this happens in only a very small number of cases, if both spouses have a history of child neglect or child abuse, the judge may decide that neither of the parents should have the care of the children. However, a judge will not consider making such a decision unless a third party – such as a social worker – raises the issue or unless it is undeniably obvious to the judge that neither spouse is fit to parent his or her children.

In cases such as this, the judge appoints a *guardian ad litem,* now known as a CAFCASS officer, to represent the children in court and to help the court determine where the children should live. Often, a grandparent or another adult relative assumes temporary care of the children until a permanent living arrangement can be established.

The Local Authority Social Services Department can enter a case if there are concerns about a child's welfare. If this occurs, as well as the CAFCASS officer, the child generally has his own solicitor representing him.

The National Youth Advocacy Service is an organisation that campaigns for children to be better represented in court. Visit their Web site on www.nyas. net; they also have a helpline: 0800 616101.

If you have fears about your ex-spouse abducting your children, see Chapter 4 for guidance.

Children divorcing their parents

A child can make an application to the court him or herself, and receive legal aid, in certain circumstances, but the judge must first deem that the child is mature enough to do so. (The child is then called 'gillick' competent, after a particular case brought by a Mrs Gillick.) In Scotland, a child over twelve is automatically considered competent to bring an action, and can do so under twelve if of sufficient maturity and understanding.

Chapter 11

Dividing Up What You Own

- -

In This Chapter

▶ Working out what you own

▶ Valuing and dividing up your property

▶ Deciding what to do with your home

▶ Dealing with your retirement benefits

▶ Sorting out your endowment and insurance policies

▶ Handling your debts

- -

*I*f your marriage has been relatively long and if you've enjoyed a reasonably comfortable standard of living, you may be surprised when you realise just how much you've managed to collect over the years and just how much it's all worth. Dividing up your property requires thought and deliberation, and possibly the advice and assistance of outside experts, because what you divvy up during your divorce has both short- and long-term financial implications for you both. The divorce court can only make one order for the division of capital and property. As you only get one bite of the cherry, it's a good idea to make sure that you aren't going to miss out.

This chapter focuses on how to handle the big stuff – your home, retirement benefits, and financial investments – as well as some of the smaller items. We also give you suggestions for dealing with your debts. How you divide up your assets needs to be seen in the context of the whole picture of your financial settlement. (Chapter 12 looks at spousal support and Chapter 13 deals with child support, two other important parts of the settlement picture.)

Getting Some Terms Out of the Way

During your marriage you may have bought a home, furniture, vehicles, computer equipment, and maybe even fine art. You no doubt own other, less valuable items, too – kitchen equipment, bedding, a television, DVD player, books, and bikes, for example. And, don't forget that pile of wedding gifts you've had stashed in the attic for years! Now that you're getting divorced, you need to do something with those things, too.

The less-valuable stuff you own can be divvied up rather informally. It's usually a matter of making sure that your children have what they need, and then seeing that each of you gets your fair share of what you need to set up new households, plus taking at least some of the items that have special meaning to you. Chapter 14, which covers some of the divorce matters you can handle without the help of professionals, suggests some ways of accomplishing this division.

Distinguishing between tangible property and intangible property

In addition to the goods you own (such as vehicles and furniture), you must also take into account your *intangible property,* such as retirement benefits, stocks, and bonds, when you are dividing up your property. (An intangible asset is an asset that has no intrinsic or marketable value in and of itself but instead represents or has evidence of value.) Your car, on the other hand, is *tangible property* that has value in and of itself (see the sidebar 'Placing a value on the vehicles you own' later in this chapter).

Identifying your marital property

Before you can divide up the value of your property, you and your spouse must first determine what property has to be included. The general rule in England and Wales is that you must take all property into account, regardless of whose name it's in or when it was acquired. Legally, you are each potentially entitled to a share of the value of any property that either or both of you own at the time of your divorce. That includes property acquired before your marriage, or after your separation if you have already separated, as well as all the property that you've acquired during your marriage. If you haven't already done so, make a list and categorise your assets. (Chapter 7 gives you some advice on how best to do that.)

If you have a pre-marital agreement, this may include provisions for the division of your property on separation or divorce and you can keep to those provisions if you both want to do so. However, pre-marital agreements are still relatively rare in England and Wales. If either of you decide not to stick to the agreement, the court can only enforce it if the judge considers it fair to you both, taking into account all the circumstances; the judge always has the ultimate discretion. However, if you do have an agreement, the judge must take it into account as one of the many factors to consider. (See Chapter 21 for more information on pre-marital and post-marital agreements.)

You may agree on a division of all your major assets, only to end up with an argument over the dinner service or your family pet. Don't lose sight of the emotional and financial cost of arguing over such things, and be ready to compromise even if you have set your heart on something.

Understanding matrimonial property in Scotland

The position on property in Scotland is different from that in England and Wales. *Matrimonial property* is all the property belonging to you and/or your spouse, or acquired by either of you during your marriage and before the *relevant date* (see below for a definition of this term).

Matrimonial property includes actual property – for instance, homes, caravans, holiday homes, time share properties, endowment and insurance policies, pensions, bank and building society accounts, savings and investments, and so on. It also covers furniture, furnishings, jewellery, cars, boats, and any other assets. A house or furniture bought before the marriage for use as a family home is also considered matrimonial property.

The relevant date

The date that matrimonial property is valued is called the *relevant date*. This date is the earlier of either

- ✔ The date when you and your spouse stopped living together

- ✔ The date when the notice of intention to divorce – usually known as the summons or the *initial writ*, that is, the document which starts the divorce action – was served on you or your spouse.

Think of it this way: If the relevant date is 1 September and you win the lottery ten days later on 10 September, the winnings aren't considered matrimonial property – meaning you don't have to share them with your spouse. However, if you won the lottery ten days before the relevant date, on 21 August, the winnings would be included as matrimonial property, and they'd be split between you and your spouse.

Exceptions to matrimonial property

There are two types of assets that you can own before the relevant date that aren't considered matrimonial propery:

- ✔ Gifts to either of you from a third party
- ✔ Inheritances

So if you were given a car by one of your parents, it isn't classed as matrimonial property. If you were left some money by your granny it's not matrimonial property. But if you used the money you inherited to buy something for the family home, what you bought becomes matrimonial property. If you gave a gift to your spouse, it's matrimonial property.

Although only matrimonial property (or it's value) is normally divided equally between you, the court can divide it unequally in special circumstances – such as if you used inherited money to purchase a substantial item, or if you agree that something should be excluded from matrimonial property. The court also has the power to deal with items which aren't matrimonial property. Bear in mind that the court divides the net total of the property in money terms. In practice, a fair share of the total of the net assets may be more or less than half.

The net value of matrimonial property

The court looks at the net value of your matrimonial property. That means the matrimonial property (including pensions or life policies paid into during the marriage) at the relevant date, after you've deducted all the legitimate debts incurred by you and your spouse during your marriage. These debts include mortgages, bank or personal loans, and outstanding transactions such as credit cards and household bills. Check with your solicitor about which debts are appropriate for consideration.

Valuing Your Assets

After you've made a list of all your property, including all property in your sole and your joint names, you need to assign a monetary value to each asset. Ordinarily, that figure is the item's *fair market value,* or what you could reasonably expect to sell the item for, assuming that you didn't *have* to sell it and that you have a willing buyer.

Although you can probably value many of your assets yourselves, you may need the help of outside experts, such as surveyors, estate agents, accountants, and actuaries to determine the worth of particularly valuable or complex assets, such as land or buildings, certain types of retirement benefits, fine antiques, a family business, and so on. You may find the services of an outside expert helpful if you and your spouse can't agree on how to value an important asset.

After you value your assets, you have to divide up the value of those assets, bearing in mind the guidelines a judge would use if such issues were to go to a full hearing in court, or by applying some other criteria that you and your spouse both agree to and that seems fair to you both.

Placing a value on the vehicles you own

Determining the value of the vehicles you and your spouse own together is relatively easy and inexpensive. You can

✔ Use one of the established car guides, such as *Glass* or *Parker*, which you can find in your local newsagent

✔ Try the following Web site: www.parkers.co.uk

✔ Ask local car dealers what they would pay you for your vehicles. Because used car

dealers tend to make low offers, you and your spouse may want to adjust the offers somewhat

✔ Read the auto ads in the classified section of your local paper for vehicles comparable to yours, or try the Web site: www.exchangeandmart.co.uk/motoring/index.php.

When you are deciding which property to take from your marriage, keep in mind your personal goals for your life after divorce, and your post-divorce financial needs.

Following the Legal Guidelines

If you involve solicitors in your property division negotiations, or if you look to a judge to decide who gets what, statutory guidelines take centre stage. The judge's personal preferences, and the persuasiveness of your lawyers, can also make a difference. Judges in England and Wales are required to give priority to your children's needs and to consider all the circumstances including the following factors. The weight and value that the judge attributes to each factor varies from case to case and is up to the judge to decide.

✔ **How much money you and your spouse each earn now and can be expected to earn in the future.** Often, a judge awards a larger share of property to the spouse who has the lower earning potential. In evaluating your earning potential, the judge may consider your age, education level, previous work experience, physical and mental health, and other factors that may have a bearing on your ability to earn a living.

✔ **The value of any property or other financial resources that either or both of you may have.**

✔ **The financial needs, obligations and responsibilities that either of you have, or are likely to have, in the future**. That includes whether you have primary care of your children, and your respective housing needs and mortgage obligations.

✔ **Your standard of living during your marriage.** A judge usually tries to allocate income and assets between you and your spouse so that there is no great disparity between you and so that neither of you suffers a dramatic reversal in your lifestyle after you are divorced. In reality, however, your lifestyle may change (probably for the worse).

✔ **Your age and health, in particular whether either of you has any mental or physical disability.** Older spouses and spouses who are in poor health often receive a greater share of the property than younger or healthier spouses.

✔ **How long you were married.** The longer you were married, the more likely it is that the court will view you as equal partners.

✔ **Your individual contributions to your marriage and family generally.** The courts recognise that paying the family's bills is only one way that a spouse can contribute to the family. Increasingly, the courts have recognised that being a full-time parent, helping your spouse advance his or her career, or supporting your spouse through university, and making other contributions to the marriage all have value, which although different should not be treated in a discriminatory way.

✔ **The value to each of you of any benefit that either of you may lose because of the dissolution of your marriage.** The most obvious example of this kind of benefit is a pension. The law specifically requires a judge to consider your pension positions, and gives powers to the judge to *attach* or *share* death in service benefits, pension lump sum, and pension income benefits between you. (See 'Dividing Up Your Retirement Benefits' later in this chapter.)

✔ **Your (and your spouse's) conduct.** A judge only takes conduct into account if it's inequitable to disregard it. In practice, that means that it rarely makes any difference, however badly you feel your spouse has behaved towards you.

Less emphasis is placed on these factors in Scotland. For instance, your marriage is considered an equal partnership and who does what won't affect the right to equal sharing of matrimonial property. There is less emphasis on what the future may hold.

If you have a new partner, the judge only takes their means into account to the extent that their means affect your position, for example if they have a home that you can share or sufficient income to support you.

Money received from personal injury claims or past inheritances is taken into account (except in Scotland), but future inheritances aren't unless they're certain and likely to be received in the foreseeable future (usually within about five years).

A 1995 Nobel Prize winner agreed to give half of his million-dollar prize to his wife in their divorce (by the way, he won the prize for economics).

Working Out Your Money Matters When You Divorce in Scotland

When compared with divorce law in England and Wales, the law in Scotland has several major and important differences relating to your money and property arrangements. If you or your spouse applies for a divorce in Scotland, the key piece of legislation is the Family Law (Scotland) Act 1985 (refer to Chapter 4 for what this law entails).

The principles for valuing and dividing your property and assets (known as *matrimonial property,* described in 'Understanding matrimonial property in Scotland' earlier in this chapter), the provisions for *aliment,* also called 'maintenance', and the kinds of orders available to regulate these matters are all laid out in this Act. The Act also contains the provisions for *interim aliment* for a spouse after separation but pre-divorce, *periodical allowance* after divorce, and aliment for a child. Financial support for children has since been taken over by the Child Support Agency (CSA). See Chapter 13 for what the CSA does.

Financial principles of Scottish family law

The Family Law (Scotland) Act has five main financial principles regarding divorce that you should know:

- ✔ You must share fairly the net value of the matrimonial property.

- ✔ The court must balance your financial and non-financial contributions (or damage) to your spouse's wealth and vice versa. For example, if you work in your spouse's business for an artificially low wage or give up work and a pension to look after your children, the judge must take that into account.

- ✔ You must share fairly the burden of caring for your children under 16.

- ✔ If you have been substantially financially dependent on your spouse, he or she may have to support you for a period of not more than three years after the divorce to enable you to adjust to the loss of that support.

- ✔ If you are likely to suffer serious financial hardship as a result of your divorce (for example if you're very ill) your spouse may have to provide for you to relieve this hardship over a reasonable period. However, this is the exception rather than the rule.

Financial orders in Scotland

The court in Scotland can make a number of financial orders. The following are the main ones:

- **Aliment:** The court can order a spouse to pay aliment, or child support, for a child of your marriage, but only if the Child Support Agency (CSA) can't make an assessment. For more about child support and the CSA, read Chapter 13. Aliment may also be ordered for the interim period until your divorce has been finalised. In some circumstances you may get an award of aliment in addition to the child support assessment.

- **Capital sum:** A lump sum paid to you by your spouse. This order can't be awarded after your divorce decree.

- **Transfer of property:** The court can order you to transfer ownership of a particular piece of property to your spouse or the other way round. Note that this order can't be awarded after your divorce decree.

- **Periodical allowance:** You may be ordered to pay a regular sum each week or month to your spouse after the divorce. Orders for periodical allowance are the exception rather than the rule and are only made if there is no other suitable remedy (such as a capital sum).

The court can also make some incidental orders before or on divorce, including orders for the following

- Valuation of property

- Sale of property

- Regulating occupation of your matrimonial home

- Regulating use of furnishings in your matrimonial home

- The date from which interest shall run on any capital sum awarded

The court can consider the following for both you and your spouse when making these orders, which provide a fair degree of discretion (though not as much as in England and Wales):

- Health

- Age

- Earning capacity

- Child care costs

- Your needs and resources

- All the circumstances of your case

Getting Up-front Advice

Before you and your spouse handle your own property division negotiations, especially if the total value of what you own together is substantial, consult with a qualified independent financial advisor before you start dividing up your assets. Though you can do it on your own, we generally recommend outside help to make sure you look thoroughly at the whole picture. (See Chapters 15, 16, and 17 about working with solicitors and mediatiors.)

With the help of computer models, financial services professionals can help you test various scenarios for dividing up what you own and what you owe together so that you can make strategically wise decisions. In essence, they can do a cost-benefit analysis of different property division schemes.

Some financial advisers specialise in providing pre-and post-divorce money management advice. They can help analyse the best way to deal with not only the division of property but also child support and spousal maintenance.

Deciding What to Do With Your Home

When everything around you is changing, you may be tempted to hold on to your home at all costs. You feel comfortable there – perhaps you spent time and energy decorating your home and doing the garden. If you have young children and you're going to be their primary carer after your divorce, you may want to stay in your own home to bolster their emotional security.

When it comes to your home, try to put your emotions to one side and approach the decision from a financial perspective. You may decide that keeping your home after you divorce isn't wise or financially realistic, or with some careful financial planning you may find a way to keep your house. The bottom line is this: Whatever you do about your home should be based on a financial decision that reflects the needs of your children and your ability to cover your costs. If you let your emotions rule, you may eventually end up losing your home because you can't afford to keep up with the mortgage payments, the bills, or with essential repairs and maintenance.

Finding out what your home is worth

The least-expensive way (free in most cases) to determine the value of your home is to ask an estate agent for recent selling prices of comparable houses in your neighbourhood and how much you could get for your house. However, the agent's estimate represents an approximation of your home's value. In the end, your home is only worth what someone will pay for it.

A better method, albeit more expensive, is to engage a property surveyor to value your home. If either you or your spouse apply to the court for a decision on your house and you can't agree on its value, you usually have to obtain a single independent professional valuation jointly

Estate agent valuations tend to be imprecise. As a result, if you and your spouse both get your own valuations, the results can be quite different. And, *don't* value your home based on its mortgage value. Mortgage valuations are often considerably less than your home's actual value and are mainly concerned with protecting the mortgagee's security.

If you do decide to get a valuation from an estate agent, it's worth your while to get a few valuations from different agents to make sure you're on target.

Evaluating your options

Most divorcing couples resolve the problem of 'what to do about the house' in one of the following ways:

- ✔ Sell the house
- ✔ Keep the house
- ✔ Retain an interest in the house

Selling your home

When your home is the only asset of real value that you own, you may have to sell it so that you can both leave your marriage with some money in your pockets. You may also decide to sell because the house holds too many unhappy memories for both of you, it's too big for you to live in and maintain by yourself, or because you can't afford to keep it. A sale may be a good solution if there's enough equity in the family home to rehouse you both.

If you do sell, remember that the selling price probably doesn't represent the actual amount of money you and your spouse can split between you. Most likely, you have a mortgage to pay off, selling costs, and possibly other costs to deduct. If you use an estate agent to sell your home, you have to pay the agent a fee, usually a percentage of your home's gross sale price (that is, the estate agent's charges). After all is said and done, when those costs are subtracted from your home's anticipated sale price (leaving the *equity*), selling your house may not appear to be a very attractive option – but it still may nevertheless be the best one.

To understand the implications of selling your home, pick up a copy of *Buying and Selling a Home For Dummies* by Melanie Bien (2004).

Keeping your home

Taking the house as part of your property settlement is an option if you can afford to buy your spouse out or you have enough other property so that your spouse can take another asset of comparable value. If your spouse agrees to transfer his or her interest in the marital home to you, the deeds have to be altered and any change of ownership registered at the Land Registry. (Refer to Chapter 3 for the process you need to go through to register ownership.) In turn, you probably either have to secure your spouse's release from the mortgage, or give an *undertaking* – a promise to the court and your spouse – that you will try your best to do so and will take full responsibility for the mortgage payments in the meantime.

Check out your mortgage capacity with an independent financial adviser or reputable lending institution and review the household budget you have projected for your life after divorce. You need to be sure that you can really afford to take over the monthly mortgage payments as well as the upkeep on your home.If you don't, you may have to sell your house eventually or you may even lose it if it isrepossessed by your mortgage provider. If you haven't already developed a household budget for yourself, Chapter 3 tells you how.

If your spouse keeps the home, takes over the mortgage, and then defaults on it, the mortgage holder can look to you for payment if your name is still on the mortgage deed, no matter what your divorce agreement says. This demonstrates why it's so important that you get released from the mortgage. Failing that, you need an *indemnity* from your spouse in the final settlement giving you the right to sue your former spouse for the money you could end up paying. However, you may have to go to court to enforce the indemnity and, even if you get a judgement against your spouse, you have no guarantee that you can actually recover what you're owed.

Retaining an interest in your home

You and your spouse may want to sell your house, but for practical reasons decide to delay the sale. For example, you may want your kids to be able to live in the same home until they complete secondary school. If you have primary responsibility for your children, you'll stay in the home with them, but your property settlement gives you both an interest in that property.

If you opt for this sort of arrangement, be sure your agreement addresses the following questions:

- ✔ How much of an interest do each of you have in the home?
- ✔ At what point must your house be put up for sale?

- Who puts the house up for sale?
- How is the asking price determined?
- How are you going to pay all sale-related expenses?
- How do you want to divide up the net sale proceeds?
- If you still owe money on the mortgage, how is it paid each month?
- How do you want to pay the homeowner's insurance, rates, and taxes?
- Who is responsible for the cost of minor repairs – and major ones, such as a new roof?

Specifying the regular upkeep your home requires in order to protect your investment in the property is a possible idea. You may also specify who's responsible for doing the maintenance and how often. Enforcing this provision, however, may be tough.

There are advantages and disadvantages to retaining an interest in your home. On the one hand, it may be the only way that you can each keep an interest in the property and safeguard the needs of your children; on the other hand, one of you may have to wait quite a few years before realising your interest, and then there may not be enough to rehouse you both, plus neither of you will qualify for public housing.

Retaining an interest in your home can be done in one of two main ways: keeping it in your joint names with a *deed of trust,* or transferring it from one to the other subject to a *deed of charge* (in Scotland it's called a *standard security*). In the first case, you remain legal joint owners; in the second, only one of you is the legal owner. However, in each case the deed should spell out the answers to the questions above, such as the size of each share and when you'll realise them. Either way, it's usually better to express your respective shares as a percentage of the value, rather than as a fixed sum. That way you each benefit from any increase in the value of the property, or share the loss, proportionately.

When making decisions about your home, bear in mind that there may be things that you and your spouse can agree between you that the court doesn't have power to order, for example taking on a new mortgage or paying the existing one. Chapter 18 tells you more about the alternatives of settling between you or asking a judge to make the decision for you.

If your home is rented, your main option is to transfer the tenancy into one spouse's name. Usually the transfer is to the spouse who has the main care of the children. Make sure that you secure the transfer before your decree absolute of divorce if you're seeking a transfer into your name and the tenancy is in your spouse's sole name.

Good news about capital gains tax

The general rule is that disposal of your family home is exempt from capital gains tax (CGT). Husbands and wives can obtain CGT relief for only one house between them. If a property ceases to be your main residence before you sell it, you get a three-year period of grace for the CGT exemption.

After separation or divorce you can still claim exemption for your home if you sell it or transfer it to your spouse. If you stop living there, and transfer your home to your spouse as part of the financial settlement, you're still exempt from CGT as long as your spouse has continued to use it as his or her main home. However, if you buy another property, you have to decide which property is going to be your *principal private residence* for tax purposes.

If, as part of your divorce settlement, you retain an interest in your property under a deed of trust on the basis that, for example, you'll realise your interest when your youngest child finishes school, you are technically liable for CGT. However, as long as you reach that settlement within three years of your separation, you don't have to pay any CGT. Be sure, therefore, not to delay settlement of your finances following separation.

If, as part of your divorce settlement, you retain an interest in your property under a deed of charge you are liable for CGT when you receive your share. You can, however, claim your annual exemption (currently £7,900 each per annum) and maybe other forms of tax relief.

Always consult with your solicitor or accountant at the time of your separation for advice on your tax position, particularly if you own more than one property between you, or if you have other substantial assets. You may also obtain a useful leaflet on CGT from the Inland Revenue – IR 281 Husband and Wife, Divorce and Separation.

Dividing Up Your Retirement Benefits

The retirement benefits you or your spouse may have earned during your marriage are treated as marital assets and will be included among the assets you have to divide up. Such benefits may include

- Occupational pension schemes, including public sector and private employment schemes
- Personal pension schemes
- The *State Earnings Related Pension Scheme*, known as SERPs, and now replaced by the State Second Pension
- Retirement annuity contracts

✔ Stakeholder pension schemes

✔ Self-administered executive pension schemes

✔ Additional voluntary contributions, known as AVCs

✔ Section 32 buy-out policies

You can claim the benefit of your ex-spouse's National Insurance contributions to enhance your own basic state pension after your divorce without any loss to your ex-spouse. Write to the Department for Work and Pensions within one month of your decree absolute, and send them a copy of your decree absolute as well as your own and your ex-spouse's National Insurance numbers. The court has no power to make orders relating to the basic state pension, although it does have powers in relation to SERPs (see 'Knowing what your pension options are' below).

In addition to getting state benefits from the government, you may earn your retirement benefits by working for an employer who either makes a retirement scheme available to you as an optional benefit or provides it to you as an automatic perk of your job.

If you've worked for several employers during your career, you may have earned retirement benefits from each. Be sure that your list of assests reflects all those benefits.

Because of the variety and complexity of pension schemes, get advice from a pension actuary, an independent financial adviser, or solicitor – or all three – before you make any decisions about how you might adjust your pensions on your divorce. (Check out Chapter 3, which gives brief explanations of the different pensions that you may be dealing with.)

You can try the following for basic help on the different types of pensions:

✔ **Citizens' Advice Bureau** (details in your local phone book) or visit their Web site at www.nacab.org.uk

✔ **The Office for the Pensions Advisory Service (OPAS)** can give you information about any aspect of occupational, personal, and stakeholder pensions. You can contact them by phone on 020 7233 8080 or visit their Web site at www.opas.org.uk

✔ **The Department for Work and Pensions** gives out free guides on pensions. You can call them on 08457 313233, write to them at Pension Guide, Freepost, Bristol BS38 7WA, or try their Web site at www.pensionguide.gov.uk

Be aware that pensions accrued after marriage and before the relevant date (see the section 'Coming to terms with matrimonial property' earlier in this chapter) are always considered part of your matrimonial property in Scotland. You may be surprised by this, especially when you can't actually get hold of the money to divide between you! Where a pension has been earned or paid into partly before the marriage a simple formula of dividing it by the number of years before and after the marriage is used.

Finding out the value of your pension

To help you or the court decide how to deal with your pensions on divorce, you must find out their value. Assessing the value of your money purchase or personal pension scheme is fairly easy (see Chapter 3 for a definition of these types of plan). In most cases, it's simply the amount of money you have invested in your plan at any given time.

To find out how much you have invested in your pension scheme, contact the pension administrator and ask for a note of the *Cash Equivalent Transfer Value (CETV* for short) or review your most recent summary statement. If you work in the private sector for an employer who offers an occupational pension, your employer is legally required to provide you with a summary annual report telling youthe value of your pension. Similarly, the provider of your personal pension scheme should provide you with an annual statement.

If you have a final salary pension scheme, valuing it can be a rather more complicated process. (Have a look at Chapter 3 for a definition of this type of scheme.) To check the CETV produced by the pension scheme trustees, you may want to employ your own actuary to calculate the true value, particularly if it's an armed forces pension scheme. The value of your final salary pension scheme can be affected by a number of different factors, such as whether there are any discretionary benefits, your age, and your health. Ask your solicitor or accountant for advice on whether you might need an actuarial valuation and to recommend a pension actuary if so.

Don't assume that getting the cash value of your pension scheme means that you can actually cash it in yet: You can't. The government restricts the percent-age of the fund that you can take in cash, and the minimum age (which depends on the type of scheme) at which you can take it. (See 'Knowing what your pension options are' later in this chapter.)

Evaluating the options for dealing with your pension

When you divorce, you basically have three alternatives for dealing with your retirement benefits (they're described in the next section). When you're considering which alternative is best for you, take the whole financial picture into account, including the following:

✔ The value of the benefits of both your own and your spouse's pension. This means not just the CETV, but also what the pension income, pension lump sum, and death benefits are likely to be

✔ The value of your potential share of the benefits

✔ The value of your other family assets

✔ How much money you need now, and will need later

✔ How close you are to retirement age

✔ The likely costs of each option

If your participation in the pension predates your marriage or postdates your divorce, you may decide that your retirement benefits shouldn't all be taken into account in quite the same way. For example, if you've been married for ten years and have been a member of a pension scheme for 20 years, it's fair to argue that your spouse should only have a share in half your pension fund, not the full amount.

Check the actual benefits that your pension fund is likely to produce. The main benefits are

✔ Income from your pension on retirement

✔ A lump sum if you choose to take part of your pension in this form

✔ Any benefits received by the benficiary on the pension-holder's death

If you need help analysing your options in light of these factors, talk with a qualified financial adviser or family law specialist.

Knowing what your pension options are

You've got several options to choose from when deciding what to do with your pension benefits. The most common options are as follows:

✔ Offseting the benefits with other assets

✔ Attaching the pension benefits so you can both receive payment on the pension-holder's retirement

✔ Sharing the benefits on your divorce

Offsetting your pension benefits

Generally, whichever spouse has earned the retirement benefits retains all rights to them. The other spouse then usually takes an appropriate amount of other assets, such as a larger share of the house. This is known as *offsetting* and is sometimes the cheapest way for you to deal with retirement benefits, especially when there aren't enough other assets to go round. For this option to work for you and your spouse, you need to have enough other assets that you can use to offset the pension.

The value of your pension isn't directly comparable to the value of your other assets, such as your house, savings, or car and you may need a specialist to help you come up with a fair division of your assets. Take these factors into account if you're planning to offset a pension against other assets:

✔ You can't simply cash in your pension until you're at least 50, and then the most that you can cash in is about 25 per cent of its value.

✔ The rest of your pension fund must be taken as income – which is taxable.

✔ You may not live until retirement age and if you don't, you won't benefit personally from the value of the fund.

✔ The value of your pension fund, if it is a money purchase type scheme, may go up or down over time depending on the investment market.

Attaching your pension benefits

This option provides each of you with a specified proportion of the various pension benefits once the spouse who is earning the pension benefits begins receiving them. The benefits can include the pension lump sum, the pension income, or the death in service benefits. This option is only available if you have a court order for pension attachment on divorce and you have to get the approval of the pension administrators in advance. There are disadvantages to this option however:

✔ You can't attach the state retirement pension or SERPs.

✔ You remain dependent on your spouse, possibly decades after your divorce, because you need a spousal maintenance order if you want to share the pension income when your spouse retires.

✔ You have to wait until your spouse retires before you can draw your pension income or lump sum benefits.

✔ You lose the pension income if you remarry, although – as long as your order specifies so – you can keep the pension lump sum.

✔ The pension benefits stop on the death of either you or your spouse.

✔ Either of you can apply to the court to vary the order so you're at risk of losing the benefit.

✔ You may not be able to control your spouse's contributions to the pension, or to prevent him or her transferring the benefits to another pension fund.

Sharing your pension benefits

Sharing your benefits means that if your spouse has a pension fund, you share the value of that fund between you in specified proportions after your divorce. You still can't cash your share in, but you can either invest your share in another pension fund of your choice (an *external transfer*), or keep it with the existing pension provider as your own distinct fund (an *internal transfer*), subject to the rules of the scheme(s) in question. You and your ex can only share a pension after you're divorced if you are granted a pension-sharing order and you get the pension administrator's approval in advance. Pension sharing isn't an option with the basic state retirement scheme, but it can be done with SERPs and most other kinds of pension.

Not all pension schemes allows you to make an external transfer; statutory schemes, for example, only allow an internal transfer. Conversely, not all schemes allows you to make an internal transfer. Where you have a choice, seek the advice of a qualified financial consultant.

The potential advantages of pension sharing over pension attachment are

- ✔ You don't have to remain financially dependent on your spouse after your divorce. (So you don't need a spousal maintenance order as far as a pension is concerned.)

- ✔ You can decide when to draw the benefits (subject to your scheme's rules).

- ✔ You don't lose the pension if you remarry.

- ✔ You don't lose the pension if your spouse dies, and you can specify your own beneficiaries if you die before retirement.

- ✔ Once the order has been made it can't be varied.

A large percentage of women in the UK don't have their own pensions, in part because women traditionally give up their careers to look after their children. If you are in this position, sharing in your husband's pension may mean the difference between living in poverty and living in comfort during your golden years.

Getting Down to Business: How to Deal with Your Joint Enterprise

If either of you owns a business or has a share in one, or if you and your spouse own a business together, its value is included in the assets to be divided between you. If you agreed to a different arrangement through a pre-marital agreement, a judge won't necessarily uphold such an agreement unless she considers that it's fair to do so, given all the circumstances. (Chapter 21 explains how pre-marital agreements work.)

In Scotland, any business owned, or partly owned, by you and/or your spouse may be considered part of your matrimonial property (you can find the definition of this term under 'Understanding matrimonial property in Scotland', earlier in this chapter). The value of this asset is how much the business is worth on the relevant date. To determine this, you must obtain a valuation of the business at the relevant date. If you remain a partner after the relevant date ordinary partnership law may also be involved.

If you and your spouse have both been actively involved in your business, you may find deciding what to do with it especially difficult. The idea that you may have to leave the business, shut it down, or sell it can be tough to accept when your marriage is ending. On the other hand, making plans for a new career may be just what you need to get over the loss of your marriage.

Your options, in a nutshell

To help you deal with the difficult decision of what to do with the business you and your spouse own, we offer you a number of options that have worked for other couples:

- ✔ **One spouse keeps the business and the other gets assets equal in value to his or her interest in the business.** Usually, the spouse who takes the business is the one who has been most actively involved in it or whose skills and knowledge are most essential to its continued success. For financial reasons or if sufficient other marital property doesn't exist, the spouse who keeps the business may buy out the interest of the other spouse over time. You need to formalise the buyout in a written agreement. Also, to help secure your spouse's payments to you, placing a legal charge on his or her real property, on the assets of the business, or on some other assets, if there are any, is a good idea.

- ✔ **You divide up the business and each of you takes a part of it.** This arrangement is practical only if you can logically divide up your business and if the division can be done without jeopardising the financial integrity of each part.

- ✔ **You sell the business and split the proceeds.** This may be your only option if all of your assets are tied up in your business. However, if the continued success of the business depends on your combined skills and know-how, the business may not be worth much on the open market unless it has significant assets that would be of value to a new owner.

- ✔ **Wind up the business.** If neither of you is interested in continuing the business and you can't sell it as a going concern, winding it up is a reasonable alternative. However, to take advantage of this alternative your business's assets must have market value. *Marketable assets* can include machinery, equipment, land or buildings, or payments due to the business. Depending on the type and value of the assets you are selling, you may want to sell the assets yourself, employ a company liquidator to sell them for you (you'll have to pay a proportion of the proceeds), or have the assets auctioned off.

✔ **Keep operating your business together.** For obvious reasons, only a relatively small number of divorcing spouses who are also business partners choose this option. Most divorced spouses don't want to continue such an important and mutually dependent relationship. In fact, doing so may actually be harmful to the business.

If you worked in your spouse's business without compensation, your contribution to the business may be a factor in your financial settlement.

Assigning a value to your business

To implement any of the options just described you may have to assign a fair market value to your business. You need the following if you want to make that determination yourself:

✔ Profit and loss statements for the past three years

✔ Balance sheets for the past three years

✔ Records of accounts receivable

✔ Records of accounts payable

✔ Tax returns and assessments for the past three years

✔ Bank statements for the past three years

✔ Contracts for future business

✔ Recent good-faith offers to buy the business, if any exist

✔ Information about the purchase price of businesses comparable to yours

When you're valuing your joint business, don't overlook its *goodwill value.* Goodwill consists of your business's reputation, name recognition, track record in pleasing its customers, role in the local community, and other factors that make it a respected enterprise.

If you're going to leave the business you've shared with your spouse, be sure to take an active role in valuing it, or engage an independent forensic accountant or business valuation expert to value it for you. As much as you may trust your spouse, it's in his or her best interest to value the business for as little as possible – either your spouse has to pay you less if he or she buys you out over time, or you end up entitled to less of the other marital property.

If you can afford to do so, you and your spouse can each engage outside experts to value your business and then you can average their estimates or otherwise agree on a value. You could also arrange for a single valuation through a mutually agreed independent expert. Getting the help of an outside expert who is familiar with your particular type of business is advisable if your business is especially large, valuable, or complex. However, be warned that the help of such experts does not come cheap.

Weigh up the risks of the business when you're considering it an asset as compared to any other assets that you're dividing between you, and don't forget to factor those risks into your settlement.

When you began your business, you and your co-owners may have decided how your share of the business would be valued if one of you decided to exit the business or sell it. Therefore, that agreement determines what your share of the business is worth, and it isn't a decision you and your spouse can make on your own.

Endowment and Other Insurance Policies

A common feature in the finances of married couples in England and Wales is endowment policies. You may have taken out an endowment policy as a savings scheme alongside an interest-only mortgage. Often this policy is considered a means of paying off the mortgage at the end of the term, maybe 20 or 25 years' ahead, or on the death of you or your spouse if sooner. Premiums are paid on a regular basis, so that the cash value of the policy gradually increases, and the policy can become a significant asset. Increasingly, however, endowment policies are not living up to their predicted targets because of the drop in the stock market in recent years, and you may now be advised to expect a shortfall between the terminal value of your policy and the mortgage that it's intended to pay off.

If you and your spouse have such a policy, whether in your joint names or only in one name, you must decide what to do with it. The main options with these and any other policies that are acquiring a capital value are as follows:

> ✔ **Surrender or sell the policy.** The insurance company with whom you hold your policy has to provide you with details of the *surrender value* of your policy on request – that is, the amount the company pays you if you decide to cash your policy in. If you cash the policy in early, you don't have to pay any further premiums but you may lose the value of any bonuses. Not all policies are sellable on the open market, but if yours is, you may get slightly better value for money selling your policy rather than surrendering it. A financial adviser should be able to advise you on your options.

✔ **Treat the policy as paid up.** Paid up means that you do not have to pay any more premiums, but you're able to receive some benefit from the policy at maturity or on death. Part of the cash value of the policy may have to go towards maintaining the death coverage.

✔ **Transfer the policy from your joint names into your or your spouse's sole name.** Transferring the policy allows one of you to retain the policy as a form of investment, or as cover for the mortgage, without losing the terminal bonuses. Some policies are formally assigned to the mortgage lender, so you may have to get the lender's consent if you want to transfer the policy to your spouse and you are retaining the mortgage. You may also have to convert the mortgage from interest free to repayment, so that you pay the capital and interest off together over time. Transferring an endowment policy can, however, be one way of providing your spouse with an immediate share of the family assets when you aren't able to sell the house until a later date and/or there are no other assets of any significance.

Dealing With Your Debts

If you owe more than you own, you're like countless other divorcing couples. In our credit-orientated society, your divorce may be more about dividing up your debts than about what to do with your assets. Although you can leave your marriage behind, you can't do the same with your debts. Divorced or not, the debts must be paid and you both must decide how to pay them.

Some of that debt may be *secured debt,* such as your mortgage or car loan. Secured debt is debt that you have collateralised with an asset. If you don't pay the debt, the creditor can take the asset that you put up as loan collateral. You probably also have *unsecured debt,* such as credit card debt, for example. For some of you, all your debt may be unsecured.

Unsecured debt has the potential to create a great deal of discord in a divorce because, unlike a secured debt, it's usually not associated with an asset of any significant value. In many divorces, if you agree to assume responsibility for a secured debt, you also get the asset that the debt is financing. But unsecured debts typically include the purchase of things like restaurant meals, petrol for your car, clothing, holidays, groceries, and so on.

Tips for avoiding trouble

Here, we offer some suggestions for dealing with what is certainly an unpleasant task – figuring out what to do with your debts:

✔ **Pay off all your debt as part of your divorce.** This is usually the best way to deal with debt, assuming that you and your spouse have enough ready cash or sufficient assets that you can liquidate easily. That means that you both begin your post-divorce lives unencumbered by financial obligations from your marriage. Paying off your debts also means that neither of you has to worry about how you'll be affected if your ex-spouse doesn't pay the debts he or she agreed to pay. Remember, creditors can look to you for payment on any debts in your joint names, no matter what your divorce agreement may say.

✔ **Trade debt for assets.** If you can't wipe out all of your debt, one of you may agree to take more than your share of the debt in exchange for getting more of the assets – the financial equivalent of taking a spoonful of sugar to make the medicine go down – because you can afford to pay more of the debts than your spouse can.

✔ **Take your fair share.** If you and your spouse own little, if anything, of real value, dividing up your debts may simply mean that each of you takes your fair share of the debt. For example, you may agree to pay off the balance on a credit card that was in both of your names but which you, not your spouse, used regularly.

✔ **Pay off your debts together after your divorce.** Avoid this arrangement – it requires too much co-operation and communication between you and your former spouse. However, if this arrangement is your best or only option, securing your spouse's obligation to pay his or her share of your unsecured debt (your credit card debt, for example) by placing a charge on one or more of your spouse's separate assets is highly recommended.

Where the law stands on your debts

When you decide the best way to deal with the money you owe, bear in mind that a judge considers the same property laws and guidelines that she applies to the division of your assets. (For an in-depth discussion of those laws and guidelines, turn to Chapter 5.) However, whenever third parties are involved the court's powers are very limited. A judge can't order either of you to pay or take responsibility for a debt to a third party. And you have to give secured creditors notice of any application you make which involves their security so that they can make representations to the court.

Chapter 12

Maintenance for You or Your Spouse

. . . .

In This Chapter

▶ Understanding what maintenance means

▶ Examining the law's stand on maintenance

▶ Understanding the pros and cons of taking capital instead of maintenance

▶ Knowing when an increase or decrease in maintenance is justified

▶ Protecting yourself against the sudden loss of maintenance

▶ The tax consequences of maintenance payments

. . . .

*E*ven if you and your spouse concur that maintenance (also known as *spousal support* or *periodical payments*) should be included in your divorce settlement, you may have a tough time agreeing on the basic terms – how much maintenance should be paid and for how long.

For example, if you're a husband who wants a divorce and your wife doesn't, she may bristle at the suggestion that she pay you maintenance, no matter how reasonable your request may be considering your ability to earn a living right away or at all. Or maybe as a wife, you're angry and hurt because your husband who's a successful business owner wants a divorce and you don't. You may retaliate by demanding maintenance, and a lot of it. You think it's the least that your spouse can do, given what he is doing to your life.

To deal with this issue as dispassionately as possible and make decisions that are fair to both of you, this chapter provides you with basic information about maintenance and the part it plays in divorce. Maintenance is just one part of the whole picture; you need to look at it alongside your decisions about your assets and child support (if you have children). Chapter 11 gives advice about dividing up your assets and Chapter 13 tells you about child support.

If you want to know what you can do to minimise the damage that a divorce can do to your money situation, see Chapter 3 for practical advice on managing your household finances and Chapter 7 for information on financial preparations for divorce.

What Is Maintenance and When Is It Paid?

Maintenance, or *periodical payments,* is the payment of money by one spouse to the other after a couple is divorced. If you separate before your divorce is final, your spouse (or vice versa) may also have to pay *maintenance pending suit* or *interim periodical* payments, which simply means payments to tide you over until the final decree of divorce or final financial settlement.

The Family Law (Scotland) Act sets the provisions for the kinds of orders available to the courts for regulating these matters. This Act also includes the provisions for *aliment* for a spouse pre-divorce and *periodical allowance* after divorce. See Chapter 11 for a description of these provisions.

In generations past, unless a man paid his ex-wife maintenance, she had no way to pay her bills. Assuming that he could afford it, an ex-husband paid his ex-wife *maintenance* for her lifetime, usually by sending her a monthly cheque for a set amount of money. In reality, however, maintenance did not really last forever because the law required, and still does, that maintenance ceases if the ex-wife remarries. In almost all cases, it also ceases if the ex-husband dies (except in Scotland, where the deceased's executors have to apply to the court to terminate the allowance).

Over the last few decades, lifelong maintenance has become much rarer and judges have to consider in each case whether maintenance should be awarded or dismissed. Spousal maintenance continues to be a part of some divorce settlements – most often divorces that involve wealthier couples or older couples who are ending lengthy marriages, or, as an added protection, where there are dependent children.

In Scotland, spousal maintenance, or periodical allowance, following divorce is unusual.

Maintenance automatically ceases on the payee's remarriage, but it does not automatically cease on cohabitation. Today, therefore, many agreements and orders expressly provide that maintenance ceases once the ex-spouse has cohabited for a specified period of time, commonly six months.

Attitudes towards maintenance have changed as the roles of men and women in our culture have changed. Whereas maintenance used to be a standard part of most divorces, today only a relatively small percentage of divorce orders or agreements provide for it. According to the Office for National Statistics, just over 175,000 petitions for divorce were filed in 2002, and in the same period there were 18,400 maintenance orders. Furthermore, the law is gender-neutral when it comes to maintenance. In the eyes of the law, men and women are equally entitled to maintenance (in actual practice, however, far fewer men receive it).

If you do receive any maintenance, be aware that it may only be for a limited period of time. Such maintenance is intended to help you 'get on your feet' and lasts for a relatively short period of time, say three to five years. If you have been based at home looking after your children, you probably need time to retrain and then to earn enough to become self-sufficient. The amount and duration of maintenance payments depend on a number of factors:

✔ Your financial needs and resources

✔ Your spouse's financial needs and resources

✔ The value of the assets you receive in your divorce settlement

✔ Your income and earning capacity both now and in the foreseeable future

✔ Your education and your spouse's education level and qualifications

✔ Your work experience and your spouse's experience

✔ Your ages and the duration of your marriage

✔ Your standard of living before the breakdown of your marriage

✔ Your health and your spouse's health – both physical and emotional

✔ The number of children in your household and their physical and emotional health

✔ The contributions that either you or your spouse have made towards the family

✔ Any other factors you want to consider if you're sorting out the terms of your divorce together, or other factors that a judge feels are relevant if that issue goes to a full hearing. Conduct is only relevant if it's *inequitable to disregard it* (if there was abuse, for example), and that is rare.

The approach to maintenance is premised on the assumption that most ex-spouses can, and eventually should, earn their own livings after a divorce. However, it also recognises that a woman (or a man, for that matter) may have put her own career on the back burner to raise the children or support the other spouse's career.

If your maintenance payments help your former spouse get the education needed to earn a good living, you may eventually be able to get a reduction in the amount, or a dismissal, of your spousal support payments.

In many situations, however, it isn't realistic to limit the maintenance to a specific period of time. If you are middle-aged or older when you divorce and have never worked outside the home or have not done so in many years, this is particularly true. As a woman, you may have a very hard time finding good employment or even getting into the job market at all. In such cases, a maintenance agreement or order may be expressed to last during your and your ex-spouses joint lives or until you remarry.

If you are a mother who views raising your children as a full-time job, you may face a dilemma. If you begin preparing yourself for the possibility of divorce by getting the education and training you need to be employable should your marriage end, you not only take time away from what you see as your primary job (child rearing) but you also get less maintenance when you do divorce. On the other hand, if you don't prepare yourself for the job market while you're still married, you receive more maintenance to begin with but will not be as prepared to support yourself when the maintenance ends (which it may eventually do).

Out of pride or a desire to be 100 per cent free of your spouse, don't summarily dismiss the idea of asking for maintenance. If you believe that you need time to become competitive in today's fast-changing and skill-orientated job market, your wisest course of action may be to swallow your pride and ask your spouse for financial help.

How the Courts View Maintenance

You may wonder whether maintenance is appropriate for your divorce, and the truth is, you won't have any hard and fast rules to go by. Maintenance-related decisions are made on a case-by-case basis, and there is no formula to help you decide the amount such as there is with child maintenance (child support). As with all decisions about finances in divorce, if you don't agree on the question of maintenance between you, the judge has a very wide discretion to decide on it for you, and that might include dismissing your claims altogether, or awarding more or less than you were hoping for.

A court rarely dismisses your own maintenance claims without your consent if you are the main carer of your children and the children are still dependent. However, a judge might only award you a *nominal* maintenance order such as 5p per annum. That nominal order, even though it has no immediate financial value, acts as a safety net because it allows you to apply to increase, or capitalise, the amount should you ever need to do so. (See 'Opting for Taking Capital Instead of Maintenance' later in this chapter.) However, once your maintenance claims have been *dismissed* they cannot be reinstated, capitalised, or varied, whether you consented to their dismissal or not. As maintenance orders are rare in Scotland, nominal maintenance orders don't exist.

If your maintenance is only going to last for a fixed period of time, the order may specify that it isn't possible for you to apply to extend that order. This is known as a *Section 28 bar*. If the order makes no such reference, it may be possible for you to apply to extend the order if you think you have grounds to do so.

When you agree to your maintenance claims being dismissed, or a judge orders it, this is sometimes referred to as an *income clean break*.

If your ex-spouse isn't living up to their maintenance obligation, you can try to enforce that obligation by asking the court to make any one of a number of orders. The most common orders include the following:

- ✔ **An attachment of earnings order,** which means that your spouse's employer will have to deduct your maintenance regularly from your spouse's wages or salary and send it to you, with payment of the balance to your spouse. In Scotland, this is known as an *arrestment of earnings*.

- ✔ **Registration of your maintenance order in the Magistrates court,** in which case the Magistrates' clerk will take over enforcement on your behalf.

- ✔ **A *garnishee* order for the arrears,** which means that you can take the money that is due to you from your spouse's bank or building society account. This is known as an *arrestment of the account* in Scotland.

- ✔ **A judgement summons, or order for committal,** which means that your spouse will be at risk of going to prison if he or she does not pay the arrears. This is only likely if there has been *wilful refusal.*

- ✔ **A charging order,** which means that you may be able to enforce the arrears through an order for sale of one of your spouse's assets.

- ✔ **Another alternative is to ask the judge to dismiss your maintenance order in return for a lump sum or asset similar in value to (or possibly slightly less than) the total amount of maintenance that you would have been due to receive.** See 'Opting for Taking Capital Instead of Maintenance' later in this chapter.

Factors a judge considers

Unless one of you makes a formal application to the court for maintenance, you and your spouse must decide on your own about maintenance, possibly with the help of your lawyers. To help guide you in your decision, the following is a list of factors a judge considers when ruling on maintenance. The greater the number of factors that apply to your marriage, the stronger your argument for maintenance.

- ✔ You have been married for a long time. You won't find a legal definition of 'long time' when it comes to marriage. However, if your marriage is less than seven years old, a judge probably won't treat it as a long-term marriage – although it may feel like an eternity to you!

- ✔ Your spouse makes significantly more money than you do and can be expected to continue doing so, at least for the immediate future.

- ✔ Your age or health status make earning a good living nearly impossible.

- ✔ You have made significant contributions to your marriage or to your spouse's career. For example, you gave up your career to be a full-time parent, you continued to work throughout your marriage and let your career take a back seat to your spouse's so that you could help him or her advance professionally, or you helped build your spouse's business.

- ✔ Your educational background or employment history puts you at a disadvantage in the job marketplace.

- ✔ You will be your children's primary carer, making the pursuit of a career immediately after your divorce a difficult task.

- ✔ You do not have other sources of regular income, such as income from trusts, property, or investments.

- ✔ You are leaving your marriage with less capital than you might normally expect.

- ✔ You will have sole care of your children and one or more of them has special needs – perhaps due to serious physical or emotional disabilities or health problems – that preclude your working or that allow you to work only on a part-time basis.

In Scotland, orders for spousal maintenance following the divorce are the exception rather than the rule, and even if otherwise appropriate, they are unlikely to be made if the situation can be dealt with by a different sort of order such as payment of a capital sum or transfer of property.

Ideally, judges would like to see the lifestyle you enjoyed when you were married continue after your divorce, but in reality, they know that most ex-spouses do not make enough money to support two households equally well, not even for a short period of time. However, a judge can try to make sure that the two of you don't end up with very different standards of living, particularly if your children are going to spend time with both of you.

Your conduct towards each other during and after your marriage rarely makes any difference to the order that a judge makes for maintenance as the judge regards your conduct as a matter between the two of you. The law says that conduct should only be taken into account if it is *inequitable in the judge's opinion to ignore it.* This means that if, for example, your spouse has injured you so badly that your earning capacity has been adversely affected, a judge is more likely to award you maintenance as a result.

Watch out for unfair arrangements

There is no 100 per cent guarantee that you'll actually see the maintenance your spouse is supposed to pay you. Depending on your circumstances, you may have little legal recourse if your former spouse doesn't pay up. So, working out the best way to structure your maintenance arrangement can be a bit of a gamble.

When it comes to income, divorce is still harder on women than men despite the large numbers of women who work outside the home. Most women, even those who receive maintenance, experience a drop in their standard of living after their marriage ends. However, some divorced men experience the same financial consequences.

Taking Capital Instead of Maintenance

You can choose to receive your maintenance in the form of a lump sum or other capital asset instead of taking it as a series of payments over time. This is known as *capitalising the maintenance.* Capitalising your maintenance can be particularly attractive if you don't trust your ex-spouse to live up to an agreement that provides for payments over time or if you're concerned that his or her financial situation may deteriorate after your divorce. It may also be a useful bargaining tool if there is a particular asset that you need as part of your settlement, such as the house, but there are not enough other assets to meet your spouse's claims. Many spouses who are at risk of a maintenance order against them prefer the certainty of giving a bit more capital now in return for a dismissal of your maintenance claims.

Be sure that the lump sum or capital asset that your spouse offers you is adequate. Don't assume just because it sounds like a lot of money that you're getting a fair amount, especially if the asset doesn't produce an income flow or your spouse wants you to take the lump sum in lieu of other capital assets. Talk with a family law solicitor or possibly an independent financial adviser as well before you sign any paperwork.

Consider the consequences of capitalising your maintenance and what you can do to mitigate those consequences before you agree to accept a lump-sum payment. If you are dependent on Income Support from the Benefits Agency for part or all of your income, the Agency treats the lump sum as if it were maintenance and deducts a corresponding amount from your Income

Support each week until they regard the lump sum as paid up, so you may end up little better off. Also, if you have had the benefit of any legal aid or public funding to pay for your divorce expenses, the Legal Services Commission expects you to pay back your costs to them out of your lump sum as part of the *statutory charge,* whereas they do not expect you to do this out of your maintenance. (An exception to this rule may be made if you have reached an agreement through the use of mediation. See Chapter 7 for more on legal aid and how the statutory charge works.)

If you take a lump-sum payment and then put the full amount in your bank account, you may end up spending it all at once. The larger the sum, the more important it is that you have an investment plan that maximises the interest you can earn on the money and gives you ready access to at least a portion of it.

If you are giving your spouse a lump sum or other capital in lieu of regular maintenance, get the help of a family lawyer and possibly a financial adviser as well before you sign your agreement. If you think that your spouse is likely to remarry in the near future, you may be better off agreeing to maintenance now because the maintenance will cease in any event on your spouse's remarriage.

Seeking a Change in Maintenance

As long as your maintenance claims haven't been dismissed, the amount of maintenance you receive may be increased or decreased after your divorce is final, under certain circumstances.

- ✔ The amount can change if you and your former spouse both agree to the change.
- ✔ The amount of maintenance you receive can also change if the court orders it.

Some couples agree to include in their divorce settlement provision for an automatic review of, or change in, the amount of maintenance every year or so, perhaps in line with inflation. If you and your spouse agree to something on those lines, your maintenance should not lose value through inflation. It's up to the two of you to implement that agreement; you do not have to refer to the court.

If you don't have any provision for an automatic change in the amount of maintenance payments, you and your ex-spouse can still agree a change, but then it's a good idea to formalise the agreement by applying to the court for a change to the terms of your original order court. You can do this by consent and by post, but you usually have to pay a court fee.

If you and your spouse are not able to agree on a change in the rate of maintenance, one or other of you may make an application to the court. You need to support your application with a statement or *affidavit* (an affidavit is a statement that you sign on oath in front of an officer of the court or any solicitor other than your own) setting out the reasons why you believe that a change is justified and what you think a fair amount is. If you think that your spouse is going to object to the application, weigh the costs of making such an application against the benefit of the change in maintenance that is likely to be ordered *before* you make your application. A family lawyer should be able to advise you on your prospects, but the judge has the ultimate discretion to decide.

Preparing for Life without Maintenance

Unless you have a *secured periodical payments order,* your maintenance payments stop when your spouse dies. Secured periodical payments orders are very rare these days and occur only when the paying spouse has substantial spare capital assets or property against which such an order or maintenance can be secured. In the absence of a secured periodical payments order, you do not have a legal right to be paid maintenance by your ex-spouse's estate. Obviously, if those payments are an important source of income for you, the death of your ex-spouse may be financially devastating for you.

If you live in Scotland and have the benefit of a periodical allowance, your payments don't automatically cease on your spouse's death, but the executors of your spouse's estate must make an application to the court to terminate the payments. Sometimes the court orders payment at a reduced rate or sets a time limit on the allowance, rather than terminating it.

Although death can come unexpectedly to people of any age, this issue may be of particular concern to you if you are ending your marriage to a spouse who is elderly or in poor health. This issue can be addressed by your spouse purchasing a life insurance policy and naming you as beneficiary or by your taking out a maintenance protection policy. A good independent financial adviser or your solicitor should be able to tell you about your options.

Another important point is that a spouse or ex-spouse who has the benefit of a maintenance order has the right to make a claim against the paying spouse's estate under the Inheritance (Provision for Family and Dependents) Act 1975, if the paying spouse did not make reasonable financial provision on his or her death. (This is not the case in Scotland, though if they're still married, they may have other rights.) The court looks at what the deceased spouse's financial position was on death and what other responsibilities he or she had in deciding what reasonable financial provision would be. If a spouse's maintenance claims have been dismissed by the court, whether by consent or not, there is almost always an order preventing that spouse from claiming against the estate as well.

Maintenance and Tax

Tax relief on maintenance payments that you *make* to your spouse has been abolished since April 2000, unless one of you is over 65, and even then the relief that you can claim is limited and modest in amount. Maintenance payments that you *receive* are not taxable, nor will they have any effect on any child support payments that your spouse is liable to pay.

Don't make your maintenance payments in cash without getting a written receipt. If you do, you won't have a record of your payments and if any question arises concerning how much you may have paid your former spouse, or exactly when you made a particular maintenance payment, you'll lack the documentation you need.

Chapter 13

Providing Financially for Your Children

*A*s a parent, you have a moral and legal responsibility to support your dependent children so that they have a roof over their heads, clothes to wear, enough food to eat, and an education – the basics, in other words. Divorce doesn't change this obligation whether your children live with you or with your ex. If you have dependent children, deciding how to share the cost of raising your children is a key issue in your divorce.

This chapter explains which parent usually pays child support to the other and how the Child Support Agency determines a minimum level of support. We also help prepare you to negotiate your child support agreement and explain when the court might become involved. We also cover what expenses beyond the basics that you should include in your divorce agreement – or that a judge orders you to pay.

Supporting Your Children

Child support is an amount of money one parent pays to the other, after the couple is separated, to help cover the cost of bringing up their dependent children.

Since 1993, the Child Support Agency (*CSA*) has been the statutory agency primarily responsible for determining the amount of child support due in each case. The CSA now has much of the power to decide child support issues that used to belong to the courts. Although it's still possible that you both can reach an agreement on child support, neither you nor your ex can prevent the other from applying to the CSA for a calculation of liability – except where an order for child maintenance has been made prior to March 2003 or if you have a written maintenance agreement from before April 1993.

You don't have to wait for divorce proceedings to apply to the CSA for a calculation of the amount; you just have to be living apart from your spouse. Either of you can apply to the CSA once you have separated and there is no fee. Historically, the CSA has been dogged by long delays; currently it has a target time of six weeks to deal with each application. Errors in the calculation of liability are likely to be less frequent now that the formula has been simplified.

Check out the CSA Web site at www.csa.gov.uk for details on the formula the CSA uses to calculate support. The principles on which the CSA base their calculations of liability are the following:

✔ The number of qualifying children the child maintenance is for

✔ The non-resident parent's net income and circumstances

✔ The number of children living with the non-resident parent (the CSA calls these children 'relevant other children')

Caring for your children all the time

Ordinarily, when one parent has primary care of the children (the *parent with care*), the other parent (the *non-resident parent*) is obliged to pay child support. If your ex-spouse was a stepparent and not the biological or adoptive parent of the child, the CSA has no jurisdiction to require him to pay child support; however, see the section later in this chapter 'Applying to the court: Special circumstances a judge may consider'. (The parent with primary care is usually regarded as meeting his child support obligation by raising the children. In fact, he typically spends as much as three times the amount of money as the non-resident parent on their children's necessities!)

The amount of child support due is based on the non-resident parent's net income and won't take account of

✔ Your income

✔ The income of either parents' current partner

✔ Either parents' housing costs

✔ Either parents' travel to work costs

Sharing your children's care

If you and your ex-spouse share the care of your children, one parent, usually the parent who receives the Child Benefit (see the section later in this chapter on 'Claiming the Child Benefit'), is designated the parent with care. The other parent is liable to pay child support at a reduced rate. The CSA bases this rate on the proportion of nights spent with each parent. Supporting your children when you share care can take two forms:

- ✔ **Splitting care equally:** If you share the care of your children on a 50:50 basis and are designated the parent with care, you will probably still receive child support from your spouse. For example, if the CSA calculates a monthly child support amount of £350 to be paid by your spouse but your children spend half of their time living with each of you, your spouse is only required to pay you £175 of support per month.

- ✔ **Sharing care in other ways:** If you and your ex-spouse share the care of the children in different proportions, then the CSA allows a reduction in their non-resident parent's child support payments in proportion to the average number of nights the children spend with him. For example, if you are the non-resident parent and the children spend an average of one night per week with you, your liability, say £350, is reduced by one-seventh to £300 and if they spend an average of two nights per week with you, your liability is reduced by two-sevenths to £250. The average number of nights is worked out over a period of one year.

Working Out What You Pay or Receive

The amount of maintenance or child support is based on the non-resident parent's net income only. For most people this means your earnings after any tax, National Insurance, and pension contributions are taken off. If you are self-employed, then it means your gross profit after tax, National Insurance, and pension contributions. For non-resident parents whose income is £200 or more per week, the rates are:

- ✔ 15 per cent of your net income if you have one child
- ✔ 20 per cent of your net income if you have two children
- ✔ 25 per cent of your net income if you have three or more children

If you have an income of less than £200 per week you pay a reduced rate of maintenance. Non-resident parents with a net income of £100 or less, and those on certain benefits such as Income Support or Jobseeker's Allowance, pay a flat rate of £5 per week (unless the child stays overnight for an average of at least 52 nights each year and then no child support payment is required).

A few people – such as full-time students and prisoners – won't have to pay anything. Payment for a non-resident parent is reduced in the same way if there are any other children living in their household, including stepchildren.

Your child support payments are also reduced if your children stay with you for at least 52 nights per year – refer to the section 'Sharing your children's care' earlier in this chapter for details.

The CSA limits the amount of net income it can consider for child support to £2,000 per month.

If you pay maintenance to your spouse voluntarily and you think the CSA may become involved, try to agree with your spouse in advance how much of these payments represent child support, as that amount can be credited to you by the CSA whilst the calculation is being carried out.

The formula for calculating child support payments can only be varied in very limited circumstances, including

- ✔ An allowance for special expenses, such as contact costs, prior debts, boarding school fees, and payment of the mortgage for your spouse. These special expenses cannot be less than £10 to £15 per week if they are to be taken into account for the non-resident parent.

- ✔ You believe, as the parent with care, that the calculation is unduly favourable to your ex-spouse because, for example, she has assets worth over £65,000 or her declared income and lifestyle are inconsistent.

If you're a non-resident parent and you don't co-operate with the CSA, the CSA can make assumptions about your income and impose an interim maintenance decision. The CSA also has wide powers, including disqualifying you from driving, to enforce child support payments.

Getting state benefits and tax credits

If you are on Income Support or income-based Jobseeker's Allowance, the CSA considers you to have made an application for child support unless you can claim 'good cause' for opting out. For example, if your ex-spouse is likely to be violent to you or the children if the CSA become involved, you may not want to apply to the CSA. If you don't have good cause and don't co-operate with the CSA, your benefits may be reduced. Once the CSA has made an assessment of your spouse's liability, you are allowed to keep only the first £10 per week that he or she pays. The rest will be taken by the Benefits Agency to help pay for your Income Support or Jobseeker's Allowance. So, if you're granted £50 per week of child support, but get £100 per week Income Support, you'll have a total of £110 per week, as £40 of the child support money goes directly to the Benefits Agency.

However, child support payments that you receive as the parent with care are ignored completely in calculating your entitlement to Working Tax Credit. If you pay child support to your ex-spouse, any Working Tax Credit you receive may be considered part of your income, depending on your net income compared with your ex-spouse's.

For more information, have a look at the Web site for the Inland Revenue (www.inlandrevenue.gov.uk/taxcredits) or visit the CSA Web site at www.csa.gov.uk. You can also try the CSA information line on 0845 600 6610, or write to the Child Support Agency FREEPOST NWW7938A Liverpool L2 6ZA.

If you're in Scotland, you can contact One Parent Families Scotland (www.opfs.org.uk) for more information. For help in Northern Ireland, visit the Child Support Agency's Web site on www.dsdni.gov/childsupportagency.

Claiming the Child Benefit

Child Benefit is payable regardless of your income to anyone responsible for, and living with, a child under the age of 16, or under 19 and in full-time education. Currently, in 2004, it amounts to £16.05 for the eldest child and £10.75 for any other child. Some lone parents may be entitled to a little more. Check the rates each year as they are subject to change.

So, if your children mainly live with you, you are entitled to claim the Child Benefit for them. If you and your ex-spouse share the care of your children equally, the Child Benefit will normally be paid to the woman unless you agree otherwise. Alternatively, you may claim the Child Benefit for one child, and your ex-spouse may claim it for another child. Contact the Inland Revenue (www.inlandrevenue.gov.uk) or the Department for Work and Pensions (www.dwp.gov.uk) for more information.

Receiving the Child Tax Credit

Like the Child Benefit, Child Tax Credit (CTC) is also paid to the main carer of children under 16, or under 19 and in full-time education. You can qualify for the Child Tax Credit whether you are employed or not, but it's dependent on your means – your income must be less than £55,000 per annum. An amount is paid for each child in the household and extra money is available if you have a child with special needs, or a child under one year old. So, as with Child Benefit, whether this extra source of income is available to you or not depends partly on whether or not you're considered the children's main carer. If you share the care of the children equally between you, the Child Tax Credit will normally be paid to the woman unless you agree otherwise.

Qualifying for the Working Tax Credit

If you are working, you may be entitled to claim Working Tax Credit (WTC), depending on the number of hours that you work and your income. Working Tax Credit is more generous if you have children and you are their main carer, and in addition you may get some help with their childcare costs. Single parents are also able to keep all of their maintenance payments and still claim Working Tax Credits. For more information, read *One Parent Families Today, the Facts* published by the National Council for One Parent Families (www. oneparentfamilies.org.uk).

Applying to the court: Special circumstances a judge may consider

The court's powers to determine child support payments (also known as *child maintenance* or *periodical payments for the child*) have been greatly limited since the Child Support Act 1991 came into effect in April 1993 and the power to determine most child support payments went to the Child Support Agency. The main circumstances in which a court can make an order for such payments are limited to the following:

- ✔ You both, as parents, agree on an amount of child support and ask the court to make an order by agreement.

- ✔ You, as the parent with care, ask the court to make an order to top up the child support calculated by the CSA where your ex-spouse has a net income of over £2,000 per month.

- ✔ Your child has special needs.

- ✔ You want an order for payment of school fees.

- ✔ You aren't the natural parent of the child but have treated the child as a child of the family.

- ✔ Your child is still in full-time education but over the age of 19, though if she's over 18 she must make the application herself.

If you have a court order for child maintenance which predates 3 March 2003, or a written maintenance agreement dated prior to April 1993, the CSA cannot get involved with the calculation of the payments (unless the parent with care is on Income Support – in this case the CSA will automatically get involved). If you want to change the level of, or enforce, child support, you have to go back to court to do it. If your court order postdates 3 March 2003, the CSA can become involved if either of you applies to it not less than one year after the order for child support was made. The CSA will then take over responsibility for calculating and enforcing the payments.

Bear in mind that when deciding whether to have a court order for support or to go through the CSA, one or both of you will be responsible for the costs of making an application to the court to vary or enforce the order, whereas the CSA doesn't charge for doing this on your behalf.

If a judge is involved in determining the level of child support, he or she has to put the needs of the children first and consider a whole range of factors including the income, needs, and resources of each of you and the children, as well as any mental or physical disability of the children, and the manner in which your children were being, or expected to be, educated.

Until the early 1990s, it was not uncommon for couples to agree a 'clean break' financial settlement on divorce which gave the parent with care the family home or a bigger share of the assets in return for an agreement that the non-resident parent would not pay any child support. Since the introduction of the Child Support Act 1993, such agreements have become unworkable (although the CSA will honour these agreements to some extent if they were made before April 1993 and part of a court order).

The reality is that the law here has never formally recognised clean break orders when it comes to children. Although it is legally possible for a spouse to agree to dismiss his or her own claims (Chapter 12 tells you more about this), you can never completely dismiss claims for a child. So now, if you as the non-resident parent agree to transfer the house to your ex in return for her not claiming child support, you won't be able to hold her to that agreement or prevent her from applying to the CSA for a calculation of your liability, and the CSA will not make any allowance for the transfer of the house.

Agreeing on Extra Expenses

There are a number of other expenses that are associated with the upbringing and support of children that you may or may not agree to pay. Among these possible expenses are

- ✔ Life insurance, where your children are the beneficiaries
- ✔ Private health care
- ✔ Disability insurance

Purchasing life insurance for your children's benefit

If you die while your children are still dependent on your financial support, life insurance proceeds help provide for their care. You may want to provide your ex-spouse with proof every year that your life insurance policy continues to be in force. If you and your ex-spouse decide to share the cost of bringing up your children, you should both purchase life insurance policies.

You must appoint a trustee – an adult who would manage the policy proceeds on behalf of your kids should you die before they're of age. Your ex-spouse is a logical choice, assuming that he or she can be trusted to manage the money responsibly. However, the trustee can be another financially responsible adult.

Providing private medical cover

Usually, if you have private medical cover, the parent with employer-sponsored medical insurance maintains the children on his or her policy. Private health insurance may not cover all medical expenses – dental or orthodontia expenses and glasses, for example, may be excluded. Nor does private health insurance pay 100 per cent of covered medical expenses. Therefore, you and your ex-spouse have to decide how those costs will be shared. If you are the parent with primary care, unless these costs are specifically dealt with during your divorce negotiations, you may end up having to cover those expenses. You may include private health care as part of your child support agreement. However, if this is the case, check the details of your spouse's health plan before you come to a final agreement about child support.

These days, some private health plans cover all medical expenses if you pay a little more each month than the standard premium, or provide a lower level of medical expense reimbursement if you use doctors 'outside the plan' – something that may be important to you if your kids are currently being treated by doctors who aren't on the list of preferred providers issued under your insurance plan. You and your ex-spouse should decide how to deal with these and other possible issues related to the scope and cost of your private medical cover.

Purchasing disability insurance

Disability insurance provides a working parent with a percentage of his or her income if he or she becomes unable to work due to illness or injury. Carrying disability insurance is more common when the parent paying child support is self-employed.

Disability insurance is especially important if a parent's business is a sole proprietorship, a partnership, or a small limited company. In such businesses, the active involvement of the business owner is critical to the business's financial success. If the owner becomes incapacitated due to illness or an accident, he or she will have little or no income and would probably be unable to meet his or her child support obligation after a period of time.

Even if your children are very young, do not overlook the issue of how you will fund their college education – you can't start saving too soon for this major expense.

Providing 'extras' for your children

Gifts, trips, clothes, and anything else that you give a child because you *want* to (and not because you *have* to) do *not* necessarily count as child support when you have a court order or CSA assessment for the support. Therefore, you can usually assume that if you're paying child support, you *cannot* deduct the value of those gifts from the total amount of support you are obliged to pay. To be certain, however, check with your solicitor if you can't agree with your spouse.

If you initiated your divorce and feel guilty about its likely effect on your children, don't try to ease your guilt by agreeing to pay more support than you can really afford. If you have a hard time coming up with the payments after your divorce, you could find yourself in legal trouble if your former spouse takes you to court to enforce the terms of your child support agreement.

Calculating your share of child support 'extras'

Under the CSA, child support is essentially a regular amount that is presumed to provide adequate support for a child. But that amount may not cover the 'extras' you want your children to have – private education, music or other lessons, holiday courses, sports gear, or extra tutoring, for example. If a judge is deciding child support in your divorce and you want certain extras to be included in the court order, you must ask the judge to consider those special expenditures in the child support amount or through an order for payment of school fees.

Even if you agree that you will be sharing responsibility for paying the basic day-to-day costs of your children's care, you still have to decide which extras to fund and how to split the cost of any big extras you both feel your children need.

It's a good idea to first calculate how you will split the cost of special activities and other extras for your kids. One easy way to calculate the split is for each of you to pay a percentage of the cost of the extras based on your individual incomes relative to your total combined income.

For example, assume that the total annual cost of the extras you want to fund is £5,000, and that you earn £40,000 a year and your spouse earns £45,000 a year, for a total combined annual income of £85,000. In this case, your income would represent 47 per cent of the total, and your spouse's income represents 53 per cent of the total. If you applied these percentages to the £5,000 total cost of the extras, in order to pay for them you would contribute £2,350 a year, and your spouse's share would be £2,650. Realistically speaking, given the cost of maintaining two households, you may not have enough money left over to give your children all the extras they've become used to or you want to provide – or paying for them will require some cutbacks in your post-divorce budgets.

Negotiating Your Own Child Support Agreement

Like almost everything else to do with divorce that you can accomplish without the help of a court, negotiating your own child support agreement has its advantages, for example

- ✔ The negotiation process encourages both of you to assume equal responsibility for deciding how you will take care of the financial needs of your children.

  Mothers often end up being their children's financial advocates in divorce court cases. Sometimes – whether it's true or not – it can appear to their spouses that mothers are really arguing on their own behalf, not for their kids.

- ✔ Negotiating together reinforces the fact that although your marital relationship is changing, you have a relationship as parents and you are both legally responsible for your children's welfare.

- ✔ Working things out together also helps increase the likelihood that once you are divorced, the parent who is obliged to pay child support will actually do so.

Your child support agreement should clearly spell out how child support will be paid, how often it will be paid, the amount of each payment, and the date by which it must be paid. Preparing a child support agreement that will meet the approval of a court requires legal help. Judges look for a tightly drafted agreement that leaves little open to question.

Increases in the *inflation rate* ultimately decrease the value of the child support you receive. A practical way of dealing with this potential problem is to build into your agreement increases in the amount of child support your ex-spouse must pay you that are in line with inflation. Or, if you have a court order for child support without any such built-in increase, you can ask a judge to order an increase. If your child support has been worked out by the CSA, the CSA will automatically review it every two years.

Ensuring that child support will be paid

Don't underestimate the importance of working out a parenting plan and using a negotiated agreement which will help ensure that your ex-spouse pays child support as agreed. (Refer to Chapter 10 for more on parenting plans.) According to the CSA there is a marked relationship between the amount of child contact and the payment of child support. Just consider the following facts:

- ✔ 93 per cent of non-resident parents who see their child at least once every two weeks, pay something

- ✔ Only 69 per cent of non-resident parents who see their children less often than once every two weeks, pay child support.

Changing the agreement as your lives change

Another advantage to negotiating your own child support agreement is that you and your spouse can craft one that readily allows you to anticipate and accommodate changes in your lives and in the lives of your children over the years. For example, you can spell out how you will deal with future possible expenses related to your children – such as orthodontics, sports, extracurricular school activities, clubs, an opportunity to study abroad, and student fees. (American research suggests that children from divorced families often suffer financially when they get beyond 18 and enter higher education.) You can also deal with salary increases or decreases either of you may experience.

Having all of this worked out ahead of time will save you time and money later on. Otherwise, every time you want to change something relating to your child support agreement, you will have to apply to the court for a variation, show good cause why you ought to get more child support, and get a new court order, assuming that the judge approves your request.

The courts aren't bound to honour provisions you include in a pre-nuptial agreement concerning the care or support of your children. The judge has the ultimate discretion when it comes to the question of care or residence, and the authority of the CSA almost always prevails now in questions of child support.

Making Sure the Child Support Gets Paid

You have no way of knowing what the future will bring, and the truth is that being single again sometimes changes the priorities of a previously devoted parent. As a result, that parent may begin to take his or her child support obligations less seriously. Or, if you and your former spouse fall out, your ex may decide to withhold child support as a way to get back at you. Other developments that can affect your former spouse's commitment to your child support agreement include the following:

- ✔ A new marriage
- ✔ Another child
- ✔ Excessive debt
- ✔ A failing business
- ✔ Substance abuse problems

Getting a court order

If you negotiate your own child support agreement, it's usually best to submit the agreement to the court for approval so that you have a consent order within the divorce. This precaution is an important one even if you believe that your spouse is totally trustworthy and you're certain that he or she will live up to your agreement.

Without a court order for child support, you will not have the full force of the law behind you should your former spouse stop making regular child support payments, begin paying less than he or she is supposed to, or fail to make any payments at all. Chapter 20 has additional information on what you can do if you begin to have trouble in getting your child support.

Using automatic deductions from wages

If your spouse fails to make the regular payments due to you either through the CSA or under a court order, you can arrange for the payments to be deducted from your spouse's salary and paid to you or the CSA by his or her employer. This is known as an *attachment of earnings order* if it's done through the court, or a *deduction from earnings order* if done through the CSA.

The errant parent's employer is served with a court order for the deduction and if that employer fails to comply with the court order, the *employer* is in breach of the order and subject to penalties. The deduction from earnings option doesn't help you collect the payments due if your former spouse is self-employed.

If your former spouse has a stable work history, the deduction from earnings option is an excellent way to ensure that you get the child support you need. But it isn't as effective if your ex-spouse regularly changes jobs – you have to be sure that each new employer is served with a new attachment of earnings court order or CSA deduction from earnings order – and it's particularly difficult to enforce if you don't know about the job changes.

To help deal with these potential problems, and if your spouse is willing, your consent order can state that your ex-spouse has to let you know whenever he or she changes jobs. Also, the court order for attachment of earnings requires your former spouse's employers to inform you and the court of any change in his or her employment status. Despite these safeguards, it's possible that you won't receive notification of any changes in your former spouse's job situation or the notification may not come on a timely basis.

Initially, your spouse may resist the idea of having child support payments automatically deducted from his or her wages (the automatic deductions may seem like an invasion of privacy or your ex-spouse may think the automatic deductions make him or her appear dishonest or unreliable). Automatic deductions are mainly used when the payer has defaulted on their payments. However, it does make paying child support somewhat hassle free and your ex may end up appreciating the automatic deduction. Plus, he or she may find it easier to manage his or her money if the child support is already taken care of and the rest of the paycheque can be spent as needed.

When Do Child Support Obligations Cease?

Ordinarily, a parent's child support obligation through the CSA ends when a child reaches 16 years of age, or until their nineteenth birthday if the child is still in full-time secondary education. However, that obligation can continue through the court while your child is a full-time college student or is attending a full-time vocational course. But, degree or no degree, your responsibility to provide child support typically ends once the child reaches his or her early twenties.

If you pay child support under a court order and your child moves in with you on a full-time, permanent basis, ask the court for an order cancelling your child support obligation. If you don't, your legal obligation to pay child support to your former spouse continues. If you are paying child support under a CSA decision, ask the CSA for a *supercession*. The CSA makes a completely new decision, backdating this to the date of your application.

Child Support and Tax

As far as adjustments to taxable income go, if you are paying child support, you *cannot* claim your payments as a tax deduction. If you are receiving child support, you do not have to claim it as income and you won't pay tax on it.

The parent who receives the Child Benefit is usually assumed by the CSA and the Inland Revenue to be the parent entitled to receive child support and the Child Tax Credit. (See the section 'Receiving the Child Tax Credit' earlier in this chapter.) Even if you're sharing the care of your children on a 50:50 basis, the Benefits Agency and Inland Revenue can't split the Child Benefit or Child Tax Credit between you. If, however, you have more than one child, you can agree that one parent claims for one child and the other parent claims for another. That way it's possible for each of you to have the benefit of the Child Benefit, Child Tax Credit, and child support for at least one child. You may each be entitled to claim Working Tax Credit as well. See Chapter 7 and the section 'Getting state benefits and tax credits' earlier in this chapter for more on the generous tax credits that are available to families with children or to families on low incomes.

Part IV
Working Out the Terms of Your Divorce Agreement

'Are you sure this is a genuine mediator?'

In this part . . .

*I*f you and your spouse hope to negotiate your divorce co-operatively and, where possible, together, this part of the book is helpful. It provides a framework for negotiating, tells you how your negotiating can be supported by both mediation and your family solicitor, and when you should get legal help. If you have children, it will help you focus on their needs as well as on your own futures.

We also explain the important role that mediation can play in helping you and your spouse avoid the expense and emotional trauma of a divorce trial. We offer tips on finding the best family solicitor for your situation, and tell you how to build and fund a mutually co-operative partnership with him or her as your divorce proceeds.

If, in the end, you fail to negotiate a co-operative divorce settlement with your spouse, the last chapter in this part gives you a taste of the divorce court process. At that point, the big decisions are left up to the judge.

Chapter 14

Doing (Some of) the Negotiating Yourself

*N*egotiating your own divorce agreement (or at least some of it) can definitely save you money on solicitors' fees and court costs. But it does require that you work in a co-operative way with your soon-to-be ex-spouse, which can be a challenge. You both have to be very sure that you are on good enough terms to attempt it. No mediator will be in the room with you to keep your meetings civilised and productive, nor will you have a solicitor to do the negotiating for you.

Although we don't tell you *what* to decide (that's up to you), we do try to prepare you to make good decisions by suggesting how to plan and organise your negotiation sessions and by offering some basic negotiating advice. In this chapter, we also provide a primer on the basic issues that you may have to resolve before you and your spouse can make your divorce legal.

First, a Word of Caution

When you read this chapter, keep in mind that the plan of action we describe is an ideal scenario to try for. Realistically, you may not have the desire or inclination to do *everything* we recommend, which is fine and understandable. Just accomplish what you can – you can still save yourself time and money.

Be warned that negotiating on your own is not for every couple and can be downright dangerous for some. When you negotiate on your own, you are less protected than in mediation, when your solicitors negotiate on your behalf, or in court. You may end up with a number of problems: A divorce agreement that gives you less than you're legally entitled to, a parenting plan that is emotionally harmful to your children, or an agreement that is completely unenforceable.

What you say to your spouse during your negotiations can be used against you if you end up in court, unless you and your spouse have a written agreement that guarantees that whatever you say during your one-to-one negotiations remains confidential. If you don't have such a written agreement, what you say to your spouse may come back to haunt you. For example, if you use mediation you must sign an Agreement to Mediate which deals with safeguarding the confidentiality of your discussions and its limits and exceptions. (Mediation is covered more fully in Chapter 16.)

Rule Number One: Be on Your Best Behaviour

Successful negotiation takes hard work on your part, a commitment to the negotiation process, and a willingness to act like mature adults. That's a tall order for many happily married couples, let alone those who are splitting up. You and your spouse have to sit down together, one-to-one, talk honestly, work out how to solve your problems in a rational manner, and be willing to give as well as take. Treat one another fairly and politely during your negotiations. If you don't, your negotiations are apt to become more than a little painful and a harsh reminder of why you are getting divorced in the first place.

Negotiating your own divorce means that both of you must

- ✔ Let reason, not emotions, rule.

- ✔ Listen without interrupting one another. Waiting to have your say can be tough to do, especially if you don't like what you're hearing.

- ✔ Resist forming a response to what your spouse is saying while he's still talking. Stay cool. If something your spouse says or does during a negotiating session upsets you, bite your tongue. Try not to respond in the heat of the moment.

- ✔ Allow your spouse to express his opinions and respect what he has to say. Ridiculing his choice of words is one way to put him on the defensive and shut down two-way communications entirely.

✔ Be open to compromise. Neither of you will get everything you want from your divorce, so be ready to make some trade-offs.

✔ Avoid using intimidation and threats to get what you want. Tactics like that will backfire on you.

✔ Be honest and polite.

When you and your spouse are negotiating, stay seated. If you stand or walk around and talk to your spouse at the same time, you are less apt to hear what your spouse is saying and more apt to get over emotional.

Starting Off on the Right Foot: The Preliminaries

If you and your spouse want to get your negotiations over with as quickly as possible, it isn't surprising. But taking the time to plan how you will negotiate can mean the difference between progress and frustration. Ideally, before you begin your formal negotiations, you and your spouse will decide the following:

✔ When and where to negotiate

✔ What issue(s) you plan to address at each negotiation session

Unless your divorce is very simple – with little to divide up, no dependent children, and no spousal maintenance – you need more than one session to negotiate it. For example, you may have to wait from time to time for information you require from different agencies, businesses, banks, and so on.

✔ How you will structure your negotiation sessions

✔ What information and documentation you need and what kind of record-keeping system you're going to use to record your progress

Working out seemingly simple things such as when and where to meet for your negotiations can easily lead to a fight. To avoid having that happen, you may want to work out the preliminaries in a public place such as a coffee bar or restaurant. If you meet in a public place, your discussion will be less likely to degenerate into a name-calling session. (Wherever you meet, make sure your conversation can't be overheard.)

Because a deadlock is always possible no matter how hard you try to come to a meeting of minds, you should also decide ahead of time what to do if your decision-making reaches an impasse, perhaps mediation or using solicitors to do your negotiating. You should also decide ahead of time where you will go to get information or clarification when a matter of law or finance arises that you don't understand.

If you and your spouse negotiated a pre-marital agreement prior to your marriage, you may well have less to negotiate. (For an explanation of how these agreements work, turn to Chapter 21.)

Planning a Method of Negotiation

There's no one right way for you to negotiate. A method that works for another couple may not be appropriate for you. However, prior to starting your negotiations, you and your spouse should come to at least a general agreement about how you will structure your negotiation sessions to make them as efficient and effective as possible. The following steps outline one plan of action that may work for your situation:

1. **Prior to tackling a major new issue in your divorce – your parenting plan, child support, or spousal maintenance, or the division of your property – share your goals and priorities with one another and discuss any special concerns you may have.**

   Try to speak in terms of your realistic needs, or your children's realistic needs. Then identify where you agree or disagree and where your shared interests lie.

2. **Develop a list of possible options for settling the issue, keeping in mind your individual goals and priorities, and your areas of agreement and disagreement.**

   When you are identifying your options, be creative and try not to censor or prejudge any ideas. A seemingly silly idea may inspire a new, more practical one that works for both of you. You may each want to develop your own list of options and then share both lists with one another.

3. **Eliminate all the ideas on your list that you both dislike or both agree are unrealistic.**

4. **Using the options that still remain, develop written proposals for resolving whatever issue you are negotiating.**

   You can each develop your own proposal for the issue, present it to one another, and respond with counterproposals, or you can write a proposal together. After you have settled on a decision, put it in writing. Each time you concur on a specific issue, you are that much closer to a final divorce agreement. However, a decision on one point may impact on another, so don't close any doors until you have got the complete picture.

The negotiating process you use doesn't have to be as formal as the one just described. Find a method that you both feel comfortable with and that facilitates a fair resolution of each issue in your divorce.

Choosing the Right Setting

When deciding on a place for your negotiation sessions, pick a quiet, comfortable (but not too comfortable) location that is relatively free of distractions. That probably rules out negotiating in front of the television or any time at home when your children are up and about. Wait until they have gone to sleep or, better still, do your negotiating away from home in a neutral location – in a corner of your local library or in a park, for example.

When you negotiate in a public place, you are more apt to be on your best behaviour, which means that you are less likely to yell at each other, burst into tears, or stomp away in a huff.

Scheduling the Time

Negotiating your divorce agreement will probably take at least a couple of sessions, depending on what you have to resolve and how quickly you and your spouse can come to a consensus on things. Therefore, fix your sessions ahead of time and make them a priority in your life. They should be every bit as important as business meetings, doctors' appointments, parent-teacher meetings, and your children's birthdays.

Set a time to begin and end each session. Generally speaking, your sessions shouldn't run for more than two hours. Longer sessions will probably become unproductive.

Chill out before you storm off

Keeping your cool can be tough to do no matter how hard you try. Old hurts and insecurities may resurface during your negotiations, especially if your spouse exhibits an uncanny knack for pushing your emotional buttons and either deliberately or unwittingly hurts your feelings. Rather than letting your emotions get the better of you or threaten to derail the negotiations, try these alternatives:

✔ Take a short 'time out'. Walk around the block, get a snack, listen to calming music, or read a magazine. Then resume your negotiating.

✔ If you need more than a quick break, tell your spouse you can't continue negotiating and rearrange your negotiation for another time.

✔ Acknowledge that you need third-party help.

Don't rush your negotiations. Take all the time that you need – you're making important decisions that will affect your life and the lives of your children for years to come.

Don't back out of a scheduled session without a very good reason. (Incidentally, wanting to play golf, having dinner with friends, or 'just not feeling like it' are not good reasons.) However, the unexpected does come up, so if one of you has a legitimate reason for rescheduling, try to provide the other with at least a few days' notice.

Deciding on the Order of Business

Develop written agendas for your negotiating sessions and determine ahead of time who will prepare them. You can take turns writing the agendas, or one of you can agree to prepare them all. Whatever you decide, make sure that both of you have a copy of the agenda well in advance of the next negotiating session. Plan to take up the major issues in your divorce in the following order:

- **A parenting plan and child support:** If you have them, your number-one responsibility in your divorce is your children's well-being. See Chapter 10 for tips on developing a parenting plan.

- **Maintenance:** You need to decide whether there is a case for one of you to pay maintenance to the other. Maintenance is covered more fully in Chapter 12.

- **Division of your property:** Remember to include any pensions and outstanding debts you may have.

Using written agendas may sound like needless work, but in fact preparing them ahead of time means that you

- Know what sort of 'homework' you should do before your next session

- Get down to business at the start of each session instead of trying to decide what you will discuss

- Stay on track during a negotiating session because you have a written reminder of what you are supposed to be talking about

When you can't resolve an issue the first time round, agree to return to it later or get outside help. An issue that initially seems unresolvable may be easier to address the next time you tackle it, especially after you and your spouse have a few successful resolutions under your belts.

Educate yourself about your divorce-related legal rights and responsibilities before you begin negotiating. You can do that by each booking an appointment with a solicitor, reading divorce-related literature (such as this book), or consulting a Web site such as www.divorce.co.uk.

Making your negotiations as painless as possible

Obviously, negotiating the end of your marriage isn't going to be much fun. We offer some suggestions that may make things easier:

✔ Start your negotiations off with some easy stuff – something both of you can probably agree on. Early success is a confidence builder and helps create momentum for continued progress.

✔ Don't lose sight of your goals: sound and co-operative arrangements for your children, a less-expensive divorce, an agreement that satisfies both of you, and a mutual commitment to making your agreement work after your divorce is official.

✔ Avoid over-reaching or posturing to gain control.

✔ When your spouse makes a concession that benefits you, acknowledge it. (Go on, swallow your pride and do it!) You will help encourage your spouse to make yet more concessions and compromises. But don't forget, in order to keep the concessions and compromises coming, you must make some of your own.

✔ Be sure that your spouse does not mistake your willingness to concede a few points as a desire to get back together, unless that is definitely what you want.

✔ Hard as it may be, try not to make important decisions 'in the heat of the moment' or when you are feeling especially depressed or guilty about your divorce. You are more apt to make decisions that you will regret later.

Acquiring (And Paying For) Expert Advice

You and your spouse must determine what sort of information you need in order to make intelligent decisions and which of you is responsible for getting that information. First, make a list of what you need, and then take turns to choose a research topic. Next, you may need to engage some of the following professionals:

✔ A qualified accountant to help you understand the possible tax implications of your financial decisions and how to plan for them

✔ An estate agent or professional valuer to help you value your home, other property, collectibles, fine art, and so on

✔ A financial adviser to help you determine what to do with the assets or pensions you may receive in your property settlement

---

Write it all down and save it

During your negotiations, keep an accurate record of what you agree on and what areas of disagreement remain.

Without a written record of your discussions, you won't know where each of you stands in the negotiating process, and writing your final divorce agreement will be difficult if not impossible.

Decide which of you will be in charge of record-keeping. If one of you agrees to be responsible, make sure that your records are always readily available to the other spouse.

If either of you has access to word processing software, enter a record of the information you acquire and your decisions electronically. You can then make hard-copy printouts and also copy them to a disk (make an extra copy so that both of you has a disk and a set of printed pages). If one of you doesn't own a computer, ask a friend or a computer service to check the disk for you.

If you are going to share the cost of outside experts, decide early how to pay for them. Any of the following options may be feasible:

- ✔ Liquidate an asset. For example, you may be able to sell one of your cars or some stocks or bonds, or dip into your savings.

- ✔ One of you pays all of the expenses involved in hiring professional help in exchange for getting an equivalently larger share of your property or taking on less of your shared debt.

- ✔ One of you pays all the expenses. The other spouse then reimburses that spouse.

- ✔ You split the expenses 50:50, 60:40, 75:25 – whatever you agree is fair.

- ✔ One of you pays the full cost of hiring one expert and the other pays for hiring another expert. However, for this to be fair, the cost of hiring each expert should be relative to your individual salaries.

So that you have no doubt about the fairness of an outside expert's advice, choose experts who have no personal or business relationship with either one of you. Meet with the expert together (not separately) and make sure the expert understands that he or she is working for *both* of you.

Bringing in a Solicitor to Help You

If you're like most people, one of the key reasons you may want to negotiate your own divorce is so that you can keep your legal costs down. However, excluding solicitors entirely from your divorce is almost bound to be pennywise and pound-foolish. Solicitors have a valuable role to play in *all* divorces, including yours. (For more on how to choose your solicitors wisely, read Chapter 15.)

You must each employ your own solicitor. No solicitor is allowed by their professional rules to accept both of you as clients. The Law Society in the UK prohibits solicitors from working with both spouses in a divorce.

Getting some basic information

Each of you should meet with your solicitor prior to starting negotiations. Use this interview to acquire an overview of the divorce law and guidelines, gain an understanding of what must be included in your divorce agreement, and determine the issues and proposals you may want to consider making during your negotiations. Unless you read law books just for the fun of it or have been divorced a number of times, these are subjects that you probably know little about.

Be sure to get advice about any special concerns you may have related to the decisions ahead of you, and find out about potential legal pitfalls or problems. After talking with your solicitor about the issues in your divorce, you may decide that your divorce is much too complicated for you to negotiate yourselves.

You may also want to use your solicitor to help you with specific tasks during the negotiating process – for example to review financial documents, to provide you with feedback about a proposal your spouse has made, or to review the counter-offer you are considering. You can talk to your solicitors about the role a mediator can play.

If money is an issue, be up front about it. For example, you may want to tell your solicitor you can only afford to purchase an hour or two of her time. Your solicitors are under a professional duty to tell you what their time costs.

Asking your solicitors to review and draft your final agreement

If you and your spouse are able to resolve all the issues in your divorce, or if you work out just some of them, before you sign anything, ask your solicitors to review what you have drafted. Having your solicitors review your draft agreement assures you that nothing important has been overlooked and that you have not created potential future problems between you and your spouse. Solicitors are more prepared to do this nowadays as long as you give them full information. In addition, you and your spouse must decide which of your solicitors will draft your final agreement. You can make that decision by tossing a coin, or you may agree that the spouse with greater financial assets can agree to engage the solicitor to prepare your final agreement, or you may agree to share the costs in some way. If your solicitor drafts the final agreement, your spouse's solicitor should review it and vice versa.

The solicitor you employ can tell you whether the agreement you and your spouse negotiate by yourselves is equitable (fair) to both of you under the law. The agreement may sound like a great deal to you, but after reviewing it, your solicitor may tell you that you're entitled to more. Although you may decide that you are happy with what's in the draft agreement, at least you'll know what you're giving up after meeting with your solicitor. Your solicitor can also make sure that your draft agreement does not overlook certain issues that may create problems (with taxes, for instance) down the road and that it is legally enforceable.

Your solicitor is trained to protect your interests and may therefore have to pose a worst-case scenario and provide legal advice to prevent or mitigate such a situation. So if your solicitor says something that alarms you or makes you question whether you should negotiate your divorce on your own, don't panic. Your solicitor is legally bound to inform you of all possible outcomes. Such a scenario that you find alarming may have little chance of actually occurring but you must consider it seriously so that down the line you do not regret that you did not listen properly.

Creating a Parenting Plan that Works for Everyone

If you are like most divorcing parents, both of you want to be actively involved in your children's lives after your marriage has ended. Plenty of research shows that your children will do best when they have two parents actively involved in their lives.

Therefore, your negotiations about your children's future care will probably focus on deciding how both of you can continue to spend time with your children, how you can continue sharing parenting responsibilities with one another after you no longer live together, and how you can both assure your children of your continued love. (For more on parenting plans and children's arrangements, see Chapter 10.)

The plan you finally decide on may not be as good as having two parents under the same roof, but it can be the next best thing. And, if your marriage was tense and full of strife, parenting under two roofs may end up being better than parenting under one. The Web site www.lcd.gov.uk/family/divleaf.htm can help you ensure that you don't overlook anything when you are developing your plan.

Working Out Child Support

If you and your spouse share dependent children, your child support arrangement may be the most important item you negotiate. The Child Support Agency (CSA) formula (covered in Chapter 13) is a useful minimum guide.

Determining a reasonable standard of living

When working out child support arrangements, you must first come to an agreement about the standard of living you want for your children after your divorce. Although you may both agree that you want the very best for your children, if you are like most couples and money was tight during your marriage, there will be even less of it to go around after you're divorced. Therefore, to provide your children with the extras that you want them to have, you and your spouse may have to agree to cut some items out of your own post-divorce budgets.

Another possibility, sad as it may be, is that after your marriage ends, you are likely to find it hard to maintain your children's current lifestyle, and you won't be able to provide them with all the extras that you hoped they could have. Deciding what to cut will probably be a tough decision to make.

When you are developing budgets for the cost of raising your children, be sure to include the cost of their share of household expenses, including the rent or mortgage, utilities, food, clothing, travel, school lunches, child care, sporting activities, music lessons, and so on. Look at the expenditure sheet we include in Chapter 3. Also, don't forget to consider how you and your spouse will pay for other expenses, such as dentistry, university or further education, any special health care, extra tuition, and even weddings. You and your spouse can decide how you will fund your children's education when you draft your agreement, or, if they are very young, you can include a clause providing that you will return to that issue as each child turns a certain age (entering secondary education perhaps), when you should have a clearer idea of his or her aptitudes and abilities and the educational or employment implications of these.

Getting a court order, even if you agree

Even if your divorce is amicable and you both agree to share the cost of supporting your children, you may want to ask for a consent order for your child support plan from the court to ensure that the agreement is upheld. If your spouse doesn't live up to the agreement, the full force of the law can help you collect it. Securing a consent order can be an important just-in-case step; without one, your options for getting the agreement enforced are more limited. Although you can get a court order for child support after your divorce, the process takes time, and while you are waiting, you and your children may suffer financially. (Chapter 13 talks more about the options for child support and about enforcing child support agreements.)

In Scotland, formal written agreements are enforced by the courts in the same way as court orders and therefore your agreement is probably sufficient there. In addition, the Scottish court can't make an order for child support if the CSA has jurisdiction even if you and your spouse are in agreement – except where *additional* payments are justified, perhaps for a disabled child.

If the spouse who will be paying child support can afford to pay more than just the minimum according to the CSA formula, your negotiations must also address how much that additional payment amount will be.

Don't forget to spell out in your agreement exactly how the child support will be paid – personal cheques, direct debit, or other arrangement. Before you sign a child support agreement, ask your solicitor to review it so that you can be sure that what you and your spouse agree to is legally enforceable and is fair to both of you.

Having a court order for child maintenance will not prevent either one of you from making an application to the CSA once the order has been in effect for a year. If one of you does apply, the CSA takes over the calculation and enforcement of child support.

Discussing Spousal Maintenance

If you feel that you need some financial support after your marriage has ended and can present solid reasons why your spouse should pay for it, then your divorce negotiations need to include discussions about maintenance. (For more in-depth information on the subject of maintenance, turn to Chapter 12.) Be aware that maintenance can be a difficult issue to negotiate, so don't give up if you can't come to an agreement right away.

If you are the spouse who needs or wants maintenance, in order to make your case compare your post-divorce financial needs and resources with your spouse's. Note the contributions you made to your marriage or to your spouse's career. Steer clear of phrases such as 'I must have', 'I require', and 'I deserve'. Don't behave resentfully about the sacrifices you may have made in the interest of your spouse or marriage. At the time you made those choices, you probably did so because you believed they were for the best.

If possible, frame your thinking in terms of how you might both benefit from any maintenance he or she may pay out. For example, perhaps you need maintenance now so that you can develop good job skills to earn a better living in the future. Depending on your circumstances, it may be that after you have a good job, not only will your spouse be able to stop paying you anything for yourself, but you may also be able to begin contributing more to the support of your children. In other words, your spouse may trade a short-term sacrifice for a long-term gain.

When you are preparing your projected post-divorce budget and are estimating your monthly income without maintenance, do *not* include in your income figure any child support you will be receiving. Child support is for your children, not for you.

Dividing Up Your Property and Debts

If you don't have young children to support, and you and your spouse both earn good money, the only decisions you may have to make may relate to the division of your property and debts. Before you can actually get down to deciding who gets what, developing a comprehensive inventory of your assets and debts (including your pensions) and assigning accurate values and amounts to each is *critical*. (See Chapter 7 for information on creating a list of your assets.)

If you and your spouse own and operate a business together, or if one of you runs a limited company, do not try to negotiate what to do about the business without the help of solicitors. The financial issues are too complicated to work out on your own – they're vexing even for solicitors!

If you are divorcing after just a short marriage, you and your spouse may be able to accomplish that division in a single negotiating session. Usually, the longer your marriage, the more you will own and owe together, and the more time you will need to reach a property settlement agreement.

Splitting it down the middle – or not

Many divorcing couples begin by thinking that they will split up their property and their debts 50:50 for practicality's sake. Depending on the circumstances of your marriage, your assets, and your debts, this method may or may not be fair. (For more information on ways to divide property, turn to Chapter 11.)

The following are some of the factors that can suggest that a non-equal split is called for:

- ✔ One of you has contributed significantly more to your family than the other. Being the main carer of your children and home is usually seen as equal to going out and earning a salary.

- ✔ One of you has a greater need than the other for more than half of the assets or less than half of the debts. For example, one of you has the main care of the children or makes much less money than the other or one of you has never worked outside the home and has little earning capacity.

- ✔ A significant disparity in your ages or your health is going to affect your ability to pay half of the debt or replace the assets you would give up.

As a point of reference or a reality check, find out from your solicitor what criteria a family law judge must use if it were up to him or her to decide how your property and debts should be divided. You can get this information if you meet with your solicitor before you start your negotiations, or you can get it from a solicitor later, after your negotiations have begun.

Regardless of what percentage split you use to divide up the value of your property and debts – 50:50, 60:40, 80:20, for example – both of you should be 100 per cent clear about the rationale for that percentage and feel comfortable with it, and preferably state your reasons for agreeing on that percentage in your agreement.

First divide the big assets, and then the miscellaneous ones. Before dividing up your assets and debts, make lists of your expected incomes and your projected needs.

Dividing up the big stuff

The first stage focuses on the division of your significant assets – your home, other real property, bank accounts, pensions, investments, vehicles, and so on – and the debts that may go with them. Don't overlook the tax consequences of your decisions during this stage. Be open to selling assets if doing so will help create a win-win situation. (You are most apt to need the help of outside professionals during this phase.)

When you divide up assets that secure a mortgage or loan – your home, vehicles, and so forth – look at both the debt associated with the asset and the asset itself. Value that asset according to the amount of equity you have in it (that is, what is left from the market value of your house or vehicle minus what you owe on the mortgage or loan).

Dividing up smaller items

Use the second phase to divide up your miscellaneous property such as your stereo system, furniture, CDs, computer equipment, kitchenware, linens, the lawnmower, power tools, and so on. You may not be able to assign specific values to these items – approximate values will probably do. During this stage you can also divide up credit card debts and other miscellaneous unsecured joint debts.

Don't overlook your family pets when you are dividing up your property. If you have children, you may want to let the pets live with whichever parent will have the children most of the time after your divorce is final. Having their pets around increases your children's sense of stability and security after your marriage has ended.

You can trade off debts for assets or vice versa. For example, you can agree to pay off more of your debt in exchange for getting a larger share of your assets; or you can agree to take less property so that you don't have to pay off as much of your debt.

If it's realistic or cost-effective, wipe out as much of your joint debt as you can by selling assets. Minimising your post-divorce financial ties is almost always a good idea. You may also want to sell joint assets to provide both of you with the cash you may need to start your lives as single people. Be careful, however, that in your quest for cash you don't sell items for less than their actual value.

Working Out What to Do with the House

Your home is probably the most valuable asset you own together. What you do with your home after a split can be tough on you emotionally as well as financially. Nevertheless, what happens to your house is a bottom-line issue that should be based, at the end of the day, on financial considerations. See Chapter 11. To help you make a sound decision, you should be asking yourself the following questions and talking over the answers to those questions with your spouse:

- How much does comparable housing cost?
- What emotional ties do each of you have to your home and to your neighbourhood?
- How much can you sell your house for?

✔ Is it important for your children to continue living in the same neighbourhood or school district?

✔ Are other houses in the same neighbourhood or school district available that you and your children can move into?

✔ If you want to keep your home, can you afford to do so, taking into account your mortgage payment, insurance costs, rates and taxes, upkeep, and maintenance?

✔ What will your spouse get in return if you keep the house?

Don't Forget Your Taxes

Don't overlook income and capital gain taxes when you are negotiating your divorce agreement (see Chapter 11). Ask your accountant, if you have one, or your solicitor to advise you on any possible tax liability. For general information on taxes, you can look at the *Which? Way to Save Tax* (Which? Books, 2002).

Other tax-related issues you may need to consider include

✔ How you will share any tax refund you may have coming

✔ How you will share responsibility for any taxes you may owe

✔ How you will share liability for any interest, penalties, and arrears you may owe if you are audited sometime in the future

Getting to a Solution

After you and your spouse think you are close to an agreement on all of the issues in your divorce, draft an agreement that reflects your decisions so far. Even if a few issues remain unresolved, start drafting anyway, noting what stands between you and your final agreement. When you see how close you are to a final agreement, you may be encouraged to get down to business and tie up those loose ends with the help of your solicitors. For help on finding a good solicitor to help you finalise your agreement, head to Chapter 15.

Chapter 15

Choosing a Family Solicitor

*R*egardless of your opinion about lawyers (solicitors and barristers) – that they're wise and informed legal advisers or a necessary evil – you almost can't escape having to use one when you are getting a divorce. If yours is a complicated and contentious divorce, the help of a solicitor is absolutely essential. If your breakup is more straightforward and amicable, a lawyer's input and assistance is advisable, even if you and your spouse handle most of the divorce negotiations yourself.

After you read this chapter, we hope you will feel a little less intimidated by solicitors and much more confident about employing one. We show you what to look for in a solicitor, how much they charge, and how to begin your search for a lawyer you can trust and afford. After reading this chapter, you'll be equipped with a set of questions to ask the solicitors you meet with and will be aware of other issues to consider when choosing a solicitor.

When to Engage a Solicitor

Assuming that you are a law-abiding citizen and have never been sued or had to sue, it's likely that you've never employed a solicitor before. Therefore, you may find the prospect of engaging and working with a lawyer downright intimidating, especially if you have always looked to your spouse to make the important decisions in your household.

Most divorces aren't simple and therefore the active involvement of a solicitor is critical. In any of the following situations, you should seriously think about employing the services of a family solicitor:

- ✔ You and your spouse have dependent children.
- ✔ You have been based in the home during your marriage and do not have the job skills and contacts you need to begin earning a good living right away, or you are an older person who has never worked.
- ✔ Your property is substantial or complicated; you have capital gains taxes and other tax issues to consider; you have made very different contributions to your marriage; or other similar factors.
- ✔ One or both of you owns your own business, or you and your spouse are business partners.
- ✔ You and your spouse share a lot of debt.
- ✔ You are reluctant to speak up when you disagree with your spouse and tend to back down when he or she disagrees with you.
- ✔ You don't trust your spouse to be honest, open, and fair.
- ✔ You and your spouse are so estranged that civil discourse and compromise are no longer part of your discussions.
- ✔ Your spouse has become physically or emotionally abusive.
- ✔ Your spouse has engaged a solicitor.

Keep in mind that professional ethics do not allow solicitors to represent both you and your spouse at the same time, even when you believe that you are going to be in complete agreement over all major issues. Ethically, the solicitor won't be able to give both of you independent legal advice if any conflict or potential conflict arises, however minor.

What to Look for in a Solicitor

A solicitor may be involved in your divorce from start to finish, or he may work with you on a very limited basis. (Generally, if you and your spouse both feel confident about your ability to work out your own divorce agreement, you can limit your use of a solicitor to initial advice and information, final evaluation and feedback, and the drafting of your final order or agreement.)

When you engage a family solicitor, it's more than a matter of running your fingers through the solicitor ads in the *Yellow Pages* until you spot the word 'divorce' or simply employing the lawyer who helped you negotiate your office lease or draw up your will.

✔ You need to engage a solicitor experienced in family law.

✔ The solicitor you engage should talk to you in plain English, not legalese, and pay attention to what you have to say.

✔ The solicitor should be someone you trust and feel comfortable with, because you may have to reveal highly personal information about yourself and your marriage.

✔ If you have young children, look for a solicitor who makes it clear that during your divorce you must put your children's needs first and that he will not pursue unreasonable demands for child support or help you pursue vindictive child residence and contact arrangements.

✔ If you call your solicitor, the phone should be answered promptly and professionally.

✔ Your lawyer should be affordable.

Appropriate skills and experience

An old adage states that 'there are horses for courses'. This saying is as true for a solicitor as for any other professional. In other words, when you select a family law solicitor, you want one with the legal skills and knowledge needed to get the job done for you:

✔ If you need help negotiating your divorce agreement, the ideal solicitor is a problem-solver, works well with people, is adept at compromise, and is comfortable in court. Although you and your spouse may have no intention of going to court, a solicitor's advocacy experience and history of success in court can have some bearing on his ability to negotiate a settlement with your spouse's solicitor.

✔ If you know from the start that you're heading for a contested hearing, you may want a solicitor who has considerable courtroom experience. Not all lawyers do. Alternatively, your solicitor should have a good working relationship with the local family law barristers. See Chapter 4 for more about the different roles of solicitors and barristers.

✔ Try to choose a solicitor who is familiar with the family law judges in your area. Knowing the court style of the judge who's likely to hear your case and how the judge has decided previous cases similar to yours helps your solicitor adapt his legal strategy and style to that particular judge.

Don't base your decision on which solicitor has the nicest office. A fancy office in an expensive building says nothing about the adequacy of a lawyer's legal skills. At the same time, don't assume that just because you pay a lot of money to a solicitor that his legal representation is appropriate to your needs or is of high quality. Also, don't let a lawyer's physical appearance influence your choice.

If your financial situation is complex, the lawyer you engage should either have a solid understanding of the issues and laws that pertain to your divorce or work closely with other lawyers or financial experts who have that knowledge, such as an independent financial adviser, accountant, or valuer. Remember, negotiating your divorce agreement is as much about financial matters as it is about ending your marriage.

Personal style

If you are relying on a solicitor to do more than simply review your divorce paperwork, you must be prepared to share details about your personal life, marriage, and finances. Therefore, you must feel comfortable with whomever represents you. In addition, your solicitor should share and support your basic philosophy or attitude towards your divorce. For example, if you want to keep things as calm, co-operative, and non-adversarial as possible, avoid solicitors who like to 'go for the jugular'.

Affordability

Most family law solicitors bill for their services on an *hourly basis*. Few agree to take a *flat fee* based on the total amount of time and work they think your divorce requires. Estimating upfront just how much time is necessary to finalise your divorce is difficult, because no lawyer knows exactly how any divorce is going to work out. Depending on where you live, on average the services of a family solicitor if you are a private client will cost you anywhere from £75 an hour to more than £350 an hour, *plus* expenses (also called *disbursements*) and VAT.

You're more apt to find a solicitor who'll take your case for a flat fee if your divorce is 100 per cent amicable and if the tasks the solicitor will perform are very well defined – for example, you just need some paperwork filled out and filed.

Among other things, a solicitor's private hourly rate (as opposed to his rate for publicly-funded work) depends on where you live in the UK and whether your community is rural or urban. If you live in London you can expect to pay the most. See the section later in this chapter 'What if You Can't Afford Your Lawyer's Fees?' for more about finding a solicitor who does legally aided, or *publicly funded,* work.

What you can (and should) expect from your solicitor

In some ways, your solicitor is like a general practitioner, in the middle of a network of services that have grown up to help you and your family during your divorce. At the same time, he must have the legal skills and a compatible approach to get you safely through your crisis.

A good family solicitor listens to your story with several things in mind. One of the first things in his mind should be to clarify how ready you are to begin divorce proceedings. If you are uncertain about whether your marriage is over, or if your partner is seeking the divorce, and you are in shock about it, a good solicitor will tell you how to contact a counsellor. If your solicitor learns from your story that you are being abused, he will take action (see Chapter 2) and may tell you how to contact a refuge.

Your solicitor should consider whether you and your family are likely to benefit from mediation. This will depend on your approach to how you want to conduct your divorce but it will also depend on how you convey your spouse's likely approach. You may think that only co-operative couples (see Chapter 5) can use mediation, but mediation can work even if you and your spouse aren't at the point of co-operating because you've stopped talking to each other. Your solicitor may think this over and suggest mediation to you if it seems a good idea in your situation (see Chapter 16 for more information on how mediation works).

If you're eligible for legal aid, you must consider mediation and meet with a mediator unless you're certain that mediation won't work – for example, because domestic abuse had occurred. Your solicitor can't be paid by the Community Legal Service to represent you until you have checked mediation out or unless there is good reason why mediation isn't appropriate.

Your solicitor can – and should – also find out whether you're eligible for any state benefits or tax credits and tell you how and where to claim them. See Chapters 10 and 13 for more information on getting state benefits.

Finding the Right Solicitor

Locating the right solicitor takes time. To start your search, you can develop a list of potential solicitors by

✔ Asking friends and family members who have gone through a divorce and were happy with their solicitors.

✔ Asking solicitors you have worked with in the past. Before requesting the name of a family solicitor, explain the nature of your divorce and the kind of legal help you think you need.

✔ Consulting the Law Society's Directory. It lists lawyers by county and city and gives details of their qualifications including the year that they were admitted as a solicitor. Your public library should have a copy. Alternatively, Chambers and Partners publish a directory called *A Guide to the Legal Profession*.

✔ Contacting the Solicitors Family Law Association (Tel: 0345 585671; Web site: www.sfla.co.uk), which can provide you with a list of solicitors in your area who specialise in divorce and family law. See the sidebar 'Specialist family lawyers', earlier in this chapter.

✔ Looking under 'Solicitors' in the phone book or *Yellow Pages*.

✔ Asking your counsellor or social worker.

✔ Surfing the Internet. Many divorce solicitors have Web sites and one of them may be located in or near your community. Some divorce-related Web sites also have links to divorce solicitor Web sites (for example, www.divorce.co.uk).

✔ If you belong to a divorce support group, asking the other members for names.

Solicitors to Avoid

If you anticipate an especially rancorous divorce, you want a solicitor who acts as your legal ally and your advocate, not one who is merely interested in collecting fees. Steer clear, therefore, of solicitors who brag about themselves a great deal, act distractedly when you speak, trivialise your questions by not answering them or telling you 'not to worry about that', or who ignore your questions entirely.

Avoid solicitors who talk down to you, don't ask you any questions, or allow themselves to be constantly interrupted by phone calls or conversations with people who come into their office while you are meeting. And make sure your solicitor does not leave other clients' files where you can see or read information confidential to them.

If any of the solicitors on your list ask you few, if any, questions about your marriage, your finances, or your divorce goals, cross that lawyer's name off your list.

Meeting Potential Solicitors

After you narrow your list of solicitors down to a small number, it is a good idea to telephone their offices to check the individual's availability and any other essential criteria (such as whether they offer legal aid if you think you might need it). By this time you should have just one or two with whom you may want to arrange a meeting to ask how they will treat your case. Don't engage a solicitor just because someone you know and respect gives the lawyer a glowing review. Make up your own mind after an in-person meeting.

During your first meeting, don't be afraid to ask questions. Find out about the solicitor's experience and talk about possible approaches to your divorce case. Make sure that you and the solicitor you decide to work with are in agreement regarding the type of divorce you want to pursue and that he concurs with your divorce goals and priorities (unless the solicitor can give you good reasons for revising them).

Request a free consultation

Many solicitors will give you a free 30-minute to one-hour initial consultation, but you may have to ask for it. Solicitors who do not offer you free consultations may charge you a nominal sum – £5 to £50 – for an initial meeting or may charge their normal hourly rate. However, the amount of money solicitors charge for an initial meeting with you has no bearing on their skills in divorce law.

Questions to ask the solicitor, and responses you need to hear

Bring a notebook with you to your meetings so that you can record the important points and how each solicitor replies to your questions. Do not be shy about taking notes. Also, as soon as possible after each meeting has ended, write down your impressions of the solicitor you've just met with.

To get you started on developing a list of questions, the following are some of the most important ones to ask. (These questions are most appropriate if you're engaging a solicitor to help with your divorce negotiations or because you need to be represented in court.)

- ✔ **How long have you been practising divorce law, roughly how many cases have you handled, and how many hearings have you been involved in?**

  Look for a solicitor who has been a family lawyer for at least three years. If you anticipate that your divorce may end up in court, make sure that the solicitor has some advocacy experience, and preferably has successfully represented other clients at contested hearings.

- ✔ **Do you take other kinds of cases as well? If so, what percentage of your practice is represented by family cases?**

  Not less than 50 per cent of the solicitor's caseload should be family cases.

- ✔ **Have you ever had a case like mine? How did you handle it?**

  Avoid a solicitor who has never dealt with the particular issues in your divorce case. Lawyers can't give you specific details about another case, but they can tell you enough for you to determine whether they have sufficient experience to deal with a case such as yours.

- ✔ **Who will actually handle my case? You, another lawyer with your firm, or both of you?**

  Don't assume that you're receiving inferior legal care if a skilled paralegal under the supervision of a solicitor works on your case. A paralegal can do a good job of handling certain aspects of a divorce for considerably less money than if your solicitor personally dealt with them.

- ✔ **What do you think about mediation?**

  If you and your spouse reach a stalemate on some aspect of your divorce and you want to give mediation a try, select a solicitor who believes in mediation and has used it successfully in divorces such as yours.

- ✔ **How do you charge, and how do you expect to be paid?**

  Find out the solicitor's hourly rate, whether they do any publicly-funded work (or *legal aid*), and get an estimate of how much your divorce will cost. If you are worried about how to pay for the legal help you need, be upfront about your concerns. See the section 'What if You Can't Afford Your Lawyer's Fees?' for more about public funding. Most lawyers require a *retainer,* or down part-payment, on the cost of their services. The cost of the time the solicitor actually spends on your case is then credited against the retainer.

✔ **How do you calculate your billable hours?**

Many solicitors bill in units of six minutes. In other words, if the solicitor spends five or ten minutes talking with you on the phone, he may round it down or up to one or two units of six minutes of billable time.

✔ **Will you provide me with an estimate of my expenses and an explanation of what those expenses may include?**

You may have to pay the cost of long-distance calls, facsimiles, copying, delivery fees, outside expert fees, court fees, and so on. Lawyers call these *disbursements*. If you object to paying certain expenses, ask for an explanation in advance of why you should be billed for them. If the expenses are not essential to your case, let the lawyer know that you are not willing to pay for them. Lawyers should not incur any substantial disbursements without your prior authorisation.

✔ **How often will I be billed for your expenses, and will I get an itemised bill?**

You should expect to receive itemised bills. It is probably best to ask for them monthly, even if little work has been done, because it will help you to budget and keep up-to-date with your costs.

✔ **If I have questions about my case, can I call you? How quickly can I expect to have my calls returned?**

It is reasonable to expect your calls to be returned within 24 hours, unless you make it clear that you are calling with an emergency. Then your call should be returned within an hour or two, possibly by another family solicitor in the team, if yours is unavailable.

✔ **Based on what you know about my divorce, what is your approach going to be?**

The solicitor should be able to provide you with a preliminary assessment of the strengths and the weaknesses of your case (and your spouse's case) and a clear explanation of how he intends to maximise your strengths and minimise your weaknesses in order to get you the best divorce possible. Steer clear of solicitors who emphasise 'playing hardball' rather than negotiating and trying mediation. Hardball tactics cost money.

✔ **If you can't negotiate a settlement and any issue in my divorce goes to a full hearing, will you or someone else from your firm represent me in court or will you recommend a barrister?**

If you think that an issue in your divorce may be fully contested, you may want a solicitor who has advocacy experience and who can handle your divorce from start to finish. Alternatively, the solicitor may use a barrister, or *Counsel,* for your representation in court. Barristers are not necessarily more expensive than solicitors, and they usually have more experience presenting cases in court. However, there will be some extra time and cost involved in your solicitor instructing the barrister on your behalf, and you may well need a personal meeting with the barrister before your hearing, for which you will be expected to pay.

✔ **What can I do to minimise my legal expenses?**

Some lawyers are more amenable than others to letting you conduct certain aspects of your case yourself – picking up documents, copying, conducting simple research, and doing other tasks a layperson can handle.

✔ **What do you expect from me?**

Any reputable solicitor expects a client to provide full disclosure of all relevant facts, provide information on a timely basis, return phone calls promptly, be honest, pay bills on time, and respect the solicitor's advice regarding what to do or not do in terms of the case. However, ultimately you are the one who makes the decisions and the solicitor must follow your instructions as long as he is within the law and the ethics of the profession.

Documents you need to produce

When you meet with prospective solicitors, try to bring along some key documents and a summary of information regarding your family's finances, including the following:

✔ Your marriage certificate

✔ A list of your assets and debts

✔ Copies of your and your spouse's current will

✔ Details and evidence of your income, both gross and net (that is, before and after deductions for tax, National Insurance, and so on)

✔ Copies of deeds to property and details of any mortgages

✔ A copy of any pre-marital or separation agreement that you may have signed

✔ Any correspondence that you've received from your spouse or your spouse's solicitor about the divorce or from the Child Support Agency

Chapter 7 provides a comprehensive list of the types of financial and other information you should have already prepared and assembled in preparation for your divorce. After you engage a solicitor, you'll probably have to provide additional background information and documentation.

What a solicitor wants to know about you

Your initial meeting is a two-way exchange – you won't be the only one asking questions. The solicitor needs to get some information from you before he can answer your questions. Solicitors must also be assured that they won't have a conflict of interest if they represent you. A conflict exists, for example, if their law firm represents your spouse's business.

The following list gives you an idea of the types of questions you can expect a solicitor to ask you:

- How long have you been married and where were you married? Why you are getting a divorce?

- Are you and your spouse still living together? If not, with whom are your children living (if you have children) and who is in the family home?

- Have there been any previous proceedings or have you used solicitors before in relation to your marriage or separation?

- Do you and your spouse have a pre-marital, post-marital, or separation agreement?

- What major assets do you and your spouse own, and what would you estimate each of those assets is worth?

- What are your family debts?

- What kind of employment-related benefits, if any, do you and your spouse have?

- Are you and your spouse retired or do either of you have plans to retire soon?

- What are your goals for your divorce in terms of spousal support, property settlement, child residence and contact, and child support?

- Do you have any dependent children from your marriage?

- What kind of relationship do you have with your children and what role do you play in their day-to-day lives as a parent?

- Has a social worker or child protection officer had any dealings with you or your children?

- What do you think will be the best arrangements for your children?

- Has there been any violence or abuse in your relationship?

- Are any third parties involved?

- Should I know anything else about you, your spouse, or your marriage?

Be prepared to provide honest answers to questions that may make you feel uncomfortable, such as: 'Do you have any present intention to cohabit or remarry?' and 'Is your spouse aware of your affair?'

Getting the Terms and Conditions of Business in Writing

After you decide on a solicitor, ask for a contract, written agreement, or a letter and terms of understanding before you pay any money over and above the cost of your initial interview. According to the Law Society's client care code, the document should detail all of the specifics you and the solicitor agreed to during any of your meetings, including financial arrangements and an estimate of the costs, certain services the solicitor will or will not provide, payment arrangements, and so forth.

Do not hesitate to take a day or two to thoroughly reread the contract or agreement before signing it. Ask the solicitor about anything you do not understand and keep asking until all your questions have been answered to your satisfaction. If you and the lawyer agree to add or delete anything, make certain that those changes are reflected in the document before you sign it. Keep a copy of the final signed contract or agreement for your files.

Changing Your Solicitor

The solicitor who helps you with your divorce is working for you. So, if you are unhappy with something your solicitor does or doesn't do, communicate that dissatisfaction to them, but be reasonable about it. If you do have cause to complain and you are not satisfied with the outcome of your complaint, you may write to the Office for the Supervision of Solicitors (OSS) at Victoria Court, 8 Dormer Place, Leamington Spa, Warwickshire CU32 5AE; Helpline 0845 608 6565. You can also contact this organisation through their Web site: www.oss.lawsociety.org.uk.

If you are sure that your solicitor is not doing a good job of representing you, and you are a privately paying client, you can dismiss him. (If you are publicly funded, see the next section.) However, you do have to pay for any work the solicitor has performed up to that point and for any and all expenses the solicitor has incurred on your behalf. Your solicitor will be entitled to hold onto your file of papers until he has received payment.

Before you dismiss your solicitor, consider getting a second opinion from another solicitor. You may find that your solicitor is doing the very best job possible under the circumstances and you may not be any happier with someone else.

Changing Your Solicitor if You're Publicly Funded

If you are publicly funded and for any reason you decide that you want to change solicitors, you will not be able to do so without the co-operation of the Legal Services Commission (LSC). If you want to change solicitors because, for example, you are moving to a different area, you need to approach your newly chosen solicitor and he will help you apply for a formal amendment to your certificate. If you want to change because you are dissatisfied with your solicitor, the LSC will probably expect you to go through the solicitor's firm's complaints procedures before they consider whether to allow you to change.

What if You Can't Afford Your Lawyer's Fees?

You may not be able to afford to pay the fees of even a relatively inexperienced solicitor. If you check your finances and come up short, some form of public funding or some other legal resources may be available to help you with your divorce.

Qualifying for public funding or legal aid

You may be able to receive public help with the funding of certain sorts of cases under a scheme operated by the government of England and Wales. The scheme is known as the Community Legal Service (CLS) and is run by the Legal Services Commission (previously the Legal Aid Board). The Legal Services Commission (LSC) has strict criteria for the granting of any sort of public funding, and it only pays firms who have been awarded the *Quality Mark* to do this work. This award means that the firms have passed through regular quality assurance tests for different areas of law. The LSC has a list of all such firms and organisations.

For more information about the legal aid scheme, contact your regional Legal Services Commission office, which you should find in your phone book or from their head office at 85 Grays Inn Road, London WC1X 8TX, Tel: 020 7759 0000, or Web site: www.legalservices.gov.uk. Alternatively, your local Citizens' Advice Bureau should be able to help. To check your eligibility yourself, and for other useful information, try www.divorce-online.co.uk or www.justask.org.uk.

If you live in Scotland and are on a low income or have no income apart from your spouse's, you may be able to apply to the Scottish Legal Aid Board, also known as SLAB (www.slab.org.uk), for financial help. This financial aid goes towards advice and correspondence your solicitor provides on your behalf. It won't cover the cost of raising a divorce action. For this you must have a certificate for full legal aid. To be assessed for legal aid, you need to fill in detailed forms about your finances and await the decision from SLAB about your eligibility.

The statutory charge

You need to regard most forms of public funding for civil and family proceedings as a loan rather than a gift. That is because you have to repay any costs that your solicitor reasonably incurs on your behalf out of any money or property worth over £3,000 that you recover or preserve in the proceedings (apart from maintenance). Your solicitor isn't allowed to release the money or property owed to you until your costs have been repaid to the LSC or you have an agreement to postpone repayment, as described in the following paragraphs. This is known as the *statutory charge* or *legal aid charge* or *claw-back*.

The rates that solicitors are allowed to charge for publicly-funded work are fixed by the government and reviewed regularly. Although they vary for different sorts of work, publicly-funded charging rates are generally a great deal lower than private charging rates. If you're publicly funded (or *legally aided*) and your spouse isn't, your total bill for the divorce is likely to be significantly lower than his or hers, even if the work that your solicitors have done is very similar.

If you do have the benefit of public funding, you may have to pay little if anything upfront to the LSC while your case is in progress. However, do not lose sight of the fact that ultimately you're responsible for your costs. You and your solicitor always need to weigh up the costs of any particular action against the benefits that you're hoping to achieve. And because you're ultimately responsible for the final bill, you are entitled to expect your solicitor to give you regular estimates and updates of your costs just as you would if you were privately paying.

Mediation and the statutory charge

You'll be pleased to know that one of the current perks of using family mediation is that the statutory charge doesn't apply. If you manage to reach an agreement on all key issues in your divorce through mediation and your solicitor puts your mediation agreement into legal form and helps you implement it, you don't have to repay any of the costs incurred by your mediator or your solicitor, which can represent a major saving to you and your spouse. The family 'pot' to be divided between you won't suffer any significant deduction for costs.

The system for public funding (legal aid) of family mediation is different in Scotland from the position in England and Wales. If you receive legal aid for advice and assistance in Scotland, your solicitor can apply to the Scottish Legal Aid Board for your share of the fees for mediation to be covered. This only applies where the mediator or the family mediation service charges mediation fees.

Varying levels of service

Many different levels of service are available for publicly-funded work even within the area of family law. Each level of service has different criteria for eligibility and scope, and different cost limits and rates of remuneration. All applications for public funding are assessed on their merits, and you will probably also be assessed on your means. To help you understand this complex topic, we set out below a simplified guide to the levels of service that you are most likely to come across in England and Wales during your divorce.

Legal Help

Legal Help is the most basic level of legal service available, and it covers you for preliminary advice and assistance on most aspects of your divorce, including the divorce proceedings themselves. Assuming that you are financially eligible under the Legal Help scheme and your divorce is undefended (which the vast majority are), this scheme enables your solicitor to prepare your divorce petition and guide you right through the court proceedings to the final decree. If your spouse has filed the divorce petition with the court, your solicitor will help you complete the acknowledgment of service and guide you through to the final decree. Be aware that Legal Help cannot cover you for representation in court.

The income and capital limits for eligibility are reviewed by the LSC each year, but if your gross income is less than about £2,300 per calendar month, and your capital less than £3,000, you may be eligible for Legal Help. Assets that are the subject of dispute between you and your spouse can't be taken into account for these purposes.

If you're financially eligible for Legal Help you don't have to pay any contribution towards your legal help costs except through the statutory charge referred to in the previous section. You are also exempt from paying the court fees (around £200) for the divorce. The rates of remuneration to the solicitor for work under the Legal Help scheme are reviewed annually and are slightly higher in London than elsewhere, but are generally in the region of £50 per hour plus VAT for preparation and attendances. Your solicitor can't incur more than £500 worth of costs under this scheme without prior authority from the LSC.

Help with mediation

If you are financially eligible for public funding , your solicitor can automatically sign you up for a certificate of Help with Mediation. This certificate means that your solicitor can give you a limited amount of advice through the mediation process and then advise you on any agreement at the end. If your solicitor advises you against any proposal that has been put forward in mediation, you can go back to mediation to try to resolve it. Once you and your solicitors are happy with the proposals, your solicitor can put the proposals into legal form (such as a separation agreement or consent order within divorce).

You won't have to pay any contribution towards your costs for the whole process. Nor will any of your costs be the subject of the statutory charge if you go ahead with an agreement reached in mediation, so you will not need to repay them at a later date. (See the previous section, 'Mediation and the statutory charge'.) The disposable income limits for eligibility are more generous than for Legal Help, and the capital limit is £8,000 instead of £3,000.

The work that your solicitor can do for you under the Help with Mediation certificate is currently limited to £150 for children cases, £250 for financial cases, and £350 for cases involving both children and finance. The solicitor cannot go beyond those cost limits on your behalf without the prior authority of the Legal Services Commission.

General Family Help

If you and your solicitor are optimistic that you can resolve issues in your divorce with your spouse through negotiation or otherwise without fully contested proceedings, you can apply for a certificate of General Family Help through your solicitor. You must undergo a financial eligibility check through the Legal Services Commission but if you're eligible, the certificate entitles you to a limited amount of advice and assistance with the negotiations or disclosure process.

You may have to pay a contribution upfront towards your costs, usually on a monthly basis, depending on your disposable income. The LSC makes you an offer of legal aid and, if you accept – which you will probably be advised to do – a certificate will be issued. As with most forms of public funding, your General Family Help costs are subject to the statutory charge, which means that you must repay your costs out of any money or property over £3,000 that you recover or preserve in the negotiations or proceedings.

The work that your solicitor can do for you under the General Family Help certificate is normally limited to £1,500. The solicitor cannot go beyond that cost limit without the prior authority of the Legal Services Commission.

Legal Representation

If you and your spouse aren't able to resolve any key issues in your divorce without going to court, you may want to apply for a certificate of Legal Representation to help with your legal costs and expenses.

The Legal Services Commission takes responsibility for assessing your means, and they may ask you to pay a monthly contribution (on a sliding scale according to your means) for the lifetime of your case, or a one-off contribution from your capital. Any contribution that you make is credited to you when the costs are calculated at the end of your case and is set against any liability you have under the statutory charge.

You don't have to undergo a means test if your children are subject to proceedings by the local authority for a care or supervision order, or if your children have been abducted abroad. You will be granted public funding for representation in those proceedings providing your case justifies it (which it usually will) without any means assessment or contribution from you.

If a certificate is granted for you, it specifies the scope of work that is covered and a limit as to costs. The initial cost limit is usually £2,500; your solicitor has to apply to the Legal Services Commission if he needs to extend the scope or cost limit for you. They may also have to get prior authority if you need to incur any extra expenses, such as experts' fees.

The rates that your solicitor can charge for work under a certificate of Legal Representation are fixed each year by the government but range from about £50 to £100 per hour, plus VAT, depending on the work done and whether your solicitor is in London or elsewhere. At the end of your case, your solicitor arranges for a bill of costs to be drawn up itemising all the work that's been done and all other expenses incurred on your behalf. You get a chance to check and comment on the bill before it's submitted to the Legal Services Commission for approval and payment. If your costs exceed £2,500 plus VAT, a district judge in the divorce court must assess the bill first, taking into account any comments you have made.

Emergency certificates

If your case is urgent (your spouse has seriously threatened or abused you, for example, or is about to dispose of a valuable family asset), your solicitor may be able to grant an emergency certificate without waiting for a full response from the LSC. You still need to fill out the application forms and your solicitor needs to be satisfied of the merits and urgency of your application, and of your financial eligibility. You have to promise to repay the LSC if it turns out, after all, that you are not eligible.

Discharge or revocation of your certificate

If your solicitor can no longer justify your continuing to receive public funding, he has a duty to notify the Legal Services Commission. This may be because your case has successfully finished, or because your means have changed so that you are no longer financially eligible. Your certificate may then be discharged.

Your solicitor also has to notify the LSC if he thinks that you are conducting your case unreasonably or that you are being dishonest about your circumstances. In that case, the LSC may revoke your certificate, which means that you are treated as never having been eligible for legal aid and you will be personally liable for all of your costs from the outset. This measure is harsh but is used only rarely.

Finding alternative ways to pay

You may have other means at your disposal to pay for legal help if you don't have sufficient cash or aren't entitled to legal aid:

- ✔ **Payment plan:** You may be able to find a solicitor who allows you to pay for his services over time, depending on your future earning potential.

- ✔ **A charge on your property:** If you own property or other significant assets that you're fairly certain of keeping as part of your settlement, a solicitor may be willing to take a charge on that property or make an agreement that you pay your costs out of it at the end of your case. If there is a charge and you sell the property, your solicitor is in line to receive all or some of what you owe him from the sale proceeds. If you have such an agreement with your solicitor, get the terms of agreement in writing and check it out with another independent solicitor before you sign.

Chapter 16

Using a Mediator to Help You Work Things Out Together

*W*hen you and your spouse are working out the terms of your divorce, no matter how hard you both may try, you're likely to encounter issues that you can't resolve on your own. If that happens, you don't have to tear your hair out in frustration or throw in the towel and prepare for a court hearing. Rather than let sticky issues derail co-operation over your divorce, you and your spouse may still be able to work out a negotiated settlement by using mediation.

This chapter explains what mediation is and how it works, and describes the characteristics of a good divorce mediator. It also describes the role of your solicitor when you use mediation (because opting for mediation doesn't eliminate your need for a solicitor).

What Is Mediation?

Mediation is a voluntary dispute-resolution method that relies on the open exchange of information, ideas, and options to help you and your spouse resolve your differences without going to court. Although mediation can help resolve a wide variety of matters, it has proven to be an especially cost-effective tool for divorcing couples. According to a recent government study, over 70 per cent of couples using mediation reached an agreement – two-thirds of those came to an agreement on all their divorce issues during mediation.

Mediation can help both you and your spouse to come out winners and avoid a court hearing in which typically one of you wins and the other loses. It also enables you, if you have children, to work together in your children's interests.

When do you start mediation?

The starting point for family mediation is when you have already separated or divorced, or you plan to do so. After you reach this point, mediation can take place at any time – before you begin to take court action, when you encounter something you cannot agree upon, or when you get as far as court and the judge suggests you consider mediation instead of having the court make a decision for you. Courts vary a great deal in their approach to mediation, but generally a judge is more likely to suggest mediation for children matters than for financial matters.

Most mediators will give you each an opportunity to find out about mediation and the mediator before you commit yourselves to the process. If either of you wants to apply to the Legal Services Commission for public funding (or *Legal Aid*) for your case, you will first be asked to meet with a mediator to see if mediation is suitable for you. In most cases, you have to consider this option before financial assistance can be granted for a solicitor to represent you in court. (See Chapter 15 and the section, 'Getting Help With the Cost of Mediation', later in this chapter for more about public funding.)

About readiness for mediation

If you are feeling a great deal of anger or other strong emotions about your divorce, you may need to go for counselling before you can sit down constructively with your spouse to make use of mediation successfully. (See Chapter 2 for a list of counselling organisations and their contact details.)

About the safety of mediation

If there has been a history of violence in your marriage or you fear that going together to mediation sessions may trigger violence, mediation may not be right for you. You can talk about this on your own with a mediator first if you still want to find out about mediation. Mediators are required by their professional Code of Practice and membership of their professional body to ensure that their practice of mediation is safe. If you opt for mediation, the mediator will discuss with you how to make it safe. See the sidebar 'Sometimes, mediation isn't such a good idea'.

What do mediators do?

At your first session, the mediator establishes the ground rules for your negotiations, clarifies the issue(s) that you want to resolve, and sets an agenda for your discussions. Your next step is to work through the agenda one item after another. Depending on the complexity of the issues you need to resolve, and how well you and your spouse are able to work together, you may be able to resolve matters in a single mediation session, or it may take three or more sessions before you reach an agreement.

A mediator doesn't take sides, interject opinions, or provide legal advice. It is unethical for a mediator, even if she is a family lawyer, to give legal advice to either you or your spouse. Nor is a mediator a counsellor. If either of you is too upset to work during sessions, the mediator may suggest counselling alongside mediation. Nor can a mediator make decisions for you or order you or your spouse to do anything you don't want to do. The mediator sets out rather to create an environment in which you and your spouse feel comfortable and are able to express your opinions calmly, talk over your differences, and work out your problems together.

You may only want to use a mediator to help you talk through the arrangements you make for your children, with or without the help of a parenting plan (see Chapter 10). You may work everything else out with your solicitors. Or you may want only to sort out finances through mediation. Increasingly, couples are using mediation to sort out everything, called 'All Issues Mediation'.

Who are mediators?

Family mediators come from either a family law background or a background in another profession that equips them to work with other people's relationships or decisions. For example, your mediator may also be a counsellor, a social worker, or a teacher. Whatever their professional background, mediators have to undergo additional training to prepare them to mediate between divorcing or separating couples.

Family mediators must meet a set of agreed standards, be deemed competent, and undergo continuing education. They are not, for example, allowed to do work in England and Wales that is paid for by the Legal Services Commission unless they have been assessed as competent by the UK College of Family Mediators or the Law Society.

Working with a qualified mediator helps you ensure that whatever you and your spouse agree to complies with the law. However the outcome of mediation isn't legally binding. You decide whether to make your decisions in mediation legally binding, through a solicitor or by other means. You are always given the opportunity to receive individual legal advice before you finalise your decisions, and it is important that you do so. (See later in this chapter for more about what happens at the end of mediation.)

Sometimes, mediation isn't such a good idea

Mediation may not be good for you if

✔ You are intimidated or threatened by your spouse.

✔ You have not really decided yet whether your marriage is over nor begun to clarify your own divorce priorities and goals, so you don't know what to negotiate for.

✔ You can't get the information you need to negotiate on an equal footing with your

spouse – you suspect that your spouse is hiding assets, for example. (A good solicitor won't let you go into mediation unprepared.)

Although mediators can help you and your spouse to communicate again if you are no longer able to do so, you both need to *want* to do so if mediation is to be effective. If you don't, mediation is not such a good idea.

Because your mediator understands the law and legal processes she is able to diffuse potentially explosive situations during your mediation sessions. For example, if your spouse threatens to storm out because you asked her exactly how much she earns, a mediator can remind your spouse that your solicitor will require that information and can get it anyway through a formal *disclosure* process if it isn't provided voluntarily.

Any reputable family mediator will tell you upfront that each of you also needs a solicitor. This is because a mediator works with you both and therefore cannot at the same time advise you individually about the proposals you reach in mediation. Because you are employing a mediator, however, you will need to make much less use of your solicitor than if he or she was doing all the work for you.

If you need any help or advice with legal issues outside of mediation, however, consult your solicitor for help as you go along. (See 'Asking for Mediation Help from Your Solicitor', later in this chapter.)

Reaping the Benefits of Mediation

It takes two to tango, to sing a duet, and to make mediation work. So, if your spouse is not serious about making mediation work, you are probably wasting your time as well as the mediator's. However, if your spouse is uncertain about whether or not to mediate, ask him or her to consider these important mediation benefits:

✔ Mediators help you focus on the needs of your children.

✔ Working out the sticky issues in your divorce using mediation can be much cheaper than going to court to resolve those issues. For example, some court cases have cost anything up to £20,000, though the average court case where there is one key issue to be decided is probably somewhere between £3,000 and £5,000.

Depending on where you live and whether your mediator works in the private or not-for-profit sector, a mediator in England and Wales can charge anywhere from £30 to £300 an hour (for example, some private mediators in London) for her services, with the average being about £80 per hour or per session for each of you. Mediators bill by the hour for both of you, so if you're splitting the cost, it's well worth the money.

Some mediators charge per session, one of which usually lasts about one and a half hours. You are likely to attend three to five sessions on average, if you mediate all issues. You're likely to attend fewer if you mediate only the arrangements for your children. And if you receive public funding, there is no cost to you.

✔ Family Mediation Scotland (FMS) services operate in the not-for-profit sector and have charitable status. The service is free to you. However, there are fees if you use them to work out your property and financial matters. You need to ask the Family Mediation Service for a note of the fees. If you're on legal aid or have legal advice and assistance, your fees may be covered, if the Scottish Legal Aid Board (www.slab.org.uk) approves the application for expenditure on mediation. Scottish solicitor mediators who work in the private sector charge fees at the commercial rate for mediation, so you need to ask them about their fees (www.calmscotland.org.uk). If you're on legal aid, these fees can be reclaimed, too. See the sidebar 'Family mediation in Scotland' for details on these organisations.

✔ A mediation session is considerably less formal, less intimidating, and less stressful than a court.

✔ You may resolve things faster. Depending on the caseload in your area's family court, it can take months – even a year or more – before your final hearing arrives. On the other hand, after you decide to mediate, your first session can probably be fixed within the month – although just how long it takes you and your spouse to work things out is in your hands.

✔ Mediation can help you and your spouse brainstorm about divorce agreement options. As a result, you may come up with fresh options for the care of your children, for the division of your assets, for maintenance for one of you, if you think it's needed, and for child support, that you may never have thought of otherwise.

- ✔ You are in control. You make the tough decisions in mediation, not a judge, and no one forces you to do anything.

- ✔ You preserve all your options. If mediation doesn't work, you can still go back to your solicitor to negotiate on your behalf, using all the information you may already have collected, or you can go to court.

- ✔ You preserve your privacy. When you use mediation, only you, your spouse, and the mediator hear what you say.

- ✔ You and your spouse are more apt to be happy with your agreement and to honour it in the future because you are working it out together instead of a judge deciding.

Finding Family Mediators

Before using a mediator, you can ask your solicitor questions about the ones she recommends, or you can contact one or two directly and ask them questions including

- ✔ How much do the mediators charge for their services? Do they charge by the hour or do they charge by the session?

- ✔ What are their professional backgrounds?

- ✔ Do they belong to the UK College of Family Mediators or are they members of the Family Mediation Panel of the Law Societies in England and Wales or approved by the Law Society in Scotland?

    The UK College of Family Mediators (01179 904 7223 or www.ukcfm.co. uk) can tell you which of their members are available in your area, as can the two Law Societies.

- ✔ Can they mediate all of the issues you need to resolve or just some of them? Some mediators handle the full gamut of divorce-related issues; not all mediate financial matters or children issues You may only want to use mediation for one or two sticking-point issues.

- ✔ Does your solicitor have good reports of their use by previous clients?

You can find a qualified mediator in your area by contacting any of the following:

- ✔ Legal Services Commission: www.justask.org.uk/leaflets/help

- ✔ The UK College of Family Mediators: 0117 904 7223; www.ukcfm.co.uk

- ✔ National Family Mediation: a network of not-for-profit services in England and Wales: 08456013034; www.nfm.u-net.com. Many of these services also provide counselling and groups for children or adults.

✔ The Family Mediators Association, private sector mediators in England and Wales: 0117 946 7062; `www.fmassoc.co.uk`.

✔ The Solicitors Family Law Association (SFLA): 0689 850227; `www.sfla.org.uk`

✔ The UK College of Family Mediators (Northern Ireland): 028 9024 3265 or 07968 756301; `www.ukcfm.co.uk`

Find out whether the mediators in your locality mediate all issues or children or financial issues only, whether they do publicly funded work and what they charge. You may want to ask whether they mediate alone or in pairs for some or all of the sessions and how many sessions there are.

Family mediation in Scotland

Two organisations are approved to provide family mediation in Scotland. These are

✔ **Local family mediation services affiliated to Family Mediation Scotland** (`www.familymediationscotland.org.uk`). Their work is directed at families with dependent children and can include children over 16 and in full-time education or further education.

✔ **Solicitor mediators accredited by the Law Society of Scotland** (`www.lawscot.org.uk`). The Law Society of Scotland is the governing body for Scottish solicitors who act as mediators, and the Society offers mediation on all issues – property, finance, and your children. They will also mediate with you if you have no dependent children. Solicitor mediators are usually members of CALM (Comprehensive Accredited Solicitor Mediators; `www.calmscotland.org.uk`).

These organisations meet standards set by the Lord President of the Court of Session (Scotland's highest civil court). They have to regulate their mediators and ensure that the mediators abide by a standard code of practice. Family Mediation Scotland is also approved by

the UK College of Family Mediators, and their mediators meet the College standards as well.

Mediators working for these organisations are protected by Scottish law from giving evidence in court. This protection means that no matter what you say in mediation, it can't be used as evidence if you go to court. There are certain exceptions – for instance, where a criminal offence has been committed or if a child's safety is at risk, or if each of you agrees that the mediator should give evidence.

All Family Mediation Scotland's services offer individual, separate, and confidential appointments when you contact the service. At this appointment you'll each hear the same information about what mediation can offer you and what other services are provided. You're also asked about your family situation and your mediator should check with you that mediation will be safe, especially if there is or has been any violence or abuse in your relationship. If mediation is a risk, you have several other options for getting help:

✔ **Contact centres:** Most family mediation services in Scotland provide contact centres. Children can spend time here with a parent

(continued)

(continued)

they don't live with, if it's difficult for parents to make these arrangements themselves. You can find more information on contact centres at `www.familymediation scotland.org.uk`, or have a look at Chapter 10.

✔ **Support groups:** Many of the family mediation services offer support groups for adults and also for children going through separation or divorce. Some services also have children's workers who offer individual sessions to children experiencing short-term difficulty. (See Chapter 2 for a list of support groups.)

✔ **Time to Talk:** This specialist service is mainly for kids whose parents can't meet in mediation, but who want to find out their children's views on matters to do with the separation or divorce. Sometimes this service is used as an alternative to the court seeking the children's views. Refer to Chapter 10 for other ways to find out what your kids are thinking.

Ask your mediator what they can offer you, your spouse, and your children, as new services are being developed all the time. For example, all family mediation services offer mediation that includes (where it is appropriate) your children, grandparents, and members of stepfamilies. However not all family mediation services offer mediation on property and financial issues. If they don't offer it themselves, they can put you in touch with a solicitor mediator in your area or a neighbouring family mediation service.

Taking Your First Mediation Step

Once you decide on mediation, and a mediator, your first contact with her is usually in person, to discuss whether mediation is truly suitable for you and the issues you want to resolve.

Your mediator should also talk to your spouse to make sure that you both choose and intend to use mediation and that you both understand what it involves.

The mediator can give you an idea of how many meetings you are likely to need – depending on the number and complexity of the issues you want to resolve – and the likely cost to each of you. (See 'Getting Help with the Cost of Mediation' later in this chapter about applying for public funding for mediation.)

You are strongly encouraged to get a solicitor each to advise you at the end of mediation and possibly along the way.

If you discuss how much your mediation will cost and decide to move forward with it, you'll be asked to sign an Agreement to Mediate before you begin to work with your mediator.

An agreement to mediate

An agreement to mediate looks something like the following, and may include some of the following statements, depending on your mediator's usual practice.

By signing this agreement we express our sincere intention to:

✔ Be fair to each other

✔ Leave fault and blame out of the negotiations

✔ Be co-operative

✔ Consider the needs of our children, our individual needs, and the needs of the family as a whole

✔ Work for the least emotional and financial upheaval

✔ Make full and frank disclosure of our finances

✔ Not transfer, change, or conceal any assets in advance of reaching an agreement

✔ Make no charges on any account unless agreed by both of us

✔ Only talk to the mediator during sessions, not at other times

✔ Agree that all communications (except the disclosure of finances which are open for use by solicitors and the court) are made on the basis that they are confidential and will not be referred to in any court evidence or affidavits

✔ Acknowledge that the Memorandum of Understanding (the concluding document) is not legally binding unless and until we choose to make it so, through our solicitors or by other means

✔ Recognise that the mediator cannot give legal or other advice, and that it is our individual responsibility to obtain any such advice as appropriate

Understanding How Mediation Works

Mediation works for you by building up mutual understanding, co-operation, and problem solving; it's *not* about winning or losing. During your mediation session, the mediator acts as coach, consensus builder, facilitator, and, if necessary, referee, and helps you to accomplish the following:

✔ Clarify exactly what you need to work out

✔ Organise your discussions by determining what you'll discuss first and how you'll approach each issue

✔ Keep your discussions moving forward

✔ Provide legal or other information as necessary (but not legal advice)

Identifying the issues and making an agenda

You are likely to enter mediation with separate agendas and may need to work with the mediator to agree on a common agenda. For example, you may think that you stand to lose everything – your spouse, children, home, and way of life, and if you have not initiated the divorce, all undeserved! Or, if you initiated the divorce, you may see yourself as managing better without your spouse, staying in the house with your children, and being generous about contact between your ex-spouse and your children. The mediator won't let you argue this out straight away, but will instead encourage you to agree on an agenda of the things that need to be tackled, such as:

- ✔ How to separate
- ✔ Arrangements for your children
- ✔ What to say to your children, when and how
- ✔ Who will live where
- ✔ How you will share out money and property
- ✔ When all this will begin to take place

Exploring the issues in detail

Unless you choose to use mediation only for settling arrangements for your children, you need to collect and share all the details of your finances just as you would if you were negotiating yourselves (Chapter 14) or through your solicitors (Chapter 15). You need to collect the information on the forms that are given to you by the mediator. These forms are similar to the forms you would use in England and Wales if you were asking a judge to decide things for you, commonly known as the *Form E*. It means that the information will be applicable and usable (or *portable*) for you in either context. (See Chapter 3 for an example of a worksheet for assembling this information.)

When you talk together about how to look after your children when you are apart, the mediator helps you to look at your kids' future through their eyes. Hopefully, looking at things from your kids' perspectives will help you begin the transition of your relationship from partners to co-parents.

You need to go through the forms together in your mediation sessions, and then the mediator can display the agreed facts from these forms for you both to see clearly.

Calculating your individual incomes

You each must fill in an income sheet on which you list

- ✔ Your monthly salary or wages from your main and any other employment

- ✔ The deductions, such as National Insurance, income tax, pension contributions, and any work-related subscriptions

- ✔ Any state benefits such as child benefit, working tax credit, child tax credit, disability benefits, rent, or council tax rebates

- ✔ Any other sources of income, such as from property, trusts, shares, dividends, fees, casual payments, or maintenance from a previous spouse, deducting your likely tax liabilities

You then need to work out your separate total net monthly incomes. (See a sample in Chapter 3.)

Working out your expenditures

You must list separately what you estimate you need to spend in the future, to work out how much money you each need after your divorce. (Chapter 3 provides a guide to help you estimate your needs.)

You need to list separately expenditures for your children. Your children's expenses are likely to include:

- ✔ Child care

- ✔ Education – travel, school meals, school trips, uniform and sports gear, any extra tuition (for example, music or sports), and support for further or higher education

- ✔ Recreation

- ✔ Clothes, including out-of-school clothes and equipment, nappies, and so on

Recording your assets

You must list all your assets, as follows (for help in establishing a full list of your assets and their values, see Chapter 7 for a worksheet):

- ✔ **Properties:** The value of your home, any other properties, and any mortgages attached to them, and brief details of the purchase date and price (for assistance, see Chapter 7)

- ✔ **Bank accounts:** The name and address, the account number and type, the balance at a given date

- ✔ **Building society and savings accounts:** Same as the preceding

- ✔ **Investments:** Name, type, size of holding, value, and date

✔ **Life insurances** – company, policy number, date of maturity and value, surrender value

✔ **Pension plans** – company, type, date of maturity, lump sum, annual pension, cash equivalent transfer value, and widow or widower benefits, if any

✔ **Cars and other vehicles**

✔ **Valuables** – such as jewellery or antiques

✔ **Other assets** – including money owed to you or any certain inheritances expected in the next few years

Listing your debts and liabilities

Make a list of how much you owe and to whom, stating beside each item whether you are jointly or solely liable (for help creating this list, see Chapter 7):

✔ Bank overdrafts and loans

✔ Other loans

✔ Hire purchase and finance agreements

✔ Credit and store cards

Verifying the details

You need to verify that you really have the assets and liabilities that you say you have. To do so, collect and bring in detailed proof or *verification* of all your income, assets, pensions, and debts (see Chapter 7). Following are some examples of the kind of proof you need to provide:

✔ **Income:** Payslips, benefit books, business accounts, and so on

✔ **Assets:** The valuation of your house and a copy of the mortgage statement for your property or properties, including more than one estate agent's estimate of its value and a record of your mortgage payments to date. From these documents, you can work out what your house is currently worth to you (that is, the capital balance or *equity*)

✔ **Bank accounts:** Bank statements and building society pass books

✔ **Pension plans:** Pension statements

✔ **Any other documentary evidence:** Details of your income, assets, liabilities, and (possibly) outgoings

How the mediator uses the financial information

As you bring in your separate and joint financial information, the mediator displays it on a flip chart so that you both can see it all put together. This way you can see where you stand and whether there is a surplus (unlikely) or a shortfall (likely) between what you have and what you need.

Negotiating your future budgets

When you both see your income, expenditure, assets, and liabilities clearly listed, you can get a measure of your future needs and resources. When a deficit exists between what you have and what you need, you have to do something to reduce that deficit – increase your income, cash in some assets, pay off some debts, or reduce your future expenditure. To work out how best to accomplish this, you need to decide on a few things:

✔ **Your goals and priorities:** You are encouraged to work towards agreeing on your goals and priorities as a basis for negotiating how you divide your assets and liabilities and your future expenses for yourself and your children.

✔ **Your options:** After you and your spouse establish some common goals, you can start thinking about the various options for meeting them. For example, if one of your common goals is that you each have accommodation large enough to house your children, you can then look at how you might achieve that, such as one of you staying in the family home and the other buying or renting elsewhere, or selling the home and each of you buying another smaller property.

The goals and options that you discuss in mediation are not just confidential to you and the mediator; they are *privileged*. That means that neither you nor your spouse – nor your mediator – may quote your discussions in court or in any court statements. The purpose of this restriction is to create an environment where you and your spouse can freely discuss any options you want without worrying that you will prejudice yourselves in any future court proceedings. In Scotland this privilege is protected by law (see the sidebar 'Family mediation in Scotland' for details).

✔ **A parenting plan:** You must decide, on the basis of what is desirable and feasible for your children, whether you share the care of them equally or whether one of you is the resident parent and if so how the other can succeed in, and sustain the cost of, staying close to the children. For more information on creating a parenting plan, see Chapter 10.

✔ **Child support:** You also need to work out how you share the cost of supporting your children. You can do this in the context of all your future income and expenditure or by reference to the formula adopted by the Child Support Agency. It is always wise to ask for an estimate of this from the CSA. See Chapter 13 for more about child support.

✔ **What to do with your home and pensions:** Some of the more common options for keeping or selling your home and for dividing your pensions are set out in Chapter 3 and Chapter 11. When you have the 'big picture' displayed plainly before you, you are able to see more clearly what options will work out best for you.

Consulting your children during mediation

One great advantage of mediation is that you and your spouse can talk together about the future of your children. If you find this a painful thing to discuss, as it often is (see Chapter 10), a mediator can help you manage your emotions so that you can continue to value and talk to each other as parents, rather than just as divorcing spouses.

As you begin to shape your plans, moving where necessary away from competing for your children to co-operating for them, the mediator is likely to suggest that you consult your children about the plans you are about to make. You can try talking to your children about the divorce in general (as we suggest in Chapter 10), but you can also involve them in your planning so that you can get their perspective, depending on their age and ability to deal with it.

If you are working on a parenting plan in mediation, you might show it to the children before it's settled. You can ask them to express their priorities on whether they'd prefer to move between two homes, or mostly live with one of you, and if so, how they want to keep close to their other parent. Children are often quite clear about some of these issues. You cannot let them make your decisions for you – you are responsible for how you parent them – but you can consult them.

If you find consulting your kids difficult for any reason, the mediator may suggest that she consults them separately and brings back their comments to you both in your next session. Not all mediators do this, but those who do have been trained to talk to children sensitively and carefully. The mediator should discuss meeting with your children very thoroughly with you beforehand and issues of confidentiality must be sorted out. The mediator only meets with your children if you all agree that this is likely to help you make decisions for their benefit.

Your children may find it a relief to see a mediator, as they can then talk fairly freely and feel that they are contributing to the arrangements being made for them, especially if it has been hard for either or both of you to listen to them.

However, the mediator is always careful to ensure that she does not become a counsellor for your children. If that is what your children need, then the mediator will suggest how counselling can be arranged.

Including other family members in a mediation session

During your mediation sessions you or your mediator may feel that other adults could usefully be included in the discussion, perhaps for a special meeting. A new adult partner may be living with your children or present at their contact visits, or one or both of you may have remarried and your children have acquired stepparents and perhaps stepbrothers and -sisters. Life, having become complicated, might have become stressful for all of you and produced disputes or misunderstandings. Your children's grandparents, who may be able to offer help or may be getting excluded, can be involved in mediation. Battle lines may even have been drawn up unhelpfully between your families of origin (see Chapter 9).

If you are in such circumstances, there may be no reason why you shouldn't use mediation, which is a method of sorting out disputes and misunderstandings in all kinds of situations, not only those associated with the actual process of divorce. You can discuss this option with your mediator and see if it is viable to include a particular person or people who may need to be heard and to listen to what you're planning. As with your children, mediation with other people in your life is done with great care, with the purpose and the ground rules clarified to everyone in advance of the meeting.

Four sisters were living with their father and his new partner. Their mother had also re-partnered. Tensions had been building up between the two households over the girls' visits to their mother. One night, two of the girls were so worked up about the phone rows going on that they ran away – fortunately to their grandparents. In the next mediation session, the parents blamed each other for causing the girls to run away, though it was clear that the problem involved more than just the two of them. They decided with the mediator that their new partners should be invited to attend a one-off meeting with them and the mediator. During the meeting, the two women began shouting at one another, each saying that the other was trying to take away the children. The mediator pointed out that they were both saying the same thing. After they realised that they shared identical fears, their relationship improved dramatically. The tension between the two households dissolved and the girls were able to spend time with both families – without so many rows.

Sometimes the children *do* know best

Richard and Jenny, 11 and 8, were invited by their parents and a mediator to have their own meeting with the mediator – without their parents – to discuss their parents' plans for sharing their care. Their parents were talking about having Richard and Jenny change households several times during the week, whereby one parent would meet them from school on certain days and the other on other days. The parents had been rowing a lot and this meant they wouldn't have to meet each other face to face.

After the mediator described the proposed plan to Richard and Jenny, they said without hesitation, 'There will be too much rushing about.'

Taking account of their separate after-school activities, Richard and Jenny suggested a series of simple adjustments, which seemed to resolve the issues for their parents and for themselves.

They asked the mediator, when she discussed with them how she was going to feed this information back to their parents, to emphasise that they loved both their parents and to ask the parents not to row in front of them. When the mediator met again with the parents to discuss their children's ideas and feelings with them, they were visibly moved and were proud that their children had been more practical than they had been.

The Memorandum of Understanding

As you negotiate your way through the big decisions together, step-by-step with the help of your mediator, she should be writing down what you propose. At the end of your sessions, your proposals are set out in written form, usually called a Memorandum of Understanding. This name is meant to draw attention to the fact that it is not legally binding unless and until you both agree to make it so through your solicitors or by other means. You may have worked together on a parenting plan such as the one described in Chapter 10; the nuts and bolts of this will be integrated into your final proposals. You either need to take this to your solicitors or your mediator will send it, with your agreement. Your solicitors can then advise you individually regarding your agreement.

Including your financial details in an Open Statement

The details of your income, assets, pensions, and liabilities, with a list of the verifying documents, are set out in an Open Statement separate from your proposals in the Memorandum of Understanding. The information is usually in schedule form, which is easy for you and your solicitors to follow.

Even if you and your spouse fail to reach agreement on any of the issues between you, you are still able to use the Open Statement in court if necessary. You shouldn't have to duplicate any of the hard work that was involved in collecting that information for the mediation.

Making your Memorandum of Understanding legally binding

After you've had a chance to discuss the Open Statement and Memorandum of Understanding with your separate solicitors and financial advisers first, you're given a chance to make it legally binding if you so desire. If you are all happy with your work, your solicitors will prepare your agreement for the court in the form of a draft Consent Order (or a Separation Deed if you aren't yet going to divorce). Your solicitors send the draft order to the court along with a short summary of your means, called a Statement of Information. If the judge accepts that your proposals are fair for the children and for you, and that you have both agreed freely to the proposals after receiving legal advice, the order is *sealed* by the court and made final, and is legally binding upon you both. Neither of you has to attend court for this process – it can all be done by post.

Asking for Mediation Help from Your Solicitor

While you are attending mediation sessions, you can consult your solicitor about the proposals you're working on at any time. If you decide to use mediation, your solicitor doesn't simply hand you on to a mediator and wait for you and your spouse to resolve all of your outstanding divorce issues. At a minimum, your solicitor can prepare you for mediation by helping you to

- Develop a list of the specific issues you want to resolve
- Work out your goals and priorities
- Assess your options
- Review any information your spouse may share with you prior to mediation so that you understand all of it and know the right questions to ask about it
- Develop a mediation plan or strategy
- Assess whether you might need any other sort of professional help, such as from an independent financial advisor, forensic accountant, or pension actuary

Depending on your ability to negotiate with your spouse during a mediation session and the complexity of the issues you want to resolve, your solicitor may also help you in other important ways:

- ✔ By serving as a sounding board on occasions
- ✔ By confirming or questioning any information the mediator or your spouse may give you
- ✔ By reviewing with you any written agreement that the mediator has drafted

Your solicitor can't discuss your situation with your spouse's solicitor nor with the mediator without your consent, as you and your spouse are the people doing the negotiation.

Getting Help with the Cost of Mediation

Over the past few years, the government has encouraged the use of family mediation in England, Scotland, and Wales, and, as part of that policy, has made public funds available to support people of low to moderate means with the cost of mediation. If you think that you might be eligible for public funding, you need to make sure that you see a mediator who is approved by the Legal Services Commission. (See 'Who are mediators?' earlier in this chapter.)

The mediator assesses your financial eligibility for mediation during your first introductory session, so you need to take details of your means to that session, along with recent evidence of your salary or state benefits or other income. If you are eligible, and mediation is otherwise suitable, the whole process including the preparation of the Open Statement and Memorandum of Understanding is free. Your spouse is assessed separately for his or her eligibility.

After the mediator confirms your eligibility, you become entitled to some free advice from your solicitor, both during the course of mediation and at the end. Your solicitor will ask you to sign a form which enables you to obtain the benefit of a certificate of 'Help with Mediation' to cover this expense. The certificate may also be extended toc over the cost of the solicitor putting your mediation into legal form and implementing it.

Family Mediation Scotland (FMS) services are free unless you use them to work out your property and financial matters. See 'Reaping the benefits of mediation' earlier in this chapter for more information.

If for any reason, mediation isn't suitable for you and your spouse, the mediator will give you or your solicitor a form CLS APP7 confirming that mediation cannot proceed. That confirmation enables you to apply for public funding to take your case to court instead if that is appropriate.

Exemption from paying your costs back to the Legal Services Commission

You'll find that most forms of legal aid for family disputes are more like a loan than a gift. So, for example, if you are granted public funding by the Legal Services Commission to take your case to court, or for your solicitors to negotiate on your behalf, you have to pay back all your court and your solicitor's costs out of any money or property that you receive as part of your settlement. This is known as the *Legal Aid Charge* or *Statutory Charge,* and it will almost certainly apply to you regardless of whether your final settlement is by consent or fully contested.

By contrast, if you're eligible for public funding for mediation, you don't have to pay back any of the costs incurred by your mediator or solicitor so long as you reach an agreement in mediation and you and your solicitors finally approve that agreement. This is as an incentive to you to reach an agreement in mediation and to stick with it.

Going to Your Solicitors if You Can't Agree in Mediation

If you don't agree on some or all of the issues in mediation, you can pass on the work you have done in mediation to your solicitors to try further to reach agreement with your spouse's solicitor. Therefore, the time and effort you've put into mediation isn't wasted (see Chapter 17).

If your solicitors also fail to find an agreement, either you or your spouse can take your case to court. See Chapter 18 for an idea of what to expect if your case goes to court.

What the court does and does not want to know

You are asked to agree before entering mediation that what you say to each other in sessions is *confidential* to you and your mediator, and that neither you nor the mediator can reveal the content of your discussions to anyone else without each other's consent. This gives you freedom to speak without being quoted, which your mediator also respects. The only, very rare time that confidentiality can be broken is when there is a real risk of harm to a child or another adult that has to be reported. You are told about this exception at the beginning of mediation.

Privilege means that the court can't inquire into the content of your mediation discussions nor can you quote each other without each other's consent. If your case goes to a hearing, neither your solicitors nor the court can enquire into or use conversations that took place in mediation. The Open Statement is the only thing that can be taken from mediation and used in court. This grants you the freedom to explore goals and options together without fear of prejudice. Here again, the exception to this rule is if there is a real risk to someone's safety.

A new development, as a result of The Proceeds of Crime Act 2002, is that mediators are also legally obliged to report you or your spouse to the authorities if they have reason to believe that either of you benefits from the proceeds of any crime.

Chapter 17

Helping Your Solicitor Get the Best Results Possible

*W*hen you engage a solicitor to represent you in your divorce, you and your solicitor become partners – you give and get, and your solicitor gives and gets – and the progress and outcome of your divorce, not to mention its cost, depend in part on how well your partnership works.

To help make your solicitor-client relationship productive and efficient, this chapter explains what you and your solicitor should expect from one another and the type of information your solicitor needs in order to represent you in the most effective (and economical) way possible.

Because the divorce process becomes more formal when you engage a solicitor, this chapter also explains how round table conferences and draft proposals work. Finally, this chapter provides some information on the preparation of the final divorce agreement.

What to Expect from Your Solicitor

You and your solicitor should understand from the outset what you need and expect from each other. At the very least, you should expect that your solicitor will do the following:

✔ **Provide a written contract or agreement that states the terms and conditions of your solicitor-client relationship and an estimate of the costs.** (Don't work with any solicitor who won't provide one.)

✔ **Live up to the terms of your written agreement or contract, or let you know ahead of time when something you agreed to needs to be changed.** (You did make sure to get something in writing from your solicitor, didn't you?)

✔ **After becoming familiar with the facts of your case, lay out a plan for, and general approach to, your divorce and explain that to you.** The plan does not need to be elaborate, but at a minimum it should give you a general sense of how your solicitor intends to proceed with your divorce to achieve an agreement that works for you. Your solicitor should also give you a rough timetable for the completion of your divorce.

✔ **Provide clear explanations of all your options as your divorce progresses, answer your questions honestly, and show respect for your preferences and decisions.**

✔ **Pull out the stops to reach a negotiated settlement.**

✔ **Give you straightforward answers to your questions.** Be prepared, however, to hear things you may not like – that your divorce expectations are unreasonable, that you should give up certain assets or pay money to your spouse, or that your spouse is unwilling to concede on an issue that is really important to you.

✔ **Tell you when your divorce priorities and goals are not legally or financially feasible.**

✔ **Return your phone calls within a reasonable period of time (24 hours is acceptable) unless you are very clear that you need a quicker response.**

✔ **Consult with you before putting an offer on the bargaining table or taking other important actions related to your divorce.**

✔ **Give you copies of all correspondence and documents sent out of her office that relate to your case.**

✔ **Keep your personal and financial information confidential.**

✔ **Store any important documents you produce for her in a safe place and provide you with copies on request.** Your solicitor should return them to you promptly after your divorce is over or if you ask for them sooner.

✔ **Act as your interim adviser, as well as your solicitor, by recommending certain services, other professionals, courses, seminars, and support groups that you may want to consider using to help you deal with the non-legal aspects of your divorce.** Good family law solicitors want to help with their clients' emotional or mental healing while they are handling the legal aspects of their divorces.

✔ **Explain to you the option of using a mediator as well as a solicitor and make a referral if you want one.**

✔ **Follow the Law Society Family Law Protocol.** You can obtain a copy of this from the Law Society, 113 Chancery Lane, London WC2A 1PL, or check their Web site: www.lawsociety.org.uk.

After your negotiations are underway, you can't rule out the possibility that your spouse's solicitor may do things that change the tenor or direction of your divorce. When that happens, your solicitor's approach will probably change and the cost of your divorce may increase as a consequence. These changes may also mean that your divorce takes longer.

Expect some disappointment and frustration along the way as the terms of your divorce are being negotiated. But don't take your feelings out on your solicitor, assuming that she has been working hard on your case. Your solicitor can't always produce instant solutions.

What Your Solicitor Expects from You

To help get you the best divorce possible, your solicitor expects you to provide information, direction, and feedback when it's needed. Respond to your solicitor's requests as quickly and completely as you can. Staying actively involved in your divorce and being responsive to your solicitor's requests is the best way to help ensure that her legal help does not cost you a fortune and that your final divorce settlement reflects at least some of your goals and priorities.

Your solicitor may tell you things that you should and shouldn't do while you are getting divorced. These instructions are intended to help protect your legal interests or your safety. Don't disregard them! If you do, you may undermine your lawyer's efforts and put your interests or your children's interests in jeopardy. The following sections of this chapter describe what your solicitor expects of you as a client.

Don't be afraid to ask questions and speak your mind

Trusting your lawyer's judgement doesn't mean that you can't ask her questions, or request an explanation when she says something that you don't understand, or speak up when you aren't sure that you agree with her recommendations.

When your solicitor provides you with advice and options, carefully weigh up what she says. Talk it through with your solicitor but, in the end, follow your intuition – only you know what will really satisfy you and how far you're willing to go to get there. Remember, you make the decisions; your solicitor only recommends the decisions that you might make.

Pay your bills on time

If you have trouble paying your legal bills, don't let them pile up. Instead, as soon as you feel financially pinched, find out if your solicitor is willing to work out a payment plan or some other financial arrangement with you. Don't just disappear or become unavailable to talk to your solicitor because of your money problem. You may hurt your case if you do. If you are publicly funded and you have to pay a contribution towards your costs (see Chapter 15 on public funding), make sure that you pay it promptly, and let your solicitor and the Legal Services Commission know if you get into difficulty.

If you don't pay your legal bills, your lawyer may well stop working on your case and make an application to the court to withdraw so that she can legally stop representing you. If the court approves the application (which it usually will if you have not paid your bills), you have to engage a new solicitor, and your divorce will take longer. You are still contractually bound to pay your solicitor's outstanding fees, as well as the costs of your new solicitor. Your solicitor is entitled to refuse to send your file of papers to your new solicitor until you have paid any outstanding costs.

Keep your solicitor up-to-date with any changes in your life

Your solicitor needs to know about any changes in your personal situation or in your spouse's life that could affect your divorce or your safety. For example, inform your lawyer if your spouse begins threatening you with a battle over the children, if your spouse's business is experiencing financial problems, if you develop a serious new relationship, or if your spouse becomes abusive.

Avoid using your lawyer as a therapist

Your solicitor is your legal adviser, not your therapist. Taking up her time with tirades about your spouse, worries about your future, or laments about what could have been is a quick way to run up your legal bills. When you are having difficulty dealing with your divorce or just need a shoulder to cry on, talk to a trusted friend or relative, or a counsellor. Refer to Chapter 2 for a list of counselling organisations and Chapter 9 has some good information about caring for yourself.

First Things First: Seeking Urgent or Interim Orders

If your divorce is contentious, one of the first things your solicitor may do is file an application asking the court to grant an *interim* or *emergency order* or an *injunction* (or *interdict* in Scotland). Such orders can help you make sure that certain things happen or don't happen while you are working out the terms of your divorce. For instance, your solicitor may request an order for

- ✔ Spousal support

- ✔ Child residence or contact

- ✔ Control of assets if you are worried that your spouse may waste or hide family assets

- ✔ The right for you to remain in your home

- ✔ An injunction against improper behaviour of many types (including physical abuse) on the part of your spouse

  If you have to apply for an order excluding your spouse from the home or to prevent abuse, you may be able to get an order at the same time that your spouse pay the rent or mortgage until the longer-term property issues are decided.

- ✔ In Scotland, the Family Law (Scotland) Act 1985 provides guidelines for *interim aliment* (maintenance). Aliment can be for a spouse or for a child, but only if the provisions of the Child Support Act do not apply. (See Chapter 13 for more information on the Child Support Act.)

If you are concerned that your spouse may disappear with your children, your solicitor can also ask the court to prohibit your spouse from doing so or ask the court to order supervised contact if there is evidence that he or she may attempt to abduct your children (see Chapter 10).

After your solicitor files the appropriate paperwork with the court, the solicitor or the court arranges for a court hearing to deal with the application. At this hearing, your spouse (actually your spouse's solicitor, assuming that one has been engaged) has an opportunity to argue why your application should not be granted.

When you need action now: *Ex parte* orders

When the need for action is immediate, your solicitor may be able to get a court order issued on an *ex parte* basis. *Ex parte* refers to a legal action ordered on behalf of one party without the other party being notified about it or having an opportunity to participate in the action. You and your solicitor will have to spell out in your application and any statement in support why the order should be granted on an *ex parte* basis. Examples are that your safety would be at risk or that your spouse might destroy or dispose of property or valuables if he or she learns of the application before an order is made.

With an *ex parte* order, your spouse will not learn about the court's decision, and a full hearing will not take place until after the court has made an initial decision on your application and granted its order. Therefore, an *ex parte* order is normally of very short duration. Both parties in the action are usually ordered to attend a hearing to determine whether the terms of the *ex parte* order should be extended or varied.

If you request an *ex parte* order and one is granted, you may be held responsible for any damage that your spouse suffers because no court hearing was held, so think through the implications with your solicitor before you make the application.

Providing Your Solicitor with Essential Information

You should provide your solicitor with basic information about your family, marriage, finances, reasons for divorcing, and so on during your initial meeting. But after your client-solicitor relationship is formalised, your solicitor needs to know a lot more about you.

Your solicitor collects much of the information we mention here through one-to-one interviews with you, and by asking you to fill out forms and provide as much back-up documentation as you can – payslips, credit card statements, title deeds to property, insurance policies, lease agreements, bills, loan applications, business profit-and-loss statements and balance sheets, records of investments, household budgets, and other documents (refer to Chapter 3 for a list of everything you should need).

Don't decide for yourself whether your solicitor needs the information she requests. Clarify with her, if you need to, why the information is necessary. Do your best to provide everything your solicitor asks for; don't hold anything back just because you think the information is unimportant or irrelevant. Failing to share that information may derail your solicitor's negotiating strategy or complicate your divorce in other ways. For example, if you with-hold information from your solicitor that your spouse's solicitor knows about, your spouse's solicitor may damage your case by introducing that information into evidence during a hearing.

If you read Chapter 7 of this book and follow its advice, you will be a couple of steps ahead of the game. But if you delay pulling together essential information because the whole process sounds oh-so-tedious and time-consuming – which it is – you won't be able to avoid assembling the necessary paperwork after you engage a divorce solicitor. Remember, the more information your solicitor gets from you or through the co-operation of your spouse, the less you need any formal disclosure or court proceedings and the less your divorce will cost. (Chapter 5 covers the disclosure process in detail.)

The following sections of this chapter provide a rundown of some of the things your solicitor needs to know.

Personal information

To help develop a constructive approach for ending your marriage and to determine what you may be entitled to in your divorce, your solicitor needs information on your personal history, your marriage, and your dependent children. Therefore, among other things, your solicitor will question you about

- Why you are getting a divorce
- The history of your marriage
- Biographical information about you and your spouse
- Your individual health histories, including whether either of you has a history of serious medical or emotional problems
- Your children – their ages; where they are living, if you and your spouse are separated; whether your children have special needs (educational, physical, emotional); whether they are attending state or private schools; and so on.

Legal and financial information

Your solicitor also spends time reviewing the ins and outs of your finances and any legal agreements you and your spouse may have entered into. Among the things your solicitor needs to know are the following:

✔ Whether you have a separation agreement. Your solicitor will want to read the agreement if you have one. (See Chapter 6 for more on separation agreements.)

✔ Whether you and your spouse own property, including homes, buildings, or land. Be prepared to provide your solicitor with copies of the title deeds and any mortgage documents relating to the property if you owe money on it.

✔ Whether you signed any pre-marital or post-marital agreements. (For full information on pre-marital and post-marital agreements, take a look at Chapter 21.)

✔ Whether you or your spouse have done any inheritance planning, such as writing a will, buying life insurance, or setting up a trust.

✔ Whether you or your spouse own shares in a limited company or have a business partnership together or separately, or if you have other shared business interests.

✔ An accounting of your assets and debts and where you got the money to pay for any of the property you may own (that is, your home and any other homes, buildings, or land).

✔ How much each of you earns annually from all income sources – including salaries, bonuses, and other employment-related income, dividends, trust income, pensions, annuities, royalties, state benefits, tax credits, and so on.

✔ Whether either of you made special contributions to the other spouse's career or business or to the family generally (for example, you helped finance the business or worked in the business; your spouse supported you through college or university; or you used your separate or inherited funds to purchase assets or to pay for your family's living expenses).

✔ Whether either of you has wasted family assets by gambling; engaging in extramarital affairs; or through addiction to drugs, alcohol, or even the Internet.

✔ Your current household budget and your projected post-divorce budget.

✔ Evidence of your spouse's fault, if you plan to petition for divorce against your spouse based on their adultery, behaviour, or desertion, or evidence of the length of your separation if you want to divorce on that basis (see Chapter 5).

Writing it all down: The story of your marriage

It may be helpful if you prepare a written narrative describing your marriage: how you and your spouse shared childcare responsibilities, what you think led to your divorce, what you want from your divorce and for your life after divorce, and what you believe your spouse wants.

A succinct narrative can be a good way for your solicitor to get at the facts and issues related to

your divorce that may not be apparent from a review of the financial, legal, and personal data forms you fill out or from your client-solicitor interviews. Furthermore, putting everything down on paper can be both cathartic and healing, and may help you put your marriage and divorce in proper perspective.

Other important information

Finally, your solicitor asks you questions about what you expect from your divorce and what you're willing to do or not do to get what you want. Your solicitor needs this information in order to meet your needs but also because she has to be certain that you have realistic expectations about the possible or likely outcome of your divorce. Given this, you can expect your lawyer to ask you about

- ✔ Your divorce goals and priorities
- ✔ Why you feel the children's arrangements you want are reasonable and why your spouse's desired children's arrangements aren't reasonable, if you and your spouse don't agree on these
- ✔ Under what, if any, circumstances you are willing to go to a full court hearing to get what you want

Hammering Out the Details of Your Settlement

Your solicitor works out the details of your proposed divorce settlement and presents them to you for your approval and then to your spouse's solicitor in detailed written or oral form. Your spouse's solicitor should do the same thing. These oral or written presentations can be little more than trial balloons to get your or your spouse's reaction to certain provisions or they can represent something closer to a final and complete divorce agreement.

After everyone feels that they are very close to a final agreement, one solicitor prepares a written draft *consent order*. Depending on the complexity of your divorce and how willing you and your spouse are to do some compromising, a single draft order may be all that is necessary before you and your spouse have something you can both approve.

Expect to review all drafts, whether they are prepared by your solicitor or your spouse's solicitor, and then be ready to provide your solicitor with feedback. Don't agree to any proposal if it makes you feel uncomfortable. You and your spouse aren't obliged to accept any draft agreement you don't like. You can accept or reject the draft agreements, or you can use them as the basis for additional negotiations.

After your solicitor fully briefs you about key points and legal issues, she may suggest that you and your spouse work out the terms of your final agreement on your own instead of working through your solicitors (assuming that you and your spouse are communicating with each other). After that, your solicitor can draft a written divorce agreement or order. She may also suggest mediation if there is a stumbling block, for example about the arrangements for your children, which you might be able to overcome by directly negotiating with each other with the help of a third party.

Evaluating the Proposal

You have to evaluate whatever agreement your spouse may propose, or that either solicitor may draft, and decide whether you like the agreement, don't like it, or like it enough to use it as the basis for your final negotiations in your divorce settlement. When you do your evaluating, ask yourself the following questions:

- ✔ Is the agreement fair to me?
- ✔ Can I afford the agreement?
- ✔ Is the agreement in my children's best interest?
- ✔ What was I looking for in an agreement that this one does not have? Are items missing that are worth the cost and the time involved in continued negotiations?
- ✔ Is the reason that I don't yet want to settle because important items are missing from this agreement or because my emotions are getting in the way?
- ✔ If I really push for any of the missing items, what may I have to give up? Is it worth it to me? What are the risks of not settling now?
- ✔ Is my spouse likely to make any additional concessions?

✔ Will I be any better off if I refuse to settle and take this case to a full hearing? What is the worst that could happen? (Your solicitor should be able to give you a strong sense of the best and the worst judgements that will be likely given the statutory guidelines and the past decisions of the judges who may hear your case.)

✔ What kind of financial and emotional toll is not settling likely to take on me and my children? Is not settling in order to gain what I want really worth it?

You and your solicitor should discuss the pros and cons of the proposed agreement. Share your thoughts and concerns with your solicitor and ask for an opinion about the agreement. Your solicitor may tell you that the agreement is about as good as you're going to get, that you can probably get a few more concessions if you keep negotiating, or that the agreement is not in your best interest. In the end, however, how you respond to whatever offer is on the table is your decision.

Making a Deal: The Final Settlement

After you and your spouse come to a final agreement about the terms of all key issues in your divorce, your lawyer or your spouse's lawyer drafts a version in the form of a consent order detailing everything you agreed to, including many standard provisions and precedents – language you may find in many consent orders. If your solicitor does the drafting, she submits it to your spouse's solicitor for review and changes, or vice versa. Children orders are drafted separately from financial orders. If there are still issues over the divorce itself, your lawyers deal with those separately as well.

Don't get impatient with all the back-and-forth negotiations. Getting everything just right is important because after you and your spouse sign the agreement it becomes a legally binding contract or order, which means that both of you are legally obliged to live up to what it says, like it or not.

A draft consent order that includes terms for your capital, property, or pensions cannot be submitted to the court for approval until after your decree nisi has been granted. The terms themselves cannot take effect until your decree absolute has been granted. Your solicitor, however, may be able to advise you on legal ways around these restrictions if there is some urgency in your case.

Attending a hearing

After you and your solicitors agree on the terms of your draft consent order, it is usually sufficient for one of your solicitors to send a copy of the draft order (and any court fee) by post to the court. If it is a draft financial order, they also must send a simple agreed summary of your respective finances and intentions known as a *Statement of Information* or *Rule 2.61 Statement*. A judge then examines the paperwork in your absence, and the court seals the draft order if it is approved by the judge, or lets your solicitors know if there are any queries.

If you do attend a hearing, your solicitor goes with you or may be able to go in your place. So long as the draft consent order is within the powers of the court and appears to be fair, the hearing should be more of a formality than anything else, and it's over quickly.

Changing the Agreement Later

After a financial order dealing with your property or capital is sealed by the court, it is almost impossible to change it, even if you and your spouse agree. It is only in the most exceptional circumstances that a judge will review such an order after it's made. Only orders concerning your children, or child or spousal maintenance, may be reviewed, but then you and your spouse will either have to agree those changes or you will have to justify why the changes should be made.

Applying for the Final Decree

If you are the petitioner, it will be your or your solicitor's responsibility to apply for the final decree of divorce – the *decree absolute* – once a final order has been made on your property and finances. Unless your finances are very straightforward, your solicitor will usually advise you to wait before applying for the decree absolute until the final financial order has been made. In most cases, a court officer can grant your decree absolute without reference to a judge, and will send a copy of the final decree to both solicitors.

Make sure that you keep a copy of your final court order and your divorce decrees in a safe place. They are important documents and you may need them for future reference, or have to supply them if you're applying for a passport or want to remarry. If you do lose them, you can apply to the court for another sealed copy, but you need to supply the court with your court reference number and a fee. You can find the court reference number in the top right-hand corner of all court documents. The number is exclusive to you and your ex-spouse.

Chapter 18

Putting the Decisions in the Hands of a Judge

. . . .

In This Chapter

▶ Analysing your options if your spouse makes you an offer of settlement

▶ Reviewing what happens at a pre-trial hearing

▶ Preparing for a fully contested hearing

▶ Understanding the role of the judge and the trial process

▶ Weighing the pros and cons of an appeal

. . . .

*W*e're going to give it to you straight: If your divorce is heading for a contested hearing (sometimes referred to as a trial), the experience is not going to be pleasant. The cost of your divorce skyrockets; you'll probably have to pay for it out of your family property (which means you and your ex will each take less property from your marriage); your stress level will soar; and you still have no guarantee that you'll like the judge's decision. If you think a contested hearing sounds like a kind of hell on earth, you're getting the idea. Contested hearings are serious business. If you're heading for such a hearing, fasten your seat belt, because you're in for a bumpy ride.

To help prepare you for some major turbulence in your life, we discuss out-of-court settlements and evaluating any offers that your spouse sends your way. We explain what happens prior to a court hearing, and offer you general advice about proper in-court behaviour. We also provide an overview of the procedure at court hearings and concludes with information on appeals, in case the outcome isn't what you'd hoped for.

Making Certain You Want to Go to Court

Before you move full speed ahead with a formal application for a court hearing on any major issue within your divorce, think long and hard about its financial and emotional costs. Putting any issue within your divorce in the hands of a judge is a gamble: The judge may not view matters quite the way you do, and you may not get the divorce order you hoped for. Never assume that you have such a strong case that the judge will automatically decide in your favour. Be prepared to be disappointed.

Before committing to a full court hearing, ask yourself the following questions:

✔ Does the risk of losing or having a disappointing outcome outweigh any benefits you may receive from going to court?

✔ Would you be better off compromising with your spouse to ensure that you get at least some of the things that are really important to you, rather than rolling the dice and hoping that you come up with a lucky number?

✔ Do you have the time for a lengthy court hearing? Getting divorced takes longer if you go to court. Preparing for the hearing take a great deal of time, and you may also have to wait for a hearing date – as long as six months or more depending on how many other cases are ahead of yours. If you want a speedy divorce, going to court isn't the way to get it.

✔ Do you want to put your children through the emotional stress of a fully contested court hearing? Although they may not fully understand what is going on, they will at least sense that you are under an unusual amount of pressure, which may scare them.

Despite all the negatives associated with a court hearing, sometimes it's your best or only option. For example, you may need to go to court because

✔ Your spouse refuses to negotiate, or negotiations haven't worked.

✔ Your spouse is hiding information essential to a fair settlement.

✔ Your spouse insists on an arrangement for your children that you do not think is in their best interest, but won't discuss it in mediation.

✔ You need more maintenance than your spouse will agree to.

✔ You think your spouse may be wasting or hiding assets.

✔ Your spouse has an alcohol or drug problem or has abused you or your children.

Settling Out of Court

Most issues within divorce never get to a full hearing, although they may get as far as the steps of the court. Therefore, while your solicitor and your spouse's solicitor prepare for your court hearing, they may also try to negotiate an out-of-court settlement.

Receiving the offer

After you and your spouse give the go-ahead to your respective solicitors, one solicitor may send the other a written offer, the other may counter it, reject it, or (if you are lucky) accept it. (By the way, your solicitor cannot accept or reject an offer without your consent.)

Eventually, all the terms of your agreement may be worked out. This back-and-forth process is a more formal version of what you and your spouse may have done if you tried to negotiate your own divorce by yourselves or during a mediation session. (To learn more about how mediation works, head to Chapter 16.)

You may get an offer during this back-and-forth process that you believe is relatively reasonable and fair. The offer may not be everything you hoped for, but it may be close. Although your solicitor should provide you with his opinions about the offer, the final decision about how to respond is yours.

If you get an offer from your spouse, read it carefully. It may not be obvious that the agreement isn't close to what you are legally entitled to, what your spouse can really provide, or what you think you need.

Deciding on the offer

Following are some questions that you should ask yourself to help you decide what to do when you get an offer:

- How close is the offer to what you are asking for, and is the offer fair?

- Does the offer reflect most, if not all, of your divorce priorities?

- Given what you know now about your legal rights and responsibilities, the value of the property you own, and how your kids are being affected by the divorce, are you likely to benefit if you reject this offer?

- How much have you spent on your case and can you afford to spend any more?

- Are you willing to take the offer just to stop the agony of going through a protracted and expensive legal process?

- Are you likely to do better if you go all the way to a final hearing than if you accept what your spouse offers?

    To help you decide what to do, your solicitor may be able to offer information regarding how the judges who may hear your case have decided cases similar to yours.

- What are the advantages and the disadvantages of settling now?

The monetary costs of a court hearing

If you go to court it can be a serious expense. The exact cost of a court hearing depends on a number of factors: what part of the country you live in (divorcing in a major metropolitan area, for example, usually costs more than divorcing in a provincial town); the specific issues the judge is deciding on; your lawyer's legal strategy; and the legal strategy of your spouse's lawyer. Your costs are likely to be higher if your own or your spouse's lawyer has a particularly confrontational strategy.

You can expect your legal bills alone to run into the four- or five-figure range – maybe as much as four times the cost of a negotiated divorce.

At a minimum, you should be prepared to incur the following expenses:

- ✔ Lawyers' fees
- ✔ Court fees
- ✔ Expert fees
- ✔ The cost of preparing evidence, bundles of documents, and witnesses for the hearing
- ✔ Miscellaneous legal expenses – copying, long-distance charges, postage, delivery fees, and so on

This list covers just the monetary costs of a court hearing. It can't begin to calculate the cost to your family's health and happiness if you're embroiled in an ugly divorce court battle.

You may think that threatening to take your case to court will pressure your spouse to give in on certain points that are important to you. Before you try this tactic, you should think about which scenario is more likely: You hold your ground and your spouse agrees to a compromise, or your spouse holds his or her ground and calls your bluff.

Settling Issues through a Pre-trial Hearing

A *pre-trial hearing* or *pre-trial review* offers you and your spouse a formal opportunity to resolve your differences and come to an agreement after you have enough information to make a decision. The judge participating in the hearing may actively push for a settlement after she knows the facts of your case. Judges have been known to instruct divorcing spouses and their legal representatives to talk over their case first. If you and your spouse aren't able to reach a settlement, the judge will note her displeasure and may give reasons for why you should have come to an agreement.

Your lawyers use pre-trial hearings to settle issues relating to the arrangements for your children following receipt of the CAFCASS report, and financial issues following full disclosure between you. (See Chapter 5 for basic information about these procedures.) Your lawyers may also try to resolve other immediate issues, such as who pays what bills while your divorce is proceeding and so forth.

The pre-trial hearing is an opportunity for both lawyers, the judge, and maybe even you and your spouse, to discuss your case outside of court and accomplish the following:

✔ Clarify the specific issues to be resolved at your final hearing

✔ Address all uncertainties that must be resolved before the final hearing

✔ Develop a timetable for interim and final hearings

✔ Determine who will be called as witnesses

✔ Decide the arrangements for preparing the necessary bundle of documents for use at the final hearing

If your case involves your children, the court will probably list a pre-trial review hearing a week or two after a CAFCASS officer has filed his or her report, and a week or two before the final hearing date (see Chapter 5 for a description of a CAFCASS officer's role). That will give you and your lawyers the opportunity to discuss any recommendations that the CAFCASS officer has made and to see if you are able to resolve the outstanding issues.

In financial cases, the Financial Dispute Resolution hearing, or *FDR*, is the main opportunity to explore the possibilities for settlement with the judge's help. This hearing is usually listed a few weeks after the first court appointment and a few weeks before the final hearing. Sometimes it is combined with the first appointment to save time and money. See Chapter 5 for more on the court procedure for children and financial cases.

The court does not usually let you postpone a court appointment without the judge's prior permission. You must have good reason if you ask for a postponement, otherwise you may have to pay your spouse's wasted costs.

Your lawyer may use the pre-trial hearing to see how a judge is likely to decide the issues in your case. If he gets the feeling that things may not go your way at a final hearing, your lawyer may urge you to settle out of court.

If you don't agree to a negotiated settlement at a pre-trial hearing, you and your spouse can agree to one later, even after the final hearing has begun.

Preparing for the Final Hearing

Getting ready for a final hearing is time-consuming work, which is why hearings are so expensive. Your solicitor reviews and gathers information relating to your case, develops and refines his legal approach, co-ordinates the production of evidence and a bundle for the court, prepares witnesses to give evidence, and makes other preparations. Often your solicitor, with your consent, will engage a barrister or *counsel* to help with the preparation and presentation of your case. Chapter 4 describes the main roles and differences between solicitors and barristers. Here we simply refer to them as your *lawyers* or *legal representatives*.

Setting the stage

Preparing for a final hearing is somewhat like staging a play, with you and your spouse as the reluctant 'stars'. The witnesses who give evidence in court are your supporting, or not-so-supporting, players depending on whether they give evidence for or against you.

To help stage your final hearing, your lawyer will outline a strategy. This serves as an overview of everything your lawyer will do to either get you a favourable out-of-court settlement as quickly as possible, assuming that is a realistic goal, or to win your case if it goes all the way to a final hearing. Your lawyer's strategy may be an aggressive or non-aggressive one:

✔ An *aggressive strategy* involves bombarding the other side with allegations of abuse, indifference, child neglect, wasting assets, infidelity, dishonesty, delay, or general instability. To a lesser extent, an aggressive strategy can involve pressuring the other side with interim applications, questionnaires, requests for disclosure, and requests to produce documents, among other things.

✔ A *non-aggressive strategy* relies more on informal disclosure to get at the facts of your case and co-operation between your lawyers to work out the terms of the issues in your divorce.

Both tactics are designed to encourage an early out-of-court settlement. Or, these tactics can make your spouse all the more determined to go to court. An aggressive strategy is almost guaranteed to make you and your spouse enemies forever, but this might be your only option.

The strategy that your lawyer chooses depends on several factors, including:

✔ Your own desires and resources

✔ What your lawyer thinks is best for the case

✔ The strategy that your spouse's lawyer is likely to use

✔ Your lawyer's style and the style of your spouse's lawyer (some are scrappy street fighters and others are wily tacticians).

If you contest the validity of a pre-marital or separation agreement, a judge may have to rule on that issue before he or she can decide how to divide up your property and debts or decide whether one of you has to pay the other spousal support. (See Chapter 21 for more on pre-marital agreements.) To save time and money, your lawyer should try to get this issue resolved as quickly as possible because the judge's decision determines exactly what issues your final hearing will address and influences how much disclosure you may need to do.

Understanding the disclosure process

In all divorce and family court proceedings in the UK, there is a duty of *full and frank disclosure* of all relevant information and documentation between the parties. In children matters in particular, this duty can even extend to information which is adverse to your own case, if it affects the welfare of your children. The judge won't permit you, your legal representatives or your witnesses to introduce at your final hearing important evidence which you haven't previously disclosed to your spouse. If one of you does produce new evidence that is essential for a fair hearing, you and the judge decide whether an adjournment (or postponement) of the final hearing is necessary, and if so, who should pay the costs of the adjournment.

One of the ways that your solicitor gathers information is by using the standard *disclosure* process, which involves the use of legal tools such as requests to produce documents, and questionnaires. (Your spouse's solicitor will do the same thing.) This disclosure is in addition to any that both solicitors may have already done – formally or informally – if you have been trying to work out a negotiated agreement on any issue in your divorce with your spouse. Chapter 5 tells you more about the disclosure process.

The current rules for procedure in financial cases – the *ancillary relief procedure rules* – are designed to make the process of disclosure less overwhelming and costly for you and require both parties to exchange all essential information and documentation in advance of the final hearing.

Disclosure costs can skyrocket in a litigated divorce. Ask your solicitor what he or she can do to keep those costs down.

Producing evidence

Your solicitor may use various kinds of evidence to bolster his arguments or to undermine your spouse's position. Your solicitor will also work out how to address evidence your spouse's solicitor may introduce that is damaging to your case. Among other things, evidence can include

✔ Financial records

✔ Police reports

   ✔ Valuations

   ✔ Doctors' records

   ✔ Photos, letters, diaries, videotapes, and audiotapes

   ✔ Psychological or medical reports

   ✔ Witness statements

Calling witnesses

Your solicitor and your spouse's solicitor may call witnesses to give evidence at your final hearing. Your friends, family members, and business associates may be called as witnesses. *Expert witnesses* who have special training, education, or knowledge, such as psychologists, business valuation specialists, doctors, valuers and estate agents, social workers, and others with professional expertise, may also be called.

If you use expert witnesses they expect to be paid for their time. Depending on the kind of witness and his or her reputation, an expert witness may charge you over a hundred pounds an hour. If these witnesses are asked to do certain things in preparation for your final hearing – review documents or write a report, for example – they will bill you for the time it takes them to do that work as well as for their time in court.

The family and civil proceedings rules expressly require expert witnesses to be *jointly* instructed by you and your spouse whenever possible. The expert's first duty is to the court, and not to either of you. You are jointly responsible for the expert's fees. If either of you want to instruct your own independent expert, you have to justify your reasons to the judge, and the judge normally allows one expert each for the particular subject in issue. You are responsible for your own expert's fees (although, if you win the case, the judge may order your spouse to pay part or all of your costs including those of your expert).

If you are worried that one of your witnesses may not turn up to court voluntarily, or your witness needs a summons or court order to attend, you may apply to the court office for a witness summons, or to a judge for a court order, requiring your witness to attend on the date and time specified. You have to provide your witness's out of pocket expenses for attending court up front at the time of serving your witness with the summons.

If you do have a witness who you think may be reluctant to attend court on your behalf, think very carefully before summonsing them. A reluctant witness may end up giving evidence that is not helpful to you, or may collapse under cross-examination. In addition, your legal representative is not allowed to ask your witness any leading questions (questions that may suggest the answer), unlike your spouse's representative who *can* ask them leading questions.

Ordinarily, witnesses are used to help establish certain facts. For example, if you and your spouse are fighting over the residence of your children, witnesses may be called to help establish which of you is their primary carer – the parent who spends most time with them, takes them to the doctor, attends parent-teacher meetings, takes them to and from school and nursery, feeds them, clothes them, and so on. Or a surveyor may be called to help decide the value of your home. Most witnesses, including you and your spouse, are expected to file and exchange beforehand a written statement or report detailing the evidence on which they are relying. Witnesses must be available to give oral evidence (and be cross-examined) at your final hearing.

Professionals who have been involved with your children, such as their teacher or doctor, rarely agree to give evidence as a witness on your behalf as they don't want to take sides. Any evidence they give should be primarily in order to help the judge decide what is best for your children, not what is best for you or your spouse. As a result, they normally meet with the CAFCASS officer instead who includes any relevant information from the witness in his report. Let the CAFCASS officer know before he prepares a report if you think there is anyone in particular he should speak to.

During the course of the preparations for your final hearing, your solicitor meets any witnesses on your behalf to get a sense of what they will say and to draft a statement of their evidence. She may advise them about the most important points that they should try to make and the best way to get those points across. However, she does *not* tell witnesses what to say.

Preparing the court bundle

Before any major hearing, particularly the final one, the judge expects your lawyers to agree on all the documents that are needed for the hearing. The documents include all the applications, orders, statements, reports, and other miscellaneous documents relevant to your case. Your lawyer has to take responsibility for collating all the documents for your application into one fully indexed and paginated bundle. The bundle also includes a chronology of all the main events relating to the issue in question (agreed if possible by your lawyers in advance), a copy of any questionnaires and responses, and a summary from each of your lawyers of the main facts, issues, and arguments in your case. Your lawyer must file the bundle with the court by a date fixed by the judge so that he has a chance to read the papers before the final hearing. Your lawyer should consult you about the contents of the bundle, but has to follow any practice directions that may be issued by the court.

Rehearsing for your big day (or days)

Prior to the start of your final hearing, your solicitor, and possibly your barrister as well if you have one, should spend time with you, preparing you for what's to come. For example, your solicitor or barrister may

- ✔ Talk you through the trial process – the procedure for the final hearing
- ✔ Review his strategy with you
- ✔ Explain the points that you should make when you give evidence, even suggesting words or phrases that help clarify your thoughts or add weight to your statements
- ✔ Anticipate questions that your spouse's legal representative may ask and help you come up with answers for the more sensitive or difficult ones
- ✔ Build your confidence by role playing or grilling you as your spouse's lawyer would if he were trying to unnerve you or make you angry
- ✔ Advise you about how to look and act in the courtroom

Tell your lawyer about any concerns you have about the hearing. She can probably help alleviate your worries. For more information about giving evidence, see Chapter 5.

Dressing the part

Appearances count and your appearance can detract from the real issues in your divorce and even undermine your lawyer's legal strategy. Be sure that you and your lawyer talk about how you should dress for your final hearing.

Most likely, your lawyer will suggest that you wear something simple and understated (for example, if you are the wife, no bright colours, plaids, or prints, that you steer clear of flashy jewellery, that your hair is clean and neat with no wild hairstyles, and that you avoid excessive make-up and too-short skirts). Even if understatement is not your style, make it yours for the final hearing – if you are the husband, this is the time to wear a shirt and tie. Judges often prefer simplicity to extravagance, and you don't want there to be any unnecessary distraction from the key issues of your case.

Acting the part

You may seethe with anger, quake with fear, or feel totally defeated when you are in the courtroom, especially when you are on the witness stand, but try to keep your cool. Also, be polite to everyone – including your spouse's legal representative and, yes, even your spouse.

Your lawyer may tell you not to worry if you cry when you are on the witness stand. You won't be the first witness who has done that, but don't be tempted to turn the tears on just for effect.

Listen attentively to the courtroom proceedings. Take notes and when you hear someone say something that you know is not the truth, let your solicitor know. The best way to do that is by passing your solicitor a note, rather than whispering in his ear. Whispering may make your solicitor miss important evidence, and someone on your spouse's side may overhear your comments.

When you're called to give your evidence, keep a few things in mind:

- **Answer the questions you are asked in as few words as possible.** Giving long, involved answers may say too much and hurt your case. If the lawyer wants to know more, let him ask you another question.

- **Pause before you answer a question so that you give yourself time to think about what to say and so that your legal representative has time to object to the question you are asked.** If your lawyer objects and the judge sustains the objection, the judge tells you not to answer the question. Otherwise, you have to answer any question you're asked.

- **If you are unnerved by a question or not sure how to respond to it, take some time to compose yourself and to think about your answer by pouring yourself some water and having a sip or by asking the lawyer to repeat the question.** A jug of water and a glass should be sitting on the witness stand. If not, ask the judge for a glass of water. You may find counting to ten before you answer helps.

- **Sit up straight; don't slouch.** Keep your hands folded in front of you on your lap. Avoid wild gesticulations.

- **Do not be rude, sarcastic, or argumentative with your spouse's lawyer, even if his or her questions are offensive or upsetting to you.** Offending or upsetting you may be part of the lawyer's strategy.

- **Address your answers to the judge slowly and clearly.** The judge records your responses, and in the end, the judge decides the case.

- **When you get off the stand, do not send dirty looks or expressions of exasperation in the direction of your spouse or your spouse's lawyer.** Maintain your dignity no matter what.

Understanding the Judge's Role

The judge who hears your case is responsible for ensuring that you get a fair hearing and that the lawyers follow the appropriate court procedures. The judge also rules on any objections the lawyers may make. If your and your spouse's lawyers get into a disagreement with one another or if someone in the courtroom gets unruly, the judge will step in.

During the hearing, the judge listens to the evidence and the lawyers' submissions and reviews any documents, statements, and reports that are entered into evidence. The judge may also ask questions of the witnesses and will almost certainly take notes, although a court transcriber or machine is also there recording every word that is said.

Many family court judges used to be family lawyers. Most judges have reputations for the kind of courtroom they run and for the way they tend to decide certain issues. For example, the judge in your case may run his courtroom with an iron hand or give your lawyers a great deal of leeway. He may have a reputation for favouring mothers over fathers in child residence battles, or be less inclined than other judges to order spousal maintenance.

If your lawyer knows which judge will hear your case and she has been practising in that judge's jurisdiction for some time, she should take the judge's style and reputation into account when preparing for your hearing. If your lawyer isn't familiar with the judge, she should talk to a lawyer who is.

In some courts, you may not know which judge will hear your case until the day of your final hearing. Therefore, your lawyer may have to 'fly blind' as far as preparing for the final hearing with a particular judge in mind.

Having Your Day in Court

You and your spouse will finally get your day in court weeks, maybe months, after your application is filed (assuming that you still haven't been able to settle the issues in your divorce out of court).

In the courtroom, you and your spouse will sit with your respective lawyers at tables or benches directly in front of the judge. If you haven't seen or spoken with your spouse in a while, the sight of him or her in the courtroom may be unnerving and upsetting; on the other hand, you may feel just plain glad that you are finally getting things resolved.

Most family proceedings are heard in *chambers*. That means that only you, your legal representatives and the judge are allowed in court. Witnesses are only allowed into court when they are giving their own evidence. Occasionally, an expert witness such as a child psychologist may be invited to stay for the whole proceedings.

Court hearings follow a very predictable sequence of events. To help you make sense of what is happening in yours, here is a brief rundown on what to expect:

1. Opening speeches

The lawyer for the spouse who has made the application outlines the agreed facts of the case to the judge and summarises the issues between you and your spouse. The lawyers should provide a brief summary of the case and issues in writing, along with a draft of the order sought. These summaries are exchanged between the lawyers and a copy given to the judge no later than the day of the hearing. These summaries set the stage for the evidence and arguments to come.

2. **The applicant's case**

   The lawyer for the spouse who made the application (the applicant) goes first. The applicant's lawyer presents evidence as to why that spouse should get what was asked for in the application – for example, residence of the children or a transfer of the house and maintenance. To help prove the case, the applicant and witnesses are called to the stand and questioned on oath, first by the applicant's lawyer (_examination_) and then by the respondent's lawyer (_cross-examination_).

   Sometimes, if an expert witness has been jointly instructed, or if a CAFCASS officer has been involved, he or she is called before any of the other witnesses and both lawyers and the judge have a chance to question him or her. The judge then usually releases the expert or CAFCASS officer to avoid any unnecessary costs and time.

   The applicant's lawyer may ask more questions of some of their witnesses who gave evidence earlier (_re-examination_). Re-examination is more apt to be used if the respondent's lawyer damages the applicant's case during cross-examination. It is used when something he or she said needs to be clarified or explained in a way that is more favourable to the applicant.

3. **The respondent's case**

   The lawyer for the respondent presents his case following the same procedures used by the applicant's lawyer, except that he doesn't have the opportunity to summarise the respondent's case orally first. The respondent's lawyer starts by calling the respondent to give evidence and then any other witnesses on his or her behalf. The applicant's lawyer cross-examines each of the respondent's witnesses in turn, and then the respondent's lawyer re-examines them if he or she needs to.

4. **Closing arguments**

   During closing arguments, both lawyers get one last chance to make their cases. The respondent's lawyer goes first. If only a few issues need to be resolved, final arguments may exceptionally be waived.

5. **The judgement or order**

   Depending on the complexity of the case, the judge may give her decision right away or take time to deliberate and return with a decision later. In most cases, the decision is given straight away. The judge also hears arguments and makes a decision on who pays for the divorce. Usually, you're each responsible for your own costs, but sometimes, if one of you has clearly lost or has conducted the proceedings unreasonably, that party is ordered to pay all or part of the other's costs.

No matter how long you think you'll be sitting in front of the judge, never bring food, drinks, or reading materials into a courtroom. And make sure your mobile phones are switched off.

Finally, the Judgement

After the judge gives her decision, she may ask one or both of your lawyers to write a written draft of the order made. Your lawyers may go straight off and do this together, or one lawyer drafts the order and sends it to the other for review and approval. When both lawyers agree, or if the given time limit expires without an objection, the order is submitted to the court for the judge's final approval.

After the judge approves your court order, you can expect the following to happen:

- The provisions of the order usually replace any interim or pre-trial court orders unless otherwise specified.

- A court officer seals the court order and sends it to your lawyers. Your lawyer gives you a copy of the sealed order.

- The solicitor for the petitioner applies for the decree absolute – the final decree of divorce – if he has not already done so. The granting of the decree absolute is usually a formality and will be dealt with by a court officer on the day of receipt.

Yes, your divorce is officially over and for better or worse, you are single again. You and your now ex-spouse must comply with all of the provisions of the court order, including transferring and returning property, paying money, adhering to a specific contact schedule, and other such terms.

Appealing the Decision

You can appeal the judge's decision if you are unhappy with it, but an appeal takes yet more time and money. In addition, you have to file your appeal within a certain period of time, usually 14 days for financial matters and seven days for children matters. How long you have to file an appeal depends on the nature of the order, who made it, and in which court it was made. If you're considering an appeal, ask your lawyer about the time limits for filing.

You can't appeal a judge's decision just because you want to, and in some cases, you may need the permission of the judge to do so. You must have a legal basis for the appeal. Generally, an appeal is entertained only if there has been some clear procedural irregularity, or it has been shown that the original judge took into account matters that were irrelevant or ignored matters that were relevant or otherwise arrived at a conclusion that was plainly wrong.

Time and money aren't the only factors you should consider when you are deciding whether to appeal. You should also consider these facts:

- Your appeal may not be heard for months, and once it is, you face another court hearing.

- While you are waiting to learn the outcome of your appeal, you, your spouse, and your children are living in a sort of limbo. You may have to delay the application for the final divorce decree yet further. The result: You're still not divorced.

- Everyone in your family already may be emotionally worn out by the first hearing.

- You may have to find a new lawyer, especially if your current lawyer thinks that filing an appeal is risky or pointless given the facts of your case.

- The judge's decision may not be thrown out, and even if it is, you have no guarantee that the outcome of your next hearing will be more to your liking. In fact, you could end up with a judgement you like even less!

Wrapping things up

You and your solicitor should review the details of the judge's decision and any aspects of your divorce that you have negotiated with your now ex-spouse so that you understand your legal responsibilities to one another and are clear about any other steps you need to take as a result. You may need to

- Transfer property, execute charges or deeds of trust, and other ownership documents

- Exchange cash and other valuables. You may want to make this exchange through your solicitor or in front of a neutral third party so that neither of you can accuse the other of dishonesty

- Amend your insurance policies as necessary or purchase new ones

- Make changes to your will and to other inheritance planning documents

- Notify or pay off your creditors

Part V
After Your Divorce Is Finalised

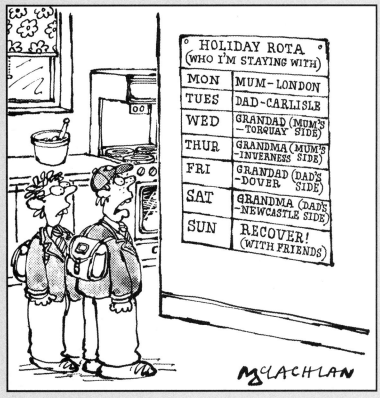

'This is what happens when both sets of grandparents are divorced too.'

In this part . . .

This part of the book helps you prepare for the post-divorce experience. We give you advice on handling your personal finances, seeking a well-paying new job, and getting the education you need to pursue that new career. We also alert you to some of the more common (and serious) problems newly-divorced people face, give you advice on how to deal with those problems, and point you toward other resources that can help. Finally, for more peace of mind the next time you marry, we offer information on prenuptial and the rarer postnuptial agreements.

Chapter 19

Handling the Practical Matters of Life after Your Divorce

- Attending to post-divorce legal and financial matters
- Rethinking or writing your will
- Managing your money after you're divorced
- Locating the job you need
- Making life okay for you and your children

*N*ow that you're divorced, what do you do first? Depending on the details of your final court order, you may have plenty to deal with in the way of paperwork and payments. You will have to begin managing your own money, perhaps find a job outside the home, and build a new social life for yourself or pick up your old one where you left off. Whether your children are living with both of you or one of you, you must work out together how you're going to care for your children now that you're on your own.

This chapter provides the information and advice you need to tie up the loose ends of your divorce and face the challenges ahead. It highlights inheritance planning issues to consider, offers information that can help you reach your educational and career goals, and suggests things you should do to manage your money wisely, no matter how much (or how little) income you have. This chapter also offers you some valuable advice about post-divorce parenting and developing new friendships.

Tying Up the Loose Ends of Your Final Court Order

Read the details of your final court order carefully, and do exactly what the order says. If you fail to carry out your legal obligations (and that is exactly what they are), the battles that may have plagued the end of your marriage are likely to continue. If your ex-spouse decides to take you to court, you may find yourself in legal trouble all over again.

Ask your solicitor which of the loose ends relating to your divorce court orders you need to deal with yourself and which he might take care of. Your solicitor should clearly advise who needs to do what in writing. Use your lawyer's letter as a checklist to make sure that you don't overlook any of your legal responsibilities.

Transferring real property

If your former spouse is to become the sole owner of real property (houses, other buildings, or land) you own together, you must transfer your interest in the property by both signing a formal deed of transfer. Your solicitor sends a copy of the deed of transfer to the Land Registry where the property is registered. If your property is jointly rented, you will need to sign an authority to your landlord to transfer the tenancy into your ex-spouse's sole name. (See Chapter 3 for more about the Land Registry.)

If the transferred property has an outstanding mortgage or charge attached to it, you are still legally liable for it, unless and until your spouse pays the mortgage off, or the lenders join in the deed of transfer and formally release you from the mortgage. That will be the case even if your final order says that your former spouse will take responsibility for the mortgage. Such an order usually contains a promise by your ex-spouse to do whatever he or she can to secure your release from the mortgage and that he or she will pay you back (or *indemnify* you) if they default on the mortgage payments. That promise is binding as far as you and your ex-spouse are concerned but not so far as the lenders are concerned. The lenders can still sue you for the debt. (See Chapter 11 for a discussion of the legal actions you can take to protect yourself legally if your ex-spouse defaults on the loan associated with the transferred property.)

If your final order obliges your former spouse to pay you a lump sum of money, you should secure that debt with an asset if you can – just as a bank or other commercial lender may do. That way, you increase the likelihood of seeing that money. For example, if your ex gets the house and, in return, he is going to pay you £30,000 within the next five years, you can secure that debt by placing a *charge* on the house by registering it with the Land Registry. If your former spouse doesn't pay up, he won't be able to sell, borrow against, or transfer the collateralised asset without paying you first.

If you place a charge on the house, and your ex-spouse defaults on payment to you, you can foreclose and sell the house. Enforcing the charge through sale is a good option if you have enough equity in the house to then pay off the mortgage, pay the costs of sale, or keep the money you're due.

Transferring other property

If you transfer stocks, bonds, policies, shares, or other funds to your former spouse, you may have to pay capital gains tax if their value has appreciated since they were first purchased. Timing may be crucial here. You need to check this out with your solicitor or accountant.

If you need to transfer ownership of a vehicle, you need to register the transfer at the DVLA, Swansea, SA99 1BL. Customer enquiries can be made by telephone on 0870 240 0010 or by e-mail at vehicles.dvla@gtnet.gov.uk. Their Web site address is: www.dvla.gov.uk.

Paying off debts

At all costs, try to avoid a divorce agreement that requires your former spouse to pay off your debt. If your ex-spouse fails to honour that agreement, your credit rating will be damaged, despite what your agreement says. This is a real concern if your ex-spouse is angry about your divorce and you think he or she may try to get revenge by not paying your debts. Chapter 11 gives you more tips for avoiding trouble.

If your former spouse does take over some of your debts, however, notify your creditors in writing and ask them to transfer those debts into your ex-spouse's name in order to relieve you of responsibility for them. Although the creditors are not legally obliged to comply with your request and although they can still collect the debt from you if your former spouse does not pay, your letters help underscore who is supposed to be satisfying those debts. And, as a friendly reminder of what you expect, send your ex-spouse a copy of those letters.

If you want to be sure that your ex-spouse is paying off the debts that used to be yours, see if you can get your ex-spouse to provide you with proof of each payment – a copy of the monthly statement will do. You may also want to ask the creditor to notify you straight away if your ex-spouse defaults.

Collecting state benefits and tax credits

Now that you are finally separated or divorced, your status will change and you may become eligible for certain state benefits or tax credits. See Chapter 7 for a summary of the main benefits and credits that may be available to you: They can make a big difference to your financial position. Make an appointment with your local Citizens' Advice Bureau to make sure that you are claiming all the benefits that you are entitled to, or for help in completing the forms. You will find their details in your local telephone directory. The sooner you apply, the sooner your application will be dealt with. Most benefits and credits will be backdated to the date of your application not to the date that you first become eligible.

Protecting your pension rights

If you have the benefit of a pension sharing or pension attachment order (see Chapter 11), there are a number of important steps that you need to take to make sure that the order is put into effect. Maybe your solicitor will deal with these for you, or advise you on the steps that you might take yourself. If you have to wait for your share of the benefits until your spouse draws his or hers or dies (that will be a pension attachment order), it is crucial that you keep the pension administrators informed of any change of address; otherwise, you may lose the benefit.

If you want to obtain the benefit of any additional contributions that your ex-spouse has made to the state pension scheme (without any loss to your ex-spouse), you must send a copy of your decree absolute to the Pension Service (www.thepensionservice.gov.uk) within one month of the grant of the decree.

In Scotland, a pension sharing order or agreement must be sent to the Pension Service within 2 months of decree of divorce – this is particularly important to remember if you have a 'Do It Yourself' divorce.

Changing your final order

If you are unhappy with something in your final order, comply with it anyway. Most of it will stand whatever you think. However, if you believe that the terms of your maintenance or pension attachment order should be modified due to changes in the circumstances of your life or your former spouse's life, you can apply to the court for a variation. Similarly, if the arrangements for your children that you agreed to or that were ordered are no longer meeting their needs, you can apply to the court to vary the order. But talk to your solicitor first to get an idea of your prospects of success.

Rethinking Your Estate Planning

If you had a will when you were married, you need to revisit that legal document now that you're divorced. Any provisions in that will appointing your then spouse as an executor or beneficiary automatically lapse on the granting of your decree absolute. (An *executor* is the adult responsible for making sure that the provisions of your will are carried out after you die. You appoint your executor in your will. A *beneficiary* is the person you name who benefits from part or all of your estate.)

If you don't have a will, now's the time to write one

Getting divorced is a good excuse for you to write a will if you don't have one already or even if you do. You may be able to get *Legal Help* for your solicitor to draft your will for you if you are financially eligible, and if you are appointing a guardian for your minor children. (See Chapter 15 for details of the Legal Help scheme.) A will isn't just for multimillionaires. You need one if you care about who inherits your property after you die. Without a will, the *rules of intestacy* determine who inherits everything you own. In England and Wales, the rules of intestacy require that your estate passes to the following people, in the order given, but subject to certain financial restrictions in each case:

1. Your spouse if you have one, but if not, to

2. Your children and grandchildren if you have any, but if not, to

3. Your parents, equally if both alive, but if none, to

4. Your full brothers and sisters or their issue, but if none, to

5. Half brothers and sisters or their issue, equally if more than one

If you don't have any of the above, your property then goes to grandparents, full aunts and uncles, half aunts and uncles, and then the Crown, the Duchy of Lancaster, or the Duke of Cornwall.

Your will can also serve the following functions:

✔ Provide for your children should you die while they are still financially dependent on you.

✔ Appoint the adults who will manage the assets you leave to your children in your will. That person is called a *trustee.* If you do not name a trustee in your will, the court may appoint your ex-spouse to play that role.

✔ Appoint the adult who will bring your children up if you and your former spouse both die while your children are still minors. This appointee is called a *guardian*, or *testamentary guardian.* Your children's guardian automatically acquires parental responsibility for them on the death of you and your ex-spouse (see Chapter 4).

Ordinarily, your former spouse becomes responsible for bringing your children up. If that's not what you want, state your preference in your will and provide your executor with a separate written statement of your reasons. However, despite your stated preference, a judge may award residence to your ex-spouse unless he or she doesn't want it or is an unfit parent, or there are other strong reasons for a non-parent to bring up your kids.

Estate planning tools to help you

In the event of your death, you can make sure that your children are financially provided for in other ways besides including them in your will. To find out which estate planning tools are most appropriate for you, talk with a wills specialist, or a trust or probate solicitor.

Trusts

A *trust* holds and manages assets for one or more beneficiaries. It can be *revocable* (one you can change later on) or *irrevocable* (a trust you won't be able to change). You must appoint a trust corporation or not less than two *trustees* to oversee and manage the assets held in trust for the benefit of young children or where real property is involved. To help you determine whether a trust is appropriate, consider the following:

- Children under the age of 18 (or 16 in Scotland) can't inherit money or property in their own right.

- Depending on the type of trust you set up, it can provide tax benefits and reduce the number of assets in your estate that must go through probate.

- Because a trust is expensive to set up and maintain, it's most appropriate when you are leaving your children a substantial amount of property.

- Trusts are complicated legal entities. To establish one, you need the help of a trust specialist or probate solicitor.

Other estate planning options

Another option is to name your children as the *beneficiaries* of your life insurance policy or nominate them for any benefits that your employer offers. Again, you have to name an adult to manage the benefits for your children should you die. Your solicitor, financial adviser, or work personnel department can provide helpful advice. If you are paying private school fees for your children, you may also want to take out a school fees policy to cover the fees in the event of your death.

Assessing Your Financial Situation

What you asked for during your divorce process and what you actually ended up with are probably somewhat different. For example, you may have received fewer assets, been saddled with more debt, and received less child support and maintenance than you had hoped for. On the other hand, if you're the one making those child and spousal support payments, those payments may be higher than you expected. Either way, money is likely to be tight now. Developing a budget helps you determine just how much you can afford to spend and where you should be cutting back. Chapter 3 can help you come up with a budget for your family.

If you are obliged to pay spousal or child support, managing your money is particularly important because the law expects you to make those payments on time and in full. If you don't, and your former spouse takes you to court to enforce arrears, arguing that you 'just ran out of money' won't cut any ice with the judge. Going back to court will cost you more time, money, and stress, and you may well be ordered to pay your spouse's costs. Ultimately, you could find yourself spending time in prison.

As a general rule, your mortgage payments (principal and interest) should not consume more than 30 to 35 per cent of your gross or pre-tax income, although some lenders are willing to lend up to five times your gross salary. Taking your mortgage and any other debt into account, you need to ensure that your budget can cope with at least a 1 per cent rise in interest rates, and preferably 2 per cent.

For help in putting your budget on track or to increase your financial skills, get in touch with your local community education college to see if they run courses on personal finance. Also, if you owe more than you think you can pay given your monthly income, a debt counsellor may be able to help you negotiate lower monthly payments to your creditors. Good sources of debt advice include

- ✔ **CAB:** www.adviceguide.org.uk
- ✔ **National Debtline:** www.nationaldebtline.co.uk or 0808 808 4000
- ✔ **Consumer Credit Counselling Service:** www.cccs.co.uk or 0800 138 1111
- ✔ **Payplan:** www.payplan.com or 0800 389 3431

Using the services of a financial adviser

Unless you are an experienced financial manager, planning and implementing an appropriate investment strategy takes the help of a qualified financial planner or adviser. When you are looking for one, as a general rule steer clear of professionals who are tied to a particular company and sell specific financial products. Instead, engage an independent financial adviser.

Working with an independent financial planner who makes money by charging you a percentage of the total value of the assets he or she manages or invests for you or employing a financial planner who charges you by the hour for advice and assistance may be better alternatives. Financial planners who charge you by the hour are most likely to consider *all* your investment alternatives – policies, stocks and shares, bonds, property, and so on. Ask the financial adviser about the different options for payment of their charges.

The Institute of Financial Planning has a search facility that will help you find a qualified financial planner in your area. You can phone them on 0117 945 2470, or try their Web site: www. financialplanning.org.uk. The sector is regulated by the Financial Services Authority

and anyone giving advice must have a Financial Planning Certificate (FPC).

One way of identifying an adviser's status without asking him or her is if they are a member of one of the financial associations that promote professionalism within the industry. If so, then the letters after their name will give you an indication of their expertise. For example, if they are a member of the Society of Financial Advisers (SOFA, www.sofa.org) or Chartered Insurance Institution (www.cii.co.uk), the following designations apply:

- ✔ **FPC:** passed the entry level examinations Financial Planning Certificate.

- ✔ **MSFA:** passed the Advanced Financial Planning Certificate and have at least two years' experience.

- ✔ **ASFA:** passed six advanced examinations, have at least three years' experience, and completed one-year continuing professional development (CPD).

- ✔ **FSFA:** passed ten advanced examinations, have at least five years' experience, and completed three-year CPD.

Finding a Job or Landing a Better One

After you take a hard look at your budget and assess all your options, you may decide that if you are going to be financially solvent, you will have to work outside the home (if you don't already) or find a better-paying job.

If you are unsure about what kind of new career you may be suited for, meet with a career counsellor. He or she can help you assess your skills and interests and discuss the types of jobs for which you may be suited. Other possible sources for this service include your local further education college and your local Job Centre or Social Security office. Look in the telephone book for your nearest social security office, for Jobcentre Plus, or Jobcentre in the social security advert in the business numbers section of the book.

Acquiring the education you need

If you already have a job but need to make more money, finding more lucrative work may simply be a matter of updating your CV and beginning a job search (especially if you have good job skills and strong qualifications). But, if you're re-entering the work world and your skills are outdated or very limited, or if you want to change careers, you'll probably need job training or continuing education to achieve your employment goals.

Financing a college degree

Depending on your job skills and education level, achieving your career goals may require getting a degree from a three- or four-year college or university course, completing a further education college course, or attending a trade or technical college (see the next section of this chapter for more on choosing a good technical college). But you may find financing the cost of higher education hard to do when money is tight, especially if you need to put money away for your children's education.

If you need help funding your education or training, the student loan, grant, or work-study initiatives may be able to help you. Extra help may be available to you if you have children or are a single parent. You may need to complete an access course to get into university if you do not have appropriate GCSEs. Fore more information, contact the DfES on 0800 731 9133 or www.dfes.gov.uk/studentsupport and try Women's Aid www.womensaid.org.uk. Or enquire about what grants are available for mature students from your local college or local education authority.

If your goal is to get a well-paying job after graduating from college, select your course of study carefully. Some college qualifications lead to a bigger and more immediate financial payoff than others.

Choosing a vocational course or college

You can find both good and bad vocational courses and providers. Attending one of the good ones can be a great way to gain very specific job skills. The bad ones will take your money and give you little in return.

Before you enrol in a privately-run vocational college, find out if your local community education college offers you the same education at a cheaper cost.

The following tips can help you shop wisely for a vocational college course:

- ✔ Visit the college. Check out its classrooms, computers, and other classroom resources. Do the surroundings look well cared for and is the equipment state-of-the-art?

- ✔ Find out if the college is accredited and by whom.

- ✔ Ask to sit in on some of the classes.

✔ Get information about the curricula, staff, costs, and refund policy.

✔ Talk to students who have completed the course you hope to enrol in. Get their opinion of how well the course prepared them for a career. If they're willing to share the information, find out what salaries they earn.

✔ Find out about the kind of career counselling and job-finding assistance the college offers its students and ask about the college's placement rate.

Searching for the right job

When you begin looking for a job many avenues are open to you. The right method for finding that perfect job depends on your particular job skills, work experience, and the kind of job you want. You may want to consider the following job search methods:

✔ Read the classified ads in your local paper, or check out their Web site.

✔ Go to job fairs. They're a great way to learn who are the potential employers in your market and what skills they're looking for.

✔ Talk with some of the larger employment or personnel agencies in your area. Some are general and some specialise in a specific industry.

✔ Work with an executive recruiter, if you are fairly well qualified already (better known as a *head hunter*).

✔ Visit your local Job Centre or public employment service agency to find out about job vacancies in the public and private sector.

✔ Tell your friends and professional associates that you're looking for a new job.

✔ Use the Internet. Searching for key words like 'job openings', 'employment', or 'careers' yields a wide variety of job openings all over the country. Narrow your search by specifying the area you want to work in or indicating the type of job you want, or go directly to the company you want to work for and click on its 'employment' link. Other sources of job information on the Internet include the Department for Work and Pensions and your local authority.

Some career-orientated Web sites offer more than just job listings. You can post your CV at these sites, conduct your own job search, arrange for a personal search agent to e-mail you information about listings that match your job criteria, and get advice from career counsellors.

- www.jobsite.co.uk

- www.connexions-direct.com

- www.proteus-net.co.uk

Dealing with Personal and Family Issues

After your divorce is over, you enter a new phase in your life. You may feel happier than you have felt in a long time, free of the tension and strife that plagued your marriage. Life after divorce can represent a time of personal growth, rediscovery, and new opportunities for you.

On the other hand, you may find being single again an intimidating and lonely experience – particularly if divorce was not your idea and you are unprepared for life on your own or if you have sole care of your children. Even if you sought this last arrangement, having full-time responsibility for your children seven days a week, night and day, can be overwhelming, not to mention exhausting. Maybe you're planning to enter a new relationship, perhaps with someone who isn't used to living with other people's children (that is, your children), or who may have kids with whom you – and your children – come to live. Or maybe your ex-spouse is entering a new relationship, and your kids have to adjust to that. In other words, your future, and your children's, could be mightily more complicated than your past.

If you need parenting support, try parentlineplus.org.uk or oneparent-families.org.uk, or look for *Co-parenting Survival Guide* by Zimmerman and Thayer (New Harbinger Publications, 2001) or *Parenting after Divorce* by Stahl (Impact Publishing, 2000).

Being easy on yourself

To help you adjust to all the changes in your life, avoid piling unreasonable expectations on yourself. Just do what you must to tie up the loose ends of your divorce; otherwise, take a breather and re-group mentally and physically. Although you may have big plans for what to do with the rest of your life, give yourself a chance to recover from what you've been through.

In other words, being a little lazy – letting your house get messier than it usually is, eating fast-food dinners once in while, skipping a few workouts at the gym – is okay. Pressuring yourself to make important decisions right away, before you can think them through with a clear head, may cause you to make some mistakes you'll regret later on.

On the other hand, maintaining those habits can make you feel good about yourself and about life in general. If you get too lazy, you may slip into a state you can't crawl out of, which definitely interferes with your ability to get on with your life.

Taking time to reflect on what happened

Try to put your recent experiences into perspective. Take time to understand why your marriage didn't work out and how you may have contributed to your marital problems. Otherwise, you may end up making the same mistakes twice. Keeping a diary is a good way to do this and counselling can be a big help, too (see Chapter 2 for advice on how to find a counsellor).

Accept the fact that your life is no longer the way it used to be and it never will be again. This doesn't mean that your new life is a disappointment – it's just different. Identify some benefits to being single again. For example, you have more privacy and time to yourself, and you can sleep better because you're no longer stressed out by your divorce.

Finding a support group

Consider joining a divorce support group. Its members can help bolster your confidence through the inevitable down times as you rebuild your life and can provide you with advice and feedback when you encounter problems you're not sure how to handle. Contact the Divorce Recovery Workshop, www.drw. org.uk, for support after your divorce. Gingerbread can put you in touch with a local group of parents on their own at www.gingerbread.org.uk, or call their helpline on 0800 018 4318.

Becoming handy around the house

You may have to take on new household chores – cooking, food shopping, balancing the accounts, home repairs, mowing the lawn – chores your ex-spouse used to do. If you need to get up to speed quickly on unfamiliar household tasks, relatives and friends may be willing to give you a quick lesson (don't be ashamed to ask them for the help you need). Reading how-to books or taking classes are also good ways to acquire new skills. Soon you'll feel proud of what you can accomplish on your own and gain confidence in your ability to learn even more.

Focusing more attention on your children

If you have children, much of your energy will probably focus on helping them adjust to life after your divorce. If you and your spouse were separated while you were getting divorced, your children most likely began making the adjustment then. Now that your divorce is final, they may have to deal with a new set of changes and will need more of your attention as a result.

Your divorce may actually provide an opportunity for you to improve your relationship with your children. Now that you are no longer distracted by the troubles of your marriage or by the process of your divorce, you can refocus some of your energy on your children.

Finding activities you and your children enjoy

Being with your children, as a non-resident parent, may be awkward for all of you at first. Seeing you living in a new place and not having you in their everyday lives may feel weird to your kids. To help everyone adjust to the new situation, avoid making every get-together a special event. Simple activities such as a trip to the supermarket, a bike ride, doing homework together, or watching a video – the kinds of things you used to do together – take some of the pressure off and help reassure your kids that not everything in their lives has changed.

If you are a non-resident parent, don't be upset if your kids don't appear overjoyed to see you when you pick them up. Their initial nonchalance may be their way of protecting themselves emotionally, or it may reflect their confidence that you'll always be in their lives and the divorce hasn't changed your love and concern for them. Don't make assumptions about the ways your children are responding to the changes occurring in their lives. Instead, try to understand the true reasons for their behaviour.

Working at rebuilding a sense of family

As you recover from your divorce, rebuilding a sense of family with your children is important for all of you. Whether you are a resident parent, a non-resident parent, or share residence with your spouse, your children need to feel that they're still part of a real family, which is essential to their sense of self-worth. To help maintain a sense of family, hold on to as many of your family rituals as you're comfortable with. Go with your children to special school festivals or arrange for holidays with your extended family.

Think about establishing new family traditions (going on an annual family holiday or taking up a new hobby with your children, for example) to make them feel as if some benefits to their new life do exist and to help your children enjoy spending time with you as a family.

Special family time doesn't have to cost a lot of money. It can be as simple as a walk after dinner, weekend bike rides, playing Monopoly, or decorating the Christmas tree. Your children will benefit from spending time together as a group and growing up in a household where open communication, humour, clear values and rules, nurturing, and respect for one another exist.

Making New Friends

When you get divorced, you will almost inevitably lose touch with some of your friends. They will probably be people you knew through your spouse, or people who may have related to you solely as one-half of a couple. Some of your friends may feel the need to choose sides in your divorce. Others may drop out of both of your lives.

But your most important and significant friendships will remain intact. Even so, making new friends can be fun and can bring new energy and hope to your life. Volunteer for a cause you care about; sign up for a class; join a singles' group (a group for divorced people is a particularly good idea), a book reading group, or a health club; or try some other new activity.

Make a point of rediscovering your local community and all that it offers you and your kids. Learn to do something you have always wanted to do but never got around to doing, or take up a hobby you put aside when you were married. Chapter 24 is full of ideas for helping you adjust to and make the most of your new life. The point is this: *Get out of the house and add some variety to your life!*

Chapter 20

The Toughest Post-divorce Problems (And How to Solve Them)

· ·

In This Chapter

▶ Your ex-spouse won't let you spend time with your children

▶ You don't get your maintenance or child support payments

▶ Your former spouse leaves the country

▶ Your ex disappears with your children

▶ You want to change your divorce settlement

▶ Your ex-spouse declares bankruptcy

· ·

*U*nfortunately, divorce may not bring to an end the problems that destroyed your marriage. Some divorced couples persist in arguing and going out of their way to make each other miserable instead of getting on with their lives. Consumed by anger and a desire for revenge, they fight over the outcome of the divorce, withhold child support or spousal maintenance, purposely delay making support payments, or interfere in each other's child residence or contact arrangements.

This chapter can't solve everyone's post-divorce problems, but it does provide you with specific information about some of the most common (and serious) problems divorced couples face and what you can do about them – if necessary.

Your Ex-spouse Interferes with Your Child Contact Arrangements

If you are a non-resident parent and your ex-spouse makes seeing or contacting your child difficult, or even impossible, your ex may be in breach of a court order, and almost certainly will put the well-being of your child at risk. Contact is the right of the child, rather than the right of either parent. If your ex is denying you contact with your child, get in touch with your solicitor for advice on the next steps to take.

On the other hand, no law requires a non-resident parent to have contact with their child. You can use your former spouse's repeated failure to stick with any order or agreement for contact as justification for why the court should modify your current arrangement. You may even be able to go to court and ask the judge to restrict your former spouse's contact if, in the end, you think that is what is best for your child.

Don't retaliate by withholding payments

If your spouse interferes with your child contact arrangements in any way, you may be tempted to withhold payment for child support. *Don't do it!* Not only will you be in breach of your obligations – just like your former spouse – but you may also jeopardise your children's well-being. Two wrongs in this case definitely *do not* make a right.

A far better course of action is to continue paying your child support and try to work things out with your former spouse. Mediation is your best bet if you want to resolve your disputes outside of court (see Chapter 16 for more on the subject of mediation); but mediation will not work unless you both are willing to give it a try. If your ex-spouse is unwilling, going back to court or to the Child Support Agency may be your only options. Talk to your solicitor to find out exactly what steps you should take next. You can also contact Families Need Fathers (www.fnf.org.uk) or the National Council for One Parent Families (www.oneparentfamilies.org.uk) for information and support for non-resident parents.

Make an application to the court

If you've already tried out-of-court resolutions without a result, consider making an application to the court – either for a fresh contact order or for a variation of a previous order. An application to *enforce* a court order is a last resort; the main remedies for breach of a court order (or *contempt of court*) are a fine or imprisonment, and they may not succeed in getting you what you really want: contact with your child. Unless your former spouse can prove that he or she has good reason to keep you from seeing your children – you've abused them, sexually molested them, you have a drug problem, and so on – your ex-spouse will probably be ordered to allow you to resume seeing your child, albeit at a pace which suits the child.

The Child Support Payments Don't Arrive

The sad reality is that literally millions of divorced parents with agreements, court orders, or Child Support Agency (CSA) assessments for child support never receive their child support, or receive it only on a sporadic basis. As a result, many of these parents struggle to provide for their children, some may lose their homes, and still others fall into poverty. If your ex-spouse falls behind with his or her child support payments, the overdue payments will become known as *arrears*. Chapter 13 tells you about the arrangements that you and your spouse might make for child support during your divorce.

If you are having trouble tracing your ex-spouse, you may be able to get a court order authorising the Benefits Agency to release the address to you. If your ex is the sort of person who can pay but won't, you can scream, cry, and tear your hair out, or you can use legal means to force your ex-spouse to pay up. The main legal means available to you are slightly different, depending on whether you have an agreement, a court order, or a CSA assessment for your child support.

Enforcing a child support agreement

A child support agreement made between you and your spouse is a form of contract, and contracts are normally enforceable by the courts according to contract law. However, if your agreement has been made in the context of family proceedings, the court is likely to enforce the agreement in one of the same ways that they would if you had a court order for child support, as described in the next section.

If your agreement has been in force for more than a year, you or your ex-spouse can apply instead to the CSA for a fresh calculation of the child support liability. The CSA then takes over all of the administration and enforcement of the child support payments. The CSA won't deal with any arrears that have accrued *before* your application to the CSA.

If you have an agreement for child support and subsequently apply to the Benefits Agency for income support, the Benefits Agency automatically refers your case to the CSA for a calculation of your ex-spouse's liability for child support and the CSA's calculation overrides your agreement. You aren't given any choice as to whether or not the CSA becomes involved, unless you can show that there is a risk of harm to you or your children.

Fulfilling an order for child support

A court order for child maintenance is also sometimes called an order for child support payments, or an order for *periodical payments for* or *to the child*. If you have an order for child support that predates 3 March 2003, you have to apply to the court if you want to enforce that order.

If your court order for child maintenance has been in effect for more than one year, either of you may apply to the CSA for a fresh calculation of child support liability and the CSA will then take over the administration and enforcement of the child support payments. The CSA will not deal with any arrears that have accrued *before* your application to the CSA. Here are some of the court's powers that you may want to make use of:

- ✔ **Attachment of earnings order:** If your ex-spouse is in regular employment, one of the most cost-effective ways of ensuring that you get your child support payments (and any arrears) is by applying for an attachment of earnings order. If you are successful, your ex-spouse's employer is obliged to deduct the child support payments directly from your ex-spouse's wages or salary and pay them to you. The court has to specify a limit of earnings below which the employer cannot deduct the child support payments, in order to ensure that your ex-spouse still gets the minimum necessary to survive.

- ✔ **Execution against goods:** The court can authorise a bailiff to enter your ex-spouse's home (or other premises belonging to him or her) and seize goods to the value of any child support arrears that have accrued. The bailiff can then sell the goods and pay the proceeds to you.

- ✔ **Charging order:** If the arrears are substantial, it may be possible to secure a charge against your ex-spouse's property up to the amount that is due to you, plus interest. Ultimately, you may be able to get an order for sale of the property and take your child support arrears from the proceeds.

- ✔ **Garnishee Order:** If you are aware that your ex-spouse has a bank or building society account, or that his or her solicitor is holding money for your ex-spouse, you may be able to obtain an order that the contents of the account be frozen until the child support arrears have been paid to you from it. This is called a Garnishee Order.

- ✔ **Bankruptcy:** If your ex-spouse has been made bankrupt, it may still be possible for you to collect the child support payments due, although you may have to compete with other creditors for a share of your ex-spouse's income. You can still apply for the arrears once the bankruptcy order has expired (normally after three years) by one of the other means referred to in this section.

> ✔ **Judgement summons or committal:** Under this method of enforcement, your ex-spouse can be committed to prison if there is evidence of wilful refusal to pay. Beware, though, of killing off the goose that lays the golden egg!
>
> ✔ **Registration of the order in the Magistrates Court:** If your child maintenance order has been made in the County Court, which is likely, you can apply to register the order in the Magistrates Court, and then the Clerk of the Magistrates Court will take over enforcement of the order for you.

An application to enforce arrears of child support payments may prompt an application by your ex-spouse for a reduction in the current payments. If he or she can show that the current payments are genuinely unaffordable, then an order may be made to reduce the payments and possibly to waive some of the arrears.

Enforcing a CSA assessment

These days, most new applications for child support are dealt with by the Child Support Agency, rather than by the court. If your ex-spouse fails to pay support based on a CSA calculation regularly, the CSA have the following powers to enforce payment.

Payment by bankers' standing order or direct debit

The CSA can order your ex-spouse to make payments by a bankers' standing order or direct debit, and direct him or her to open a bank account for this purpose if he or she does not already have one. The frequency of payments usually matches your ex-spouse's salary or wage payments.

Deduction from earnings direction

Your ex-spouse can either agree to a deduction from earnings voluntarily or, if there are arrears, the CSA can require your ex-spouse's employer to deduct the child support payments at source and pay them directly to the CSA. The deduction from payments direction has two main parts: a normal deduction rate to cover the current child support payments and any arrears, and a protected earnings portion which states the minimum amount of take-home pay your ex-spouse is left with after making the deduction – 60 per cent of his or her net earnings for that employment. Any shortfall can be carried forward to the next pay period.

A liability order

If none of the above methods of enforcement are appropriate, the CSA can apply to the Magistrates Court for a liability order. The order can include interest, penalty payments and fees, as well as child support payments. The court must make an order if it is satisfied that the payments are due and unpaid. It cannot question the basis of the child support calculation.

Once a liability order has been made, the Secretary of State can try to recover the debt by various means:

- ✔ **Distress action,** using bailiffs to seize and sell goods and household items
- ✔ **Third party debt order,** requiring a bank or building society to release funds to the amount of the liability order
- ✔ **Charging order on property or assets,** so that when the property or assets are sold, the monies due will be paid to the Secretary of State
- ✔ **Registering the liability order in the Register of County Court Judgements,** which will affect your ex-spouse's credit rating and possibly his or her membership of a professional body
- ✔ **Committal to prison,** for a maximum of six weeks
- ✔ **Removal of driving licence,** or disqualification from obtaining one for up to two years

Ultimately, the court decides which means of enforcement is most appropriate. The court is unlikely to disqualify your ex-spouse from driving if he or she needs to drive to earn a living. But if your ex-spouse is committed to prison or disqualified from driving, and at the end of the prison sentence or disqualification still hasn't paid the arrears, the CSA can make a further application to the court.

Your Ex-spouse Leaves the Country

Unfortunately, some parents are so intent on not paying their child support that they move out of the country, often without leaving a forwarding address. When that happens, enforcing a child support court order and collecting that support can be particularly difficult.

There are means of enforcing maintenance orders abroad, but they can be expensive and time consuming, and will not apply to all countries in the world. Ask your solicitor for some preliminary advice before you launch into any enforcement proceedings abroad.

Scotland is a different legal system, so taking the children out of England into Scotland, or vice versa, may raise many of the same problems, such as having to return the children to the country they were taken from so the courts can decide where they should live.

Your Ex-spouse Disappears with Your Children

If you have residence of your children and your ex-spouse kidnaps them or refuses to return your children to you, he or she is committing both a criminal and a civil offence. *Leave no stone unturned if your ex-spouse takes off with your children.* The longer you wait to act, the harder finding them will be. You should

- ✓ **Call your local police station immediately.**
- ✓ **Contact your solicitor straight away.**
- ✓ **Hire your own private investigator.** *Private enquiry agents* who track down missing persons using national computerised databases can be very effective at turning up missing people through Social Security numbers, driver's licence numbers, and plenty of asking around.

If you suspect that your spouse may be thinking of taking off with your kids, you should also alert your children's childminder, nursery, or schools about your concerns. However, unless there is a court order forbidding your ex-spouse to remove the children from your care, the school, childminder or nursery won't have the power to prevent your ex-spouse from doing so. The best they may be able to do is to call you and stall your ex-spouse until you arrive.

If you think that your ex-spouse may be planning to leave the country with your children, and you have a residence order, contact the Passport office and ask that your child not be granted a passport if your ex-spouse applies for one. Should your former spouse manage to get out of the country with your children, contact the Department for Constitutional Affairs Child Abduction Unit, who will put you in touch with a solicitor who is authorised to take abduction proceedings on your behalf. *Do not delay.*

The organisation Reunite will be helpful should your child ever be taken out of the country without your permission. Contact Reunite at: PO Box 24875 London E1 6FR, Tel: 0116 2555 345, e-mail: reunite@dircon.co.uk.

Your Ex-spouse Owes You Maintenance

Many former spouses who are legally obliged to pay spousal maintenance fail to make the payments or don't make them consistently, often because they resent having to pay the money or because a new spouse pressures them not to pay. Other ex-spouses don't pay because they develop serious money troubles after their divorce and instead of asking the court to let them pay less they simply stop paying or pay only when they can afford to.

Your best option when your spouse owes you maintenance is to contact your solicitor, who can both lay out your options and help you carry out a plan of action. Refer to the section headed 'Fulfilling an order for child support' earlier in this chapter for a list of what some of your options are.

The best time to ask your solicitor about potential problems with your spouse's payment of maintenance is when the terms of your divorce financial settlement are being written.

Your Ex-spouse Fails or Refuses to Sign Property Over to You

If you have an order that your ex-spouse is to sign the house or other valuable property over to you, and he or she fails or refuses to do so, your solicitor can apply to the court for an order allowing a district judge or a partner in your solicitor's firm to sign the deed of transfer in your ex-spouse's place. You have to give your ex notice of the application, and serve a copy of the original order on him or her, endorsed with a penal notice – that means the order will state that if your ex-spouse doesn't comply with the order, he or she will be guilty of contempt of court and may be committed to prison. If your ex-spouse still does not respond and you have to proceed with your application for the judge or solicitor/partner to execute the deeds, you may get an order that your ex-spouse pays the costs of your application.

You Want to Change Some Terms of Your Divorce Settlement

Sometimes things change, and the agreement or judgment that seemed fine at the time it was written may no longer be what you need or want now. Or maybe you've never been happy with the outcome of your divorce – you've done your best to abide by your order or agreement but have decided it's time to do something about it.

If you and your former spouse see eye-to-eye on the changes, then modifying your agreement or the judge's order may be relatively hassle-free, assuming that the judge shares your perspective and assuming that the changes will not harm your dependent children in any way. However, if one of you wants things changed and the other doesn't (which is more likely), then you may be in for a replay of your divorce battles.

Demonstrating a change in your circumstances

Ordinarily, if you ask the court to vary the terms of an order made within your divorce proceedings, you must justify your request by demonstrating that a definite change in your circumstances exists. It's unlikely that a judge will regard your simply 'not liking' the terms of your court order as sufficient justification for a change.

To vary the terms of your child residence and contact arrangement, you must be able to demonstrate that the proposed change is in the children's best interests. On the whole, the court does not like to disturb the status quo unless there is a legitimate need for the change due to significant changes in your life, in your former spouse's life, or in the lives of your children. Those changes may include the following:

- ✔ You're moving a long distance away.
- ✔ Your children are not being properly supervised when they're with their other parent. This may be due to a substance abuse problem, because his or her work hours have changed and the children are left alone for long stretches of time, because your former spouse is busy partying into the wee hours of the morning, or other similar situations.
- ✔ Your child has become seriously ill and the present arrangements are unsuitable.
- ✔ One parent has become seriously ill, been arrested for a violent crime, or has been accused of child molestation or child abuse.
- ✔ You and your teenage children are in constant conflict, and you can no longer control them.
- ✔ Your ex-spouse's new spouse is improperly relating to or influencing your children.
- ✔ You believe that your former spouse is abusing or sexually molesting your children.
- ✔ The arrangements are simply not working out.

Whatever the reason(s) you give to justify your request for a variation, the judge makes his or her decision according to what's in the best interests of your children.

After you're divorced, you or your former spouse may also want to make changes in your child maintenance court order. Usually, the parent who is receiving the support wants more money, and the parent who is paying the support wants to pay less. What a surprise! The parent who is requesting the variation must provide the court with proof that changes in his or her life, changes in the life of the other parent, or changes in the lives of the children merit the variation. Remember, though, that if your court order was made after 3 March 2003, and it has been in effect for more than one year, there is nothing to stop either of you from applying to the CSA instead for a calculation of liability. If you have more children with another partner after you get divorced, a judge may view that as a valid reason for lowering the amount of child support you are obliged to pay to your former spouse. The CSA formula will also treat your net income as reduced by a certain percentage for each new child that you have. See Chapter 13 for more information on child support.

Courts are not permitted to agree to a variation of a couple's capital settlement or property settlement once it has been made into an order, save in the most exceptional circumstances.

Securing a court order if you change the agreement yourselves

If you and your ex-spouse informally decide to change your child residence and contact arrangement, you will not need to tell the court unless you are changing the terms of a court order. If you do want to deviate from the terms of an existing court order, you may be well advised to get a new order that reflects all of your changes. Otherwise, if you and your spouse have a later disagreement over the arrangements, you may have more difficulty persuading the court that the original order should be changed.

Put your new agreement in writing and, to be certain that it is enforceable, get a solicitor's help in wording it. Make sure that you both get copies of the new agreement.

If you are paying court-ordered child support and you and your ex informally agree that you can begin paying less child support than what was ordered, that you can suspend your payments for a while, or that you don't have to pay any child support at all, the court may view your new informal agreement as nonbinding, even if you put it in writing. In that case, the court order for child support remains in effect.

Even if your requested changes are mutual, a judge may not consider them to be in the best interests of your children. Therefore, if you and your ex-spouse reduce, cease, or suspend your child support payments, the court may consider the non-paying party to be in breach of the order and that parent could end up in legal hot water. If you want to vary your current court order, do so by applying for a new one.

Your Ex-spouse Files a Bankruptcy Petition

Given that consumer debt is an ever increasing feature of modern life and the finances of many people take a turn for the worse after divorce, the possibility exists that your former spouse, or his or her creditors, may file a bankruptcy petition. Your ex-spouse can file his or her own bankruptcy petition if he or she owes any one creditor more than £750 and cannot afford to pay.

If you believe that your ex-spouse may be thinking about filing a bankruptcy petition, and if he or she is currently paying you maintenance, child support, or both, or there has been a consent order transferring money or property to you from your ex-spouse within the last three to five years, get in touch with your divorce solicitor or a bankruptcy solicitor immediately!

Support obligations – theory and practice

Here's the theory: Although going bankrupt wipes out many of your ex-spouse's debts, including some of the debts he or she may have agreed to pay according to your divorce agreement or court order, the bankruptcy will *not* affect his or her obligation to pay you maintenance or child support.

However, in practice, the trustee in bankruptcy, who takes over all of your ex-spouse's financial affairs, can apply for an order from the court to help discharge some of the debts, and that order may mean that your own order for maintenance or child support may be reduced during the period of bankruptcy. Although you can apply to enforce any arrears once the bankruptcy order has been discharged, the courts do not normally enforce arrears which are more than 12 months old.

Capital and property orders

If an order has been made within the divorce proceedings for your ex-spouse to pay you a lump sum, filing a bankruptcy order means you can't enforce payment of the lump sum whilst your ex-spouse remains bankrupt, although you are entitled to try and enforce it once the bankruptcy order expires, usually after three years.

If you've already received the lump sum payment , the trustee in bankruptcy can apply to the court to 'set aside' the order and reverse the payment, if he can show that the order was considerably better value to you than it was to your ex-spouse, your ex-spouse appeared to be favouring you over his or her other creditors, or he or she was attempting to defraud the creditors in some way. The same risks may apply to property or other assets which have been transferred to you by your ex-spouse within the last three to five years.

If your ex-spouse has applied for the bankruptcy petition, and you think that the petition may be an attempt to frustrate an order made in your favour, you can try to prove that your ex-spouse is not really bankrupt at all. Alternatively, if you think that your ex is genuinely in difficulty financially, you may be able to persuade him or her to enter into an *individual voluntary arrangement* or *IVA* with his or her creditors. This is cheaper than bankruptcy, does not carry the same stigma, and may be agreed by the creditors so long as your ex-spouse keeps up with promises of payment.

It is usually considered good practice for your divorce solicitor to include in the final divorce settlement a declaration that your spouse is solvent. Although this may not prevent a trustee in bankruptcy later questioning the true nature of the order, it may help.

Chapter 21

Thinking Ahead: Pre-marital Agreements

- -

In This Chapter

▶ Bringing up the subject of pre-marital agreements with your spouse-to-be

▶ Sorting out what to put in your pre-marital agreement

▶ Making your agreement legally acceptable

▶ Calling on a solicitor to help you with your agreement

▶ Negotiating a post-marital agreement

- -

Sooner or later, you'll probably meet someone new, fall in love, and maybe even think about tying the knot again. If you've been divorced before, you may know that marriage can be something of a gamble, and when it ends it can drain your emotions and your bank account. So you may wonder if you can do anything to make splitting up a little bit easier, just in case things don't work out the way you hope the next time around.

A pre-marital (or *pre-nuptial*) agreement may help you achieve some peace of mind because it lets you and your future spouse work out some of the details of your divorce *before* you get married. Although it may seem somewhat cynical (let alone unromantic) to discuss such an arrangement with your spouse-to-be, drafting a pre-marital agreement may make good sense given today's divorce rate. (Of course, we hope you won't need to use it.)

This chapter tells you all about what a pre-marital agreement can and can't do, what gives the best chance of making such an agreement legally influential, and the role that solicitors play in the drafting process. (We also offer you some advice for raising the subject with your intended.)

Pre-nups: They're Not Just for the Wealthy Anymore

The legal status of pre-marital agreements in England and Wales has been the subject of recent court cases and political debate. Currently, pre-marital agreements cannot exclude the jurisdiction of the court, and the judge decides how much weight, if any, is given to a pre-marital agreement in each case. Judges are increasingly prepared to take a pre-marital agreement into account as one of the factors they have to consider, particularly with shorter marriages, if it's fair to you and your spouse to do so.

In Scotland, pre-marital agreements are generally valid and binding if they are entered into without coercion or intimidation, consent has been freely given by both parties, and the terms were fair at the time they were entered into. Anyone in Scotland of sound mind and over the age of *legal capacity* – that is, of sufficient age to enter into a contract – can enter into a legally binding agreement, including a pre-nuptial agreement.

Traditionally, pre-marital agreements have been associated with very rich people, especially when a wealthy person is marrying someone with a lot less wealth or earning power – such as with Michael Douglas and Catherine Zeta Jones (before she got the Oscar).

In recent years, people of more-average means throughout England and Wales have begun using pre-marital agreements in the hope that they will have some effect. For example:

- ✔ People who have already gone through a difficult and expensive divorce and want to make any future split less divisive and distressing – and cheaper.

- ✔ Spouses-to-be who own their own businesses and want to protect their enterprise from the potential repercussions of divorce.

- ✔ Older people heading into marriages with a substantial amount of property, stocks, shares, and other valuable assets.

- ✔ Couples, especially older ones, who want to write their own inheritance rules so that they can ensure that their children from a previous marriage, and not their future spouse's children, inherit certain assets when they die. (By law, when a spouse dies, the remaining spouse has a legal right to claim a share of the deceased's estate, no matter what his or her will says.)

- ✔ Couples who want to negotiate the rules of their marriage – how they will share in the housework, what religion their children will be raised in, and other issues relating to the management of their marriage and family life. (However, the courts don't usually enforce such lifestyle provisions.)

In the pre-marital agreement signed by American magician David Copperfield and supermodel Claudia Schiffer, she agreed to never reveal Copperfield's 'tricks of the trade' should they divorce.

You may feel you're tempting fate, but working out the details of your divorce before you get married by negotiating a pre-marital agreement can be one way to minimise the potential negative financial and emotional repercussions of divorce. Doing most of the end-of-your-marriage negotiating at the start of your relationship – when everything is still rosy – can make your divorce negotiations more straightforward, less emotional, and cheaper, and can help protect important assets in the aftermath of divorce (if there is one). It can even improve the quality of your relationship because you feel more secure and certain about your future.

Broaching the Subject with Your Spouse (Delicately)

You like the idea of a pre-marital agreement, but you're wondering how to broach the subject with your intended. You realise that your soon-to-be spouse may not consider negotiating a pre-marital agreement to be the most auspicious way to begin a marriage. We can't guarantee you a risk-free way to raise the subject. Nevertheless, we can give you some general ground rules for opening the discussion:

- **Be honest without being hurtful about your reasons for wanting a pre-marital agreement.** If you've had a bad previous experience, cite this as the reason for your request rather than doubt about the honesty or commitment of your future partner. If you sound as though you are being evasive or are lying, or if you appear to be acting out of greed, you may have a tough time getting to the negotiation stage and you may even derail your marriage before it's begun.

- **If you are nervous about bringing up the idea of a pre-marital agreement or you try and the discussion becomes heated, consider using a session with a counsellor to explore the pros and cons together.** A good counsellor does their best to ensure equal participation in the discussion and work to prevent either of you putting unfair pressure on the other. (See Chapter 2 for advice on how to find a counsellor in your area.)

- **Be absolutely clear with yourself as well as with your future spouse that your desire for a pre-marital agreement says nothing about any doubts about your love for and commitment to him or her.**

- **Explain (having considered fully) how your spouse can also benefit from the pre-marital agreement.**

- **Avoid becoming defensive or angry if your spouse becomes upset.**

✔ **If you and your future spouse try to draft your own pre-marital agreement and reach a stalemate, consider arranging a session or two with a trained mediator.** (Mediation is discussed in detail in Chapter 16.) If mediation helps you resolve your differences and you end up with an agreement, give your draft agreement to a solicitor so you can be sure that it has the best chance of being enforceable. You and your intended should each engage your own independent solicitor to review the agreement from your perspective.

Deciding What Goes in Your Agreement

The provisions you include in your agreements should reflect your individual interests and financial concerns. You may have some thoughts already about what to include, and your solicitors can also make some suggestions. Think about how long you want the agreement to last. In addition, think about the following questions: The answers you come up with may give you some fresh ideas.

✔ If you're making a sacrifice by agreeing to give up your career to help build up your spouse's career or business, or to raise your children, how will you be compensated?

✔ Will one of you pay the other maintenance in the event that your marriage ends? If so, how much will the payments be and how long will they last?

✔ Who will pay the legal fees if you get divorced?

✔ If you purchase property together, what will be the nature of your joint ownership? (See Chapter 3 for the different options.)

✔ Who will get the house and any other significant property if you get divorced?

✔ How will you deal with inheritance issues?

✔ How will you share expenses during your marriage?

✔ What will you do about your debts if you get divorced?

✔ If you intend to support your spouse while he or she goes through university, medical school, or another training course, how will you be compensated if your marriage ends?

✔ Will your spouse have any interest in your business if you get divorced?

✔ How will you be compensated if your spouse-to-be has bad credit and, therefore, during at least the early years of your marriage all credit has to be in your name? (You will be responsible to your creditors for that debt, even if your spouse agrees to pay off some of it should you get a divorce.)

If you and your spouse-to-be are buying a property together, and one of you is putting in a much greater contribution than the other, your main concern may be to protect that greater interest. In that case, the solicitor who is dealing with the purchase for you can word the purchase deed in such a way that it reflects your respective contributions. In addition you can draw up a deed of trust spelling out your respective contributions, and your intentions regarding your joint ownership and responsibilities. If you have such a deed, you may not have to go to the trouble and expense of a pre-marital agreement. (However, as always with divorce and pre-marital agreements, the divorce court has the ultimate power to adjust your respective interests in any property.)

Negotiating the terms of your pre-marital agreement may have an unexpected effect. Depending on what you learn about your future spouse by going through the process, you may decide to call off your marriage instead of signing on the bottom line.

After you have prepared your pre-marital agreement, read it periodically to make sure that it continues to reflect your interests and needs. If things have changed, you and your spouse can agree to amend the agreement or to cancel it. The amending or cancelling process has legal implications, so talk with a solicitor if you are thinking about doing either.

Making Your Pre-marital Agreement Courtroom-ready

The laws of England and Wales guide judges when they are making decisions about how to divide up a divorcing couple's joint property and debts. Bear these laws in mind if you are thinking about having a pre-marital agreement. Chapter 4 summarises the main factors that a judge has to take into account during divorce proceedings if he or she is asked to decide on a division of your property.

If you and your future spouse write a pre-marital agreement, you can include whatever terms you wish (with the provisos we state next) as long as they are acceptable to both of you. But to have any chance of your pre-marital agreement being taken into account on divorce, you need to ensure that the following guidelines are observed. Although there is no guarantee that the court will enforce your agreement even if you follow these guidelines, you can be pretty sure that the court won't enforce it if you haven't.

✔ **The agreement must be in writing, and the terms of the agreement must be clear.**

✔ **Both of you must sign your agreement – because you want to, not because you are being threatened or coerced, or because of other**

external pressures. Pregnancy might be regarded as such a pressure unless the implications of the pregnancy are recognised between you. Neither of you should exploit a dominant position.

✔ **Your agreement should be negotiated and finalised well before the date of your marriage.** This lessens the likelihood that either of you feels pressured to agree to your partner's requests in order to avoid jeopardising your impending marriage. The more distance you can put between the date of your marriage and the signing of the agreement, the better.

✔ **You must both be involved in negotiating the agreement, although you can use solicitors to do the negotiating for you.** The court is more likely to enforce an agreement if you both have proper independent legal advice.

✔ **You must be 100 per cent forthcoming with one another about your assets and liabilities.** Both of you must be aware of what the other is giving up or getting before you sign the agreement. The more information you share with one another, the better. If you don't have full disclosure, the court will want to know who made that choice, and *why*.

✔ **You must both fully understand what you are agreeing to.**

✔ **You should expressly consider whether the agreement will still apply, or will differ in any way, if you have children.**

✔ **The agreement shouldn't be likely to create any injustice to either of you.**

If you or your spouse can prove that one or more of the characteristics just listed were missing from your pre-marital agreement negotiations, the court is more likely to change or reverse certain provisions in the agreement or, after holding a hearing, disregard your pre-marital agreement entirely.

Reciting in your agreement the reasons why you want to make such an agreement (for example, to avoid litigation in the event of divorce), whilst recognising that you can't exclude the jurisdiction of the court, may help you win the support of the court.

You may be able to include provisions for spousal support in your pre-marital agreement. However, family courts won't necessarily be bound by those or by provisions relating to the care and support of any children you have during your marriage because those provisions may not be in your children's best interests.

Getting Legal Help with Your Agreement

Each of you should engage your own solicitors to help you during the pre-marital agreement negotiation process. Engaging your own solicitor is always a good idea any time you negotiate the details of an important legal document that has implications for your financial well-being.

A solicitor can help you ensure that the agreement is fair to you and can explain how the agreement can affect you if your marriage ends in divorce. He or she can also make certain that the agreement has the best chance of being taken into account by a judge.

The solicitor you use should be a family law practitioner, preferably with specific experience in the area of pre-marital planning (although few solicitors in the UK have this expertise because pre-marital agreements are still so rare). Depending on the circumstances, you may also need the assistance of a lawyer with special expertise outside the area of family law or the help of other professionals. For example, if you own a business, you may want a business law specialist or a business valuation expert involved in your pre-marital planning. Or, if you want to set up a trust as part of your planning, the assistance of an estate planning solicitor is advisable.

You and your spouse should discuss your pre-marital goals and concerns and what each of you thinks is fair before you meet with your solicitors. Then you can determine if writing a pre-marital agreement is even possible. You need to identify and categorise the issues you agree on, the issues that need legal clarification, and what you want your solicitors to help negotiate. Using a solicitor to help you work out the terms of your pre-marital agreement can cost you anywhere between £500 and £5,000, depending on where you live, the complexity of the issues you address in the agreement, and the value of the assets involved. For most couples, the solicitor fees are at the lower end of the scale. If you consider the cost of a litigated divorce, spending money now on a pre-marital agreement may save you some money in the long run.

Drafting a Post-marital Agreement after You're Married

Just as its name implies, a *post-marital agreement* is one that you and your spouse draft after you are married. Although this type of agreement is even more rare than a pre-marital agreement, it is useful on occasion.

Understanding how to use a post-nup

You can use a post-marital agreement pretty much the same way that you can use a pre-marital agreement. For instance:

- ✔ If you or your spouse decides to start a business after you are married, you can spell out in a post-marital agreement what will happen to the business if you get divorced or if you die while you are still married.

- ✔ You can use the post-marital to try to ensure that all of your estate goes to your children when you die, instead of a portion of it automatically going to your spouse.

- ✔ You can use a post-marital to work out most of the details of your divorce but, as with pre-marital agreements, you can't exclude the jurisdiction of the court.

Doing your best to make your post-nup stand up in court

Post-marital agreements are very rare in England and Wales, and the guidelines regarding what makes a post-marital agreement most likely to be taken into account by a court tend to be even less well-defined than those that apply to pre-marital agreements. Basically, neither are necessarily legally enforceable. Generally however, the guidelines mirror one another. Therefore, when you negotiate your post-marital agreement, abide by all the same rules that apply to pre-maritals, including full disclosure, no coercion, and honesty.

Because a post-marital agreement is relatively rare, using separate solicitors can help ensure that your agreement will stand up in court if one of you contests its terms further down the road.

If you want your post-marital agreement to be considered by the court, you're better off negotiating it while your marriage is still on solid ground, not after your relationship begins to fall apart. Otherwise, if you do split up and one of you later contests the terms of the agreement, the court may view the post-nup as little more than an effort by one of you to take advantage of the other. Also, if you petition for divorce too soon after you finalise your post-marital agreement (and what constitutes 'too soon' is up to a judge to decide), the agreement may not hold up in court if your soon-to-be-ex challenges it.

Part VI
The Part of Tens

"'My goodness, Snow White,' said her friendly, kind, generous, loving & <u>extremely</u> beautiful stepmother, "I wouldn't eat that apple if I were you.'"

In this part . . .

The Part of Tens contains quick and handy bits of advice and information, packaged ten to a chapter, including

- ✔ Divorce-related Web sites that put you in touch with a world of accessible information (for you and your kids) about going through a divorce, including ways of meeting other people who are experiencing the same things you are.

- ✔ Things you can do to help make your children's lives as happy and stable as possible.

- ✔ Suggestions for how to put your divorce behind you, get on with your life, and jump back into the social swim.

- ✔ Because you never know when you'll meet someone new, tips on how to make your next marriage or serious relationship a happy and lasting one.

Chapter 22

Ten (Or More) Divorce Web Sites

*A*lthough surfing the Net is no substitute for solid legal advice, you can quickly get hold of basic information about divorce-related issues online. In this chapter, we list some of the most useful Web sites dedicated to divorce issues. The first two Web sites are privately run and aim to provide up-to-date legal and financial information to those in the midst of a divorce.

www.divorce-online.co.uk

You can download much of the legal paperwork necessary for a divorce from Divorce Online. Just about everything you need is here (except for detailed legal advice), and costs anywhere from £15 to £85. In addition to general advice and links to lawyers and mediators in your area, you'll find:

✔ Applications for a decree absolute, name change, and Form E (A form used by the courts to collect financial information. See Chapter 7 for more information.)

✔ Samples of separation, prenuptial, and co-habitation agreements

✔ 'Children Act legalpac', including documents for use in residence and contact applications

✔ Calculations to help you work out if you're eligible for Legal Aid and child support

www.divorce.co.uk

This excellent, practical, small, and very user-friendly site has been compiled by an experienced family law practice in Cambridge. Here you'll find step-by-step guidelines to help you plan what you want to do about your divorce and how to do it. The site is updated regularly to reflect recent changes in the law and is divided into four main sections:

- **Legal and financial** – You can download financial worksheets that will help you sort out your settlement, as well as find information about independent financial advisers, mortgage information, and property sales. Chapters 3, 5, and 7 also have more information on these topics.

- **Personal and emotional** – Here you'll find help with finding marriage and relationship counsellors and other resources. Also have a look at Chapter 2 for information about locating a counsellor and Chapter 9 about taking care of your emotional health.

- **Children** – You can find advice on what to tell your children, how to help them, and what to avoid. Chapter 10 also has this covered.

- **Mediation** – Links to family lawyers, mediators, and CABx (Citizens Advice Bureaux) in your area can be found here. Chapter 16 also goes into detail about mediation.

www.itsnotyourfault.org

The best thing about this Web site is that your children can use it. www.itsnotyourfault.org has been produced by NCH (once known as National Children's Home), a charity that provides mediation and children's counselling services. The colourful, engaging material and resources, including a diary where kids can record their thoughts and feelings, can help your children feel normal and not alone while you are going through a divorce. Information on how to cope with the experience of separation is directed to three groups of people – parents, teenagers, and children.

www.justask.org.uk

This Community Legal Service (CLS) government Web site gives you a directory of the widest range available of names and addresses in your area for CLS-approved solicitors, mediators, and divorce information providers. The site operates quickly, is updated regularly, and is linked to a range of other

Web sites, so it can almost be a one-stop shop. For example, here you can easily access the Scottish Legal Aid Board on www.slab.org.uk and the Child Support Agency on www.DSSgov/uk/CSA, plus other national organisations and professional bodies for further information.

The 10,000 professionals in the directory have all been awarded the Legal Services Commission Quality Mark, which means that they have been given a stamp of approval by the CLS. You can also find a legal aid calculator to work out if you are likely to be eligible for legal aid, as well as definitions and descriptions of the types of aid available. You can download Consumer Association leaflets on divorce-associated topics, including legal help, mediation, and buying and selling a house.

www.dca.gov.uk/family/divleaf.htm

You can download a range of excellent, attractive, well-designed and well-written leaflets for parents and children of all ages about divorce and separation from this Web site. What we've found most useful is the downloadable Parenting Plan – we refer to it in more detail in Chapter 10. This Web site also takes you to a directory of services for the family compiled by the Department for Constitutional Affairs. This directory includes a link to contact details for ethnic and faith community groups on www.lcd.gov.uk/family/marsup/famtxtfr.htm.

www.ukcfm.co.uk

This specialist family mediation site run by the UK College of Family Mediators is primarily directed towards mediators, but it is also useful for anyone who wants to know about mediation. The UK College promotes and regulates the best practice of family mediation, and the site gives you full information about family mediation as well as access to the contact details for College member mediators in areas throughout the whole of the UK.

You'll also find a listing of the College's policies and guidelines for the consultation of children in mediation, cross-cultural mediation, and for their recommended screening and safe handling procedures where there have been incidents of domestic violence and abuse. (See Chapter 16 for more on mediation.)

www. sfla.org.uk

Solicitors belonging to the Solicitors Family Law Association (SFLA) seek to conduct divorce cases, as well as other family legal issues, in a constructive way. The primary aim of their code of practice is to reduce emotional and financial costs. Have a look at Chapters 15 and 17 for more info on the SFLA. This Web site offers the following:

- ✔ SFLA member solicitors in your area
- ✔ Detailed fact sheets on arrangements for children, financial arrangements, divorce procedure, making the best use of legal advice, and living together
- ✔ News of changes in divorce law
- ✔ Details of regional groups you may find helpful
- ✔ Publications and news of events

www.womensaid.org.uk

This excellent Web site begins with a definition of domestic violence and reports relevant research and developments, including updates on government policy and initiatives on domestic violence. (You can also access government policy information directly at www.homeoffice.org.uk.)The site also allows you to use it privately without leaving any evidence on your computer that you visited.

The multi-lingual site adds to the emergency information provided in Chapter 2. It also points you to financial information (covered in Chapter 3) and to the Web site of the Department of Further Education and Science (DfES) for government policy and initiatives for children at risk of violence. If you want to begin or re-enter further education or training, this Web site links to others offering practical information such as how to apply for grants and teacher training from your Local Authority, referred to in Chapter 19.

www.fnf.org.uk and www.matchmothers.org

Families Need Fathers (FNF) gets a lot of publicity for the often unrecognised experience and views of fathers separated from their children by divorce. Because the feelings of fathers denied contact can run high, the publicity often provokes controversy.

This site aims to ensure that fathers can gain access to a range of information about family courts, including court forms and other information. You'll also notice a direct link to the court Web site: `www.courtservice2.net`. Most importantly, you can find contact details for local FNF groups, where you can find even more information and support. To complement this site, MATCH (Mothers Living Apart from their Children) also has a good Web site (`www.matchmothers.org`).

Sites for Single Parents

Gingerbread (`www.gingerbread.org.uk`) co-ordinates local groups for separated and divorced adults; **Parentline** also offers information for parents, including stepfamilies (`www.parentlineplus.org.uk`). The **Council for One Parent Families** offers a wide range of statistical, research, and practical information on `www.oneparentfamilies.org.uk`.

Ten (Plus One) Web Sites in Scotland

Following is a list of Web sites with information specific to getting a divorce in Scotland. As the laws are slightly different, these Web sites can help if you need information on what steps to take if you're Scots. Or perhaps you're just looking for some local help.

- ✔ `www.familymediationscotland.org.uk`: A one-stop shop for family services related to separation and divorce, providing a video clip of a mediation session to help you see what mediation is like.

- ✔ `www.calmscotland.org.uk`: This Web site gives you information on mediation and how to find a mediator.

- ✔ `www.dial-a-law.org.uk`: At the dial-a-law site, you'll find all kinds of information on many parts of Scottish law as well as tips on finding a solicitor in Scotland.

- ✔ `www.fla-scotland.co.uk`: This Web site, for the Family Law Association in Scotland, provides details of its member solicitors specialising in family law.

- ✔ `www.slab.org.uk`: The Scottish Legal Aid Board Web site provides general information about Scottish law. You'll find info on how to find a solicitor specialising in family law, getting legal aid, and general information about navigating through various legal issues.

- ✔ `www.sclc.org.uk`: This site for the Scottish Child Law Centre provides specialist information on the law relating to children and young people in Scotland.

✔ www.couplecounsellingscotland.org: This site is a great resource if you're interested in trying counselling. Couple Counselling Scotland is the Scottish equivalent of Relate.

✔ www.opfs.org.uk: The One Parent Family Scotland Web site is useful if you want information, help, or support on being a single parent.

✔ www.children1st.org.uk: This site is the Scottish equivalent of Parentline, with information on parenting – whatever your family situation.

✔ www.scottishwomensaid.co.uk: The Scottish Women's Aid Web site is extremely helpful if you're considering a divorce, or need help in an abusive situation.

✔ www.cas.org.uk: The Citizen's Advice Scotland Web site has details of Citizens's Advice Bureaux throughout Scotland.

Ten (Almost) Web Sites in Northern Ireland

As with Scotland, here's a list of Web sites with information specific to Northern Ireland.

✔ www.relateni.org: Relate Northern Ireland.

✔ www.niwaf.org: Northern Ireland Women's Aid Federation, for information and help on domestic violence.

✔ www.barnardos.org.uk: Barnardos (Northern Ireland).

✔ www.gingerbreadni.org: Gingerbread (Northern Ireland).

✔ www.dnausers.d-n-a.net/pacbelfast: Parents Advice Centre.

✔ www.mediatorsinstituteireland.ie: Mediators Institute Ireland, for advice on mediation.

✔ www.irish-counselling.ie: Irish Association for Counselling and Psychotherapy.

✔ www.domesticviolenceforum.org/malevictims.htm: Men's Advisory Project, for men experiencing domestic violence.

Chapter 23

Ten Ways to Help Make Everything Okay for Your Kids

. . . .

In This Chapter

▶ Being there for your children when they need you

▶ Supporting your ex-spouse's parenting efforts

▶ Not burdening your kids with your worries

▶ Keeping your promises

▶ Being sensitive to the issue of dating

. . . .

*T*hree out of every five divorces involve at least one child under the age of 18. So to say that nearly every child these days knows someone his or her own age whose parents are divorced or divorcing isn't stretching the truth. Even so, few children expect that divorce will happen in *their* family, but when it does, the effects can be devastating.

At first, your kids may feel as if their lives have been turned upside down, with everything that they know and love being taken away from them. Your divorce is your children's divorce, too. As a parent, you have the responsibility of helping your children cope with the profound changes that are happening in their lives. This chapter provides suggestions for how you can bring some stability to an otherwise uncertain situation.

✔ **Show your kids that you still love them:** Tell your children that you love them and prove it by your actions. Spend time with them, show them affection, and be ready and willing to listen when they want to talk and share their feelings with you.

✔ **Encourage your children to respect and love their other parent:** Give your kids permission to love their other parent. Don't paint such a negative picture of your ex that your children feel guilty about their love for their mum or dad. Instead, support your ex-spouse's parenting efforts and speak in positive terms about each other.

For example, tell your children funny or affectionate stories about your family, or about how you and their other parent met, or about your former spouse's relatives. Such conversations demonstrate that you're comfortable talking about your ex-spouse and give your children a sense of pride in their family history and roots, something all children need.

✓ **Don't burden your kids with your problems:** Treat your kids like children, not like grown-ups. Although they may have to assume more responsibilities in the home after your divorce – maybe even getting a job – never forget that they aren't yet adults.

Be careful not to burden them with your problems and avoid sharing all your worries with them. If you're going through a rough time, your children will probably sense it and may feel scared about what could happen to them as well. If you're feeling stressed – perhaps you're concerned about how to pay the bills – let your children know what's going on but don't go into lurid details. Assure them that no matter what, everything will be all right. Chapter 8 suggests some books that might help your children, and don't forget about your local library – it's a great free resource.

✓ **Try to agree with your ex-spouse on the ground rules for parenting:** If you and your former spouse are sharing the day-to-day care of your children equally, try to agree on the big issues such as curfews, discipline, schoolwork, and homework. Living by one set of rules in one home and by a totally different set of rules in the other can be tough on your children – and in turn tough on you and your ex-spouse. Refer to Chapters 4 and 10 for tips on how to make this easier.

On the other hand, if your former spouse does not parent your children as you do, don't complain about it to your children or argue about it unless his or her parenting style is, in your view, clearly doing emotional or physical harm to your children.

✓ **Make your children feel at home in your new place:** If you have moved out of your old home and now have a new one, make sure that your children have a special place there that's all their own. If your finances allow, let them decorate that space. At the very least, make your new home as comfortable as possible for your children so that they will enjoy visiting or living with you.

Your kids will feel much better if you and your ex agree to maintain a supply of their clothes, toiletries, and toys – within reason – at each of your homes. Then your children don't have to pack and unpack a full suitcase each time they travel from one parent's place to the other.

✓ **Avoid manipulation:** Don't argue with your former spouse in front of your children, using your children as go-betweens if you're fighting with your ex, or trying to prevent your ex or his family from seeing them.

If your ex-spouse starts dating, don't attempt to sabotage that relationship or make your children think that you would disapprove of their liking your ex's new girlfriend or boyfriend. Kids can't have too many caring, supportive adults in their lives. Besides, if you behave resentfully because your former spouse has a new love relationship, you're inadvertently giving your children a lesson in jealous behaviour.

✔ **Keep your promises:** This helps to make their lives as predictable as possible. For example, if you say you'll pick them up at a certain time, be there; if you tell them you're going to do something together, do it. If you have to change your plans, give your children as much notice as possible and – if your ex is agreeable to it – re-arrange the planned activity.

If you live too far away from your children to see them regularly, the next best thing is to write to or phone them as often as possible.

Many non-resident parents dread seeing their children because it is so painful for them to say goodbye and return their children to the other parent at the end of each visit. If you are feeling this way, try to take comfort in the fact that over time saying goodbye becomes easier. Don't let these feelings prevent you from seeing your children. It is important that they can depend on spending time with you on a regular basis.

✔ **Wait to date:** Avoid bringing home new partners straight after your divorce is final and certainly avoid introducing your children to multiple dating partners straight afterwards. When you first begin dating, your children may resent you spending time with new people so soon or feel threatened by the presence of these strangers. For a while, you may want to arrange times with someone you're dating for when your children are staying with your ex-spouse if you think that will make your children more comfortable. (For more re-partnering advice, turn to Chapter 24.)

If you begin dating someone regularly, your kids may become emotionally attached to that person, treating him or her as a regular and special adult in their lives. Be aware that if your relationship then ends, your children may have a tough time accepting the fact that it's over (especially if your ex-spouse is no longer an active participant in your children's lives).

✔ **Make your children's lives stable and predictable:** Maintain as many routines, rules, and traditions from your past family life as you can. Children thrive on predictability. After your divorce, try these tips for creating stability for your children:

- Serve their meals at the same time

- Let them keep their pets if possible

- Be available to help them with their homework

- Maintain the same standards of discipline

- Don't interfere in your children's relationships with the parents, brothers, sisters, and other relatives of your former spouse

- Your children have already experienced a significant loss – don't compound it by attempting to scuttle new friendships your kids may need and value.

✔ **Avoid becoming a 'super parent':** If you feel guilty about the effect your divorce may be having on your children, or if you're angry because they live with your ex-spouse, don't try to compensate for your feelings by becoming a 'Saturday treats' dad (or mum) who lavishes them with gifts and money or becoming a smothering and over-protective parent.

As difficult as it may be, try to maintain the same relationship with your children that you had before the divorce. They need predictability and stability at this moment, not excessive gestures. The best way to provide them with what they need is through your simple love and affection.

Chapter 24

Ten Tips for Putting Your Divorce Behind You and Moving On

In This Chapter

▶ Finding moral support

▶ Seeking counselling if necessary

▶ Meeting new people

▶ Getting your finances under control

▶ Putting some fun back into your life

*I*f you feel like crawling into a hole and hiding until your divorce is over, it's no wonder. But life definitely does go on and things will get better (sooner, rather than later, we hope). You may even fall in love again and your next marriage may be a perfect match. To boost your spirits a bit, we offer ten tips for moving forward with your life and planning for happier times.

Find an (Adult) Shoulder to Lean On

Find someone with whom you can talk openly and honestly about your situation. It doesn't matter who it is – as long as that person is a good listener. Pick someone you trust who has given you good advice in the past.

Express your thoughts in the safest way you can. In other words, don't rant and rave to your former spouse or to your children. Get rid of those negative feelings so that you can get on with your life. (See Chapter 9 for help understanding the emotions you may be feeling.)

Above all, avoid loading all your worries on your kids. They have their own insecurities, and you need to put up a strong front for them (see Chapter 10).

Start Keeping a Diary

An excellent way to get a handle on your emotions is by starting a diary or journal. Keeping a diary is an effective way of confiding your thoughts and keeping track of how they change from week to week and may even make you less reliant on friends and family to help you get your head together again.

Write as though you're talking to your best friend or to yourself. Draw pictures to illustrate your thoughts. Every week, read what you wrote the previous week. You may be surprised at the depth (or the triviality) of your emotions, or you may discover that – in just a week – your feelings about things have changed quite a bit.

Seek Help if You Need It

If you're crying all the time, harbouring a lot of anger toward your ex-spouse, feeling depressed, or having a tough time getting on with your life, you need more than a shoulder to lean on – you need professional counselling. An accredited counsellor or therapist can give you the objective feedback and encouragement you need to deal with your emotions in a constructive manner.

If you don't already have a counsellor that you like and respect, your family doctor should be able to recommend someone, possibly attached to their practice. Contact your local Relate office. Relate offers individual divorce counselling as well as couple counselling. Your solicitor, mediator, or a trusted friend or relative may also be able to give you the name of a local counsellor. Or try the British Association of Counselling and Psychotherapy Web site – www.counselling.co.uk to find a counsellor in your area. (See Chapter 2 for more information about counselling.)

Fight the Urge to Return to Your Ex

If you feel desperately lonely after your divorce, which happens to many people, stay away from your ex-spouse except when necessary – such as when making arrangements for children. Endings should remain as endings. Do not attempt to look for comfort in those old, familiar arms no matter how much you would like to. It's time to move on. You may feel that reconciling is the only way to stop the heartbreak and ease your loneliness, but don't be fooled. None of your old problems are likely to be solved that way unless you both have very serious doubts about the decisions you have taken.

Focus on Your Work

Your work or professional life may have suffered while you were going through your divorce. You may have used every ounce of your energy and concentration just to accomplish the most basic tasks of your job and to get through each day. Now that you're divorced, re-focusing your energies on your work can provide the ordered routine that you need in your life just now. Plus, your professional accomplishments can make you feel good about yourself and may even land you a pay rise or a promotion. If you've been out of the workforce for a while and want to re-start your working life, Chapter 19 offers some useful advice.

Don't look to your colleagues to provide you with the physical closeness or the emotional understanding that you crave – dating or sleeping with colleagues is always dangerous territory. What you want is security, not uncertainty, in your job.

Get in Touch with Your Spiritual Side

If you believe in God or some other higher power, don't be ashamed to pray for guidance and understanding. You may also want to try meditation or yoga, which can give you a renewed sense of calmness and added self-awareness. Mary Kirk's book *Divorce: Living through the Agony* draws on the spiritual aspects of divorce, including a chapter on forgiveness.

Clean Up Your Debts

Try to get debt-free as quickly as possible. Just now, you don't need the extra worry of dealing with unpaid bills and debt collectors. Plus, the sooner you can wipe out your debts, the sooner you can start saving money for the things you really need or want. If you don't have a spending plan or budget, develop one now. It will help you determine if your monthly income is sufficient to meet your monthly outgoings. If your living expenses and debts exceed your income, carefully analyse your expenditures to see which ones you can reduce or eliminate. Chapter 3 provides detailed instructions for developing a personal budget.

If you have enough income to cover your monthly expenditures and debts, focus on paying off those debts that carry the highest interest rates and service charges. Those usually include credit card debt, store cards, and finance company loans.

Try Something Entirely New

Seek out activities you'll enjoy as a newly single person – join a gym or take a dancing or cookery class where you can meet other people who are also looking for new activities. Dare to try something alone that your ex-spouse never wanted to do with you – go skydiving or backpacking, or go on that cross-country drive you've always dreamed about. (A change of scenery may be just what the doctor ordered!) If outdoor activities don't sound appealing, discover the artist within you. Singing in a choir will concentrate your mind, or painting, sculpting, or photography will keep your hands and mind busy and you'll have something to show for your efforts.

Save Money by Sharing Your Space

If you are financially strapped, you may consider getting a lodger. By sharing your home with another adult, you can reduce some of your monthly expenses and your living space may seem less lonely. Another option may be to move back in with your parents temporarily. Returning to familiar surroundings where you will be around loved ones can provide you with a safe place to regroup and save money until you're back on your feet. However, it is probably important that this does not last long or you and your parents may begin to lose the independence gained from each other.

If your children are living with you full- or part-time, try to put their needs first whenever you can. Though a lodger, particularly a student, may work out well with your children, they may equally not welcome sharing their home or you with anyone else – at least, not too soon. Make sure you consult them thoroughly to find out how they feel before making any decisions (see Chapter 10).

Re-start Your Social Life

Get out of the house and meet new people. Join a support group or a singles' club for the formerly married. Meeting other divorced people and doing fun things together is good therapy, not to mention a way to meet people with whom you may want to make friends or new relationships.

Tips on using dating agencies

If you've been out of the dating scene for a while or have difficulty meeting people of the opposite sex, using a dating service can be a worthwhile option. But watch out: These services are in business to make a profit, so choose a service carefully. Make sure you're comfortable with the service's approach to matchmaking.

If you decide to try your luck, you will need a sense of humour and an open mind. The Association of British Introduction Agencies recommends that you ask the agency how many introductions you can reasonably expect given your parameters, and that you remember that a successful introduction may not happen right away. Sometimes it takes a few tries before you meet the right person, and if you're not happy with the way things are going, tell the agency sooner rather than later. They may be able to redefine the criteria they're using to match you with someone else for a more successful introduction. Dating agencies operate in a number of different ways:

✔ **Dating agencies:** These take your details and attempt to match you with another person. They vary enormously in their methods and effectiveness. Some use hunches, others computerised matching. Agencies' client lists and the number of appointments they offer you can vary greatly, and they can also differ in their fees. For example, one woman we know paid £900 and had only one introduction. Another friend did rather better for £250 with a different agency and met her new partner after a few introductions.

✔ **Supper clubs:** Some agencies set up supper clubs where six or so people are booked to a table in a restaurant or the pub. Sitting down to supper with six strangers can test your conversational skills and it's a great way to meet new people of both sexes.

✔ **Online dating:** Nowadays, many dating agencies, like Match.com or Udate.com, are based solely on the Web. You can upload your picture, a description of yourself, and what you're looking for in a partner, and then scan through as many other people's profiles as you like. Usually you pay a monthly fee for the service, which allows you unlimited access to the site's database of profiles as well as a contact e-mail address within the site. It's then up to you whether you take the next step of giving an e-mail address outside the site to someone you've met and 'talked' to, or moving up to a phone call, meeting, and so on.

✔ **Speed dating:** This low-risk, low-cost, and highly social method gives you anywhere from three to eight minutes to talk with one person and at the ding of a bell move on to the next person. By the end of the evening, you hand over a list of all of the people you'd like to meet again. The agency then compares all of the lists and sends you e-mail addresses for all of the people you've chosen who have also chosen you. At the very least, it's a good laugh trying to figure out which questions to ask to find out what you need to know – all in the space of three minutes.

At some point you'll want to get back into the social swim. But don't begin dating as soon as the ink has dried on your divorce decree. Statistically, the majority of divorced men and women remarry within a few years of getting divorced. Most counsellors suggest not dating anyone seriously until you have been divorced for at least a year.

After you have decided that you are ready to date, you may be in a quandary about how to meet new people, especially if you have been away from the social scene for some time or didn't socialise or go to clubs much before you were married. Meeting potential partners may require some resourcefulness.

- ✔ **Tell your friends that you want to start making new relationships.** They may be eager to introduce you to someone, perhaps by inviting both of you to a dinner party or to join them in some other low-stress group activity.

- ✔ **Attend a class.** A car repair or language class is usually a good place to meet both men and women.

- ✔ **Take up a sport.** Joining a volleyball team, tennis club, or bowling league that attracts both sexes can be a healthy, relaxed way to meet people you may want to get to know better.

- ✔ **Do some voluntary work.** Giving your time and energy to a cause you care about can put you in touch with like-minded men and women.

- ✔ **Join a singles' group.** Contact Gingerbread in your area. You may find some groups listed in your *Yellow Pages* or local newspaper. Your place of worship may also have an organised singles' group.

- ✔ **Try a dating agency, online dating, placing a personals ad or answering one.** Read the sidebar 'Tips on using dating agencies' to see if one of these methods is right for you.

If you use personal ads to meet potential dates, for safety reasons always choose a public place for your initial meetings and steer clear of bars. A meeting at a lunch place, coffee shop, or bookstore is usually a good choice. Don't give anyone you meet your home phone number or address until you feel comfortable and safe with that person.

Chapter 25

Ten Strategies for Next Time

*B*efore you can get behind the wheel of a car, you must pass a test on your driving skills and knowledge of the rules of the road. But no such tests exist to determine your fitness for marriage. Many couples fail to realise that a good marriage doesn't just *happen* – it takes work.

Both parties to a marriage must nurture and care for that relationship. Those who manage to work that out often come to this realisation the hard way – through trial and error, living through failed marriages, going through a divorce, and trying again. With that in mind, this chapter offers you several key ingredients that relationship specialists have found in just about every successful marriage.

Don't Just Talk – Communicate

Failure to communicate is at the root of many marriages gone sour. Poor communication manifests itself in many ways. You may have a tough time speaking your mind or broaching uncomfortable subjects with your spouse, or you may have assumptions and expectations that are completely unknown to your marriage partner.

If you want to talk with your spouse about something that you know is a sensitive or difficult issue, carefully choose the time and place for the discussion. You may also want to rehearse what you're going to say to avoid inadvertently using words that may make your spouse angry or defensive.

When you tell your spouse about something that's bothering you, avoid using statements that begin with 'you' and asking 'why' questions, both of which will almost certainly put your spouse on the defensive. Many relationship educators and couple counsellors suggest writing down a three-part statement that begins with how you feel, followed by what you would like changed, and ending with what you would like your spouse to do instead. For example: 'I feel frustrated when you tell me that we're going to the cinema and then you don't get home from work until 10 pm. I wish you would phone me if your plans change.' Men and women tend to differ in their communication styles, which can sometimes cause problems in relationships. If you want help with understanding what your spouse is really saying, pick up a copy of Deborah Tannen's best-selling book, *You Just Don't Understand: Women and Men in Conversation* (Ballantine Books), or try *Men are from Mars; Women are from Venus* by John Gray (HarperCollins).

Make Time for Each Other

Maybe you and your ex-spouse were inseparable at the start of your marriage. But over time, as you got caught up in the day-to-day details of your lives and struggled to balance career and family, you began to have less and less time for each other. Some studies show that people talk for longer in the day to their work colleagues than they do to their spouses. Gradually, couples can drift apart, emotionally and physically.

You may feel that in this time-deprived, high-pressure culture of ours, you have too little time for yourself, much less for your spouse. Yet, if you want your marriage to stay healthy, you must create regular opportunities to be together, show that you care for each other, and demonstrate how much you appreciate your spouse's company. Here are some suggestions for showing your spouse how you feel:

- ✔ **Say 'I love you'.** Don't assume that after you marry your spouse doesn't need to hear those words any more. A woman once accused her partner of never telling her that he loved her, to which he responded 'But I buy you flowers every week'. Sometimes, your different ways of expressing yourselves pass each other by.

- ✔ **Eat at least one meal together each day.** Talk to one another during your meal and don't watch TV while you're eating.

- ✔ **Go on a date together at least once a month.** Mark the day on your calendar like you would any important meeting or appointment. Your date doesn't need to be expensive – it can involve a walk in the woods, a film, a picnic, or a drive in the country. What you do is less important than your taking the time to be alone and to enjoy one another.

✔ **Don't sit in front of the TV every night.** Instead, have a conversation with your spouse. Do a puzzle together, play a game, or just share the silence of reading and enjoy simply being with one another.

✔ **Don't assume that the way you like your spouse to demonstrate his or her love for you is also what your spouse desires.** Ask your spouse to make a list of the caring behaviours he or she would welcome in order to feel loved. Give your spouse a list of your own preferences. You may be surprised at how the two lists compare.

Fight Fair

Arguing is a healthy way for you to clear the air and resolve problems. Good fighting is fair fighting. When you fight fair, you avoid personal attacks, insulting language, finger pointing, recriminations, and threats. Any one of those things is apt to put your spouse on the defensive, increase the emotional level of your argument, and make your spouse less willing to listen to what you are saying and less open to compromise. The goal of a fair fight is not to have a winner or a loser, but to resolve your disagreement in a way that makes you both feel good about the outcome. If your tempers are flaring, take time-out and cool down. Fix a time to discuss the subject later when you both will be more calm and collected.

Try New Ways of Resolving Old Problems

In every relationship, certain problems seem to occur time after time. Even if the problems that keep repeating themselves are quite minor, over months and years they can create a considerable amount of anger and resentment in your marriage. Often, the solution to recurring problems, both big and small, is to find a new way of dealing with them. For example, you like the tube of toothpaste to be squeezed from the bottom and rolled tight as it's used up. Your wife drives you crazy because she is a free-form tube squeezer. You have had countless arguments over the toothpaste tube – you don't know why she can't remember to do what you ask, and she can't understand why you're making such a big deal out of what she considers to be a very petty issue. The solution? Buy two tubes of toothpaste – one for her and one for you.

Although the solution to every recurring problem may not be quite so easy as resolving the toothpaste debate, creative problem solving can work wonders for a marriage.

Maintain Your Sense of Humour

Laughing together is one of the best experiences you can have in a marriage and you can find ways to make it happen. Tell jokes, look for the humour in everyday situations, go to a comedy film, recount amusing situations from home or work, or simply smile more often whether you feel like it or not. Making light of a problem is a gentle way of letting your spouse know that something he or she is saying or doing (or *not* saying or doing) is bugging you and it's time to talk about it.

Forgive and Forget

In a relationship as close as marriage, occasionally you're going to get on each other's nerves. Although these minor irritations don't usually signal the end of your marriage, if you over-react by making them more significant than they really are you can damage your relationship over time.

When your spouse's behaviour irritates or angers you, try to understand why. Is it because you had a bad day at work or because you are really worried about one of your children? Does your spouse's behaviour remind you of something your ex-spouse used to do or remind you of the way one of your parents used to treat you?

Try to keep your spouse's behaviour in perspective. Ask yourself: 'Is what my spouse said or did *really* that important?' Try to remember all the good things about your spouse. Also, consider the things you do that drive your spouse crazy and how much you've appreciated a forgiving attitude. If your spouse's behaviour is really a problem for you, try talking about it together. If the problem is serious, get professional help (see Chapter 2 for more on relationship counselling).

Resolve Problems Quickly

If you and your spouse have had a big row, it may be up to you to swallow your pride and say 'Let's talk' or 'I'm sorry' even if you still feel hurt, vulnerable, or angry. Resolving your marital differences sooner, and not later, helps to minimise the likelihood that your relationship will be infected by hurt feelings, festering anger, and unresolved conflict.

Attend Pre-marriage Counselling to Avoid Surprises

Too often, the euphoric pleasure of falling in love and planning a marriage overshadows the truly important preliminary work you should be doing – ensuring that your new relationship is the real thing and that you both have what is needed to make it work. That means getting to know one another, warts and all, making certain that you share the same basic values and priorities, and building the relationship skills necessary to weather love's slings and arrows after the newness and excitement of your relationship has worn off.

A growing number of marriage or couple counselling agencies offer help in this area. For example, Relate provides pre-commitment workshops called 'Couples' at many of their centres. Their workshops on 'Moving Forward' include giving you skills to help you move on and have better relationships in the future. You can also check out `www.lcd.gov.uk/family/marsup/famtxtfr.htm`, for contact details for various faith community counselling centres.

Attend a Marriage Enrichment Course

You can attend a marriage enrichment course with your new partner in a relaxed setting over a weekend in company with other couples and the guidance of course leaders. Marriage enrichment is a process of education about the improvement of close relationships in general and marriage in particular. It involves learning by experience in couple groups with the aim of achieving change in attitudes and behaviour to increase the couple's sense of satisfaction with the relationship.

The main emphasis in marriage enrichment courses is on commitment to growth, communication, and constructive resolution of conflict. As a couple, you're shown how to work through your own problems and conflicts more effectively and set your own goals for your marriage realistically. Visit the Web site of the Association for Marriage Enrichment at `www.ame-uk.org.uk`, or head to Chapter 2 for more on these helpful courses.

Support Your Spouse's Outside Interests

Some newly marrieds, including those marrying for the second time round, assume that after they become a couple they have to do everything together. Although 'being joined at the hip' with your new husband or wife may be fun at first, after a while at least one of you will want to do things on your own, or spend time with your own friends. If your spouse suddenly wants to do his or her own thing, don't assume that your spouse loves you any less. And, don't be resentful over your spouse's newfound interest or hobby. Instead, support your spouse in pursuing new interests, maintaining old friendships, and making new ones. Those things that make your spouse happier and more satisfied will produce positive feelings that transfer to your marriage. You may find that your conversations are more interesting and you're laughing more often. You may even discover new things to appreciate about your spouse, which can deepen your love for the person you married. Don't let fear of another marriage failure make you restrict the freedom of either of you.

Attempting to control how your spouse spends every waking hour can make a once-happy marriage feel suffocating and create needless anger and resentment in your relationship. If you're feeling threatened by the changes taking place in your relationship, try to understand why they bother you or make an appointment to talk with a counsellor about it (see Chapter 2 on how to find a relationship counsellor).

If you sense that your spouse feels saddened or threatened by the activities you want to do by yourself, talk with your spouse about your interests, make sure that your spouse meets your new friends, and reassure him or her with your love and affection that everything is fine in your relationship.

Glossary of Terms

Abduction: The removal of a child from the parent with care without their permission.

Acknowledgment of Service Form: The form by which the respondent (or co-respondent) acknowledges having received the divorce petition.

Actuary: A professional who estimates the current or future value of an asset such as a pension.

Affidavit: A formal statement signed on oath or affirmed to be true by the person making it in support of an application to the court, for example in relation to financial matters.

Alimony: See *Maintenance.*

Ancillary relief: The financial relief that the court may provide on divorce, including maintenance (or *periodical payments*), lump sums, property and pensions for you, and child support or lump sums for your children.

Annulment: The legal end to a marriage that has been ruled void or voidable. A religious annulment does not have the force of law whereas a legal one does.

Answer: A formal response to a petition for divorce, separation, or annulment. In the response, the person who is served with the petition admits or denies the allegations made by the petitioner as the cause of the breakdown of the marriage.

Anti-stalking order: An order made by a judge or magistrate to protect a person from the following: being followed, waiting outside a person's home, making threatening or harassing phone calls, or displaying other sorts of behaviour in order to harass, intimidate or frighten.

Appeal: The process by which the losing party in a court action asks a higher court to review the decision of a lower court and determine whether a legal reason exists to order a new trial or to change some aspect of the lower court's decision.

Assets: Things of value. Depending on the type of asset, you can use it to purchase something else, you can sell it, or you can use the asset as collateral for a loan. An asset can be tangible – such as cash, property, vehicles, antiques, fine jewellery, or art; or intangible – such as stocks and shares, bonds, or pension benefits.

Attachment of Earnings Order: An order which requires that an employer deduct maintenance regularly from wages or salary in order that it be sent to a spouse or former spouse (known as an *arrestment* of earnings in Scotland).

Barrister: also known as *counsel,* a lawyer instructed by solicitors to give an opinion or to represent solicitors' clients in court.

CAFCASS officer: also known as Family Court Adviser: A person who prepares an independent report to assist the court in deciding what arrangements are in the best interests of the children, where there is a disputed issue relating to them. He or she normally meets with both parties and the children themselves. The CAFCASS officer or Family Court Adviser has different titles according to proceedings: In orders in separation and divorce – Children and Family Reporter; in Care Proceedings – Children's Guardian.

Calderbank offer: An offer made without prejudice, in which the person making the offer reserves the right to produce a copy of the offer letter to the court after a decision has been made, to support an application for costs.

Capital Gains Tax: A tax payable on any profit made on the disposal or transfer of an asset.

Capitalising maintenance: Paying a lump sum or other capital asset in return for a final dismissal of spousal maintenance claims.

Cash Equivalent Transfer Value (CETV): The cash value given to a pension fund at any time, based on the value of the fund if it were transferred from one scheme to another.

Chambers, in: When a court sits 'in chambers' the proceedings are heard in private, so that only you, your legal representatives, and the judge are allowed to be present. Witnesses are only allowed to be present while giving their evidence. 'Chambers' can also refer to the workplace where barristers are based.

Charging order: A court order to enforce the payment of a debt against an asset, usually real property, which may lead to an order for sale of the asset.

Child support: Money paid by one parent to the other parent to help meet the financial needs of their children. Ordinarily, the support continues until a child completes full-time secondary education, although a parent may have to provide support while a child is a full-time college student or attending a further education course. Sometimes referred to as child maintenance or child periodical payments.

Child Support Agency: A government agency with statutory powers set up to calculate, collect, and enforce child support payments from the non-resident parent to the parent with care of the child.

Children's Guardian: A court-appointed trained social worker, who represents the interests of children (or occasionally vulnerable adults) in divorce proceedings. This person is a CAFCASS officer operating in this particular role.

Class F: The formal means by which a non-owning spouse's rights of occupation of the matrimonial home are protected in a property which is not registered at the Land Registry.

Clean break: A financial arrangement where it's agreed or ordered that the husband and wife will make no further financial claims against each other. A clean break may be expressed to relate to claims for income, capital, property, or pensions.

Common law marriage: A popular expression for the relationship between couples who are living together without being married. This has no legal status in UK law, although it is a commonly used term and does have some legal status in Scotland.

Community Legal Service: The service set up by the government to deal with the provision of legal aid and legal services.

Consent Order: The order made by a judge once arrangements are agreed and settled.

Contact: The right of a child to keep in touch with another person, usually a parent, and the arrangements made for him or her to do so. The word replaces the previous term 'access', although the general public and the media still regularly use the old terminology.

Contempt of court: A wilful and deliberate violation or breach of a court order, judgement, or decree (for example, breach of a non-molestation order). Spouses who are in contempt of court may be punished by the court.

Co-respondent: A person with whom the respondent is alleged to have committed adultery. The law no longer requires that person to be named in the divorce proceedings.

Counsel: An alternative term to 'barrister'; it describes the role of a particular kind of lawyer rather than a title. A barrister or counsel is usually engaged to act as the advocate in court or to advise on the law.

Court order: A legally binding written document issued by a court and made by a judge.

Cross-examination: The questioning of a witness by the lawyer representing the opposing party to ascertain the truthfulness of what the witness said or to further develop the witness's testimony. Witnesses are cross-examined during a trial or court hearing.

Current market value: The amount an asset is worth if you sell it at the present time.

Custody: This term is no longer in use in UK courts. It has been replaced by the concept of *parental responsibility* whereby each parent continues to be legally responsible for their child after divorce, and by *residence* which is where the child shall live. The term 'custody' is still used by the media and in the international context.

Decree absolute: The final legal stage of a divorce.

Decree nisi: The first stage of a divorce, when you prove your ground for divorce.

Deduction from earnings order: An order at the disposal of the Child Support Agency (CSA) requiring an employer to deduct child support from a non-resident parent's wages and pay it direct to the CSA.

Deed: A legal document signed by the maker, and sealed.

Default judgement: An order or judgement made on the basis of the claimant's information only because the defendant or respondent failed to respond, didn't respond on time, or did not appear in court.

Defendant: The person being sued; usually known in family and divorce proceedings as the *respondent.*

Desertion: When one spouse moves out of the home that the couple shares without the consent of, or against the wishes of, the other spouse. To be a basis for divorce, the desertion must have lasted for at least two years.

Diligence: The Scottish term for enforcing maintenance orders.

Disbursements: Usually, the out of pocket expenses a solicitor incurs on your behalf.

Disclosure: The process through which information and documentation is exchanged between spouses or their solicitors within, or with a view to, court proceedings.

Dissolution: The end of a marriage (in other words, a *divorce*). The term does not include annulments.

Domestic abuse or violence: Domestic abuse or domestic violence is understood to include emotional and verbal abuse between couples as well as physical harm.

Duxbury calculation: The formula for working out the lump sum appropriate for a clean break, based on the amount of maintenance payable and life expectancy of the recipient.

Emergency applications: Applications that are urgent, such as applications for injunctions.

Equitable distribution: A legal system of dividing up the value of a divorcing couple's property based on what is fair to both of them.

Evidence: Relevant testimony, documents, videos, tape recordings, and other information offered to and accepted by the court to prove or disprove an allegation.

Examination: The questioning of a witness on the stand by the lawyer representing the spouse on whose behalf the witness is testifying.

Ex parte: An application for relief from the court made without the other party being present, being notified, or having an opportunity to participate in the action.

Financial Dispute Resolution Appointment (FDR): An appointment with a judge to try to resolve financial disputes without a full hearing. They are on a *without prejudice* basis, so that a different judge deals with the final hearing without being privy to what went on in the FDR.

First Directions Appointment (FDA): The first appointment with a judge in financial proceedings to assess the issues and what needs to be done before the final hearing. The judge gives directions for the future conduct of the case.

Form E: The form used by the courts and also by solicitors and many mediators to collect financial information for or within divorce proceedings.

Garnishee order: An order allowing money to be taken from a spouse's bank or building society account in order to pay a debt, typically arrears of maintenance (known as an *arrestment* of the account in Scotland).

Get: A Jewish religious divorce.

Ground: The legal basis or reason for a divorce.

Hague Convention: An international convention whose philosophy is that decisions about child custody or residence should be made in the jurisdiction in which the child was habitually resident prior to an abduction.

Hearing: A proceeding before the court that attempts to resolve an issue through testimony, legal arguments, and the introduction of evidence.

Injunction: A court order prohibiting someone from acting in a way that's likely to harm someone else, for example by causing a financial loss for that person or hurting that individual emotionally or physically, or requiring a person to do something such as allow a spouse back into the home.

Intangible property: An asset that has no intrinsic or marketable value in and of itself but instead represents or has evidence of value (for example, stocks and shares, bonds, or pension benefits).

Interim hearings: hearings for a judge to hear applications for interim court orders, for example for personal protection, child contact, or spousal maintenance. Decisions are for the short term.

Intestacy: where no will has been made.

Joint custody: See *Parental responsibility.*

Joint property: Property legally owned by two or more persons, a husband and wife for example.

Joint tenancy: A form of joint ownership of property under which the survivor automatically inherits the whole property.

Judgement summons: An application for an order for committal, for example if arrears of maintenance are not paid. Committal to prison is only likely if there has been *wilful refusal* to pay.

Judicial separation: A formal separation sanctioned by the court which releases the spouses from the duty to cohabit and enables the courts to make orders about money and property. In Scotland only orders for maintenance can be made.

Jurisdiction: The authority of a court to rule on a particular legal matter. Different types of court have different jurisdictions. For example, certain county courts can deal with divorce but Family Proceedings Courts cannot.

Land Registry: The office where the ownership of property is registered.

Legal aid: A form of public funding available to assist parties with the costs of a legal dispute. Currently administered by the Legal Services Commission in England, Wales, and Northern Ireland, and by the Scottish Legal Aid Board in Scotland.

Legal separation: A legal agreement or court judgement formally authorising a couple to live apart and spelling out the terms for their living apart. The couple is still married to one another.

Maintenance: The regular payment of money by one spouse to another for their financial support. Maintenance may be provided for only a limited period of time or can last until the payee spouse dies or remarries. Also known as *spousal support* or *periodical payments.*

Maintenance pending suit: A court order for temporary financial support while a couple's divorce is pending.

Matrimonial home: Any property in which a married couple live together, whether or not they own or rent it.

Mediation: A non-legal means of resolving a divorce-related dispute with the assistance of a neutral third party. Decisions made in a mediation session are arrived at by mutual agreement and not ordered by a judge The issues discussed in mediation can be about children, finance, or property.

Memorandum of Understanding: A non-legally binding statement of proposals, used in mediation, and agreed upon by the parties.

Money purchase or defined contribution scheme: A type of retirement scheme. The final amount you receive depends on how much is contributed to your scheme and how much the value of the assets in the scheme appreciates over time.

Nikah: Muslim marriage contract.

No-fault divorce: A divorce that is granted with no requirement to prove that one of the spouses was guilty of some marital misconduct. The UK does not grant a divorce without fault, unless there has been either a two-year separation with consent to divorce or a five-year separation.

Non-molestation order: An order forbidding a person to abuse, harass, threaten, or molest another person.

Non-resident parent: The parent who does not live with his or her children most of the time. Ordinarily, this parent is obliged to pay child support.

Nullity decree: A decree that the marriage has been declared null and void. Also called annulment.

Occupation Order (or ouster order or injunction): A court order that can force your spouse to leave your home, allow you to return or forbid your spouse to enter or come within a certain distance of your home or restrict his or her rights within the home.

Order: A ruling by the court on an application that requires the parties in a divorce to do something or not do something or that establishes the parties' rights and responsibilities.

Parental responsibility: All the rights, duties, and responsibilities which by law a parent of a child has in relation to that child. If you are or have been married, you both have joint parental responsibility for your children before, during, and after divorce or separation.

Periodical payments: Regular maintenance for a spouse or child.

Petition: The legal document filed to initiate a divorce.

Petitioner: The person who files a petition or initiates a couple's divorce proceedings.

Pleading: Formal written application to the court for relief and the written response to it. Among other things, pleadings can include petitions, answers, and replies.

Post-marital agreement: Sometimes called a post-nuptial agreement. A legal agreement made between spouses after marriage that spells out their present and future rights and responsibilities towards one another should they divorce or should one spouse die. Rarely used and not always enforceable in the UK.

Power of Arrest: A power which allows a police officer to arrest your spouse if he or she breaches or violates the terms of an injunction.

Pre-marital agreement: A legal agreement between a couple made before they marry that spells out their rights and responsibilities towards one another in the event that they later divorce or one of them dies during their marriage. Not automatically enforceable in the UK. Sometimes called a pre-nuptial agreement.

Pre-trial hearings: Pre-trial hearings are held by the judge before the final hearing to settle issues or give final directions, for example relating to the arrangements for the children following receipt of the CAFCASS report.

Privilege: The court can't enquire into the content of your *without prejudice* negotiations or mediation discussions nor can you quote each other without each other's consent.

Prohibited Steps Order: An order prohibiting specific steps in relation to a child, for example a change of surname or removal from the jurisdiction.

Property Adjustment Order: An order that a husband or wife should transfer property to the other, or that a property be sold or that the spouses' shares in it be adjusted.

Real property: Homes, other buildings, and land and any attachments to those assets.

Request for Directions: An application to the court for a decree nisi.

Residence Order: An order stating the arrangements about with whom a child is to live.

Respondent: The defendant in a divorce.

Rule 2.61 Statement: See *Statement of Information.*

Secured debt: Debt that you have collateralised or secured with an asset. If you don't pay the debt, the creditor can take the asset that you put up as loan collateral.

Secured Periodical Payments Order: An order that ensures that your maintenance payments continue on the death of your ex-spouse. Such orders are very rare, only occurring when the paying spouse has a lot of capital assets.

Separation Agreement: A document setting out the terms agreed for separation, usually before divorce proceedings are considered.

SERPS: State Earnings Related Pension (now replaced by the State Second Pension).

Service: A term for delivering a legal document, for example by post or in person.

Settlement: A written agreement between spouses resolving the financial issues in their divorce. It is also sometimes used to refer to the final financial order made by a judge in court proceedings.

Shariah: A system of Muslim law. The Muslim Law (Shariah) Council can deal with Muslim divorces in the UK.

Specific Issue Order: An order determining a specific issue relating to a child.

Statement of Arrangements: The form which has to be sent to the court with the petition if there are children of the family, setting out the current arrangements and the arrangements proposed for the children when the divorce takes place.

Statement of Information or Rule 2.61 Statement: The statement which accompanies a draft consent order to the court, in the form of a simple agreed summary of your respective finances and intentions.

Statutory Charge: The means by which the Legal Services Commission recoup any costs that you have incurred under the legal aid scheme.

Subpoena: A legal document served on a witness requiring that he or she appear in court. Ignoring a subpoena can result in punishment by the court. Sometimes referred to as a witness summons.

Summons: A written notification to the defendant or witness in a lawsuit that the lawsuit has been filed and that a response is needed.

Talaq: Muslim divorce. A *bare talaq is* a single unilateral declaration of divorce by a husband.

Tangible property: Property that has value in and of itself, such as a house or a car.

Tenancy in Common: A form of joint ownership, often used by cohabiting couples, in which each owner has a distinct share. If the size of the share is not defined, then it is usually assumed that it is 50 per cent. Either joint owner can leave his or her share by will or intestacy.

Testamentary guardian: a person appointed to hold parental responsibility in the event of both parents' deaths.

Testimony: Statements or evidence provided by a witness under oath in court.

Transcript: A typed record of the trial or court hearing.

Trial: A formal court hearing presided over by a judge to resolve the issues. Sometimes referred to in this book as a final or fully contested hearing.

Trust: A legal entity established to hold and manage assets for one or more beneficiaries.

Undertaking: A solemn promise to the court to do or not to do something. Breach of an undertaking is punishable as a contempt of court.

Unsecured debt: Debt which is not secured against an asset (see *Secured debt*), such as credit card debt.

Without prejudice: An opportunity afforded by the courts to make offers or proposals which will not be revealed to the court without the maker's consent nor taken account of by (will not prejudice) a court if agreement is not reached.

Index

FOR DUMMIES®

The easy way to get more done and have more fun

FOR DUMMIES

The easy way to get more done and have more fun

FOR DUMMIES®

The easy way to get more done and have more fun
